Refugee Performance

Refugee Performance
Practical Encounters

Edited by Michael Balfour

intellect Bristol, UK / Chicago, USA

First published in the UK in 2013 by
Intellect, The Mill, Parnall Road, Fishponds, Bristol, BS16 3JG, UK

First published in the USA in 2013 by
Intellect, The University of Chicago Press, 1427 E. 60th Street,
Chicago, IL 60637, USA

A catalogue record for this book is available from the
British Library.

Cover designer: Clare McFadden
Copy-editor: MPS Technologies
Production manager: Bethan Ball
Typesetting: Planman Technologies

ISBN 978-1-84150-637-1

Printed and bound by Bell & Bain, UK

Contents

Acknowledgements

I would like to thank all the authors who have contributed to the collection. It is no mean feat to deliver manuscripts on time and with such professionalism, as always the deadlines were tight and the turnaround vicious.

Research and compilation for this book was undertaken with the support of an Australian Research Council (ARC) Linkage grant and generous sabbatical time given by Griffith University, Brisbane, Australia.

Thanks to Griffith colleagues for their generous support. Thanks to Nina Woodrow, our wonderful research assistant on the ARC grant, who creates miracles out of very little time and resources. I'd also like to thank Natalie Lazaroo for her efficient support on the book production.

Grateful thanks to Mercedes Sepulveda from Multilink Community Services, Logan, who took the effort to seek us out in the first place, and collaborated with us closely over a number of years. To Shona Doyle for her long-standing commitment to the project, and to Peter Forday (ex-CEO) and Helen Coyne, the current CEO, for working hard to make the partnership work despite a thousand other commitments.

Thanks also to my colleagues at the University of Manchester and the In Place of War team without whom I doubt this book or the current ARC project would have happened.

My acknowledgement and thanks also to Niz Jabour for his inspiration and tenacity.

Sincere thanks to the team at Intellect, in particular Melanie Marshall for her encouragement and belief in the project and Bethan Ball for her hard work on the manuscript.

Finally, my gratitude to the individuals and groups I continue to work with from a refugee background. To your openness and willingness to join in and have some fun.

Permissions

The editor wishes to thank the authors and publishers for their permission to use their work.

Balfour, Michael, 'Refugee Performance: Encounters with Alterity,' *Journal of Arts and Communities*, 2: 3 (2010), pp. 177–195.

Burvill, Tom, '"Politics Begins as Ethics": Levinasian Ethics and Australian Performance Concerning Refugees,' *Research in Drama Education: The Journal of Applied Theatre and Performance*, 13: 2 (2008), pp. 233–243.

Conquergood, Dwight, 'Health Theatre in a Hmong Refugee Camp: Performance, Communication, and Culture,' *TDR*, 32: 3 (Autumn 1998), pp. 174–208.

Dennis, Rea, 'Inclusive Democracy: A Consideration of Playback Theatre with Refugee and Asylum Seekers in Australia,' *Research in Drama Education: The Journal of Applied Theatre and Performance*, 12: 3 (2007), pp. 355–370.

Edmondson, Laura, 'Marketing Trauma and the Theatre of War in Northern Uganda,' *Theatre Journal*, 57: 3 (October 2005), pp. 451–474.

Kurahashi, Yuko, 'Theatre as the Healing Space: Ping Chong's *Children of War*,' *Studies in Theatre and Performance*, 24: 1 (2004), pp. 23–36.

McMahon, F. F. (Felicia Faye), 'Repeat Performance: Dancing DiDinga with the Lost Boys of Southern Sudan,' *Journal of American Folklore*, 118: 469 (Summer 2005), pp. 354–379.

Nikčević, Sanja, 'Rape as War Strategy: A Drama from Croatia,' *PAJ: A Journal of Performance and Art*, PAJ 77, 26: 2 (May 2004), pp. 110–114.

Schininà, Guglielmo, 'Far Away, So Close: Psychosocial and Theatre Activities with Serbian Refugees,' *TDR*, 48: 3 (T183) (Fall 2004), pp. 32–49.

Sliep, Yvonne, Weingarten, Kaethe, and Gilbert, Andrew, 'Narrative theatre as an interactive community approach to mobilizing collective action in Northern Uganda,' *Families, Systems, & Health*, 22: 3 (2004), pp. 306–320.

Illustrations

Front and back cover: Clare McFadden, www.claremcfadden.com/

Clare McFadden is a designer, producer and facilitator of arts-based programmes for children and communities. She works in schools, kindergartens and cultural institutions across Australia. Clare has designed for theatre, film and music productions and her illustrations have been exhibited in group and solo shows, most recently, at the 2011 Bologna Children's Book Fair, Italy. In 2010, Clare was the recipient of the Lord Mayor's Young and Emerging Artist's Fellowship – enabling her to investigate international best practice methods of engaging children in the arts. In 2011 she was a recipient of the May Gibbs Children's Literature Trust Fellowship. She wrote and illustrated *The Flying Orchestra*. The book was awarded the 2011 Children's Book Council of Australia Crichton Award and was selected as one of the '50 Books You Can't Put Down' as part of the Australian Government's 'Get Reading' Campaign.

'Encounters in the Aida Refugee Camp in Palestine: Travel Notes on Attending Alrowwad Theatre's Production of *Handala*' (2011). Rand T. Hazou. Figure 1: Copyright the Naji Al-Ali Family, *Handala*, reprinted with kind permission. Figure 2: Alrowwad Cultural and Theatre Training Society (ACTS), *Handala* (2011), reprinted with kind permission. Figure 3: Alrowwad Cultural and Theatre Training Society (ACTS), *Handala* (2011), reprinted with kind permission.

'Refugee Performance: Encounters with Alterity,' Michael Balfour. Figure 1: Copyright Wendy Ewald, *Towards a Promised Land*, reprinted with kind permission. Figure 2: *Waste Man* 1–4. Copyright Anthony Gormley, *Waste Man*, reprinted with kind permission. Figure 3: *Towards a Promised Land* 1. Copyright Thiery Bal, 2006, reprinted with kind permission. Figure 4: *Towards a Promised Land* 2, Wendy Ewald, *Towards a Promised Land*, reprinted with kind permission.

'Drama and Citizenship Education: Tensions of Creativity, Content and Cash,' Sarah Woodland and Rob Lachowicz, *Venuste with suitcase*. Reprinted with kind permission, Sarah Woodland.

'Hospitable Stages and Civil Listening: Being an Audience for Participatory Refugee Theatre,' Alison Jeffers, *Afrocats performing in* Nyubani Wapi? Where is Home?, Manchester, 2006. Reproduced with the permission of Community Arts North West.

Author Biographies

Michael Balfour is Chair, Applied Theatre, Griffith University, Brisbane, Australia. His research expertise is in the social applications of theatre – theatre in communities, social institutions, and areas of disadvantage and conflict. He is the recipient of four current Australian Research Council-funded projects: *Refugee Performance,* developing drama-based projects with refugee new arrivals; *The Difficult Return,* creating new approaches to arts-based work with returning military personnel and their families; *Captive Audiences,* evaluating the impact of performing arts programmes in Australian prisons; and *Playful Engagement*, exploring applied theatre methodologies with people with mid- to late dementia in aged-care facilities. Previously, Michael was a researcher on *In Place of War*, a four-year Arts and Humanities Research Council (UK) project. He is the author of a number of key publications in the field of applied theatre, including *Performance: In Place of War* (co-author with James Thompson and Jenny Hughes) (Seagull Press, 2009), *Drama as Social Intervention* (co-author with John Somers) (Captus Press, 2006), *Theatre in Prison* (Intellect, 2004) and *Theatre and War 1933–1945: Performance in Extremis* (Berghahn Books, 2001). Contact: m.balfour@griffith.edu.au.

Tom Burvill is Senior Research Fellow in the Department of Media, Music and Cultural Studies, Macquarie University, Sydney, Australia. His research concentrates on Australian alternative, political and community theatre practice, and particularly the work and history of the Sidetrack Performance Group, an Australia Council-funded multi-ethnic innovative community theatre company based in Marrickville (since 1979) and similar groups. Components of this work include theatre and performance concerning refugee asylum-seekers; and in general the politics and ethics of cross-cultural and intercultural performance. Tom's research has centred around performance as social practice and as a form of cultural negotiation of themes of social justice and inequality. Contact: tom.burvill@mq.edu.au.

Dwight Conquergood served as a professor in Northwestern's Department of Performance Studies from 1983 until his death. He was named department chair in 1993 and held this post for six years. He also served as the Director of Graduate Studies for the Department of Performance Studies and as the director of Northwestern's Center for Interdisciplinary Research in the Arts from 1990 to 1995. Throughout his career, Conquergood's work focused on those marginalized by society. In 1981 he began his work with Hmong refugees at Camp Ban Vinai in northern Thailand. In Chicago, he helped new Hmong immigrants find housing and employment, and served as their advocate in court cases and other dealings. In the mid-1980s Conquergood worked with Palestinian refugees at the Jabaliya camp on the Gaza Strip. Later Conquergood relocated to the North Side Chicago neighbourhood of Albany Park to conduct research in the community. The 'Big Red' tenement Conquergood selected was located in an area known as Little Beirut, rampant with gangs, graffiti and civil disorder. He became an active member of the community, befriending and tutoring gang members while he studied their culture and daily life. This research led to his work *Life in Big Red: Struggles and Accommodations in a Chicago Polyethnic Tenement*. Conquergood also researched the purpose, rituals and societal implications of the death penalty in America. His 2002 paper, *Lethal Theatre: Performance, Punishment, and the Death Penalty*, was published in *Theatre Journal*.

Rea Dennis is currently a senior lecturer (drama) at the University of Glamorgan, UK. She has a particular interest in psycho-physical performance methodologies and works with a number of playback companies focusing on ensemble development and artistic repertoire from this perspective. Rea is co-director with Magda Miranda from Brazil of Lembrança, a bilingual company who perform relic-montages of located memory and autobiography using physical and interactive forms, their work has been shown in the United Kingdom, Australia, the United States and Brazil. An international teacher of improvisation and playback theatre, Rea works with companies in Australia, the United Kingdom and Brazil. Rea has previously studied for a Ph.D. in playback theatre at Griffith University, Australia (2004), and has a range of experiences in using theatre and arts in different contexts (development, business, refugee and disability and mental health). Contact: rdennis@glam.ac.uk.

Laura Edmondson is an associate professor in the Department of Theater at Dartmouth College, where she is also affiliated with African and African American Studies. Her articles on East African theatre and performance have appeared in *Theatre Journal*, *Theatre Research International*, *TDR*, and the anthologies *African Performance Arts* (Routledge, 2002) and *Violence Performed* (Palgrave Macmillan, 2009). Her book, *Performance and Politics in Tanzania: The Nation on Stage*, was published by Indiana University Press in 2007. Her research has been supported by grants from the National Endowment of the Humanities and the American Association of University Women. In 2008, she co-organized 'Eti! East Africa Speaks!' a residency for East African theatre artists at Dartmouth and in New York City, which received funding from the Ford Foundation, Dartmouth College, 651 ARTS, and the Martin E. Segal Theatre at the CUNY Graduate Center. Also a playwright, she is currently collaborating on a performance piece, *Forged in Fire* with Ugandan performer and playwright Okello Kelo Sam and Tanzanian musician and dancer Robert O. Ajwang', which integrates music, dance, and text to explore Okello's personal experiences of the civil war in northern Uganda. She has also taught theatre history and playwriting at the Bagamoyo

College of Arts in Tanzania and Makerere University in Kampala, Uganda. She is currently at work on her second book, *Genocide Performed: Narratives of Violence from Uganda, Rwanda, and the DRC*. Contact: laura.edmondson@dartmouth.edu.

Rand T. Hazou is a lecturer in theatre and drama at La Trobe University, Victoria, Australia. He completed a Bachelor of Arts in Geography, Media Studies and Drama at the University of Queensland in 1998. In 2004 Rand was commissioned by the UNDP to travel to the Occupied Territories in Palestine to work as a theatre consultant, running workshops for Palestinian youths. In 2009 Rand was awarded a Ph.D. in Theatre and Drama at La Trobe University. His thesis examined the theatre interventions staged in Australia dealing with Asylum Seekers and Refugees. In 2011 Rand was awarded a Cultural Leadership Development Grant by Australia Council for the Arts to develop The 7arakat |'ḥarakāt' Project which seeks to develop a series of theatre-related initiatives between Australia and Palestine. Contact: r.hazou@latrobe.edu.au.

Niz Jabur was born in 1962 in Najaf in the South of Iraq. Niz was a young child at the coming to power of the Ba'ath regime in 1968 and a late teenager at the inception of Saddam Hussein's leadership in 1979, during which time he was a university student, refugee and exiled artist between the time of the economic sanction and the invasion of Iraq. Niz has been in political prison and in a detention centre and has lived through the experiences of crossing borders and knows the stories of the stories. He works in the creative arts as a way to communicate his and other stories with wide range of audiences. Niz has studied theatre for the last 23 years and worked as a theatre writer, director, lecturer and currently as a Ph.D. student in Australia. Contact: survivalfire@hotmail.com.

Alison Jeffers is a lecturer in applied theatre and contemporary performance at the University of Manchester, UK. Her book *Refugees, Theatre and Crisis: Performing Global Identities* (2011) is based on research in theatre and performance with and about refugees. She carried out theatre projects with refugees and asylum seekers at the Medical Foundation for the Care of Victims of Torture in Manchester between 2005 and 2009 and worked with a group of refugee participants to write and perform a verbatim theatre piece on refugee issues called *I've Got Something to Show You* in 2005. This project is discussed in 'Looking for Esrafil' (2011) in *Get Real: Documentary Theatre Past and Present*, edited by A. Forsythe and C. Megson. Other publications in this area include 'Half-Hearted Promises or Wrapping Ourselves in the Flag: Two Approaches to the Pedagogy of Citizenship' in *Research in Drama Education: The Journal of Applied Theatre and Performance*, November 2007; 'Performance in place of war: refugee artists and communities in the UK' in *Changes in Museum Practice: New Media, Refugees and Participation,* edited by H. Skartveit and K. Goodnow (2009); and 'Dirty truth: personal narrative, victimhood and participatory theatre work with people seeking asylum' in *Research in Drama Education: The Journal of Applied Theatre and Performance*, June 2008. Contact: alison.jeffers@manchester.ac.uk.

Okello Kelo Sam is the founder and director of Mizizi Ensemble, a dance and music troupe based in Kampala, Uganda. He has led workshops throughout Europe and the United States on Ugandan dance and music. A gifted actor, he played starring roles in the films *Abducted: War Child*, directed by Robert E. Altman, and *White Light*, directed by Jean van de Velde. Both films address the crisis of child soldiers in Uganda. He also appeared in *The Last King of Scotland* as well as serving as a choreographer and composer. He is also the founder of Hope North, a resettlement centre in northern Uganda for victims of the war between the Lord's Resistance Army and the Ugandan government. Contact: samokello@gmail.com.

Yuko Kurahashi is an associate professor of theatre at Kent State University. She is the author of *Asian American Culture on Stage: The History of the East West Players* (Garland, 1999) and *Multicultural Theatre* (Kendall/Hunt, 2004 & 2006). Her interest has been in community–based theatre and outreach programmes which led Kurahashi, in 2009, to work as a videographer for *Beyond the Mirror*, the collaborative production by Bond Street Theatre (New York City) and Exile Theatre (Kabul, Afghanistan). Contact: ykurahas@kent.edu.

Robert Lachowicz is a community lawyer and educator. He is currently education coordinator at the Refugee and Immigration Legal Service (RAILS) in Brisbane and also teaches clinical legal education through Griffith University. He has worked as a principal solicitor at a youth community legal service and as principal solicitor and director at RAILS over many years. Robert has created training packages on cross-cultural justice, communication, conflict resolution, law and citizenship for the judiciary, Government, universities, schools and community groups. Robert has worked as a Government policy adviser on Indigenous justice, convenor of an Aboriginal Reconciliation group and has been president of his local resident's association. He maintains his interest in the arts as a film-maker, street performer, puppeteer, musician and is a board member of a local Arts Cooperative. Contact: robert.lachowicz@rails.org.au.

Felicia Faye McMahon is research associate professor in Anthropology, Maxwell School, Syracuse University. She is a former Fulbright scholar to eastern Germany (1995–1996) and an elected board member and past president (1998–2001) of the Fulbright Association Chapter of Central New York. Her published research focuses on public folklore, specifically in the Adirondacks of northern New York State, reunified Germany and, most recently, with new refugee communities in Central New York. Felicia also works professionally with several non-profit organizations in Cayuga, Seneca, Delaware, Chenango, Oneida, and Onondaga counties to coordinate folk arts programmes. Currently she is working with refugee resettlement agencies on projects relating to cultural intervention. Contact: frmcmaho@syr.edu.

Sanja Nikčević is a theatre critic, associate professor and head of Theatre History in the Drama Department at The Academy of Arts in Osijek, Croatia. She has twice been awarded a Fulbright scholarship. Sanja has edited *Anthology of Croatian War Plays*, *Anthology of American Plays* and *Theatre Criticism Today* (a collection of essays in English) in Croatia, and *Anthology of Contemporary Croatian Drama* in Macedonia. She has also published six books: *The Subversive American Drama or Sympathy for Losers* (1994), *Affirmative American Drama or Long Live the Puritans* (2003), *Losers' Genius in Our Town* (Zagreb, 2006), *What is Croatian Drama to Us?* (Zagreb, 2008), and *Theatre Criticism or Inevitable Companion* (Zagreb, 2012). Her book *New European Drama or Great Deception* (2005) received a Croatian award and was translated in Slovak, English (in *New Theatre Quarterly,* 2005), Hungarian and Polish. Sanja is founder and the first president of the Croatian Centre of the International Theatre Institute (ITI), and was editor of special editions of *The Series Mansions* and the journal *Theatre*. At present she is the president of a national theatre critics' organization and adviser for the European Theatre Award. Contact: sanja.nikcevic@zg.t-com.hr.

Robert Ombalassasa Ajwang' is a musician, dancer, and choreographer from northern Tanzania. He received his early dance education through performing in local ceremonies and rituals and went on to study East African music and dance at the College of Arts in Bagamoyo, Tanzania. Since moving to the United States in 1999, he has performed and/or taught workshops in Georgia, Florida, California, Vermont, New Hampshire and New York. He has also taught as a guest lecturer at Makerere University in Uganda, and his choreographed version of Malivata was performed at the National Theatre of Uganda in 2004. In the summer of 2008, he participated in *Eti! East Africa Speaks!*, a residency of East African performing artists at Dartmouth College and in New York City. Most recently, he performed his original choreography at the Centre X Centre festival in Kigali, Rwanda, and in Kampala, Uganda. He holds an MFA in dance from Bennington College. Contact: robert.ajwang@dartmouth.edu.

Guglielmo Schininà (MA, MSc, MBPsS) is a Social Theatre scholar and practitioner, and an expert in psychosocial and cultural integration activities in war-torn situations and natural disasters, with vulnerable migrants and victims of trafficking. He currently leads the International Organization for Migration's (IOM) global Mental Health, Psychosocial Response, and Intercultural Communication Section. He has worked in more than 30 Countries in East and West Europe, the Middle East, East Africa, Asia and the Caribbean and developed relevant academic courses at the University of Pristina in Kosovo, the Lebanese University, the University of Tripoli in Libya, and directs the Summer School in 'Psychosocial interventions in Emergency Displacement' at the Sant'Anna University in Pisa. He has written on Social Theatre and Theatre of the Oppressed in *The Drama Review, Research in Drama Education, Psychosocial Notebooks, Comunicazioni Sociali,* and others. Contact: gschinina@iom.int.

Yvonne Sliep, Ph.D., School of Psychology, University of Kwa-Zulu Natal, Durban, South Africa; **Kaethe Weingarten**, Ph.D., Department of Psychiatry, Cambridge Health Alliance,

Cambridge, Massachusetts, and the Witnessing Project, Newton, Massachusetts; **Andrew Gilbert**, Ph.D., Psychology Department, Rhodes University/Fort Hare University, East London, South Africa. Contact: sliepy@ukzn.ac.za.

Zlatko Topčić was born in Sarajevo on 30 April 1955. He graduated from Law School of the University of Sarajevo. He has published the following collections of short stories: *Životno pitanje/ The Vital Question*, (1981), *Ptica iz drugog jata/Bird From Another Flock*, (1995), *Bogumilske legende* (Bogomil Legends, (1997) and *Izabrane priče* (Selected stories, (2000); novels *Čovjek niotkud /A Man From Nowhere*, (1986), *Kulin* (1984) and *Košmar/Nightmare* (1997). His stories have been translated to English, Polish, Italian, Slovenian, French, Czech, Turkish and German, and they were included in several anthologies. He is the laureate of several prestigious B&H literary awards: The B&H Writers' Association Annual Award for Best Book Published in 1997 (novel *Košmar/Nightmare*), the first award at the anonymous concourse for film scenario awarded by the Association of Film Makers of B&H (*Remake*, (1999), *Čovjek niotkud/A Man From Nowhere* and *Gola koža/Bare Skin*, 2004) and the first award at the anonymous concourse for theatre play (*Time Out*, 2000, and *Glavom kroz zid*, 2004). Contact: xxyz@lol.ba.

Sarah Woodland is a facilitator, educator and researcher in Applied Theatre, Participatory Arts and Community Cultural Development in Brisbane, Australia. For the past seventeen years, Sarah has been instrumental in developing and facilitating programmes in a broad range of contexts, using drama and other arts-based and experiential group processes. Sarah graduated from Queensland University of Technology with a Bachelor of Arts (Drama), completed a Master of Drama Education (Hons) at Griffith University and is currently completing a Ph.D. in Prison Theatre, exploring devised drama with women and Indigenous participants in correctional contexts. Sarah has worked extensively in both the United Kingdom and Australia – she spent four years from 2001 as a core ensemble member of Geese Theatre Company, UK, and has since been a freelance facilitator in Brisbane with partners such as Brisbane City Council's Youth Team, Brisbane Youth Detention Centre, Edmund Rice Education and Mission Australia. Sarah tutors on a range of courses within Griffith University's applied theatre programme, including *Applied Theatre Project* and *Applied Performance*. She is also the Director for Griffith University's Theatre Scope programme that aims to enhance learning and teaching through partnerships and outreach projects. Contact: s.woodland@griffith.edu.au.

Nina Woodrow has a background working in welfare, community arts and community cultural development, and education in Australia, with some stints overseas. She has a history of involvement in oral history, community theatre and storytelling projects, engaging with community groups and facilitating workshops using a framework that integrates social, cultural and artistic processes and outcomes. She also has had a parallel career as an adult literacy and English as a second language (ESL) teacher within the vocational education and training sector in Australia. As a language and literacy teacher she worked with a wide range of people including young people and refugees. It is with these learners in particular that she embraced drama and digital storytelling methodologies as a way of engaging those with stories to tell and language and literacy (particularly digital literacy) skills to learn. An interest in exploring these kinds of processes further – looking at how cultural identities are inscribed in narratives, the relationship between wellbeing and creative expression, and the way participative processes facilitate this kind of creativity can be employed in educational and community based contexts – led her to research work. In 2010 she moved from language teaching to a research position at Griffith University, and she is commencing a Ph.D. programme in digital storytelling at Queensland University of Technology. Contact: n.woodrow@griffith.edu.au.

Preface

The title of this book, *Refugee Performance,* suggests there is a constituency of practices that might be unified under a definite term or god forbid to propose a new field of study. This is far from the intentions of the collection. No one chooses to be a refugee, and certainly it is a tag that new settlers seek to transcend as swiftly as possible. There are significant issues with labelling the work directly as refugee performance. So the title of the book is inherently a paradox, but a paradox is not always a bad place to start a story. Nor is it improper to investigate something that combines contradictory qualities and features, as long as the paradox, the uncomfortable elements, hold their form. The objective is not to resolve the contradiction, but to understand it better.

This collection has grown out of an interest in performance and theatre in sites of war and the impact of conflict on diasporic communities. My personal connection to these themes started in Northern Ireland where I was at University during the tail end of the troubles (early 1990s). During this time I worked with some other graduates to run a children's theatre company and got cross-community funding to run workshops with teenagers from Catholic and Protestant backgrounds (groups of 16, 8 from each religious background). It quickly became apparent that the groups were sick of issue-based work, and really just wanted to do some drama. So we did. Inspired by Bread and Puppet and Welfare State International we designed large-scale street parades with giant puppets that reinvented common myths and popular stories. The work pushed us to consider the ways in which aesthetics worked with groups who were supposedly in conflict with each other.

More recently with an Arts and Humanities Research Council project *In Place of War* (www.inplaceofwar.net/) and an Australian Research Council Linkage grant exploring arts-based approaches to supporting newly arrived refugees transition to a new culture, I have been directly involved with a range of individuals, groups and communities from refugee backgrounds. It is these experiences and encounters that have given rise to this book, for though there has been considerable activity by writers, artists and researchers discussing their insights into work for, by and with refugees the work is scattered and sometimes hard to find. The premise of this collection was to create a space in which the key issues, experiences, observations and passions could be shared. The chapters are designed to be in dialogue with each other, not to construct a finite discourse, but to suggest, provoke and, importantly, disseminate stories and insights. Borrowing from

Elssas (1992) the process is about complimentarity (contributors with similar experiences grouped together) and congruency (contributors with varied experiences grouped together to help understand differences among them). These two principles have governed the selection and commissioning of chapters and writers. Some chapters have been previously published, others have been commissioned, and further writings have been sent to me by writers interested in being part of the collection. I have made a deliberate choice of combining perspectives from artists, individuals with refugee backgrounds, academics, researchers and non-theatre practitioners who have sought out performance as a tactic in their work. I hope this adds richness to the dialogue.

The chapters represent stories from a range of countries and war contexts, including Iraq, Thailand, Burma, Uganda, Palestine, Croatia, Serbia, Australia, the United Kingdom, and the United States of America. This is by no means a comprehensive guide to performance and refugee work, or a representative sample of current and recent conflicts. There is no background information to the wars and their genealogy, unless the authors explicitly draw this into their work. This collection is a tentative first step of complimentarity and congruency, focused on thematics, commonalities and divergencies in refugee-related work. The authors offer a range of possibilities for performance, and in equal measure underline the problematics of practice. Too often in refugee performance work it is the well-intentioned practitioner/agency that unravels a social dynamic and leaves behind scar tissue, hidden behind silent, polite smiles. All too often I have learnt what not *to say*, and what not *to do* with the refugee individuals and groups with whom I have had the privilege to work.

The chapters therefore provide a summation of performance tactics with different analytical frameworks and certainly different conclusions and outcomes. Niz Jabour sets the scene provocatively and poetically detailing in *dreamatic* terms his personal homecomings, departures and arrivals to Iraq (the motif of The Rooms provided the inspiration for the front cover). 'On Stitches' attempts to provide an overview of some of the key tensions in refugee performance both in terms of the sociopolitical realities of refugees as well as the ways in which artists have attempted to conceptualize their work. Dwight Conquergood's chapter was one of the first and in many ways one of the landmark papers dealing with refugee theatre. It is derived from sustained ethnographic field work in a Hmong refugee camp (Thailand) and details the development of a communication project that sought to build strong ownership and community participation through prolonged engagement and dialogue. Conquergood's ethnographic observations are marked by an intense humanity, combined with attuned analyses of the dynamics of camp life and the divergent cultural relationships between the insider (Hmong) and outsider (NGO volunteers and workers) individuals/groups.

'Forged in Fire' (a play extract), Yvonne Sliep, Kaethe Weingarten and Andrew Gilbert's 'Narrative Theatre as an Interactive Community Approach to Mobilizing Collective Action in Northern Uganda,' and Laura Edmondson's 'Marketing Trauma and the Theatre of War in Northern Uganda' all reflect recent issues from a specific context – northern Uganda.

Sliep, Weingarten and Gilbert describe an interactive community approach that addressed the issue of domestic violence in a refugee camp in northern Uganda. Domestic violence had emerged at the time as one of the residents' most significant health problems. Based on principles of narrative therapy and Forum Theatre, this community-based approach, named Narrative Theatre by the community workers themselves, sought to address the causes and alter the trajectory of the potential outcomes of domestic violence at both the individual and community levels. Edmondson's significant chapter discusses the creative work of the World Vision Children of War Rehabilitation Centre. The centre provides a safe place for children who have been abducted by the notorious Lord's Resistance Army (LRA) to serve as child soldiers, porters and/or so-called wives of the rebels. Edmondson critiques the use of creativity, questioning the ways in which local acts of theatre and performance can be used in a range of ways, both positive and problematically, by a variety of players on the global stage.

Rand Hazou's 'travel notes' mark out some of the dichotomies at play in the Palestine context. Personal, questioning and conflicting, the journey reflects Rand's encounter with Alrowwad theatre company, and their definition of how creative arts act as a beautiful resistance to communities in the Aida Camp. Sanja Nikčević's 'Rape as War Strategy: A Drama from Croatia' details the history of a play, *Maria's Pictures,* based on true stories told to the playwright, Lydia Scheuermann Hodak. The chapter discusses the play and its subtle exploration of war-related themes and its reception (or lack of it) by Croatian theatres and reflects on why there was a refusal to mount a production either during the war or after it. The chapter is followed by a powerful extract from *Refugees* by Zlatko Topčić (trans. Davor Diklić). In 'Far Away, So Close: Psychosocial and Theatre Activities with Serbian Refugees' Guglielmo Schininà discusses his experiences in Serbia in 1999 in which he worked as a workshop facilitator, as part of emergency relief services focusing on the persistent problems caused by the wars. The chapter details his work on rituals, on construction and reconstruction of the individual, group, and collective roles, on community building, on creative re-elaboration of mourning and anger among the International Displaced Persons (IDPs) in communities around Serbia, using his theatre experience not to impose but to create communication and interaction.

Tom Burvill's chapter, '"Politics Begins as Ethics": Levinasian Ethics and Australian Performance Concerning Refugees,' begins by outlining Emmanuel Levinas's radical conception of ethics. Levinas invokes/declares an absolute and primary obligation of responsibility to the human Other, whom he figures hyperbolically as invoked by the epiphany of the encounter with 'the face of the Other.' This encounter with alterity founds not only ethics, but subjectivity itself, in Levinas's conception. He applies Levinas's concept to the refusal of responsibility, of unqualified hospitality and asylum exercised by the Australian Government under John Howard. The chapter argues that the rich and varied response of Australian theatre and performance to this refusal was, however, broadly ethical. Its form of politics was to produce affective rather than ideological transformations in the audience. Burvill examines a selection of performance and theatre work that uses different performance strategies to explore how this was achieved.

Michael Balfour's chapter, 'Refugee Performance: Encounters with Alterity,' explores the ethics between aesthetic representation and refugee experience, examining two practical projects one in Logan, Australia, the other a site-specific mini festival in Margate, UK. The chapter explores the potential promise of performance in the promiscuous traffic between different ways of knowing. Balfour argues that these ways of knowing involve engaging the arts to help transcend the process of mapping secure forms of knowledge onto others, through avoiding victimhood narratives, and foregrounding the importance of listening for stories that emerge in their own time and in their own ways.

McMahon's 'Repeat Performance: Dancing DiDinga with the Lost Boys of Southern Sudan' highlights the ways in which in folklore studies, there is a dearth of information about the transnational processes by which diasporic communities actively negotiate their identities. The author examines the variables that affect the cultural performances of the DiDinga, an understudied group of southern Sudanese refugees, known in the United States by the moniker the 'Lost Boys.' In today's world of globalization and transnationalism, documentation and interpretation of recontextualized performances is more critical than ever before. Part of this inquiry seeks to make explicit the tensions that affect ways by which this small group of parentless male youth come to consensus about appropriate and meaningful traditions performed for the public in a new context. Drawing on public sector work with refugees, McMahon explores how folklore research contributes to identifying internal and external forces that act on the aesthetics of recontextualized performance of diasporic groups, as well as how folklorists work effectively to present and interpret recontextualized traditions of people now residing in the United States.

Yuko Kurahashi's chapter, 'Theatre as the Healing Space: Ping Chong's *Children of War*,' examines the empowering/re-authoring function of *Children of War*, a play that was presented in Fairfax, Virginia. The play comments on both past and current political conflicts in the homeland of each participant, and on the effects those conflicts have on their personal lives. The chapter examines the therapeutic effect of this project – how, for example, the participants' recollections were used to lead them into self-reflection, communication and negotiations that often resulted in insights. The goal is not, however, to evaluate the production in psychotherapeutic and medical terms. The intention, rather, is to show that the piece created a site for expressing the 'unspeakable,' and, symbiotically, a kind of communal healing, a kind of understanding, that allows both participants and audiences to re-author those horrific experiences.

Sarah Woodland and Rob Lachowicz's chapter, 'Drama and Citizenship Education: Tensions of Creativity, Content and Cash' explores the key tensions of an applied theatre project, *The Good Citizen Ship*, designed to assist refugees in passing the Australian citizenship test. The project aimed to explore in an interactive and dynamic way the key values, privileges and responsibilities underpinning Australian citizenship, as well as other more factual details contained within the test. The authors illuminate some of the challenges that face interdisciplinary approaches and explore the project's position in the context of contemporary applied theatre theory.

Community-based performance often facilitates participation through story-based processes and in this way could be seen as enacting a form of inclusive democracy. Rea Dennis' chapter examines a playback theatre performance with a refugee and asylum-seeker audience and questions whether inclusive, democratic participation can be fostered. It presents a snapshot of the political/social/cultural climate in Australia, as well as the refugee and asylum-seeker sector in Brisbane, at the time of the performance by referencing discourses of multiculturalism and stranger danger in the wake of 9/11. Specific moments from the performance are analysed to reveal the way the momentum of ritual performance clashes with the tenuous status of the refugee participant and the structural power dynamics within the audience. Alison Jeffers important chapter, 'Hospitable Stages and Civil Listening: Being an Audience for Participatory Refugee Theatre' concludes the collection. In the chapter Jeffers suggests that there is a need to shift the focus from refugee participants onto the audience in order to challenge ethical assumptions. The chapter aims to do this by examining *the practice of being an audience* at a refugee theatre event. Using writing on theatre audiences helps to develop an understanding about the relationships between audience members and refugee performers and shows how the act of *listening* at a refugee theatre event can be construed as a civil act that simultaneously challenges notions of togetherness and opens up tough questions about responsibility.

The material in the book asks questions. The writers attempt to provoke uncertainties that chip away at the paradox of refugee performance; illuminating and eliding the shades and nuances of this unexpected practice. The practical encounters between experience, reflection, action and aesthetics are grounded in the direct observations of the authors and the imperative to create affective possibilities through performance. Theatres of resistance, of creative exchange (and barter), and of representing the impact and consequences of mass social upheavals.

Chapter 1

Iraqi Memories. A Personal and Poetic Exploration of Homecomings, Departures and Arrivals from a Theatre Director Who Fled Iraq in 1987 and Returns Home Again

Niz Jabour

Prelude

I use the word *dreamatic* (not dramatic), because dreams in language are my only hope to reach out for the understanding with which to develop creative narratives in time and place. This is a process that can be described thus: 'To take hold of our own existence, our own history, and make it into *a dream* that was there from the beginning when we were called into this space' (Pelias et al. 2008: 254, emphasis added).

The poet Omar Khayyam asks a question about time travel in our dreams, about the meaning behind (us) being born and why (we) come to live:

> *If my coming were up to me, I'd never be born*
> *And if my going were of my accord, I'd go with scorn*
> *Isn't it better in this world, so old and worn*
> *Never to be born, neither stay, nor away be torn?*

> (Omar Khayyam, *Rubaiyat*)

In answer to the Persian poet, I found myself a refugee without any given options, and if I had known that I would become a refugee, I would have wished I had never been born.

Background

I was born in 1962 in a city called Najaf, which is the centre and holy place for Muslims of the Shia faith. It is a small town known as the home of the largest cemetery in Iraq and the shrine of Imam Ali Bin Abi Talib.

My unique position as an artist stems from my upbringing, education and training in arts (specifically in theatre) in Iraq, my subsequent lengthy and involved experiences in exile and my work with local and exiled multi-ethnic communities in Iraq, Pakistan and Australia (since 1998). I was a young child when the Ba'ath regime came to power and was a university student at the inception of Saddam Hussein's leadership in 1979. As an Iraqi artist, I studied theatre and directing for years, only to see any possibilities for a future disappear. I lived through the sacking of libraries and destruction of books, and I have witnessed it all again, with different targets, in more recent years on visits home since 2004.

I lived the multiple complexities of cultural identity during my journey as a refugee, crossing borders between Iraq, Iran, Pakistan and Australia.

The power of narrative

We narrate what we see and experience either in our inner reality or in our imagination. The power of narrative is the power of our voices to maintain memory in all forms and patterns. The re-telling of stories becomes a real option for making human voices heard through forms of conversation and performance. Words form stories that can store history. Words have power, and this is why, under tyranny and in dictatorship, specific words are officially banned and others suffer from self-censorship.

We participate in actions and we get involved in the outcome of events, whether we are or have been the oppressed or the oppressor, victim or witness, powerful or powerless. We engage in the processes that generate the re-telling of collective or individual memory.

We reconstruct frameworks of events, memories and imagination corresponding to historical and/or cultural frames in our memories. The reconsideration of history no longer remains a chronicle of the powerful but becomes an account of the voiceless (powerless), silent and dismissed voices of the people.

I like the attention Ricoeur pays to the role of mediation or mediator, where history is the mediator between memory and forgetting. I am, however, more interested in having artists – singers, painters, poets, mimes, actors, writers, directors, film-makers, musicians, dancers, composers, performers – stand as mediators between *memory* and *remembrance*. To give them the means to narration based on the experiences, imaginings and interpretations that may bring some light to their truth and sense of justice.

In *Memory: an Anthology* (Wood and Byatt 2008: 203) the poet Craig Raine wrote: 'Memory is like metaphor in its operation [...] I see almost every narrative, every performance as form of metaphor in which I encounter narrative in the structure of thematic designs through one's self.'

I agree with this, and find here an exposition of the interaction between the self and poetic and everyday languages as a means to further the exchanges between personal and historical narratives.

Personal memory and historical events in an everyday-life narrative

I invite you to visit *The Rooms* [of my story] with me. 'Room[s] of imagination, room[s] of memory' are metaphors to narrate stories within a poetic narrative in which 'the event itself operates as a lightning rod that allows us to see clearly for a brief moment.'

At home: 13 November 2008 – 8.17 a.m.

I am at home now. I am at home, in a circle of unfinished thoughts and doubts about the future. It is just a huge dust in Iraq all day and every time. Dust awaits and welcomes me, across the border, into the city and at home, like a monstrous salute for an absent return. It is enough to be alive. I have arrived in a country that is like a big prison, where concrete blocks prevent the eye from looking to the other side of the street, where the city is like a detention centre with Iraqis volunteering in the police and armed forces. Passing one checkpoint after another, when the road to home is like a train of endless checkpoints, when the sentence, 'show me your identity certificate,' is a common welcome, and where fear stands like faceless thoughts in the eyes of passengers from the Kuwaiti border to Najaf city in the south of Iraq.

Here I am in a neglected land, in the suburb of Al-Ansar, where cholera is enemy of the poor, nesting in the drinking water like a dream in the desert. I have arrived, but where to now? I meet with my brothers, sisters and the rest of the family one after another, and news of my arrival is like fire eating dry leaves. 'He is back!' my sister shouts, and it is like I never left, or it was a short while ago and not the 21 years of the exiled life of a refugee. Nothing has changed, the same houses, streets and shops with high levels of corruption among police, army and government officials. Huge wires connect all the houses and buildings to electric power generators like spider-houses, hanging on walls, fences and over roofs.

Welcome home, with no drinking water, no electricity. These are the typical thoughts and conversations in every house. People are talking and saying that one of the reasons we do not have electricity and water is the occupation policy. This argument is used against Iraqi political parties. This answer is one of the most common answers you get here, even if you interviewed the entire population, while others believe that the vast driftnets of Iraq's government corruption are beyond description and consider Iraq the most corrupted place on Earth.

The first piece of advice I always receive is, 'Do not talk about God and politics!' but every conversation is about the politics of religion. People still believe that the invasion took place because the United States and its allies had come to liberate them; others think it is because God is not happy with the Iraqi people's faith and beliefs. 'What is God and do I believe in God?' No one is interested in talking about the future because the future is like a black spot of confusion on the white page of the country's history and the life of Iraqi society. What can I do, and how and where do I start?

Let me hope tomorrow is not the same as the days that have marked the passage of centuries here up until the present?

Okra: 13 November 2008 – 10 p.m.

I spend some time with my family with lots of joking and food. The Iraqi lifestyle is, of course, very different from the Australian. The people's dreams here are about security, jobs and the desire to be able to express their opinions without political or social repercussions or even a bullet in the head. In the midst of all kinds of pressures, people are (still) looking towards the future.

Every little detail here is a special moment of peace and harmony in memory, which I have missed before, after and between departures and arrivals.

From Baghdad: 18 November 2008 – 4.26 p.m.

Walking around the streets is like reading a poem written by an unknown poet. People's stories are jumping from one corner to another and they have lots of thoughts to share when they come sit and share my silence with me. People are thirsty to tell me about what happened to them in their everyday life. Here, I do not ask anyone any questions. I just keep listening and they do the talking. Sometimes all it takes to make people talk is to say hello. 'Hello,' and little bit of respect is what people need to express without stopping.

I am listening to everyone's sorrow and pain and trying not to ask any questions, because the connections I have with those stories are alive in my memory.

Timing: 25 November 2008 – 10:37 a.m.

I am trying to sleep but I cannot, because of the social pressure from my family surrounding me now and environmental issues, such as water shortage, dirty or infected water or air dusty with depleted uranium. There are daily confrontations between people and government officials about meeting their daily requirements for water and food. Sometimes these confrontations lead to fearless or desperate acts and end in death, in prison or in a garbage bin. Life here is not a joke or a drama research project. Not even an objective academic study. What I see and witness is related to the *dreamatic* vision about *one's own* self-reality, when real and not real are very hard to separate.

The rooms

I need to use the metaphor of a room to retrieve the complexities of war, refugees and exiled worlds. These are memories and experiences I dwell on. They are raw, performative materials, and I am sharing this journey with you.

I acknowledge that I am a learner with located experiences in time. I wake up in the morning thinking in Arabic. I start thinking in Farsi after a few moments, and a little bit later I (re)start, thinking in English. I am living (in) a variety of languages and cultures. I am living (in) many rooms.

The room as a metaphor comes from a mystical structure in the *One Thousand and One Nights*. The room is a metaphor of and for story-content in real-life experiences. Remembering the *One Thousand and One Nights* brought back to me this narrative: a person went to meet the king in Baghdad, seeking to find an answer to a question. The king listened to his request and said, 'I will give you a key that opens fifty-one rooms in my palace and if you can't find the answer, we will talk.' The fellow took the key and went from one room to another. There was an empty room, a room with one chair, a room with dead people, a room with princes holding flowers, a room with swords and costumes, etc., and the king said, 'You can name anything to be found in these rooms!' But at the end, in the last room, there was only a mirror that stood as a door without a room.

I do not have to tell the reader what to read or how to enter these rooms at this stage of the journey, because I/We are the stories, and they are told with our own and other voices.

A story is enclosed in a room and I ask you: 'What are you going to do?'

Room 1: Bleedings of imprisonment

I threw the door of mercy away
and kept a mirror in my pocket
for the dictators and those sleeping in the brothel of politics.
I threw the door of the house away
I carried the prayer of ascetic fasting.
The Spirit is a key for a lost lock.

Throw all the land and bleeding imprisonment
on the threshold of exile.

Naked I called those who were not in spirit.
Oh strange! It is naked life!
Leave clothes and outdated land here –
The land and wasteland,
Each question for justice and annihilation –
I have thrown my limbs on the side of the road
And the way that led me to fast.

I've thrown everything
And calm, I hope to depart.

Room 2

There is a beautiful pain, lying in the bottom of self-
burning (burning inside) of all affiliation.
There is a beautiful hope, placing seeds of light in every step of our life.
Pain and hope are the keys to presence.
In the interval between them
I become a citizen.

Room 3

Tell me what you remember and I will tell who you are because I don't know, and none know what we would or could forget and why.

Room 4

Each one of us is allowed to make our own history and history is what we make.

I went to Baghdad four times: the first time was on 24 April 2004 – there was no state and the streets were full of blood and shades of sorrow were painted on people's faces.

I went to find out about my family. How old were they? What do they look like after nineteen years of exile within and without? Is it valid or true to say that the memories of having being born here arose like a burning fire inside me, making me feel like a lost child? I saw the destruction of cities, houses, buildings and human bodies. Breath was screaming alive in the air. I have 19 years of life, looted or shared, that was spent crossing borders to survive. The problem I had was bigger than my memories of my family, and it no longer exists; it is merely an illusionary mirror echoing the silence of the unknown.

When I arrived the first man to recognize me was my father. He was sitting as I left him, in the same spot. I stood and looked at five people sitting in front of our old house and my brothers were sitting there too, but they had never met me before because they were born while I was living in exile. My father shouted like a wounded soul, and his tears told me how long he had been waiting for that moment to see me again.

Where shall I start? The entire street wakes up. This young boy who departed from his home is coming back to his family and friends. Welcome home, welcome to the grave of memories under occupation, welcome now. I have with me a camera, I open the bag and show the children how to use it anywhere and anytime they want it.

Room 5: Private Room

During the day, I frame my dreams
At night, I burn all the frames of me.

It's the coldness marching across all borders.
Like the child waking up to bring some water to the family,
early in the morning.
He didn't know that there was a bomb waiting for him, a nine year-old child.
What the father said: it's night time, the soldier is asleep.
When he wakes up, I will ask him if he really meant to kill my son or not?
Have a nice dream then, in the coldness of a dead child.
My mirror broke a long time ago and my voice is getting old.
But I could sing sometimes for myself and the shadows in my mirrors.
My fingers are not bleeding any more.

Room 6

The second visit to Baghdad was on 23 February 2006 when there was civil war and fighting in the streets of Najaf, and when my memory was bleeding for answers. What could I do?

This was a time when the entire society and culture had collapsed, and when Iraqis were fighting among themselves and killing one another. This was when unknown and re-discovered diseases began to be born in the bodies of families. It is unfinished, and there is nowhere to go.

Room 7

On my third visit, on 24 April 2008, I am in urgent need of finding peace within my soul, of finding what it is all really about? Why the Iraqi memories? Is it because I was born in Iraq? What are the impacts of war and dictatorship regimes on the social fabric? Am I still the researcher who is living the experiences?

Thoughts grow like seeds in the soil of lived experiences and in time they manifest in questions. I started to learn more and more about myself and my relationship with a country called Iraq or HOME. Where can a researcher and an artist stand, witnessing a real and unreal world of war?

Room 8

The conversation sleeps in the bed of silence,
No word in or out
Just the eyes
Looking in a dark room for a candle's light to come.
Alone like a sick bird
Lying on the ground thirsty….

Room 9: Eyes

Two eyes, one on the door and the other one on the road, waiting for absent returns.
Two eyes like road stones,
like twins slapping death,
and swinging swings for a stranger.

Two eyes cried until they became blind,
and white sand walked in them, into white windows,
story and memory,
as if history is repeated twice.
as if they are the laughing wars
Or coffins hanging in the sunset.

Two eyes,
the wooden stick is the sight of a blind man
who reads pictures on the ground
and visions he has seen.

Two eyes
Like yours, Baghdad.
Whenever a blind man fails, the river dries up and the palm tree dies, Baghdad
Stay like us, two rivers and a third river of human beings
We will meet like two eyes ….

Less and more, I am Ok.
The moon is a room for rent
and the sun is not my heater, nor have I a bag.
What to take with you to see drying rivers?
War time, war zones, war thorns.

Room 10

On Wednesday, 7 April 2010:

We have had bloody days and nights when explosions shook the heart of the nation again.
More than eleven explosions danced in the mirror of hope, where greetings slaughtered
the meanings of the time in my face and I became a bird:

that deletes innocence in old houses
and churns the cement with the blood of children,

while missiles shattered stones and homes.
Havoc in the cities, and the river runs to escape the desert.
Does no one else remain but you Baghdad?
Blood moves in the cracks of destroyed buildings
Aging and the Spirit are melted on the gates of hell.
No gods or prophets,
I'm here, like roses of fire
crown the house of nothingness drowsiness.

Room 11

How many times were refugees and Gypsies forced to leave their home or native land? The war against Jews and Gypsies looks similar to the current war against Gypsies and Muslims in the West.

To the moment you listen, to the moment you speak ....
To this and that moment, welcome and goodbye
And to you, Gypsy stranger,
Oh, Gypsy 'stranger,' how it happened, you sink before your empty ship,
How come you sink empty?
My breath is my country, my identities and the whole world. The most
distinctive means of identity to me comes with maintaining
living memories.

Like a Black door, a Black window in a grave.
Shading of lost sorrows in the mountain of being.
extinguishing the lights of options
And hanging the best dreams on the wall of societies
While the fool with his mirror walks jauntily.

Room 12: Hello

She said, 'My husband was killed while we were having breakfast with the kids; and here I am as you see, living with my seven children in this public terminal for cars (public car park). A blanket as a roof and a wooden stick with three metres of rope as wall, we are refugees in our own homeland and refugees in our own cities. We don't know anyone who can help us, we wrote to the Major of the City of Najaf; to sheikh and mullah, but no one gives us any food. I am really trying hard to let my kids go to school; I don't want them to live in the streets because we have nowhere to go. The old kid is nine years old and no school wants him, they think he is mad, and there you go, what to do?'

Questions from the rooms

There are thousands of stories of widows and orphans, of people living in silence and fear of death. Those widows have been at the heart of a single unresolved problem in Iraq since 1917, when Great Britain's last ship of slaves went from Africa to Iraq.

There are thousands of stories about the unknown diseases spreading among the population, of deformed children and risky pregnancies because the United States used depleted uranium. It is said that the Iranian's puppet (the Iraqi government) is calling for women not to have children in Al-Anbar province. The future of the country is unclear. Is it going to be an Islamic state with Iranian domination in the region, or will the Americans withdraw, or will there be open conflicts between Israelis, Arabs and Americans against Iranians and a repeat of the story of the Iraq–Iran war (1980–1988)?

What is the future of a country during an undecided period of reform of a government or a state? What price do civilians pay for unresolved political violence?

There has been conflict in the region since the formation of Iraqi borders around its mixed populations, religious and ethnic groups. The ongoing struggle of these communities and their memories is complicated by the conflicting interests of local and international denominations. The people of Iraq have lived for three decades through social trauma. First there was the period of Saddam Hussein (1979–2003), then the economic sanctions and isolation (1991–2003), followed by multiple wars – the first Gulf War (1980–1988), the second Gulf War (1991) – and now an occupation and ongoing military strikes and actions led by the USA and its allies since 2003.

People are shocked by inexplicable events that have made their world an unspeakable place: hostile and death-ridden.

The Iraqi people over centuries have been persecuted and their voices have been silenced by the dominant power. There has never been a time for the Iraqi people to establish their own state without Western or regional interference in the economic and political process of (re-)building their country. The Iraqi people have lived for a long, long time within the cycles of violence and war. The fight was and will be about the dominant power of ethnicities or ideologies over water rights in the Tigris–Euphrates river system

The words *remember* and *memory* have been associated with permanent pain and suffering in Iraq from the dawn of its history to the present day. The people are living at the edge of a complete loss of social justice, culture and memory and are 'too scarred by the past, too wary of the future to believe that their long nightmare may have ended' (Brockmeier 2008: 15). This failure of hope is due to the absence of independent mediation and the people's lack of confidence in the dialogue between components and sectors of society.

'Remembering the past becomes the struggle for the truth' (Brockmeier 2008: 15). Equally, turning a blind eye to the past becomes a struggle for truth, and even the struggle to forget becomes a struggle for the truth. Every passing moment becomes a struggle for truth, a moment of truth. In remembering and forgetting there are many attempts to hide one truth at the expense of another. Effective communication processes between the self and others rely on the complexities of re-remembering the forced changes in the social fabric during peace and war, on the one hand, and reflecting on forgotten personal memories, on the other. The ability to communicate with these live entities of memory is the ability to re-localize 'ourselves in […] time and history' (Brockmeier 2008: 28). Where can we create our space on common ground in order to understand the impact of events on everyday life and the continuing interplay of meanings in historical events?

What common ground can we find on which to create our spaces in order to understand the impact of events on everyday life and the continuing impact and interplay of meanings from historical events. How can memories be (re-)constructed through the re-creation of art? If there is no artist, no arts of life, how can we reflect on our thinking, our future? I agree with Barba (2006: 108) in his response to exile in *Paradox of the Sea*: 'I tell myself: my country can be defined as a voluntary exile. The country in which I dwell is the theatre.'

I have experienced a multiplicity of exiles, and the meaning of exile has come to me from my own shattering. I see exile as:

Exile within one's own culture because of the economic
and political repression.
Exile without one's own culture because of the sense of
displacement/rootlessness, with no belonging.
Exile within and without because of the lost direction within one's
own soul, a spiritual exile. Exile of the whole planet, because of
the abuse of names such as God, nation, democracy, to justify a
war; this is total exile, on in which the self/entity is forced to exist
in a world where identities collapse on the walls of arts.

My exiles brought to light my memories of languages, cultures and history and opened a great gateway to negotiate cultural and creative narratives in performance. In my creative journey, I focus on ways that stories are heard, shared and expressed peacefully among communities and individuals.

References

Barba, Eugenio, 'The Paradox of the Sea,' *New Theatre Quarterly*, 22:2 (2006), pp. 107–11.

Brockmeier. J., 'Remembering and Forgetting: Narrative as Cultural Memory,' *Culture Psychology*; 8:15 (2008), pp. 15–43.

Khayyam, O., *Rubaiyat*, www://en.wikipedia.org/wiki/Mesopotamia (accessed 26 August 2011).

Pelias, R., Richardson, L., Ellis, C., Bochner, A., Denzin, N., Lincoln, Y., and Morse, J., 'Talking and Thinking About Qualitative Research,' *Qualitative Inquiry,* 14 (2008), p. 254.

Wertsch, James V., and Roediger, Henry, L., 'Collective Memory: Conceptual Foundations and Theoretical Approaches,' *Memory*, 16:3 (2008), pp. 318–326.

Chapter 2

On Stitches

Michael Balfour and Nina Woodrow

In May 2003 it was reported that a Kurdish asylum seeker, Abas Amini, had sewn up his lips, ears and eyelids as a way to protest the decision made by the UK authorities to deport him back to Iran. The decision to give asylum to Amini, a poet, was given and then subsequently challenged by the Home Office. Several days later, an independent tribunal rejected the appeal and the Iranian national was allowed to stay in the United Kingdom. At a press conference announcing the success of the tribunal, Amini's interpreter read out a poem:

> He sewed up his lips so that he could speak out.
> He sewed up his eyes to make others see.
> He sewed up his ears to make others hear.
> You whose eyes, ears and mouths are free, see, hear and speak out.

The image of the stitched asylum seeker, and the subsequent unstitching created an act that was theatrical and spectacular, recording the invisibility of a personal testimony, as well as a bold and conscious political act. The image was a counter-narrative to the normative stories of fear and suspicion that were (and continue to be) in circulation about (legal and illegal) immigrants. The stitched face startles, as it brings us quite literally into an encounter with 'the Other's' psychological and physical pain. As Soguk (2006) notes, it's Amini's recognition and reclamation of his body as 'a hidden site' of political-poetics that fuels the potency of the act:

> Read against the literal background of his body as a canvas of torture, Amini's poem has the effect of a political act in space already infused with power relations and meanings. ... As an 'event' in space, his poem necessarily contains (emanates from and reflects) the traces of the material and metaphorical conditions of the social space Amini resides in but cannot unproblematically inhabit. ... Thus, fundamentally his poem functions as a historical political act on life, recording what might otherwise be relegated to nonhistory.
>
> (Soguk 2006: 390)

Political and performative events, or biopoetics as termed by Soguk (2006), such as Amini's sewing of his eyes, ears and mouth can act as violent disjunctions to normative representations of refugees. Amini's body-as-a-poem presents a radical trauma to the present rationalization of refugees, in that it disrupts and re-tells a powerful story of nonhistory, forces an encounter with the other that personalizes the anguish without victimizing the subject. Kristeva quotes Khlebnikov to describe the potential efficacy of such an aesthetic:

> Short [poetic] pieces are important when they serve as a break into the future, like a shooting star, leaving behind a trail of fire. They should move rapidly enough so that they pierce the present. … [They] set the present ablaze.
>
> (Kristeva 1980: 61)

Unfortunately, Amini's public act of self-mutilation is no longer a rare act, as marginalized individuals attempt to make visible their histories, often in fatal ways. Soguk (2006) argues that the increase in corporeal interventions (immolation, suicide, riots, stitching of the body) are resorted to 'in order to thwart the techniques of disappearance utilized by state apparatuses, which reduce their stories to statistics and then consign them to the labyrinths of governmentality' (Soguk 2006: 391). He concludes that Amini's action is a survival act:

> It is only by radically altering the disposition of their bodies in relation to the spatial political and governmental orders that refugees can reclaim their agency. In this context, sewing lips, ears, and eyelids becomes an effective available strategy by which to highlight the actual violence that the often-invisible politics of disappearance performs on refugees and asylum seekers. In this way, mutilation stops being a self-mutilation: It emerges as a violence pointing to the violence inflicted on refugees when their agency is taken away step by step, document after document, in detention centers, refugee houses, and court appearances. Step by step, a refugee is stitched voiceless, sightless, and soundless.
>
> (Soguk 2006: 392)

Amini's poetic act serves as a useful metaphor for the kind of material conditions of the artists and practitioners who are writing in this book. The conceit of calling this book 'Refugee Performance' is at once problematic and ethical. It fixes the experiences of individuals to specific and quite often troubled representations marred by the trope of victimhood. As Shuman (2005) warns, terms like refugee performance can establish a familiar, reductive scaffold that 'shores up the promise of mutual understanding and the redemptive power of empathy, a scaffold built on the necessary central positioning (and presence) of the refugee subject in relationship to a non-refugee witness (or audience) and a particular conception of representation' (Dennis 2008: 212). This is particularly difficult as there is often an emphasis on personal narrative in refugee performances, for example verbatim theatre (performance of refugee or asylum seeker transcripts), testimonial theatre (refugees 'performing' their experiences on stage) or playback theatre (improvised interpretations of personal refugee stories).

The reliance on personal testimony is often part of an effort to empower refugees through the sharing of subaltern experiences with a wider audience. However, as Jeffers (2008) warns, these stories can also be interpreted as problematic representations of victimhood.

Preoccupied with personal narratives and particularly drawing on the traumatic past, these theatrical representations can be conditioned by 'bureaucratic performance' (Jeffers 2008: 218), the judicial context within which stories are constructed. 'These structures require narratives of persecution if the asylum seeker is to be successful in his or her claim for asylum, and such narratives often make their way into participatory work' (Jeffers 2008: 217). The very category of refugee performance creates an essentialist frame from which the extrication of practice is almost impossible. The effort to construct a discourse about refugee performance is enmeshed in an unwavering paradox. Put simply, how may practice deal with refugee stories when the stories themselves (bureaucratic performance, personal stories as victimhood, suffering as spectacle) make an encounter with alterity more elusive?

In discussing accountability in playback theatre with refugees, Dennis argues for a rich aesthetic in overcoming the 'dampening effect of empathy' (Dennis 2008: 212). By this she means the presentation of 'injury' as 'reductive and potentially re-violating' (Dennis 2008: 214). The obvious danger of this kind of performance is that these representations of personal narratives produce 'suffering as spectacle' (Salverson 2001: 123).

A rich aesthetic is one that, perhaps, plays with levels of meaning and interpretation, and can redefine an encounter with the other in new and transforming ways, rather than reinforcing preconceived values. In order to elide the paradox of refugee performance and the production of a secure map of experience, the theatre practitioner needs to offer tactics about how to 'sneak up' on the paradox, by exploring 'the Other' in different ways:

> This is [...] not necessarily so much about knowledge of the other, or information about their situation [...] as [it] is about the ethical quality of the experience itself, about a certain kind of affect. It is not perhaps even about, in the first instance, empathy or sympathy with the other, as these forms of relationship may be more about seeing in the other what is like oneself (what Levinas calls the Same). It is perhaps something more purely embodied than that, less explicit.
>
> (Burvill 2008: 236)

In this chapter, we would like to offer an overview of some of the key tensions in refugee performance work, both in terms of the lived sociopolitical realities of refugees, and the ways in which artists and refugee-artists have negotiated the complex terrain of aesthetic representation. Refugee-related performance is often an attempt to direct itself to the broader sociopolitical context, to seek affirmation, understanding and acceptance and/or to protest. In broad terms, it seeks to insert unfamiliar narratives into familiar bureaucratized or mediatized stories, to produce what de Certeau defined as 'novel citations' (de Certeau 1997: 31). Suffice to say that some of the problems encountered in refugee performance question the notion of theatre activities as something that always lead to positive results or outcomes (see Chapter 6 by Laura Edmondson). Nevertheless, the practices and practitioners writing in this book also suggest the ways in which performance can re-inscribe the contours and contents of the refugee experience both as a mode of survival and as a tool for sociopolitical dialogue.

Definitions

On 28 July 1951, the United Nations approved the convention relating to the Status of Refugees. Along with the 1967 protocol, the Convention is one of the key international legal documents defining who is a refugee, their rights and the obligations of states. The convention entered into force on 22 April 1954, and defines a refugee as:

> [a] person who owing to a well-founded fear of being persecuted for reasons of race, religion, nationality, membership of a particular social group or political opinion, is outside the country of his nationality and is unable or, owing to such fear, is unwilling to avail himself of the protection of that country; or who, not having a nationality and being outside the country of his former habitual residence as a result of such events, is unable or, owing to such fear, is unwilling to return to it.
>
> (UNHCR 1979)

The question of 'who is a refugee?' has been posed and argued about by various scholars, policy-makers and agencies before and after the Convention. The legal, financial and political ramifications of defining the term in particular ways mean that the semantics of every word are weighed and carefully scrutinized, especially by State governments. The field of refugee studies is a broad one, and includes specialized researchers in international law and politics, as well as those from anthropology, economics, geography, psychology, sociology and development studies. The diversity of the field reflects the complexity of the phenomena. Research in the field has focused on scope, definition and causality of the refugee issue, as well as exploring the impact of practical and policy solutions. The UN Convention is a useful and in some ways remarkably progressive statement to emerge from an intergovernmental process. It points to the violent act of separation that an individual or group goes through from their 'home' State, and forces them into transition, and into a state of legal limbo or liminality. The betwixt and between state is one that is simultaneously legal, psychological, social and economical. The label of refugee also brings with it a moral status of dependency, with large numbers of stateless individuals and groups at the mercy of international relief agencies and the benevolence of, often, indifferent (or hostile) neighbouring countries. Relatively few get the option of relocating to a Western country for repatriation. As Rizvi notes: 'Once an individual, a human being becomes a refugee, it is as though he has become a member of another race, some subhuman group (Rizvi quoted in Dunbar-Ortiz and Harrell-Bond 1987: 232).

Displaced

TOUR GUIDE: Here we are
entering into the habitat of that peculiar species
the internally displaced.

20

They are increasingly common in this area
there are now 1.9 million of them in northern Uganda.
But please don't confuse them with refugees
the markings are quite distinct.
That's what the UN says
and they are the experts.

Come on. Keep your cameras ready! Why must I keep
    reminding you of that?

Look! There!
Two males of the species are fighting.
Fighting with so much anger and passion.
Can you see what they are fighting over?
Put on your binoculars!
A half litre of sunflower oil.
Aren't they funny creatures?

Over there. Excellent.
A prime view of their mating habits.
You can see the parents over there having sex where the
    children see them.
A fascinating example of what happens to this species
when an entire extended family is forced
into a six-foot-wide hut.

What are you all looking at?
Oh, yes, that one over there is missing its mouth.
Remember what I told you about the renegade buffalo we
    saw earlier?
That is what they do to their victims.
That one got off easy.
They can do so much worse.

His delivery gradually becomes more rapid fire.

You are looking confused.
You do not understand what you are seeing.
The swollen stomachs of the children?
Protein deficiency, of course!
That skinny woman?

She is not just skinny. Haven't you heard of AIDS?
Why is that man holding the child upside down?
Trying to stop her convulsions.
Why are those people digging?
Can't you figure that out for yourself?

(Sam, Edmondson and Ajwang', extract from play
Forged in Fire, Chapter 4 in this collection)

The consequences of placing refugees in camps are often negative, not only for the refugees themselves but also frequently for the national populations and governments of receiving states (Black 1998). In discussing the negative consequences of 'encampment' of refugees, it is both common and quite important to be specific about the elements of 'camp life' that are most problematic. For Bowles (1998), it is the increased dependence of camp dwellers that is perhaps of most concern. For Yousif (1998), while it is partly the association of camp-based settlements with overcrowding, also important is an apparent link with the withdrawal of international aid. For scholars concerned with environmental issues, it is again population densities that are often seen as important. Black (1998) has stressed social and organizational issues, especially the extent to which refugees are cut off from local populations. Refugee camps are intended as places of sanctuary. However, conditions within them can often be as dangerous and traumatic as those from which refugees have fled (McKelvey and Webb 1997). The refugee camp experience can have both acute and long-term effects on refugee mental health. Factors affecting its impact include age and gender, length of time spent in the camp, camp conditions, refugees' cognitive orientation toward the future and social support available to refugees within the camp. Bauman (2004) has argued that refugees are the wasted lives of globalization, stripped of all identities except that of being stateless, statusless and functionless. The flight to camps or temporary shelters is the beginning of a liminal process, in which loss accumulates. These large groups are at the mercy of (often) indifferent neighbouring states, and the charity of non-government organizations (NGOs) struggling to maintain basic living standards or what Agamben (1998) calls bare life.

In the context of Palestinian camps, Hazou observes: '[T]he camp is a constant reminder of homes left behind. Like the keys of return, Feldman argues that refugee camps also 'operate as forms of visible commemoration' (Feldman 2008: 500). They are visible reminders not only of 'Palestinian losses', but also of 'their claims to their homes' left behind' (Hazou, 2012: Chapter 7 in this collection).

Conquergood's (1988) ethnographic approach to understanding the lived realities of a refugee camp led him to living in a camp itself, something that other NGO agency workers rarely did. The experience shaped an understanding of both the complexities of how individuals and groups dealt with dislocation and the somewhat diffident relationships with NGO workers and agencies. Conquergood (1998; and Chapter 3 in this collection) discusses the ways in which the organization of camp life subordinates the inhabitants to specific values and systems of knowing that in some instances reinforces the lack of status in their situation:

The dialectic between the perception of 'difference' and 'dirt' is interesting. I suggest that so much focus on the 'dirtiness' and 'difficulty' of the Hmong is actually an expression of Western expatriates' uneasiness when confronted with Difference, the Other. A Western aid official's encounter with the Hmong is a confrontation with radical difference-in cosmology, worldview, ethos, texture of everyday life.

(Conquergood, Chapter 3 in this collection)

People and actions that disturb order, violate categories, mess up the system are branded unclean: 'The unclear is the unclean' (Turner 1967: 97). Labelling someone or something 'dirty' is a way of controlling perceived anomalies, incongruities, contradictions, ambiguities – all that does not fit into our categories, and therefore threatens cherished principles. 'Dirt', then, functions as the mediating term between 'Difference' and 'Danger'. It is the term that loads the perception of 'Difference' with a moral imperative, and enables the move from description to action, from 'is' to 'ought'. Defining something as unhealthy, harmful, dangerous establishes the premise for 'moving in', for control, making it 'illicit to intervene [...] in order to exercise the rights of guardianship [...] to impose "the good" on others' (Todorov 1984: 150).

(197)

In re-negotiating the outsider–insider relationship between inhabitant and NGO worker there was an immediate sharpening of Conquergood's perspective that whatever theatre work he created would disavow the approach of simply using performance as a way to 'get refugees to do what bureaucrats think best for them' (181). Conquergood was interested in working with, and as far as possible, within the cultures he was living among. As he observes, these were cultures in stasis, pulled between a traditional past and an uncertain present:

Betwixt and between worlds, suspended between a past and future, they fall back on the performance of their traditions as an empowering way of securing continuity and some semblance of stability. Moreover, through performative flexibility they can play with new identities, new strategies for adaptation and survival. The playful creativity of performance enables them to experiment with and invent a new 'camp culture' that is part affirmation of the past and part adaptive response to the exigencies of the present.

(180)

The complexities of inter-camp social relationships and the ways in which culture remains a dynamic and evolving process are repositioned when considered against the ways in which displaced lives evolve through settlement to another (or third) country.

Newly settled refugees: Concepts of resilient ecologies

In 2011 the number of people forcibly displaced worldwide reached 43.7m people, the highest number in 15 years (United Nations High Commission for Refugees 2011). The statistics show a rise of internally displaced people (IDP) – up to 27.5m at the end of 2010. The UNHCR says that by the end of 2010, three quarters of the world's refugees were residing in a country neighbouring their own.

The settlement experience for many refugees can be a very difficult time with feelings of homesickness, isolation and culture shock compounding people's abilities to start a new life in a new country. Many refugees have experienced extremely difficult pasts, high levels of poverty, low levels of formal education, suffered from the effects of torture and trauma and have low levels or no knowledge of English. Their day-to-day existence before arriving in a new country may have been in a refugee camp (where the average stay can be as long as ten years). Many may have never rented a house, paid a bill, gone to work or have had any concept of engaging with institutions such as banks, real estate agents or government departments. The significant settlement issues include high unemployment, housing issues, English language barriers, the effects of trauma and general health issues. In Australia, for example, data from the Longitudinal Survey of Immigrants to Australia (LSIA) reveals that outcomes for humanitarian entrants are 65 per cent poorer than for other groups of migrants, across a range of economic, social and wellbeing indicators (Department of Immigration and Citizenship 2009). The LSIA also indicated that outcomes for humanitarian entrants have deteriorated in recent years. These entrants are finding it more difficult to establish themselves than their earlier counterparts and, in particular, are experiencing lower levels of employment, lower workforce participation rates, lower levels of income and more health problems and psychological distress (Department of Immigration and Citizenship 2009).

Depending on the country that refugees are sent to they might receive support from government or non-government agencies to help with the process of adaptation and settlement. These programmes vary enormously in scope and range, and are characterized by 'diversity' rather than a 'single logically consistent effort' (Haines 1985: 7). There is a growing body of research that has indicated the need for refugee programmes that are culturally appropriate and community based, with any intervention being dedicated to the key principle that it must reflect the priorities of the refugee community itself (Miller and Rasco 2004). Linked to this is research that aims to illuminate the resilience of particular refugee communities and individuals, to highlight culturally embodied perspectives and to examine the coping strategies and forms of strength that allow new settlers to thrive.

Linking arts practice to research that privileges contextualization as a form of knowing and understanding, and that honours our collective human capacity for transformation and renewal, offers a potentially productive link between inquiry, creativity and activism. Many practitioners in community development, welfare and settlement programmes, for example, would find Papadopoulos's (2007) observation reflected in the refugees communities they work with. According to this view there are those within our communities who have survived and have even become strengthened by their traumatic experiences. This view offers an important alternative perspective, and a more hopeful framework for working outside the paradigm of trauma and a Post-Traumatic Stress Disorder (PTSD) diagnosis. Papadopoulos, describing a phenomenon he calls 'adversity activated development,' argues that,

> having come so close to death or having experienced the unbearable anguish of substantial losses, people often emerge transformed, reviewing life, themselves and their relationships. This means that, paradoxically, despite their negative nature, devastating experiences (regardless of the degree of their harshness and destructive impact) may also help people reshuffle their lives and imbue them with new meaning.
>
> (Papadopoulos 2007: 304)

Studies which have focused intently on illuminating culturally embodied experiences and understandings of survival and adaptation, which are often hidden from view, can offer valuable insight for creative arts practitioners into the complexity of acculturation. Marlowe's (2010) qualitative study, for example, based on interviews with 24 Sudanese men resettled in Australia highlights the value of these 'untold stories.' This research suggests that picture painted for by the biomedical model is dangerously incomplete, as only part of the story is told:

> From an exclusive trauma-focused understanding, a thin description of the individual is created where other important considerations of identity and history (social, political, cultural) are easily lost or hidden. Thus, the story of a person's experience(s) of trauma associated with forced migration and how it has negatively influenced his/her life can overshadow other co-existing stories which can emphasize something very different about what a person values and readily identifies with.
>
> (Marlowe 2010: 183)

This study gained an insider's perspective into what helped these men through hardship that included: 'their culture, parental teachings, spirituality and how they maintained hope.' The source of resilience here can be seen to reside outside the trauma story, located in culture, history, values, stories and traditions, along with dreams and aspirations for the future (Marlowe 2010: 195–196).

If the general understanding within our communities is that refugees are universally and permanently depleted by their traumatic histories, then we may be missing something important, underestimating the potential for transformative renewal. We may also miss the opportunity, as members of a hosting society, to mobilize a more collective contribution towards sustaining a healthy, supportive and hopeful social ecology. The importance of recognizing this potential is supported by surveys of the research in refugee wellbeing. Murray et al. (2010), for example, conducted a review of refugee mental health interventions that surveyed the empirical research, evaluating therapeutic interventions in resettlement contexts around the world. This study concludes with a call for inventions based on psychosocial models that promote personal change. The final assessment here was that positive interventions of this nature

> ... may best be achieved by engaging individual clients, families, and whole communities in programs that place emphasis on individual and social growth and change in response to adversity. Programs (should) give due acknowledgment to community leaders and indigenous wisdom, help build community capacity, ensure cultural salience and significance, and work to minimize power differentials between health professionals and local healing.
>
> (Murray et al. 2010: 582)

Ungar (Ungar et al. 2007) describe how, 'a second wave' of resilience research focused on protective factors and processes and how more recent work has introduced a more ecological interpretation of resilience. Learning more about culturally determined indicators of resilience is critical in this view since resilience in this context depends on the, 'capacity of the environment to provide access to health enhancing resources in culturally relevant ways' (Ungar et al. 2007: 288). We can also learn to appreciate how, 'culture provides meaning to a person living through adversity' (Ungar et al. 2007: 306). This research shows how survival, resilience and hopefulness can arise from the highly creative process of negotiating a transition amid the interplay of experience, culture, context, and the availability of individual and community resources. Meaning-making of this nature then – constructing reformulated identities, developing new connections to place and engaging with a new community – is negotiated within a particular cultural milieu and may be best appreciated within an ecological framework.

As much as we may search for it, desire it, wish to depend on it, there are no definitive answers to be found in the research. Refugee-related performance work draws from the intricate and subjective tangle of human experience and meaning-making. So although we know that refugees frequently begin their new life in a place of permanent settlement having survived extremely traumatic experiences, we also know that there are enormous variations in the reported rates of psychopathology (Fawzi et al. 1997). In some context early symptoms of distress may be suppressed (Goodman 2004; Beiser 2009), and in others mental health may deteriorate sharply immediately following resettlement with symptoms of depression and an elevated risk of PTSD persisting for more than a decade (Tran et al. 2007). All of these studies recommend remaining alert to such symptoms while honouring a survivors' own 'timetable to healing.'

These ecologies of hope are fragile and vulnerable. Creative artists working with refugee groups post settlement need to be highly attuned to the nuances and silences that exist. The focus and content of drama-based group work cannot afford to make any assumptions, the settlement process is one of forgetting as much as remembering. To be identified and asked about defining stories is not always empowering. As important is the preoccupation with the here and now, the lived experiences and the day-to-day realities of making and sustaining new constructions of home.

Drama-based group work, where the emphasis is on opening up spaces for dialogue, building relationships and enhancing a sense of agency within participants, is a practice that may therefore be particularly well aligned with strength-based approaches to settlement support. It also has the potential to link with more recent research into cross-cultural and ecological concepts of wellbeing and resilience. Having finally arrived in a country of permanent settlement, performance work can provide a sanctified space for refugees to seek meaning, restoration and reconnection. Theatre can provide a forum and a medium for addressing four key recovery goals, identified with a framework for recovery developed by the Victorian Foundation for Survivors of Torture (Kaplan 1998) and adopted by the UNHCR (2002): restoring safety, restoring attachments and social connections to others, restoring meaning in life and restoring dignity.

Creeping up on the paradox

One way of untangling some of the key tensions threaded through refugee performance work is to begin with an appreciation of the way theatrical and performative practices have the capacity to bridge different kinds of meaning-making. As Conquergood (2002) notes, '[T]he constitutive liminality of performance studies lies in its capacity to bridge segregated and differently valued knowledges, drawing together legitimate as well as subjugated modes of inquiry' (Conquergood 2002: 151). This means that analysing refugee performance work can pull us into different knowledge systems, inviting a kind of Foucauldian inspired observation of different ways of understanding and perceiving.

If we move from 'who is a refugee?' to 'what does it mean to be a refugee?' and if we then question whose definitions we are hearing or appreciating, then some of these tensions emerge more clearly. The creative practices and analytical viewpoints of practitioners and artists working in the area of refugee work, reflect a movement between embodied and intellectual understandings, smoking out these subjugated and dominant knowledge systems.

Attempting to define the refugee experience and explore refugee identity means traveling through contested and disputed terrain. Even as a purely intellectual inquiry refugee studies embraces a wide range of epistemological frameworks. Researchers have struggled for decades with the task of developing an organizing framework to describe and study the impact of dispossession and flight, the drawn out process of seeking asylum, refugee resettlement and adaptation/acculturation processes. Currently it appears that there is little consensus and the debate spanning several disciplines is more controversial and complex than ever.

There is, however, an historical acceptance in the mainstream refugee literature of the biomedical perspective, and this has shaped much of the research into the repercussions of forced migration as a result of political violence and persecution. Pathologizing refugee experiences is an established framework for conducting research. Within this discourse, trauma and PTSD are the most commonly used descriptors for refugee experiences, and the outcomes in terms of health and wellbeing. It is generally understood that experiences such as war, torture and other human rights violations, threats to life, traumatic losses, dispossession and eviction, the experiences of flight, refugee camps and final resettlement in a third country will expose individuals to significant, multiple stressors and result in refugees demonstrating higher levels of psychological disturbance that the general population (McKelvey and Webb 1997; Steel et al. 2002; Terheggen et al. 2001).

The way performance work for, by and with refugees is constructed and viewed is inevitably circumscribed by these understandings of refugees as traumatized victims. Popular, political and academic definitions of the meaning of refugee status and refugee identity inevitably form the back-story for theatrical practices. In this way the testimonies/life stories/narratives of refugees are framed and defined before a word is spoken or gesture made. Aesthetic representations and performed testimonies about experiences of war, violence and forced migration, as well as stories about the process of seeking asylum, resettlement, survival, and maintaining a transnational identity are all set against such discourses.

At the same time, however, refugee performance, located at the juncture where aesthetics and politics meet, where embodied and intellectual understandings entwine, can be viewed as having a potential to generate a new, negotiated third space (Bhabha 1994; 1996). The notion of a third space, despite (or in spite of) its contradictions and ambiguities, provides a spatial politics of inclusion rather than exclusion that 'initiates new signs of identity, and innovative sites of collaboration and contestation' (Bhabha 1994: 1). Those engaged in refugee performance work (as artists, performers, practitioners, students, settlement professionals, researchers and so on) may be inspired by the moments of potency and hopefulness that appear fleetingly in this space. In these moments there is a potential for resisting bureaucratic, dehumanizing portrayals of refugee trauma, for undercutting a media driven appetite for suffering and spectacle, for supporting communities to celebrate cultural identities, for activism and agency, and for offering a vision of our collective, human capacity for survival and transformation.

The possibility of performance

The disruptive potential of performance work, according to some activists, exists in the creative tension between 'theory and theatricality, paradigms and practices, critical reflection and creative accomplishment' (Conquergood 2002: 151). Theatrical projects can be seen to hold a 'radical promise' that arises from 'a commingling of analytical and artistic ways of knowing that unsettles the institutional organization of knowledge and disciplines' (Conquergood 2002: 151). This kind of knowing, for example, can be generated by performances involving refugee testimonies since public storytelling has the capacity to collectivise these experiences where they may otherwise be depolitized and labeled as individual. If there is a thread running through the chapters collected here, it is how they each document contextualized and responsive theatrical practices in which refugee identity may be reconceptualized from victim to agentic self, from criminal and problematic 'outsider' to new citizen, new settler.

Several of the chapters in this collection have highlighted this interplay, between the hopeful, transformative potential of refugee performance and the tendency for configurations of power operating in the host country to frame our reading of what it is to be a refugee in a reductive way. Acknowledging these tensions can yield some illuminating results. Dennis (2008), for example, draws our attention to an inescapable paradox when she offers a careful analysis of how conflicting discourses are at play in the context of a playback theatre project with refugee and asylum seekers in Brisbane, Australia. The playback theatre event sought to 'enact a form of inclusive democracy,' and in doing so it highlighted the presence and impact of power relationships. In this setting the presentation of biographical material is loaded up with the discourses on border control, 'illegal' entry, the criminalization of asylum seekers and detention in tension with discourses that refer to human rights, multiculturalism and social inclusion. The performance space mimics the 'real world' as a site of a struggle for power and survival, and these conditions are inescapable. Bureaucratic procedures colonize this storytelling place since 'the refugee context is structured around the repeated requirement to tell within a culture of institutional disbelief; a story is presented as currency to earn the next stage of entry' (Dennis 2008: 361).

The playback theatre method, as Dennis explains, is often seen as a collective public event equated with inclusive democracy. It is attributed with the capacity to empower participants and 'liberate the disenfranchised voice' (Dennis 2008: 356). The reliance of the form on personal storytelling from participants/spectators, however, presumes a level of social and artistic freedom. For asylum seekers, the climate of the conservative Howard government's immigration policies and the dismantlement of multiculturalism Australia in the early 2000s, did not constitute such an environment. Since, as Conquergood (2002: 146) has observed, 'subordinate people do not have the privilege of explicitness, the luxury of transparency, the presumptive norm of clear and direct communication, free and open debate on a level playing field,' then we may observe an example of how the unwavering paradox at the centre of refugee performance work is embedded in the premise.

Dennis also suggests, however, that there is a potential within the playback theatre performance method for the practice to function as a 'bridge,' where stories may be 'exchanged for entry into the new world; exchanged for access to a new future; exchanged for a chance to re-story a life that has been disassembled by war and terror' (Dennis 2008: 366–367). The struggle here is to hold the practice up within a consciously balanced analytical/critical as well as artistic framework. Refugee participants are unlikely to be in a position to take advantage of opportunities to 're-storying' in this context without, as Dennis articulates, 'a kind of deliberate and thoughtful practice that repeatedly makes explicit who is there, who is missing, who has told, what voices are absent, what stories are absent, what assumptions we are making' (Dennis 2008: 367).

The intractable nature of the tensions surrounding refugee subjectivities on an international stage, and the complexity of the ideological landscapes they inhabit, is excavated with great insight by another writer in this collection. Laura Edmondson applies a sharp analytical focus using the concept of 'marketing' in her report on her research based within the World Vision Children of War Rehabilitation Centre in Northern Uganda. This chapter traces the 'bewildering complexities' (see Edmondson's chapter in this book: 99) of the cultural forces intersecting in this terrorized and forsaken part of the world, which has been brutalized by an eighteen-year-old civil war. This is a place that Edmondson acknowledges 'could too easily be categorized as an economic wasteland isolated from the transnational flow of corporate capital' (453).

Children abducted and inducted into warfare, to serve as 'soldiers, porters, and/or so-called wives of the rebels,' are rescued and brought to this rehabilitation centre. In such an environment art, stories, dance and drama are employed as part of a Western style 'counselling' approach, but also, as Edmondson reveals, as a marketing strategy. These cultural/art forms serve as vehicles for the discourses of rebels, international humanitarian organizations and civilians. A master narrative of rescue and restoration, an 'heroic tale,' is appropriated and fiercely guarded as a matter of survival by a range of stakeholders. This narrative is also embraced by the local civilians, the Acholi people, since they are restricted to the 'discourse of warfare and humanitarianism as a means of entering the global market.' For this group the investment is clear since the narrative 'serves as one of the most crucial resources that they possess' (453).

Edmondson also, however, describes witnessing disruptions to this dominant narrative of war, small gestures among a group of former female captives demonstrating their strengths, moments of triumph over these forces that silence and oppress. Spontaneous dance performances by the girls at the centre expressed an, 'enthusiasm and passion for their culture (which) defied the tropes of humanitarian discourse that situated them as hapless victims' (470).

In this way spaces for cultural memory and for displays of resilience and creativity and survival were carved out of the 'epistemic murk' and the intractable, insidious politics of globalization and warfare (474). This observation draws out, and places a fine point on, the power and potential of refugee performance work to stratify different discourses, to resist domination, and to offer alternatives. As Edmondson explains:

> In the uncontainably hybrid cultural landscape of northern Uganda, the dances simultaneously serve as fodder for the imperialist international gaze and nourish a vibrant subculture in which the children can commemorate their strength. Even after the official guests had departed, the dances frequently continued, constructing an alternative narrative that exceeds the representational frame of marketing trauma.
>
> (473)

The performance of traditional dance is also the subject of McMahon's chapter, and here the focus is on interpreting how traditions are recontextualized in new locations. From her perspective as a folklorist, McMahon analyses the expression of transnational refugee identity within a place of permanent asylum, a third country, through the performances of the DiDinga, a group of southern Sudanese refugees, resettled in New York, and known locally as the 'Lost Boys.' These young men, having lost connection with their parents and elders, actively select and reformulate traditions 'as a means of identifying, affirming, and valuing uniquenesss and personal history' (355).

McMahon, in this study, identifies a role for folklorists in mediating the aesthetic reformulations of culture and traditions within the critical early period of refugee resettlement. Performing a ritual in a new context requires a particular kind of support since, as McMahon notes:

> globalization has created a global commons a performance space where there are few guidelines to help facilitate interactions. But folklorists today are in a unique position to make valuable contributions with long-term effects. Public folklorists, in particular, are in a critical position to facilitate ways for newcomers to maintain cultural identities and thus avoid being overwhelmed by American culture.
>
> (see McMahon's chapter in this book: 243)

This kind of lens helps us to appreciate that resettlement is a dynamic, creative and transformative process. Tracking the finely nuanced process that this group of newcomers traversed to find a new expression for performing traditional dance, is a study in the complex negotiations involved in acculturation. The delicate to-and-fro between shared knowledge and playful improvization, between individual memories and group interaction, all within dynamic interaction with external forces, is a creative process that ultimately holds the promise of delivering a new form of authenticity for these refugees.

Within the field of refugee studies, there is now a growing body of qualitative studies published within the last decade that aim to illuminate the resilience of particular refugee communities and individuals, such as this group of 'lost boys,' and to highlight culturally embodied perspectives (Goodman 2004; Khawaja et al. 2008; Marlowe 2010; McMichael 2002; Mitchell et al. 2006; Sonderegger and Barrett 2004; Westoby 2008). This allows us to examine the coping strategies and forms of strength that allow diasporic groups to thrive. In performances, such as those of the DiDinga boys and the Acholi girls, the source of resilience can be seen to reside outside the trauma story, located in the energy, the creativity and the adapted traditions that these survivors bring with them, along with their dreams and aspirations for the future. In occupying this 'third space,' this kind of performance work privileges the expression of valued and hybridized traditions and the processes of negotiating a new transnational identity.

These kinds of artistic expressions can open up new areas of knowledge, and indicate potentially powerful directions for future research and exploration. They indicate the possibilities for working outside the paradigm of trauma and PTSD and for creeping up on the paradox at the heart of refugee performance work. Where performance work functions as a form of inquiry and activism that prioritizes the subjective perspectives of refugees themselves, it can lead to a deeper appreciation of the phenomenon itself. In this way we are afforded the benefit of

> thinking about, through and with performance; performance as a lens that illuminates the constructed creative, contingents, collaborative dimensions of human communication; knowledge that comes from contemplation and comparison; concentrated attention and contextualisation as a way of knowing.
>
> (Conquergood 2002: 152)

Refugee performance work, and the chapters in this collection, speaks to the existential, core questions about what makes any of us capable of transcending trauma. What it takes to remake ourselves, our communities, our cultures in the aftermath of unspeakable, unseeable, unknowable violence and what makes us capable of creatively employing new symbols and metaphors, new embodied artistic representations of human experience and creativity. Finally, we may see suspended in those fleeting moments, what capability we have in reworking our definitions and transforming the world just a little.

References

Agamben, Giorgio, *Homo Sacer: Sovereign Power and Bare Life*, trans. Daniel Heller-Roazen, Stanford: Stanford University Press, 1998.

Bauman, Z., *Wasted Lives: Modernity and its Outcasts*, Cambridge: Polity Press, 2004.

Beiser, M., 'Resettling Refugees and Safeguarding Their Mental Health: Lessons Learned from the Canadian Refugee Resettlement Project,' *Transcultural Psychiatry*, 46:4 (2009), pp. 539–583.

Bhabha, H. K., 'Frontlines/Borderposts,' in A. Bammer (ed.), *Displacements: Cultural Identities in Question*, Bloomington: Indiana University Press, 1994.

———, 'Cultures in Between,' in S. Hall and P. Du Guy (eds.) *Questions of Cultural Identity*, London: Sage Publications, 1996.

Black, R., 'Putting Refugees in Camps,' *Forced Migration Review*, 2 (1998), pp. 4–7.

Bowles, E., 'From Village to Camp: Refugee Camp Life in Transition on the Thailand–Burma border,' *Forced Migration Review*, August 1998.

Burvill, T. '"Politics Begins as Ethics": Levinasian Ethics and Australian Performance Concerning Refugees,' *Research in Drama Education: The Journal of Applied Theatre and Performance*, 13:2 (2008), p. 233.

Certeau de, Michel, *Heterologies: Discourse on the Other*, Minneapolis: Minnesota University Press, 1997.

Conquergood, D., 'Health Theatre in a Hmong Refugee Camp: Performance, Communication, and Culture,' *TDR*, 32:3 (Autumn, 1988), pp. 174–208.

———, 'Performance Studies Interventions and Radical Research,' *TDR* 46:2 (Summer 2002), pp. 145–156.

Dennis, R., 'Refugee Performance: Aesthetic Representation and Accountability in Playback Theatre,' *Research in Drama Education*, 13: 2 (2008), pp. 211–215.

Department of Immigration and Citizenship, *Longitudinal Survey of Immigrants to Australia*, Commonwealth of Australia, 2009.

Dunbar-Ortiz, R., and Harrell-Bond, B. E., 'Who Protects the Human Rights of Refugees?' *Africa Today*, 1st/2nd Quarter (1987), pp. 369–374

Fawzi, M. C., Murphy, E., Pham, T., Lin, L., Poole, C., Mollica, R.F., 'The Validity of Post-traumatic Stress Disorder among Vietnamese Refugees,' *Journal of Traumatic Stress*, 10: 1 (1997), pp. 101–108.

Feldman, I., 'Refusing Invisibility: Documentation and Memorialization in Palestinian Refugee Claims,' *Journal of Refugee Studies* 21: 4 (2008), pp. 498–516.

Goodman, J. H., 'Coping with Trauma and Hardship among Unaccompanied Refugee Youths from Sudan,' *Qualitative Health Research*, 14: 9 (2004), pp. 1177–1196.

Haines, D. W., 'Refugees and the Refugee Program,' in D. W. Haines (ed.) *Refugees in the United States*, Westport, CT: Greenwood Press, 1985.

Jeffers, A., 'Dirty Truth: Personal Narrative, Victimhood and Participatory Theatre Work with People Seeking Asylum,' *Research in Drama Education: The Journal of Applied Theatre and Performance*, 13: 2 (2008), p. 217.

Kaplan, I., *Rebuilding Shattered Lives*, Victorian Foundation for Survivors of Torture Inc. Australia, 1998.

Khawaja, N. G., et al., 'Difficulties and Coping Strategies of Sudanese Refugees: a Qualitative Approach,' *Transcultural Psychiatry*, 45: 3 (2008), pp. 489–512.

Kristeva, J., *Desire in Language: A Semiotic Approach to Literature and Art* New York: Columbia University Press, 1980.

Marlowe, J. M., 'Beyond the Discourse of Trauma: Shifting the Focus on Sudanese Refugees,' *Journal of Refugee Studies*, 23: 2 (2010), pp. 183–198.

McKelvey, Robert S., and Webb, John A., 'A Prospective Study of Psychological Distress Related to Refugee Camp Experience,' *Australian and New Zealand Journal of Psychiatry* 31 (1997), pp. 549–554.

McMichael, C., '"Everywhere is Allah's Place": Islam and the Everyday Life of Somali Women in Melbourne, Australia,' *Journal of Refugee Studies*, 15: 2, (2002), pp. 171–188.

Miller, K., and Rasco, L., 'An Ecological Framework for Addressing the Mental Health Needs of Refugee Communities,' in Miller, K., and Rasco, L. (eds.), *The Mental Health of Refugees: Ecological Approaches to Healing and Adaptation,* Mahwah, NJ: Lawrence Erlbaum, 2004.

Mitchell, J., Kaplan, I., and Crowe, L., 'Two Cultures: One Life,' *Community Development Journal*, 42: 3 (2006), pp. 282–298.

Murray, K. E., Davidson, G. R., and Schweitzer, R. D., 'Review of Refugee Mental Health Interventions Following Resettlement: Best Practices and Recommendations,' *The American Journal of Orthopsychiatry*, 80: 4 (2010), pp. 576–585.

Papadopoulos, R., 'Refugees, Trauma and Adversity-Activated Development,' *European Journal of Psychotherapy Counselling*, 9: 3 (2007), pp. 301–312.

Salverson, J., *Performing Testimony: Ethics, Pedagogy, and a Theatre beyond Injury,* Unpublished PhD dissertation, University of Toronto, 2001.

Shuman, A., *Other People's Stories: Entitlement Claims and the Critique of Empathy*, Champaign, IL: University of Illinois Press, 2005.

Soguk, N., 'Splinters of Hegemony: Ontopoetical Visions in International Relations,' *Alternatives: Global, Local, Political*, 31 (2006), pp. 377–404.

Sonderegger, R., and Barrett, P. M., 'Patterns of Cultural Adjustment Among Young Migrants to Australia,' *Journal of Child and Family Studies*, 13: 3 (2004), pp. 341–356.

Steel, Z., Silove, D., Phan, T., and Bauman, A., 'Long-term Effect of Psychological Trauma on the Mental Health of Vietnamese Refugees Resettled in Australia: A Population-based Study,' *Lancet*, 360: 9339 (2002), pp. 1056–1062.

Terheggen, M. A., Stroebe, M. S., and Kleber, R. J., 'Western Conceptualizations and Eastern Experience: A Crosscultural Study of Traumatic Stress Reactions among Tibetan Refugees in India,' *Journal of Traumatic Stress*, 14, (2001), pp. 391–403.

Todorov, T., *The Conquest of America: The Question of the Other*, New York: Harper & Row, 1984.

Tran, T. V., Manalo, V., and Nguyen, V. T. D. 'Nonlinear Relationship Between Length of Residence and Depression in a Community-Based Sample of Vietnamese Americans,' *International Journal of Social Psychiatry*, 53: 1 (2007), pp. 85–94.

Turner, V., *The Forest of Symbols*, Ithaca, NY: Cornell University Press, 1967.

Ungar, M., Brown, Marion, Liebenberg, Linda, Othman, rasha, Kwong, Wai Man, Armstrong, Mary, Gilgun, Jane, 'Unique Pathways to Resilience across Cultures,' *Adolescence*, 42: 166 (2007), p. 24.

United Nations High Commission for Refugees, *2011 Global Trends: Refugees, Asylum-seekers, Returnees, Internally Displaced and Stateless Persons*, Geneva: Division of Operational Services, Field Information and Coordination Support Section, 2011.

Westoby, P., 'Developing a Community-development Approach through Engaging Resettling Southern Sudanese Refugees within Australia,' *Community Development Journal*, 43: 4 (2008), p. 483.

Yousif, Tarig Misbah, 'Encampment at Abu Rakham in Sudan: a Personal Account,' *Forced Migration Review*, 2 (1998), pp. 4–7.

Documents

Refugee Resettlement: An International Handbook to Guide Reception and Integration—Chapter 3.3 Investing in the Future. UNHCR 2002. http://www.unhcr.org

Handbook on Procedures and Criteria for Determining Refugee Status under the 1951 Convention and the 1967 Protocol relating to the Status of Refugees HCR/IP/4/Eng/REV.1 Reedited, Geneva, January 1992, UNHCR 1979. (See also the website of the Office of the United Nations High Commission for Refugees for other handbooks and guidelines: http://www.unhcr.org.)

Chapter 3

Health Theatre in a Hmong Refugee Camp: Performance, Communication, and Culture

Dwight Conquergood

A Hmong widow walks to a crossroad in Camp Ban Vinai, surveys the scene, and then
   settles herself on a bench outside the corner hut. Bracing her back against the split-
   bamboo wall, she begins to sing. At first softly, as if to herself, she sings a Hmong *khy
txhiaj* (folksong). Aware of a gathering audience, she raises her voice to fill the space around
her. She sings a lamentation, carving her personal anguish into a traditional expressive form.
With exquisitely timed gestures, she strips and peels with one hand the branch of firewood
she holds in the other. Tears stream down her face as she sings about the loss of her husband,
her children, her house, her farm, her animals and her country. She sings of war, and flight,
and breaking and of a time when she was a wife and mother in the Laotian village where
silver neck-rings were worn. She punctuates each refrain by tossing away a sliver that her
strong fingers have torn from the wood she holds across her lap as if it were a child.

The sad beauty of her singing attracts a crowd. She never makes eye contact but
acknowledges the crowd's presence in her spontaneously composed verses, subtly at first, and
then more confidently. She is both lamenting and entertaining. With nothing left to tear away,
she makes the final toss of the last splinter, rises and begins to sway with the rhythm of her
song. People set out food for her. I give her the few baht I have in my pocket. Her face still wet,
she breaks into a broad smile. Strange laughter interrupts her otherwise balanced verses.

She thanks us for listening to her sadness and tells us how happy it makes her to sing for
us. Then she crosses the road to where I am standing and gives me a blue sticker the size of a
nickel, with a crescent moon on it. It is one of the stickers the camp hospital puts on medicine
bottles to indicate when the medicine should be taken, morning or night. With her thumb she
presses it onto the page of my journal in which I am writing field notes on her performance.
I notice that she has blue moons and golden suns stuck to her cheeks and forehead.

I came across this performance on my first day of fieldwork in Refugee Camp Ban Vinai in
Thailand, where I had been assigned by the International Rescue Committee as a consultant
for their environmental health education programme. In many ways this opening image
cathects the themes that would become salient in my fieldwork: performance, health and
intercultural exchange between refugees and expatriate health professionals.

I arrived in Thailand in February 1985 having just completed, with Taggart Siegel, a
documentary on Hmong shamanism and the Sudden Unexpected Death Syndrome that
has reached epidemic proportions among the Hmong resettled in the United States (Siegel
and Conquergood 1985).[1] My intention was to do straightforward field research on cultural
performance, particularly shamanism, in refugee camps, but the refugee situation had

become so politically sensitive in Thailand that all camps were closed to outsiders, particularly researchers. Therefore, I sought employment with the international aid voluntary agencies that administer health care and services to the camps. Fortunately, I was hired by the International Rescue Committee (IRC) as a health worker in Ban Vinai, a hilltribe camp not far from the Mekong River that divides Thailand from Laos, and the oldest and largest refugee camp in Thailand. During the time of my fieldwork, the official population of the camp was 45,231 with an additional 2000 to 3000 undocumented 'illegals' living in the camp without rice rations. I offered my services as an ethnographic consultant in exchange for the official papers that would legitimize my presence in the camp. My major assignment was to help design and direct an environmental health education programme for this camp which was represented in many agency reports as the 'filthiest', most 'primitive' and 'difficult' in Thailand.

Working with the refugees and a local Thai IRC employee, I helped design and direct a health education campaign based on native beliefs and values that was communicated in culturally appropriate forms. Specifically, we started a refugee performance company that produced skits and scenarios drawing on Hmong folklore and traditional communicative forms, such as proverbs, storytelling and folksinging, to develop critical awareness about the health problems in Ban Vinai.

The Ban Vinai performance company

Camp Ban Vinai may lack many things – water, housing, sewage disposal system – but not performance. The camp is an embarrassment of riches in terms of cultural performance. No matter where you go in the camp, at almost any hour of the day or night, you can simultaneously hear two or three performances, from simple storytelling and folksinging to the elaborate collective ritual performances for the dead that orchestrate multiple media, including drumming, stylized lamentation, ritual chanting, manipulation of funerary artefacts, incense, fire, dancing, and animal sacrifice. Nearly every morning I was awakened before dawn by the drumming and ecstatic chanting of performing shamans. During the day women everywhere would sew *pa ndau* (flower cloth), an intricate textile art that sometimes takes the form of embroidered story quilts with pictorial narratives drawn from history and folklore. Performance permeates the fabric of everyday life in Ban Vinai.

A high level of cultural performance is characteristic of refugee camps in general. Since my work in Ban Vinai, I have visited or lived for short periods of time in eleven refugee camps in Southeast Asia and the Middle East, not counting a shantytown for displaced people in Nigeria. In every one of them I was struck by the richness and frequency of performative expression. One explanation for this is that refugees have a lot of time on their hands to cultivate expressive traditions. But I think there are deeper psychological and cultural reasons for the high incidence of performance in the camps. Refugee camps are liminal zones where people displaced by trauma and crisis – usually war or famine – must try to regroup and salvage what is left of their lives. Their world has been shattered. They are in passage, no longer Laotian, certainly not Thai, and not quite sure where they will end up or what their lives will become. Betwixt and between worlds, suspended between past and future, they fall back on the performance of their traditions as an empowering way of securing continuity and some semblance of stability. Moreover, through performative flexibility they can play with new identities, new strategies for adaptation and survival. The playful creativity of performance enables them to experiment with and invent a new 'camp culture' that is part affirmation of the past and part adaptive response to the exigencies of the present. Performance participates in the re-creation of self and society that emerges within refugee camps.

Through its reflexive capacities, performance enables people to take stock of their situation and through this self-knowledge to cope better. There are good reasons why in the crucible of refugee crisis, performative behaviours intensify.

And, of course, even before the Hmong became refugees, oral traditions and cultural performance were the primary ways of educating the young and promoting beliefs and values among adults, as is the case in most Third World cultures (see Ong 1982). Any communication campaign that ignored the indigenous cultural strengths of performance would be doomed to failure.

There is always the danger, however, of appropriating performance and using it as an instrument of domination. I wanted no part of the puppet-theatre approach used by some expatriates as simply another means to get refugees to do what bureaucrats think best for them. Instead, I hoped that performance could be used as a method for developing critical awareness as an essential part of the process of improving the health situation in the camp. My project was aligned with the popular theatre approach to development and political struggle that is being used with success throughout the Third World, particularly Africa, Latin America and Asia. This theatre movement frequently draws inspiration from Paulo Freire's fieldwork as documented in *Pedagogy of the Oppressed* (1986). Augusto Boal (1985) and Ross Kidd (1982, 1984) are perhaps the best-known names associated with the popular theatre, or people's theatre movement. Fortunately, a sizable body of literature is developing around this kind of Third World theatre (Bustos 1984; Desai 1987; van Erven 1987; Eyoh 1986; Kaitaro 1979; Kidd and Byram 1978; Thiong'o 1981, 1983, 1986). In *Helping Health Workers Learn* (Werner and Bower 1982) – which is the companion volume to the widely distributed *Where There Is No Doctor: A Village Health Care Handbook* (Werner 1977) – there is an excellent chapter on politics, health and performance entitled, 'Ways to Get People Thinking and Acting: Village Theater and Puppet Shows.'[2] This work perhaps more than any other inspired my efforts in Ban Vinai.

The critical/political component of popular theatre enacts itself in the process of developing the performance as much as, if not more than, in the final presentation to an audience. The backstage processes of researching and developing culturally appropriate materials along with the participatory involvement of the people are experiential/processual dimensions as significant as any explicit 'message' communicated in a skit or scenario. For popular theatre to work effectively as a tool of critical awareness and empowerment for oppressed peoples it must be rooted in and begin with their cultural strengths. Instead of aesthetic distance and other concepts of elite theatre, popular theatre is contingent upon what Kenneth Burke calls rhetorical processes of 'identification' and 'consubstantiality' (1969: 19–23).

The health worker uses popular theatre must, perforce, become a participant fieldworker. Getting to know the people well is important not just as a technique for collecting appropriate materials and dramaturgical ideas to be worked into performance programmes but as a way of earning their trust and respect. No matter how flashy and entertaining your health show, village people are wary of outsiders – experts who drop in for a day or two and then leave. Refugees, even more than villagers, have good reason to be sceptical of officials who keep themselves at a distance. The Hmong have a proverb: 'To see a tiger is to die: to see an official is to become destitute' (Tapp 1986: 2). When a health worker gets involved, becomes part of the struggle, it speaks as forcefully as any line in a performance script. Ndumbe Eyoh said it clearly: 'There seems to be no other better way than associating fully with them, meeting them in the villages, joining them in their daily chores and sharing with them their lifestyles' (1986: 23). That is why it was crucial for me to live in the camp with the Hmong, although that was considered a great oddity by the other expatriate agency workers who commuted from Chiang Kham village, an hour's drive away. Indeed, it was one of the camp rules that agency workers had to leave by 5.00 p.m. every day. Nevertheless, through delicate negotiations with the camp commander, a Thai colonel, I was able to stay overnight in the camp.

I hoped to break the pattern of importing the knowledge of 'experts' and distributing it to the refugees, who were expected to be grateful consumers. I wanted to help demonstrate to both expatriates and refugees that *dialogical* exchange between the two cultures, the two worldviews and sensibilities, was possible (see Bakhtin 1981; Todorov 1984; Conquergood 1985).

One of the things that worked well for me as a health worker was to barter recommendations and health practices with traditional healers. This kept the programme from being too one-sided. Because of the camp conditions, I personally had frequent trouble with intestinal disorders. For this discomfort, I went to the women herbalists who gave me a root to chew that was quite helpful. Early in my fieldwork I fell through a bridge and gashed my toe when a rotten board gave way. Herbalists treated my wound with soothing poultices from a glossy-leaved plant. Within a week the jagged wound had healed and I was able to go without a bandage. Because of the rugged terrain, however, I stubbed my toes repeatedly and reopened that wound more than once. I became quite dependent on the herbal healers – they knew that my trust and respect for their medicine was genuine. Their pleasure in my trust was overwhelming. Never have I received such devoted attention. However, when I came down with Dengue fever, a somewhat serious illness, I spent a week in a Singapore hospital taking advantage of the best that modern medicine had to offer in order to get back on my feet as soon as possible. My friends, of course, were curious about the hospital, and I shared the details of my treatment with them. What I tried to do in my fieldwork was enact an example of dialogical exchange, or barter, wherein each culture could benefit from the other, approaching health care issues within a both/and embrace instead of an either/or separation of categories; this approach was particularly important because the refugees were accustomed to having expatriates undermine, even outrightly assault, their traditions.

The first test was whether or not the Hmong would accept a popular theatre approach. Quite simply, could we gather an audience? That test came earlier than I had planned when five rabid dogs rampaged through the camp biting several children. The solution proposed by the camp commander was to go to the Thai market, buy five machetes, and kill all the dogs. To his great credit, the director of the International Rescue Committee in Ban Vinai persuaded the colonel against this course of action. He proposed instead that IRC use its funds to buy rabies vaccine and inoculate all the dogs in camp. The vaccine was purchased and IRC personnel were at their stations ready and poised with needles to vaccinate the dogs. No dogs arrived. The problem centred on communication. The Hmong were not boycotting the rabies programme. They simply were baffled by this strange procedure, or unaware of it. There was no effective way of getting the word out as to where, when and why dogs should be brought to the IRC stations for injections.

I had just arrived in camp and was beginning to establish a rapport, recruit and work with refugee performers/health workers. We had developed some characters based on stock figures in Hmong folklore and were designing and constructing costumes and masks. We had started improvisation and confidence-building exercises, but everything was still very tentative. The group was very young; all but one were under twenty. We were just beginning to mesh as a group when the IRC director approached me and asked for help with the rabies vaccination project. Time was running out. The camp dogs would have to be vaccinated soon or Ban Vinai might have a serious rabies epidemic.

I certainly did not feel confident about putting the fledgling actors to this kind of major test so soon. We met and discussed the seriousness of the situation and collectively decided what would be the best strategy for quickly communicating this important message to as much of the camp population as possible. We soon agreed on a grand, clamorous, eyecatching 'Rabies Parade' that would snake its way through all the sections of the camp. The tiger costume – appliqued cotton fabric with a long rope tail – was almost finished, so it was agreed that the tiger would be the lead figure in the parade. The tiger is a trickster figure in Hmong folklore and mythology, a very dramatic and evocative character. We knew the tiger would draw attention, inspire awe. The tiger would be followed by a nature-spirit, a ragged costume with long coloured strings for hair, that would sing and bang on a drum. That noise, we hoped, would reach the people inside their huts and bring them out to see the commotion. We agreed that the chicken, a feathered costume with a striking cardboard mask that covered the entire head, would be the pivotal figure. After the dancing tiger and the clamorous nature-spirit got people's attention, the chicken would talk through a bullhorn and explain in terms the Hmong would understand the seriousness of rabies and why it was important for every family to round up the dogs and bring them for injections. The chicken couched all this in an appeal toward protecting the children and then gave specific instructions for each neighbourhood in the camp as to where and when they should bring the dogs. It was culturally appropriate for the chicken to be the leading speaker because in Hmong lore chickens have divinatory powers. They are frequently offered up in spirit ceremonies as guides to lead the way to the sky kingdom. Three days after a baby is born, chickens are used in an augury ceremony to determine the child's future. Hmong naturally associate the chicken with divination because, as was explained to me, 'Who is the one who knows first when the sun comes up every morning?'

We had some pep talks among ourselves to build confidence to go on the road the following morning. Not only would this be the performance company's first show, it would be the first time any member of our young group had performed in public. The ones who seemed to be the most extroverted were selected for the key roles of tiger, nature-spirit and talking chicken. The rest would don masks and come along as backup and as moral support for their comrades. Without assigning them specific roles, I encouraged them to do whatever they felt comfortable with in the parade. This would be an opportunity for them to get exposure in front of an audience before assuming more demanding roles.

Our casting instincts for the critical roles of tiger, nature-spirit and chicken turned out to be inspired. At first, everyone was extremely self-conscious and inhibited. I was prepared for the worst. But as we kept banging the drum and hanging together, some children began pointing their fingers and laughing at the listless tiger. This brought him to life. The young fellow turned out to be a natural acrobat. Drawing on the media influence of Chinese movies that Thai entrepreneurs show in the open air once a month, he created a highly physical 'Kung-Fu Tiger' to the joy of the people who streamed out of their houses to see such a sight. The fellow playing the nature-spirit turned out to be quite a musician. In addition to the drum, he brought along a folk instrument, a reed pipe organ, that his grandfather had made. He spontaneously danced as he blew the pipes, a great hit with the crowd. The chicken enjoyed the importance of his role and took it quite seriously. Understanding the power of word-of-mouth networks, the young actor instructed his audiences to go and tell their neighbours and relatives what they had just heard.

In terms of ability to gather an audience, the Rabies Parade was a huge success. Also, the novice performers had acquitted themselves beyond my highest expectations. However, the real test of our communication effectiveness was whether or not the Hmong would bring their dogs to the vaccination stations.

The next morning, full of nervous anticipation, I staked out the first vaccination station. It was a heartwarming sight. Dogs came pouring in – on rope leashes, in two-wheel pushcarts and carried in their owners' arms. We could not vaccinate them fast enough. I myself vaccinated scores of dogs. The vaccination stations became a sort of street theatre. As you can imagine, the dogs did not submit willingly to these injections. It is a rather intricate operation to hold a struggling dog up in the air – we had no veterinary tables – and get it injected properly. There was a lot of scuffling and abortive thrusts of the needle – the stuff of farce. Also, with so many nervous dogs concentrated in one area, fights broke out. For a week this part of the rabies programme was performed before rapt audiences, drawing crowds equal to those for the parades. We vaccinated almost 500 dogs.

We took advantage of the performance company's initial outing to elicit direct audience feedback as part of the process of testing, developing and refining our concepts. The drum that was used belonged to a shaman, and some of the older people objected to its use. When the young performer brought the gong from home, I recognized it as a shaman's and questioned the company about the appropriateness of using it. Everyone said there would be no problem, and that a shaman had donated it. In any event, we never again used a shaman's instrument in our performance.

Throughout the development of our health theatre programmes, we actively solicited feedback from Hmong elders. We received excellent, helpful criticism. After we had rehearsed our first set of acted scenarios we showed them to a Hmong leader. He critiqued the performers on three points: (1) the performers and stage managers not in costume should wear traditional Hmong clothes, and not Western-style T-shirts and trousers available in the camp through charity outlets; (2) the backup music for the dances should be authentic Hmong, not Thai or Western-influenced melodies; (3) the rhymed chants were a little off from the traditional Hmong prosody, he taught the young performers the correct speech patterns. These criticisms were very useful because many of the members of the performance company were quite young and had grown up in the camp, exposed to outside influences. Moreover, the critique demonstrated the concern of Hmong leaders for maintaining their cultural integrity against the forces of assimilation.

There was one other criticism regarding the masks and the tiger. The oldest member of the performance company declined to wear a mask of any kind. The masks were too real for him. He was unable to frame the wearing of a mask as make-believe and worried about problems with spirits as a consequence of wearing the mask. We, of course, gave him roles that did not require wearing a mask and he remained a dedicated and important member of the performance company. But, soon after the Rabies Parade, a few of the people said that the masks and the tiger were scary and worried that some of the children's spirits might be scared away and they would fall sick. This response struck terror in me. As many anthropologists have noted, the political influence and power of shamans lies in their role as interpreters of the source and cause of illness. Shamanic ceremonies for a patient are in two phases: first, the divination/diagnosis, then the cure. A shaman can influence the politics of a village by interpreting certain actions as the cause of illness or calamity. There is no lack of children falling sick every day in Ban Vinai. Fever and diarrhoea are prevalent. Hundreds of children had enjoyed our parades. If one shaman attributed the sickness of one child to spirit-flight precipitated by the parade, the Ban Vinai health and performance company would be destroyed. One accusation could ruin us.

It was a tense week for me, but no accusations came. However, we decided to modify our staging techniques based on this feedback. Powerful characters like the tiger would no longer play directly to the audience in open form. Using theatre-in-the-round staging, we would direct the energies of the tiger and other masked characters inside the circle, using onstage focus. We would have these dramatic characters interact in an animated way with one another, but not directly confront the audience.

However, we did not want to lose the power of open-form communication, so we needed a narrator character who could safely and directly address audiences. Proverbs are an important communication form in all oral cultures and particularly popular with the Hmong. We wanted to use a character who could recite health proverbs and tell stories and who would have a special rapport with small children. Almost a quarter of the camp's population is under the age of five, the most vulnerable group with a high rate of disease and death.

Appealing to them would also be a way of involving their parents; Hmong families are tightly knit and children are greatly loved. This led to the creation of our most successful character who became the symbol for the entire health communication programme: the beloved Niam Tsev Huv/Mother Clean, our cleanliness clown. She was the collective creation of the entire performance company. Inspired by Peter Schumann's Bread and Puppet Theatre, I introduced the idea of a huge muppet figure constructed on a bamboo frame. The performance company took it from there. Someone designed her face, a pleasant smile painted on a cloth-stuffed dummy's head tacked atop the bamboo frame; someone else did her costume, a colourfully striped dress that made her look larger than life; another member made her hair out of dyed yarn. The performance company worked collectively on all phases of the performance process, from research for scenarios to composing songs and proverbs to costume construction. Except for the tiger's mask which I purchased in Loei, the provincial capital, all of the costumes and props were handmade from local materials.

The performer who eventually assumed the role of Mother Clean was a late starter – not one of the precocious three who emerged during the Rabies Parade. Several members of the company tried out the role, but he was the one who brought Mother Clean to life. Mother Clean, as he created her, was as gentle and loving as she was physically huge and imposing. She was a narrator-character who set the stage for the performance and, during the performance, could negotiate back and forth between direct address to the audience and dialogue with onstage characters. Mother Clean particularly loved little children and always had special words for them. They adored her; sometimes during a performance they would run on stage to peek underneath her muppet skirts. Mother Clean always handled these moments with tender dignity, improvising skillfully. She also was very, very funny. Adults would double over with laughter at her antics. The incongruity between her size and her feigned daintiness was very farcical. Mother Clean grew in popularity so that the sight of her coming down the camp road would immediately draw a huge crowd for a performance. As she would walk through the camp, small children would shout her name. Hundreds of T-shirts were printed with her image in the Ban Vinai Print Shop run by a Japanese Refugee Relief Agency. The camp literacy project used her image on posters. She was perhaps the most visible figure with the highest name recognition in the camp and she became the linchpin of our communication campaign. People believed that Mother Clean was on their side and the side of their children and they listened to what she told them about health and sanitation.

Performance, garbage, and the environmental setting

Once we had demonstrated that performance was an appropriate and successful way of communicating with the Hmong, we set out to work on the environmental health problems of the camp. Ban Vinai has serious hygiene and sanitation problems. The cause, however, lies in the environmental circumstances, not any innate character flaw of the Hmong. Simplistic health messages imported from Western middle-class notions of cleanliness simply would not work for Ban Vinai. What was needed was a health education and consciousness-raising programme that was sensitive to the history and specific environmental problems and constraints of the camp.

Ban Vinai is located in an isolated, hilly region of northeast Thailand, the poorest sector of the country. The camp has a population larger than any city in this remote area of Thailand, surpassing even Loei, the provincial capital. It is the most populous refugee camp in Asia. All these people are crowded onto about 400 acres of undeveloped land. The camp space is intensively used because refugees are forbidden to go outside the camp without the express permission of Colonel Vichitmala, the Thai camp commander. Armed guards enforce this policy. During the time of my fieldwork more than one refugee was shot for venturing outside the camp.

The overcrowding in the camp, not to mention the sanitation level, is compounded by large numbers of animals. The Hmong were sturdy peasant farmers before they became refugees. Resourceful by nature, they supplement their diet by raising a variety of animals within the confines of the camp. Purchased as inexpensive chicks, and a valuable ceremonial animal, chickens scratch about everywhere. Every family seems to have at least half a dozen. Ducks and geese are also raised. Pigs are a common sight, and dogs and goats roam freely throughout the camp. Because space is at such a premium, there is little room for separate livestock pens. During the day they roam outside and at night they are often brought inside the house. In one of the thatched huts where I regularly slept overnight, I shared a corner with seven chickens – they were kept underneath wicker baskets at night – and the neighbour's pig. Inside many of the homes of very poor families you could find guinea pigs scurrying about, an inexpensive source of protein. Ban Vinai boasts a herd of more than twenty dairy cows, a gift from a well-meaning but uninformed charitable organization with the intention of raising the nutritional level of the camp. The Hmong do not drink milk; like many Asians, some are lactose intolerant. Because the cows were donated for the common good, no individual is authorized to butcher them. Therefore, completely useless, the cows wander freely throughout the camp, contributing to the hygiene and sanitation problems of the camp.

Housing is extremely crowded and inadequate. The United Nations High Commission for Refugees built 395 tin-roofed buildings, each one with ten small rooms. The camp was established in 1975 for 12,000 refugees; the population has nearly quadrupled since then. The 1984 birthrate was 5.5 per cent, one of the highest in the world. 25 per cent of the Ban Vinai population was born in the camp. The refugees have responded to the housing shortage by building more than 2,250 thatch/bamboo huts. But it costs more than $50 for the materials to build a house. That kind of money is hard to come by in a refugee camp, so extended families crowd together in congested living quarters. During the rainy season, some of these dirt-floor huts are in danger of getting washed away, so families use partially buried discarded glass bottles to bank up the earth around their huts.

Camp Ban Vinai is the largest gathering of Hmong in the world. The tragic events of war and global politics have led to this artificial urbanization of the Hmong with dizzying speed. Traditionally, the Hmong lived in small mountaintop villages in the forbidding terrain of northern Laos where they tended their animals and grew dry rice and corn in fields cleared from the forest. F. M. Savina reported that the Hmong in Laos 'do not seem to like big settlements. They prefer to live in little groups making up hamlets rather than real villages' (1930: 182). A peaceful mountain people who kept to themselves, they had little contact with even the lowland-dwelling Lao, much less the rest of the world, until they were pulled into the war in Southeast Asia. In the 1960s they were recruited by the CIA and trained by the Green Berets as anticommunist guerrilla fighters.[3] In proportion to their population, they suffered casualties ten times higher than those of Americans who fought in Vietnam (Cerquone 1986). When US forces withdrew in 1975, Laos collapsed and came under the rule of a government hostile to the Hmong who were viewed as collaborators with the hated enemy. Thousands fled their beloved mountain homes to seek asylum in Camp Ban Vinai, just across the Mekong in Thailand. Almost overnight they were thrown into a densely populated camp with no time to develop the adaptive cultural traditions and folkways, not to mention garbage disposal systems, that societies in the West have had centuries to evolve. It is any wonder, then, that there would be severe environmental health problems in Ban Vinai?

Moreover, there is no running water or adequate sewage disposal in the camp. The camp commander lists the water shortage as one of the major problems. Water has to be carried long distances in buckets balanced on shoulder yokes or in 10-gallon cans strapped to the back, a job usually done by teenagers. Sewage disposal is also a chronic problem. There are not enough pit toilets for the camp population. The latrines are distributed unevenly throughout the camp and are clustered together in long rows – convenient if you happen to live close to a cluster but the trade-off is the overwhelming stench. Because there is a shortage of toilets, they are kept locked and families have to obtain keys from the camp administration. Keys get lost, and there are never enough keys to go around, particularly for all the children. Further, you need to bring along a bucket of water to flush the shallow pit, water that is scarce and has to be carried on the back of some family member. Obviously, there are many disincentives for using the pit toilets; the stench alone is often a deterrent. Because gaining access to and using the pit toilets is a rather complex operation, most small children (one-fourth the population) simply cannot manage.

I go into detail about the camp toilets in order to give an infrastructural explanation for what has become a topos in reports about Ban Vinai from Western journalists and visiting relief workers. Ban Vinai is notorious for the image of refugees relieving themselves in the open space. This act, so shocking to 'sophisticated' sensibilities, functions discursively as a sign of 'the primitive.' Before I left Bangkok en route to Ban Vinai, I heard stories about this behaviour from other aid workers and came across this motif in written reports as well as oral anecdotes. This recurrent image is psychologically and rhetorically interesting for what it reveals about our discursive projections of the Other. My observations are that the Hmong are a very modest people. The act does not occur with the frequency the stories imply.

However, you have only to spend three days and nights in the camp in order to understand the environmental circumstances that produce such behaviour even occasionally. Living in the camp with the refugees and experiencing these environmental constraints and indignities was instructive for me.

The following excerpt from an unpublished report written by an agency health worker is representative:

> The first week I arrived in Ban Vinai, a refugee city, a city without discipline, I strolled around the camp and realized the important need for basic health education. No one looks after the children playing cheerfully in the streams. The streams in which they defecate, take a bath, and throw garbage including drainage from houses and toilets. The refugees use sticks for cleaning after defecation and throw them behind the toilets. When it rains, the sewage goes into the streams. Also, a lot of children wear nothing when it rains.

Instead of blaming the Hmong for the poor health conditions, our performance company situated the problem in the environmental setting. Instead of didactic health messages instructing the Hmong to change their behaviour, we developed performances that would stimulate critical awareness about the camp environment, particularly how it differed from the natural mountain villages of the Hmong in Laos. Once their radically changed living conditions could be brought to consciousness through performance, the Hmong might understand the need for changing some of their habits to adapt to this altered situation. Such a line of thinking was not alien to them. One man offered me an environmental explanation for the high suicide rate in Ban Vinai. He argued that, in their homeland, family tensions and pressures could be relieved by the troubled person leaving home temporarily to stay with relatives or friends in the next village until the situation cooled down. Without this outlet in Ban Vinai, pressures sometimes mount until suicide seems the only escape. Also, there is a traditional Hmong proverb that encourages adjustment to change of venue: 'When you cross a river, take off your shoes / When you move to another place, you must change your headman' (Conquergood 1989: 46).

We mounted a series of performances focused on the problem of garbage in the camp. The first thing we had to do was problematize 'garbage.' In a traditional Hmong village, garbage would not be the problem it was in Ban Vinai. If all disposable waste is organic, and you live in a small hamlet on a windswept mountain slope, then pitching waste out the door is not a problem. It becomes instant feed for the household pigs or is biodegradably reabsorbed into the natural ecology of the environment. Within the context of a crowded refugee camp, however, traditional ways of waste disposal entail radically different consequences. We wanted to get this message across without demeaning the people, suggesting that they were dirty.

Our 'Garbage Theme' month featured Mother Clean in one of our most successful scenarios. Drawing on the *poj ntxoog* evil ogre character from Hmong folklore, we created an ugly Garbage Troll in soiled ragged clothes and a mask plastered with bits of garbage and dirt. The Garbage Troll would lumber into the centre of the playing space and begin dramatizing the behaviour we wanted to discourage – peeling eggs and other food and throwing the waste on the ground, picking up dirty food from the ground and putting it into his mouth, and so forth. After a few minutes of this improvisation, the tiger would charge on stage and rebuke the troll for such unseemly behaviour. The tiger would growl and snarl and pounce at the impassive troll, all the while making verbally explicit how bad this behaviour was. The tiger would give up and leave but then the pig would run out on stage and fuss at the troll for his disgusting conduct. The young performer who played our pig was a gifted clown and there would be much farcical business between the pig and the Garbage Troll until the troll drove the pig away. Then the chicken would follow suit and sagely admonish the troll about the environmental consequences of his behaviour and how he would make children sick by throwing garbage all about. The troll would respond by throwing more garbage on the ground and at the chicken, driving the latter away.

From a considerable distance, Mother Clean would slowly sweep toward the dirty Garbage Troll. The children forming a circle around the playing space would have to open up their ranks to permit Mother Clean's passage. They would call out, warning her to beware of the nasty Garbage Troll. But Mother Clean would be unaware of the danger; absorbed in sweet thoughts she would sing to herself and dance as daintily as her bulk would permit. The children in the audience would increase the volume of their warning cries until Mother Clean heard and caught sight of the Garbage Troll. Unafraid, slowly, triumphantly she would sweep toward the nasty troll huddling in the dirt making menacing noises. She'd reach down, pull him up by his hands, then, in a moment of redemptive grace, remove his dirt-face mask and wash his face and hands. Transformed, the troll and Mother Clean danced as music was played from our battery-operated cassette player. Tiger, pig and chicken rushed back on stage to dance and sing with Mother Clean and the redeemed troll. Our health workers, wearing sandwich-board posters with the health theme boldly lettered, would join the circle, and Mother Clean would slowly spell out and read the poster proverbs for those in the audience who were nonliterate. She would talk and invite comment and discussion about the theme.

The theme we developed in proverb form and painted on the sandwichboard posters was this:

Thaum peb nyob pem roob cua thiab nag
Tshoob yam khoom qias neeg pov tseg.
Tam sim no muaj neeg coob coob nyob hauv zos vib nai,
Peb txhua leej txhua tus yuav xyuam xim
Cheb yam khoom qias neeg kom huv si

[When you lived in the mountains
The wind and the rain cleaned the garbage.
Now with so many people in Ban Vinai
We all must be careful to clean up the garbage]

Mother Clean would lovingly amplify the message of the proverb, explaining how a small village on a mountain slope with plenty of space for everyone could absorb organic refuse naturally through the elements of wind and rain. She pointed out that Ban Vinai is very different from the mountaintop villages in which the Hmong used to live. Consequently, customs and habits, particularly regarding garbage, needed to change accordingly. She exhorted a change in behaviour without degrading the people whom she was trying to persuade, locating responsibility in the environmental circumstances. Everyone could agree that indeed Ban Vinai was very different from their former home. After establishing that premise, Mother Clean then could make the point about the need for an adaptive response to this new situation.

This scenario was staged three or four times a week, each time in a different section of the camp. In this way we could reach most of the camp population in a month's time. Each day we would find a wide place in the road, or a clearing between houses, and use that empty space for the performance. One of the company members would walk around the area with a bullhorn announcing the performance. The performances were so popular that we sometimes had crowd control problems, with people pressing in so close that there was no room for the performers to move. One of the company members, usually the one who made the initial announcements over the bullhorn, would serve as 'house manager'. He would draw a large circle on the ground with a pointed stick and declare that area the players' space, off-limits to curious children. This strategy worked, except for the occasional dog that wandered on stage.

It was hard work performing in the open air under the tropical sun. I admired the dedication of the refugee performers. I was particularly touched by the young man who played Mother Clean. Lee Neng (his name means 'human being' in Hmong) was malarial and every month or so would run a fever, have a stomach-ache and pass blood in his urine. I insisted that he not perform during these bouts and proposed that we use an understudy when he was sick. Besides, the roles of the pig, chicken and tiger were passed around among the company members. But Lee Neng knew that he had a special rapport with the children and that his character Niam Tsev Huv was doing good in the camp, helping the little children so that they would not get sick so often. He said it made him feel very good when he was Niam Tsev Huv and he refused to surrender the role, even when he was ill. Sometimes he was so weak he could barely be heard. I would give him aspirin and lighten the performance schedule when I knew he was feverish.

We included a participatory dimension to the performances by teaching health and sanitation songs to the children. Initially, young children performers were trained as role models who travelled around the camp with our troupe, singing and dancing the sanitation songs. However, we incurred 'labour problems' with the young actors when their parents complained about the taxing performance schedule. We discontinued the Chorus of Children and used members of the performance company, particularly the young women, as sanitation song leaders.

The children of the camp loved to learn and sing these sanitation songs. They particularly enjoyed a call-and-response style of singing in which the audience would alternate the singing of verses with a leader, Mother Clean or one of the refugee health workers. We put some of the songs on cassette tapes, and distributed them throughout the camp in that way as well. Most of the Hmong have access to battery-operated cassette players because many of them correspond with relatives resettled in the West by sending cassettes through the mail. I also gave cassettes of these songs to the 'Hilltribe Broadcast Program', Radio Thailand. Later, when I toured their studios and facilities in Chiang Mai and interviewed the Hmong broadcasters, they reported that the Ban Vinai Health Songs were very popular with their listening audience.

Here is a sample health song composed for our campaign:

Yog koj mus yos hav zoov tsam ysov tom
Yog koj tsis ntxuav muag ntxuav tes, taw ibce
Koj yuav tau kab mob
Yog koj mus tom tej hav tsaub liab koj yuav tau mob

[If you play in the jungle
The Tiger will bite you
If you don't wash your hands, face, and body
You will get sick
If you play in the garbage
You will fall ill]

Another sanitation song, 'Using the Latrine', turned out to be one of the most durable songs in the repertoire. Mother Clean led a parade of 40 singing children throughout the camp, with the message visually reinforced on posters that graphically depicted the appropriate behaviour. There was follow-up to the parade with activities such as colouring pictures and a game called 'Take Your Small Brother or Sister to the Latrine'. Once again, reaching and involving the children was an important way of communicating with adults.

Mother Clean was the anchor for the performance company. A variety of performance materials and activities could be organized around her character. She seemed to embody something very appealing to the Hmong. Adults as well as small children were delighted by her messages. I will never forget the image of a very thin, elderly man doubled over his walking stick with uncontrollable laughter during Mother Clean's performance. His neighbours told me they had not seen him laugh in a long time.

Expatriate health professionals and the Hmong: Perceptions of difference, disorder, dirt, and danger

The more I learned about the history and cultural dynamics of the camp, the more I came to believe that the expatriate health professionals needed consciousness-raising messages as much as the Hmong. The Hmong are perceived by Western officials and visiting journalists as the causal, producing agents of the unsanitary and unhealthy conditions in the camp. Instead of seeing the Hmong as struggling within a constraining context of historical, political and economic forces that have reduced them from proud, independent, mountain people to landless refugees, the Hmong are blamed for their miserable condition. In her brilliant and incisive analysis of refugee assistance programmes, Barbara Harrell-Bond notes this sad pattern: '[I]t is alarming to observe that assistance programmes are dominated by an ethos in which the victims of mass exodus are treated as the villains' (Harrell-Bond 1986: 305). It is easier to scapegoat than to historicize a complex problem.

I began to collect the phrases used regularly to describe the Hmong by agency officials who worked in Ban Vinai. The word I heard most often was 'filthy', followed closely by 'dirty', and often part of a cluster of terms that included 'scabies', 'abscesses', 'faeces', and 'piles of garbage'. A phrase regularly employed to cover a multitude of perceived sanitation sins was the following, 'They're one step out of the Stone Age, you know'. A meaning-packed word heard about the Hmong almost every day was 'difficult', and its ramified derivatives: 'difficult to work with', 'the most difficult group', 'set in their ways', 'rigid', 'stubborn', 'you cannot get through to them', 'backward'. One dedicated humanitarian agency employee who had worked with the Hmong for several years told me that 'the hand of God is on this place', but as for the Hmong living here, 'they're a fearful lot … you cannot work with them'. These perceptions surface in official discourse as well. Senator Alan Simpson, ranking minority member of the Senate Subcommittee on Immigration and Refugee Affairs, visited Ban Vinai for a day during the time of my fieldwork. He introduced a new metaphor into this complex of discursive denigrations of the Hmong. He called the Hmong 'the most indigestible group in society' (Simpson 1987: 4). Ambassador Jonathan Moore, the new U.S. Coordinator for Refugee Affairs, was more diplomatic when, in a 1987 interview, he singled out the Hmong as 'the people with special problems' (Moore 1987: 5).

The dialectic between the perception of 'difference' and 'dirt' is interesting. I suggest that so much focus on the 'dirtiness' and 'difficulty' of the Hmong is actually an expression of Western expatriates' uneasiness when confronted with Difference, the Other. A Western aid official's encounter with the Hmong is a confrontation with radical difference – in cosmology, worldview, ethos and texture of everyday life. The difference is exacerbated if the relief workers are devout Christians. The three relief agencies that have been in charge of the camp hospital have all been Christian organizations which have perceived the animism of the Hmong as 'devil worship'.

For medical health officials with a professional commitment to the tenets of Western science, the equally strong Hmong belief in spirits and shamans challenges fundamental Western assumptions about the nature of the world. What is frustrating for agency workers is that the acceptance and cooperation of the Hmong are essential for the successful delivery of healthcare programs and services. The Hmong are the clear majority in Camp Ban Vinai, of course, and they continue to control their symbolic universe. Much to the distress of agency workers, they have not acquiesced to the new scientific epistemology presented to them as a 'superior' form of knowledge. Visible affirmations of their traditional way of understanding the world are displayed everywhere. Here are excerpts from a report by Dr. Ronald Munger, an epidemiologist who did research in Ban Vinai:

> The striking issue in regard to traditional Hmong health practices is how visible these practices are in Ban Vinai Refugee camp in Thailand. [...] Shamanism was widely practiced. [...] There were other more common everyday rituals which reflected pervading belief in the spirits in every aspect of life. Ritual figures or heads of sacrificed animals set on poles were common. Wooden boards on the floor at the doorway of a home were intended to confuse unwanted spirits and prevent them from entering the house. [...] Pleasing the spirits was a primary goal. For example, bracelets, necklaces, and other devices were often placed on babies and small children to contain the spirit of that person and avoid its loss. [...] Many Hmong homes [...] contained small altars with the items needed to interact with spirits. There were buffalo horns [...] rings and rattles used during rituals.
>
> (Munger 1984)

All this display of 'difference' and 'strangeness' is quite dramatic to Western eyes and makes a vivid impression. Unfortunately, as Tzvetan Todorov reminds us, 'The first, spontaneous reaction with regard to the stranger is to imagine him as inferior, since he is different from us' (Todorov 1984: 76). All too easily, 'difference is corrupted into inequality' (Todorov 1984: 146).

Mary Douglas' ideas about the social relativity and symbolic functions of dirt help explain how 'Difference' and 'Dirt' are conjoined in perceptions of the Hmong. Inspired by William James' insight that dirt is 'matter out of place' (Douglas 1966: 164), she argues:

> [D]irt is essentially disorder. There is no such thing as absolute dirt: it exists in the eye of the beholder. [...] Dirt offends against order. Eliminating it is not a negative movement, but a positive effort to organise the environment.
>
> (Douglas 1966: 2)

Perceptions of what is clean and unclean are contextually variable and culturally specific. Habits of cleanliness and rites of purification are the manifest expressions and protections of deep structures and fundamental classificatory schemes that maintain order and help hold a society together. People and actions that disturb order, violate categories, mess up the system are branded unclean: 'The unclear is the unclean' (Turner 1967: 97). Labelling someone or something 'dirty' is a way of controlling perceived anomalies, incongruities, contradictions, ambiguities – all that does not fit into our categories, and therefore threatens cherished principles. 'Dirt,' then, functions as the mediating term between 'Difference' and 'Danger.' It is the term that loads the perception of 'Difference' with a moral imperative, and enables the move from description to action, from 'is' to 'ought.' Defining something as unhealthy, harmful, dangerous establishes the premise for 'moving in', for control, making it 'licit to intervene [...] in order to exercise the rights of guardianship [...] to impose "the good" on others' (Todorov 1984: 150). Perception, language and politics cathect in the encounter with the Other: 'the perception of the other and that of symbolic (or semiotic) behavior intersect' (Todorov 1984: 157; see also Foucault 1973; Said 1979).

The communication between expatriate camp officials and the refugees in Ban Vinai is so clouded by the perceptual transformations which I call the Difference-Disorder-Dirt-Danger Sliding Continuum, that other explanations for the poor health conditions of the camp get filtered out. I quote a revealing passage from one of the monthly reports submitted to the Bangkok office by a Ban Vinai health officer:

> Three refugees in Center Five had just died before my arrival. [...] We walked around that area. It was muddy; piled with garbage, sticks thrown behind toilets and sludge appeared from place to place. [Agency] garbage pits and sewage treatment lagoons were situated above and close to the buildings. 'It's a horrible smell when the wind blows especially from that garbage pit down to our houses, sometimes we can't eat anymore,' [a refugee said]. [...] [He] asked me to convey this problem to [the agency], hoping we could move the pits to another place. However, [the agency] can't move it at all because of the limitations of land and budget.

This is a remarkable passage. After the obligatory faecal imagery of the toilets, mud, sludge and ooze, there is almost a recognition scene. The health official notes the 'garbage pits' and 'sewage treatment lagoons' his agency has situated dangerously close to the living quarters. The refugee accompanying him on this site tour follows up on the perception and complains. We are presented with a marvellous glimpse of a refugee talking back to a camp official, resisting the unhealthy and degrading circumstances in which he and his people are caught. The responsibility for the problem almost gets shifted from the refugees to the environment, with the expatriate agencies even held accountable for contributing to the creation of a harmful scene.

This rupture in the discursive text about refugees gets sealed off quickly, however. Scarcely a page later, the perceptual blinders are back in place: 'Even though some have had public health training, it is evident that the training has had little effect – their homes are untidy and stuffy and their children are dirty. They have no picture of community.' We are comfortably refocused on the dirtiness of the refugees. This ideology of blaming the victims, and thereby legitimizing domination and control over them, is displayed transparently in the final section of the report, ominously subtitled 'Submission for Discipline':

> We all realize that even though lots of refugees have been trained about hygiene and sanitation by volags [voluntary agencies], they still behave as they used to. [...] No refugees really take care of the environment. [...] They live freely wandering around without any responsibility.
>
> In my own opinion it'll take a long time to change their habits which detract from their health. One thing that might help is a 'system of discipline'. [...] For example, the

refugees can be told what will happen if they throw garbage everywhere, defecate into the streams, etc.

It's an idea that we might think about carefully and which might work in the future.

This text is paradigmatic of the documents produced by the bureaucracy and institutional apparatus of refugee relief agencies. It is an avatar of the twin themes of discursive power and institutional control that Michel Foucault discussed in *The Birth of the Clinic: An Archaeology of Medical Perception* (1973) and *Discipline and Punish: The Birth of the Prison* (1977). Because the 'limitation of land and budget' forecloses the consideration of infrastructural change in the camp environment, attention is diverted to the 'change [of] their habits which detract from their good health.' Refugee subjects are discursively represented in a way that reduces them to the unhealthy and/or passive Other who is to be managed, administered and, if need be, changed. Their resistance, interpreted as recalcitrance, only legitimizes and further sustains the institutional power and authority that are enacted upon them. Harrell-Bond deconstructs the strange, self-reinforcing logic that underpins refugee programmes in Africa where she did fieldwork: 'Often interpretations of compassion seem to define those in need as helpless, and then work in ways which makes sure that they are useless' (Harrell-Bond 1986: 82).

One of the motives that would prompt doctors and nurses to volunteer for stressful work in an alien, harsh environment is concern for the refugees' souls as well as their physical bodies. I heard horror story after horror story from the refugees about people who went to the hospital for treatment, but before being admitted had their spirit-strings cut from their wrists by a nurse because 'the strings were unsanitary and carried germs.' Doctors confidently cut off neck-rings that held the life-souls of babies intact. Instead of working in cooperation with the shamans, they did everything to disconfirm them and undermine their authority. Shamans were regarded as 'witch doctors.' Here are the views of a Finnish nurse who worked in Ban Vinai: 'They have their bark and root medicines and rites to appease the spirits. Most of it is worthless, and some of it is positively harmful' (Evans 1983: 111). Is it any wonder that the Hmong community regarded the camp hospital as the last choice of available health care options? In the local hierarchy of values, consulting a shaman or herbalist, or purchasing medicine available in the Thai market just outside the entrance to the camp, was much preferred and more prestigious than going to the camp hospital. The refugees told me that only the very poorest people who had no relatives or resources whatsoever would subject themselves to the camp hospital treatment. To say that the camp hospital was underutilized would be an understatement.

As I critique my work in the camp I realize that I should have developed more consciousness-raising performances specifically for the expatriate health professionals. They needed to develop a critical awareness about health problems in the camp at least as much as did the Hmong. Directing most of the performances to the Hmong resulted in a one-sided communication campaign and subtly reinforced the prevailing notion that the Hmong were primarily responsible for the bad conditions.

I did develop one performance event that was designed especially for the agency health workers, the 'IRC Health and Sanitation Celebration.' All the voluntary agency personnel were invited to a showcase of skits from the refugee performance company culminating in a shared meal. The ostensible purpose of this event was to let the other agency workers know what we were doing so that they would not be surprised if they came across one of our health shows in the camp. The implicit agenda was to promote better understanding of Hmong culture and traditions. To this end, we capped the series of performance sketches by bringing a Hmong shaman on stage who enacted a traditional soul-calling ceremony of blessing and tied string around the wrists of expatriate personnel who voluntarily came up to the stage. Given the history of hostility between shamans and the hospital, this was a radical move. Those who participated in this intercultural performance found it deeply moving. However, they were a small, self-selected group who were already the most open-minded. Most of the expatriate guests politely remained in their seats but observed attentively. The most dogmatic agency workers – for example, the Christian nurse who refused to allow any Thai calendars in her ward because they had pictures of the Buddha – did not even attend this event.

I should have been more assiduous in attempts to reach the expatriate personnel who were most ethnocentric in their dealings with the Hmong. My sympathies were with the refugees. My interests and energies were devoted to understanding and working with the Hmong. It was easier to identify with the Hmong; the dogmatic Christians became the Other for me.

It is important to speak out against the repressive practices of some refugee relief agencies, however, in the interest of searching for a solution to this sad situation, I do not want to substitute one scapegoat for another. I agree with Harrell-Bond that 'it is unproductive to blame' the agency fieldworkers for the enormous communication breakdowns that occur in refugee camps. By nature a refugee camp is a highly volatile, stressful, politically intense, multicultural arena, usually located in a harsh environment. In matters of communication and intercultural sensitivity, relief workers 'are not trained. Within the agency bureaucracy they are not rewarded for involving themselves with individuals. In fact, fieldworkers are often warned against "getting involved"' (Harrell-Bond 1986: 305). The agency workers I met in Ban Vinai were all dedicated, caring people. Even though they commuted to the camp from a Thai village an hour away, their living conditions there were quite basic. Many of the workers were volunteers, working in the camp at considerable personal sacrifice. The problem cannot be so easily contained at the level of the agency personnel. The root of the problem goes much deeper into institutional bureaucratic practices and the ideologies that empower and sustain them.

The ideal is for the two cultures, refugees and relief workers, to enter into a productive and mutually invigorating dialogue, with neither side dominating or winning out, but both replenishing one another (see Bakhtin 1981). Intercultural performance can enable this kind of dialogical exchange between Self and Other. Eugenio Barba talks about performance as 'barter':

Otherness is our point of departure. Imagine two very different tribes, each on their own side of the river. Each tribe can live for itself, talk about the other, praise or slander it.

But every time one of them rows over to the other shore it is to exchange something. One does not row over to teach, to enlighten, to entertain, but rather to give and take: a handful of salt for a scrap of cloth. [. . .] Otherness is our meeting point.

(Barba 1986: 161)

As a medium of exchange, performance draws us to the margins, the borders between Self and Other. Bakhtin affirms: 'The most intense and productive life of culture takes place on the boundaries' (Bakhtin 1986: 2). Conceived of as barter, a site of exchange, performance is a key to understanding 'how the deeply different can be deeply known without becoming any less different' (Geertz 1983: 48). The value of the exchange is in the encounter, the relations that are produced, not the objects: 'It is the act of exchanging that gives value to that which is exchanged, and not the opposite' (Barba 1986: 268).

Postscript

I returned to Camp Ban Vinai for a brief follow-up visit in September 1987, anxious to see what had become of Mother Clean and the Ban Vinai Performance Company in the two years since my departure. IRC had hired a Thai university graduate who worked with me on the health education programme and she was to take over the project after I left. Although she left IRC to work for another agency in the camp, Mother Clean and the performance approach to working with refugees survived this transfer to another agency. I was delighted to see that Mother Clean had been fully integrated into the culture of Camp Ban Vinai. Literacy textbooks produced in the camp print shop were illustrated with images of Mother Clean. Mother Clean hand puppets were made in the camp and used for entertainment and instruction. Mother Clean puzzles delighted children. The ultimate test was that Mother Clean had been invited by the Hmong leaders to perform at the New Year Festivities, the most important and elaborate celebration of Hmong culture.

The character had been through three reincarnations and several performers in the two years I had been gone. Two bamboo frames and costumes had been worn out by heavy use. Her yarn hair was more purple than I had remembered it, but other than that she looked very much the same as when I left in 1985. I was pleased to see her again, as well as the young man who currently performed her. Nuanjan Charnwiwatana, the Thai worker in charge of the programme after I left, told me that during her change of employment from IRC to another agency, there was a period of time when Mother Clean did not perform. She said that children would come to the IRC office in camp and ask worriedly, 'Where is Mama Clean? Is Mama Clean sick?' And they had begun to ask about Mother Clean's children. Construction was underway during my visit for a child-sized Mother Clean, and the performance company talked of eventually having a Mother Clean family. Mother Clean's success as a communicator had reached personnel in other refugee camps, and I was told that she had been cloned for some of these.

A new participatory theatre strategy was highly successful: Mother Clean now made home visits. The performers were quite confident with the character and could improvise lines that directly addressed the problems of a particular household or neighbourhood in the camp. These home visits also involved a great deal of interaction between Mother Clean and her hosts. The home visits were still highly entertaining because Mother Clean would have to manoeuvre her considerable bulk through the crowded living quarters and underneath low-hanging thatched eaves. This required a good deal of awkward bending and turning on Mother Clean's part and sometimes she would get stuck in a narrow passageway, to the glee of the onlookers.

It was heartening to see Mother Clean still being performed by Hmong actors, supporting Hmong identity, and blending with Hmong cultural traditions which still flourished in the camp. My return visit was celebrated by a shamanic performance. Hmong friends positioned me on a shaman's bench in front of his altar, tied me with a cord to a live pig, while the shaman circled me chanting and beating a gong. The pig's soul was released on my behalf through a deft cut at the throat, while the shaman covered his face with a dark veil and entered ecstatic trance, leaping back and forth between the bench and the ground.

Conditions had not improved in the camp since 1985. If anything, the camp was even more tense. There was a new camp commander who imposed more rules and restrictions. The presence of soldiers was greater. Throughout my stay during 1985, I was never stopped by the military. On my second day in camp during the return visit, I was challenged by a patrol. The camp was even more crowded, particularly with 'illegals,' estimated to be as many as 10,000. Still, it was gratifying to see the Mother Clean character bringing some joy to the camp inmates, particularly the children, while attempting to address in a positive way the difficult situation.

References

Bakhtin, M. M., *The Dialogic Imagination*, Holquist, M. (ed.), translated by Emerson, C., & Holquist, M., Austin: University of Texas Press, 1981.

———, *Speech Genres*, Emerson, C., & Holquist, M. (eds.), translated by McGee, V. W., Austin: University of Texas Press, 1986.

Barba, E., *Beyond the Floating Islands*, New York: Performing Arts Journal Publications, 1986.

Boal, A., *Theatre of the Oppressed*, translated by Charles, A., & McBride, M. L., New York: Theatre Communications Group, 1985 [1979].

Burke, K., *A Rhetoric of Motives*, Berkeley, University of California Press, 1969.

Bustos, N., 'Mecate, the Nicaraguan Farm Workers' Theatre Movement,' *Adult Education and Development*, 23 (September 1984), pp. 129–140.

Cerquone, J., *Refugees from Laos: In Harm's Way*, Washington, DC: U.S. Committee for Refugees, American Council for Nationalities Service, 1986.

Conquergood, D., 'Performing as a Moral Act: Ethical Dimensions of the Ethnography of Performance,' *Literature in Performance*, 5 (April 1985), pp. 1–13.

——, *I Am a Shaman: a Hmong Life Story, with Hmong Text and Ethnographic Commentary*, Minneapolis, MN: Center for Urban and Regional Affairs, Southeast Asia Refugee Studies, 1989.

——, 'Hmong Proverbs: Texts and Ethnographic Commentary,' in Johns, Brenda, & Strecker, David, *The Hmong World*, New Haven, CT: Yale University, Council on Southeast Asia Studies, 1987.

Desai, G., 'Popular Theatre, Participatory Research and Adult Education in Africa: A Preliminary Bibliography,' unpublished manuscript, Northwestern University, 1987.

Douglas, M., *Purity and Danger: An Analysis of the Concepts of Pollution and Taboo*, London: Routledge and Kegan Paul, 1966.

van Erven, E., 'Philippine Political Theatre and the Fall of Ferdinand Marcos,' *The Drama Review*, 31:2 (1987), pp. 58–78.

Evans, G., *The Yellow Rainmakers*, London: Verso, 1983.

Eyoh, H. N., *Hammocks to Bridges: Report of the Workshop on Theatre for Integrated Rural Development*, Yaounde, Cameroon: BET & Co., 1986.

Foucault, M., *Birth of the Clinic: An Archaeology of Medical Perception*, translated by Sheridan Smith, A. M., New York: Pantheon, 1973.

——, *Discipline and Punish: The Birth of the Prison*, translated by Sheridan Smith, A., New York, Pantheon, 1977.

Freire, P., *Pedagogy of the Oppressed*, New York: Continuum, 1986 [1970].

Geertz, C., *Local Knowledge: Further Essays in Interpretive Anthropology*, New York: Basic Books, 1983.

Harrell-Bond, B., *Imposing Aid: Emergency Assistance to Refugees*, New York: Oxford University Press, 1986.

Holtan, N. (ed.), *Final Report of the SUNDS Planning Project*, St. Paul, MN: St. Paul-Ramsey Medical Center, 1984.

Kaitaro, T. (ed.), 'Theater as Struggle: Asian People's Drama,' Ampo, 11:2–3 (1979).

Kidd, R., *The Popular Performing Arts, Non-formal Education and Social Change in the Third World: A Bibliography and Review Essay*, The Hague: Centre for the Study of Education in Developing Countries, 1982.

Kidd, R., *From People's Theatre for Revolution to Popular Theatre for Reconstruction: Diary of a Zimbabwean Workshop*, The Hague: Centre for the Study of Education in Developing Countries, 1984.

Kidd, R., & Byram, M., *Popular Theatre and Participation in Development: Three Botswana Case Studies*, Gaborone: Bosele Tshwaraganang Publications, 1978.

Moore, J., 'Interview with Jonathan Moore: U.S. Coordinator for Refugees,' *Refugee Reports*, 8, (June 1987), pp. 1–5.

Munger, R., 'Synopsis of Comments to the Wilder Foundation Refugee Projects,' in Holtan, N. (ed.) *Final Report of the SUNDS Planning Project* St. Paul, MN: St. Paul-Ramsey Medical Center, 1984, pp. 37–39.

———, 'Sleep Disturbance and Sudden Death of Hmong Refugees: A Report on Fieldwork Conducted in the Ban Vinair Refugee Camp,' in *The Hmong in Transition*, New York: Center for Migration Studies, 1986.

Ong, W., *Orality and Literacy: The Technologizing of the Word*, London: Methuen, 1982.

Said, E., *Orientalism*, New York: Vintage, 1979.

Savina, F. M., *Histoire des Miao*, Hong Kong: Société des Missions Étrangères de Paris, 1930.

Siegel, T., and Conquergood, D. (producers), *Between Two Worlds: The Hmong Shaman in America*, video-documentary, Siegel Productions, 1985.

Simpson, A., cited in 'Senate Holds Midyear Hearings on FY 87 Refugee Missions,' *Refugee Reports*, 8 (July 1987), p. 4.

Tapp, N., *Hmong of Thailand: Opium People of the Golden Triangle*, The Indigenous Peoples and Development Series Report, no. 4, London: Anti-Slavery Society, 1986.

Thiong'o, N. W., *Detained: A Writer's Prison Diary*, London: Heinemann, 1981.

———, *Barrel of a Pen: Resistance to Repression in Neo-colonial Kenya*, Trenton, Africa World Press, 1983.

Thiong'o, N.W., *Decolonising the Mind: The Politics of Language in African Literature*, London: J. Currey, 1986.

Todorov, T., *The Conquest of America: The Question of the Other*, New York: Harper & Row, 1984.

Turner, V., *The Forest of Symbols*, Ithaca, NY: Cornell University Press, 1967.

Werner, D., *Where There is No Doctor: A Village Health Care Handbook*, Palo Alto, CA: Hesperian Foundation, 1977.

Werner, D., and Bower, B., *Helping Health Workers Learn*, Palo Alto, CA: Hesperian Foundation, 1982.

Notes

1 More than 100 Hmong refugees, almost all men, have died suddenly. Autopsy reports show no cause of death (see Holtan 1984; Munger 1986).

2 *Helping Health Workers Learn* should be read as a model of praxis. It is designed for village health workers, but it has much to say about action and reflection and the development of a critical consciousness. Although the authors draw extensively on the methods of Freire, they provide an incisive critique of his work. I recommend this book particularly for academics whose social and critical theories get abstracted from the lived struggles of poor people.

3 Through the Freedom of Information Act a CIA film depicting the recruitment, training and guerrilla warfare of the Hmong in Laos is now available. This media text documents how the Hmong were recruited and used by the CIA during the war in Southeast Asia. It sets forth vividly the political-historical circumstances that led ultimately to the Hmong becoming refugees.

Chapter 4

Play Extract: *Forged in Fire*

A performance text created by Okello Kelo Sam, Laura Edmondson, and Robert Ajwang'

Introduction

In 2005, Okello Kelo Sam, a performer, playwright and musician from northern Uganda, Robert Ajwang', a Tanzanian musician and dancer, and I embarked upon a collaboration to develop a performance text around the crisis in northern Uganda. The result was *Forged in Fire*, a quasi-solo performance piece during which Okello plays three characters: (1) Okello himself, who tells the story of his brother, Omony Godfrey Sam, who was abducted by the Lord's Resistance Army in 1996; (2) the Tour Guide, who provides an ironic commentary on the sensationalism and machinery of war; and (3) the Rebel Commander, who gradually forges a friendship with one of the children in his unit.

The piece relies upon an intimate relationship with the audience, who are variously cast as Okello's confidant, a crowd of American tourists or recently abducted Ugandan children. In the excerpt provided below, the Rebel Commander has faded from the story as the play moves into an exploration of the aftermath of immediate trauma. Okello, in particular, laments the loss of his homeland as the place where his umbilical cord is buried. In his monologue that opens the play, he explains: 'We do not celebrate birthdays. We celebrate the burial of the umbilical cord. Every year, they build a shrine around the spot where the child's umbilical cord is buried.' The image of the buried umbilical cord resurfaces throughout the play as a haunting symbol of the cultural loss that permeates the landscape of war.

In the United States, *Forged in Fire* has been presented at Florida State University, Dartmouth College and the Martin E. Segal Theatre Center at the CUNY Graduate Center in New York City. Future plans for the script include performing it for East African audiences and revising the text to reflect the present realities of post-conflict Uganda.

TOURIST GUIDE: I've never seen anything like it!
An entire herd
as if they were waiting for us.
Why have you put down your cameras?
Keep filming! The footage is remarkable.
I'd say there were at least fifty of them.
We caught them right during the migration to the rebel camps in Sudan.
They are still wearing their school uniforms so they are quite early in the journey.

They still have several hundred kilometers to go.
Their endurance amazes wildlife biologists given the lack of
    food
water
sleep
and the abundance
of threats
beatings
fear.
Can you believe that any of them make it to Sudan at all?

What are you doing? Your tears will fog up the lens of the
camera.

Transition to **COMMANDER.** *This transition is very quick; he just drops the tour guide hat.*

COMMANDER: Recruits
Look around you.
The weak ones were cut down like vegetables.
You are the only ones left.

You have pulled many thorns from your feet.
You have drunk urine when there was no water.
You have learned not to cry when you are beaten.
You have killed with your hands.

You have persevered.

You understand our mission.
You understand that for decades the government has tried to
    decimate the Acholi people. They sent soldiers.
They sent AIDS.
They sent Ebola virus.
They wanted to do to us what they did in Rwanda.
They wanted genocide.

But the Acholi are God's creation whom he loves very much.
So he has chosen you.
And you have answered that call.
You are the saviors of your people.

You can lay an ambush.
You can set a landmine.
You can shoot down a motorcar.
A military helicopter.
A neighbor.
Your aunt.

You are no longer recruits. You are soldiers. And as soldiers, you
    deserve a reward.

Kadogo!

KADOGO/ROBERT: Yes sir!

COMMANDER: *Weka muziki!* [Play the music!]

*He beckons to Kadogo, who begins to play a tape of soukous music and brings soda to the commander,
who begins to distribute it among the audience. The Commander and Kadogo, and perhaps any
brave audience members, begin to dance. The tone should be one of utter celebration.*

Transition to **OKELLO.**

OKELLO: In 1998, my cousin Susanna Adon saw him.
            She lives near Lagoro Hill
            a hill that is a symbol of the god of the Acholi people from Jule
                region.
            You can see the hill from anywhere in Acholi-land.
            It acts as our compass
            each side is unique.

            The rebels came and abducted children from her village
            and that is when she saw him.
            She begged them to leave him with her.
            They refused and they took her husband.
            A child has been abducted from every single extended family in
                northern Uganda.
            You read in the newspaper
            that twenty rebels have been gunned down by a military
                helicopter.
            You read this and think

what a good job the Ugandan army is doing to bring this terrible
   war to an end.
But an Acholi reads this and thinks
was it someone I knew?
A schoolmate
a cousin
a sister
a son?

We began to hear rumors that he was in Sudan.
Some of his fellow students who were abducted
came back and told stories about him. He had become a
   commander.
He was known by many people who returned.
He was known because he participated in so many escapes.
Especially children from our village.
He would bring them to his group and allow them to escape.
There are many people from my own village
who gave testimony
about how he helped them to escape.

Transition to **COMMANDER**.

COMMANDER:	Omera.
KADOGO/ROBERT:	Omera.
COMMANDER:	We are close to home.
KADOGO/ROBERT:	Where?
COMMANDER:	You can see Mt. Moroto and Lagoro Hill from here.
	Lagoro! Have you been to those caves?
KADOGO/ROBERT:	My grandfather said they are haunted.
COMMANDER:	No, no. There are no bad spirits there. It is a very special place.
	There are two caves.
	One always has honey and the bees don't sting.
	And the other has such fresh, sweet water
	you cannot imagine.
	But if you dare to carry it with you, you will get lost.
	You will never find your way.
KADOGO/ROBERT:	I do not remember the last time I had honey.
COMMANDER:	We will go there.
KADOGO/ROBERT:	How close are those caves?
COMMANDER:	So close. I feel as if I could touch them. *Omera!*

KADOGO/ROBERT:	*Omera.*
COMMANDER:	Things are happening. I know it.
	We will capture Gulu and we will finally go back home.
	We will sit by a real fire not these little fires we build in the bush.
	We will sit by a real fire
	and we will drink pots and pots and pots
	of porridge.

Transition to **OKELLO.**

OKELLO:	In 2000, I heard there was a group of children in Kitgum
	he had helped to escape from around Karamoja.
	I went there to talk to the children.
	One of them said that my brother told a group of children, about four of them,
	that it was time to go back home.
	They were close to Acholi-land
	and it was time to escape.
	They started running
	he was running ahead
	his colleagues noticed them.
	One of the commanders started chasing and shooting.
	One of them
	a little girl
	was shot in the leg
	and my brother turned back.
	My brother turned back.
	The others kept running.
	They didn't see what happened.

Transition to **COMMANDER.** *He ties Kadogo's hands behind his back and brings him to stand before the audience.*

COMMANDER:	Soldiers.
	The Lord's Resistance Army is your mother and your father.
	And today your parents are very, very proud.
	You saw that this man
	this traitor
	this hyena
	was missing
	and you raised the alarm.

To Kadogo:

You made it so easy. Your fire filled the sky with smoke. You crashed through the papyrus reeds like a stupid cow. You led us right to the caves. Did you not learn anything I taught you?

You have shamed me.

To the audience:
We are lovers of peace.
We love the Acholi people.
We love all Ugandans.
That is why we must chase the evil out,
so that only peace will remain.
The Holy Spirit has told us what to do.

He takes stones out of the small canvas sack and distributes them among the audience.

The stones should be clean.
They should be the size of your fist
the size of your heart.
It is time to show your love.
Who will go first?

Transition to **OKELLO.**

OKELLO: When the war ends
I will look for his body.
I'm hoping that these children
will know the area around where he was killed
and can show me the place.
The girl who was shot was around 10 years old
I will look for the bones of a ten year old and an adult.

We held the funeral for him last January.
We could not have it at home.
We held it in the IDP camp in Pagule.
At least 600 people came.
That is not so many
if you know that there were about 36,000 people in the camp
altogether.

I know you want details.
I can see it from your faces.
You always want details.
This is what I will tell you.
It was as painful as the moment when you lower the body into
    the grave.

Robert starts to play music; just as Okello is about to begin singing, he stops himself and speaks to Robert.

No. We do not have music at the funerals of young people.

Transition to **TOUR GUIDE.**

TOUR GUIDE: I'm so pleased with all of you.
                    You have such sharp eyes.
                    You have already seen a rebel commander
                    a herd of abductees and we haven't even reached the IDP
                        camp yet.
                    A few of you have expressed dissatisfaction
                    about not spotting Joseph Kony
                    and I really must apologize for this.
                    Next time, we will make arrangements and go to Sudan
                    we might see him there.
                    But don't worry
                    even those who have seen him
                    pretend that they haven't.
                    He will only be seen when the development of the park is over.

                    Here we are
                    entering into the habitat of that peculiar species
                    the internally displaced.
                    They are increasingly common in this area
                    there are now 1.9 million of them in northern Uganda.
                    But please don't confuse them with refugees
                    the markings are quite distinct.
                    That's what the UN says
                    and they are the experts.
                    Come on. Keep your cameras ready! Why must I keep reminding
                        you of that?

Look! There!
Two males of the species are fighting.
Fighting with so much anger and passion.
Can you see what they are fighting over?
Put on your binoculars!
A half liter of sunflower oil. Aren't they funny creatures?

Over there. Excellent.
A prime view of their mating habits.
You can see the parents over there having sex where the children
    see them.
A fascinating example of what happens to this species
when an entire extended family is forced
into a six-foot-wide hut.

What are you all looking at?
Oh, yes, that one over there is missing its mouth.
Remember what I told you about the renegade buffalo we saw
    earlier?
That is what they do to their victims.
That one got off easy.
They can do so much worse.

His delivery gradually becomes more rapid fire.

You are looking confused.
You do not understand what you are seeing.
The swollen stomachs of the children?
Protein deficiency, of course!
That skinny woman?
She is not just skinny. Haven't you heard of AIDS?
Why is that man holding the child upside down?
Trying to stop her convulsions.
Why are those people digging?
Can't you figure that out for yourself?

Transition to **OKELLO**.

OKELLO: Every single hut at the IDP camp is surrounded
with graves of children.
Instead of shrines for the umbilical cords
you have graves.

The people have been betrayed.

You think that once you have spoken nicely
condemned the war
that is the end of it.
The UN official says
this cannot go on.
The UN official says
it's the worst humanitarian tragedy of the world today.
And the people applaud
and the official feels proud that he gave a powerful speech.
Then he doesn't think about it
it is gone
it is erased from his mind.
He doesn't know that that speech
has created hope
in the minds of the people.
And one year
two years
twenty years from now
the people will still be waiting for him to help.

To raise people's expectations is a kind of betrayal.
Why do you think that time is limited to your life span?
Don't you care about the legacy you're leaving behind?

The world uses people like sugar cane. You chew it, and when the sap is finished—

He spits. Transition to **TOUR GUIDE.**

TOUR GUIDE: You seem tired, poor people.
So I have a nice surprise for you.
I've booked rooms for you at the Acholi Inn in Gulu town.
You will be treated very well.
You'll watch CNN in the bar

You'll eat tilapia and vegetable curry
in the privacy of your rooms.
You can recharge your cell phones and camcorders.
Now don't be worried if you hear gunfire at night.

The hotel is owned by a colonel of the Ugandan army
so you are safe.

There is even an internet café in town
so you can check your e-mail if you want.
But be careful walking in the town.
It is a mysterious place.
Many centuries ago
a snake came out of a hole
and created a rainbow.
Usually, when a snake comes out from underground
it leaves a hole that is filled with water.
But this particular hole was filled with a magical city
a city that exists beneath this very town Gulu.
Perhaps you will see lines of people
walking along the side of the road
lying on the verandas of the shops
crowded into bus stations
fighting for space to sleep.
These are the ghosts from that magical city.
Now listen to me closely.
If you see that city if you see these ghosts
You must not tell anyone.
Otherwise you'll disappear.
And we would miss you very much.

Transition to **OKELLO**.

OKELLO:

I have three children.
My first born, a girl, is named Laweno.
It means princess.
She was born with the umbilical cord around her neck
as if she was wearing a necklace.
My second born is my son Omara
which means love.
I named him after my great grandfather
who was a pillar for the family.
He kept the family together.
My third born is named Ochieng.
It means the sun shining.

I witnessed his birth
I was with my wife Marian from the time she went into labor
    until he was born.
It was the best feeling that had ever happened to me
and gave me even more respect for my wife and all mothers.
To produce life
what women go through
to have periods and have people look at them as if they were dirty
that is the source of life!
And to carry a child for nine months
and then to give birth
a moment when they themselves are between life and death
because they could easily die.
How can someone take away that life from her?
I was so tired after Ochieng was born.
I was more exhausted than Marian
those of you ladies who have given birth will not agree with me
but that is what I am telling you.
I was so tired I couldn't stand
I got into my car and found myself in Entebbe
43 kilometers away,
and I parked the car
and lay down on the ground
and slept.

I have kept my children's umbilical cords.
I cannot bury them because I am not at home.
I can't do the ritual, I am in a foreign land.
I am hoping that one day I will be able to do the ritual for my
    children.
But it is taking so long
they are getting too used to Kampala as home.
Sometimes
when I am talking to them on the phone on my travels
they say
daddy, when are you coming back home?
I think,
that is not home.

Here in America
people leave their home and get a new job

and that place becomes their new home.
I can live in Kampala and work in Kampala
but that is not my home.

Here you pledge allegiance to the flag
there you pledge allegiance to the place
where your umbilical cord is buried.

If the time comes
if the war ends
and the children and the mother tell me we are not moving
because that is not where we belong
we belong to Kampala
we do not belong to Gulu
do you know what that would do to me?
That would just kill me.

*Transition to **TOUR GUIDE**, who holds the clay pot out to the audience.*

TOUR GUIDE: I've seen you looking at this pot.
You like it, don't you?
It would make a nice souvenir.
You can see how sturdy it is.
It would pack well for the journey home.
You can take one home with you.
But if you take one you must do something for me.
Don't just leave it on a shelf
and hope your friends will ask you about it.
You must use it.
Really use it.
Use it to cook a spinach casserole
to water the garden
to honor a loved one who has passed on.
Use it to bless your children. Use it to bless life.
I hope to see you again.
There are so many beautiful things here that you have yet to see.
This is the pearl of Africa.
Tell them about us back home.

Transition to **OKELLO**.

OKELLO: I was driving my mother to Kampala
where so many of us live in exile in our own country.
I was taking her away from her home
where she lived her entire life of some fifty years.
She had lost her husband
her second-born son
and now her home.
She could not even protest when I insisted that she leave
she was in such a state of shock about the evil going on around
    her.
The rebels were leaving pots
burning over fire at the side of the road.
Pots that held body parts of their victims.

Two things happened on the trip.
She cried
and I composed this song.

He places the pot on his head and picks up his harp.

We must all find a way to go on.
There is a Swahili word *kuvumilia*.
It means to endure the pain.
This way
is mine.

He exits singing.

Chapter 5

Narrative Theatre as an Interactive Community Approach to Mobilizing Collective Action in Northern Uganda

Yvonne Sliep, Kaethe Weingarten, and Andrew Gilbert

Although strong frameworks exist for working with issues of social health that bridge the individual and society, such as those of the World Health Organization (1986, 1991), many interventions end up focusing either on the individual (e.g., interventions aimed at changing attitudes and beliefs; United Nations Programme on HIV/AIDS 1999) or on structural change within society (World Health Organization 1995). Grappling with the processes that operate recursively among individuals, families or households,[1] communities and society is much more difficult and, consequently, often avoided (Sliep 1996). However, understanding these processes is crucial if there is to be an authentic shift of control of health issues from external agencies to the family and community, as advocated by the frameworks just mentioned (Labonte 1994).

The developing world dynamically illustrates the shortcomings of a medical or an individual approach to health-related issues. For example, in the First World, HIV/AIDS has become a chronic disease controlled by access to antiretroviral drugs. Drug compliance and a healthy lifestyle are the central issues. However, dealing with the virus as the focus of the problem obscures the personal and social effects of living with HIV/AIDS (Sliep 1994). In the Third World, inadequate access to antiretroviral drugs makes the critical issue, rather than one of focusing on the virus itself, one of helping individuals, families, communities and health workers to collectively understand the effects of the epidemic and develop local actions designed to address these effects.

Despite the importance and advantages of using an approach that applies a framework in which the problem is understood to exist at recursively linked levels of the individual, the family or household, the community and society, few programmes operate in this fashion (Sliep 1996). Players in health promotion interventions often fail to conceptualize the effects of these interventions at more distant levels from those in which they play a central role (Sliep 1995). Thus, for example, in relation to the AIDS epidemic, those involved in voluntary counselling and testing may be sensitive to psychosocial issues at the individual level but fail to see how actions at this level may have an impact at the family or community level. Similarly, programme directors and policymakers may be aware of implications for policy and social transformation but are insensitive to effects at the family level.

The most effective strategies and tools for dealing with health-related issues in developing countries incorporate linkages among different ecosystemic levels (Sliep 1996, 2003b). This is certainly true with regard to domestic violence, the health issue considered in this chapter. These types of strategies and tools can expose the individual, household and community processes that have particular effects on individuals and can mobilize collective voice and action (Sliep 2003b). They can also provide the means for closing the gap between individuals struggling with problems in isolation and a collective response that addresses the underlying features of problems that are socially rooted. With regard to domestic violence, for instance, focusing on the family in which the abuse takes place in isolation from the greater collective can perpetuate shame, blame and secrecy. It is only in highlighting the effects of domestic violence on the individual, the family, and the community concurrently that a shared response and, therefore, a shared responsibility can be mobilized to address both the cause and the perpetuation of the problem.

To help people make the linkages across system levels, it is important to shift the locus of control for addressing the effects of a health issue from the external agencies, which implement interventions, to the people who are directly experiencing the effects. This means that those within the local context, not those outside of it, have the power to determine processes, gain access to resources, and achieve needed outcomes (Ankrah 1991). This shift toward greater local control can operate on at least two levels: mobilizing the power that operates interrelationally at micro levels and examining and marshalling the social controls that exist within the collective at a more macro level (de Guzman 2001).

Shifting interrelational and social control to the local level where effects are experienced is not about shifting the responsibility of addressing the disease or social problem onto the shoulders of the local community. Rather, it is a strategy designed to engage the strengths and abilities of people. The enormity of health problems such as HIV/AIDS and domestic violence in resource-poor settings can create hopelessness and despondency. It is important, therefore, that strategies focusing on local dynamics actively avoid the trap of helplessness. Instead, strategies must enable people to bring forth their own strength and power and see the power they have to determine the processes of engagement with those who abuse their socially granted power.

The role of community health workers is crucial in these strength-based approaches. Community health workers are often caught in a difficult dilemma, however, precisely because they are at the intersection between the community and outside agencies. They either become the representatives of the external intervention, which distances them from their community context, or become trapped by the despair felt by the community (Gilbert and Rankin 2000; Sliep 1998). Any community-focused approach must take into account the effect of the problem and the intervention on health workers and incorporate them into the collective processes.

In this chapter, we examine a community-based approach in the particularly difficult social context of a displaced refugee community in northern Uganda with a history of trauma arising from that displacement and armed conflict. During the work involved with this project, the community identified domestic violence as its most pressing problem.

Setting the scene

Domestic violence in a refugee camp in northern Uganda

To place this social health issue in some perspective, domestic violence – which we define here as physical, emotional, sexual or financial abuse of women and children perpetrated by partners, ex-partners, relatives or close friends in either public or private spaces – occurs in all countries and affects people of all classes, religions and ethnicities (Coomaraswamy 1999; Krug et al. 2002; World Health Organization 1997). Domestic violence is linked to multiple short- and long-term negative health outcomes that relate to its severity, frequency and duration (Follette et al. 1996; Koss et al. 1991). It is a leading cause of injuries to women and girls around the world (Human Rights Watch 2000).

It is common that women who have had to escape violent political conflict by leaving their home countries are subsequently subjected to domestic violence in refugee camps. Domestic violence is a frequent aftermath of political violence (Jacobs et al. 2000; Weingarten 2003, 2004). The pressures of life in the camps are difficult for all who seek refuge there, but particularly so for women who are responsible for maintaining households under conditions of extreme scarcity. Sadly, these very stresses strain remaining relationships, contributing to domestic violence (Human Rights Watch 2000).

It is also the case that domestic violence is widespread in rural areas of Uganda, where the workshop described here took place. It is estimated that one in three women in rural Uganda experience domestic violence, with about half of these incidents leading to physical injuries (Koenig et al. 2003). No Ugandan laws prohibit domestic violence, although international law now recognizes that violence against women constitutes a violation of human rights (United Nations High Commission for Refugees 1999).

Organizational context

Yvonne Sliep carried out the workshop described in this article in a refugee camp in northern Uganda under the auspices of and in collaboration with the Transcultural Psychosocial Organization (TPO). TPO, a collaborative centre of the World Health Organization, is associated with the Vrije Universiteit in Amsterdam as a nonprofit organization. The Netherlands Ministry of Foreign Affairs finances the majority of its worldwide projects. TPO, formerly the Institute for Psychosocial and Socio-Ecological Research of Amsterdam, was founded in 1995. The organization deals with refugees and other groups of people who have been traumatized by war, human rights violations or other forms of organized violence. It mainly works in refugee camps or communities that have been affected by violence.

Uganda, a land-locked country, is located in East Africa (Majuga 1999; Nzita and Niwampa 1997). To the west, it borders the Democratic Republic of Congo, formerly known as the Belgian Congo and Zaire; to the north, it borders Sudan. It is from these two borders that refugees migrate, hoping for a safer life. TPO established itself in northern

Uganda in 1994 to respond to the needs of 230,000 Sudanese refugees living in the West Nile area. The main objectives were to provide high-quality psychosocial and mental health interventions and to build the local capacity of the refugee and national communities (TPO 2003).

The most common forms of crises were gender-based violence, especially against women, along with child abuse and neglect. Combined with family disputes, gender-based violence ranks highest in terms of the frequency with which it causes problems dealt with by counsellors; more than 1400 cases were reported in the year 2002 (TPO 2003).

The approach outlined here was implemented in March 2003. In brief, it consisted of training in, and practice with, Narrative Theatre (NT), a form of Forum Theatre (as described subsequently). Training was provided to 35 psychosocial workers and middle-management personnel including assistant field coordinators, assistant training coordinators, trainers of trainers and a few selected senior counsellors (Sliep 2003c). The TPO members largely came from conflict areas themselves and lived around, but not in, the refugee camps.

Yvonne Sliep developed NT as a participatory and contextually sensitive means of working at both an individual and a collective level while keeping the focus on local dynamics. As such, NT is an appropriate strategy for addressing the causes of domestic violence and exploring possibilities that can alter its course.

Narrative theatre

NT draws on ideas and concepts found in narrative therapy (Dulwich Centre 2003; White and Epston 1990; Zimmerman and Dickerson 1996) and Forum Theatre (Boal 1992, 1995). After learning about both of these approaches, psychosocial workers at the workshop in northern Uganda coined the label 'Narrative Theatre.' By using their term, we keep alive the richness that emerged when formal theory interacted with community activities rooted in local contexts.

NT blends aspects of narrative therapy and Forum Theatre; thus, we provide a description of the areas of significant overlap. Narrative therapy is an approach to counselling and community work that views people as the experts regarding their own lives and views problems as separate from people. Narrative therapy assumes that people have many skills, competencies, beliefs, values, commitments and abilities that will assist them in reducing the influence of problems in their lives. The term *narrative* refers here to an emphasis placed on the stories of people's lives and the differences that can be made through particular tellings and retellings of these stories (White 1995; White and Epston 1990).

'Externalizing' is a concept that was first introduced to the field of family therapy in the early 1980s. Initially developed in work with children, externalizing has always been associated with good humour and playfulness (as well as thoughtful and careful practice). There are many ways of understanding externalizing, but the focus is on facilitating a process in which the problem is seen as separate from the person (White and Epston 1990).

One of the more well-known examples of community 'externalization' occurred during HIV/AIDS projects conducted in Malawi. Problems such as stigma and silence surrounding HIV/AIDS that have contributed to division within the community were externalized, and AIDS itself was personified ('Mr./Ms. AIDS'). The effect of this externalizing was that communities were able to have conversations with characters playing the role of 'Mr./Ms. AIDS.' In these externalizing conversations, 'AIDS' articulated its strategies, hopes and dreams. Confronted in this fashion with the intentions and effects of 'AIDS,' communities have been able collectively to take an opposing position. The identification and personification of an externalized counterplot, 'Mrs. CARE,' have also galvanized collective action (in this instance, CARE was an acronym for 'Community Action Renders Enablement'; Sliep 1995).

As mentioned, NT also draws on Forum Theatre, or 'Theatre for the Oppressed,' developed by Augusto Boal in Brazil (Boal 1995). According to Boal (1992), he used the term 'theatre' in its most archaic application. In this usage, all human beings are seen as able to act and can therefore be viewed as actors (this view has links to that espoused by the exponents of performative psychology; see Holzman 2000). Similarly, everyone in life observes and thus takes on the role of a spectator. The purpose of Forum Theatre is for everyone to be involved, as actors and 'spect-actors' (the latter are seen as active spectators). Boal used this technique to create change and to actively unmask and address practices of power. The methodology is participatory, nonjudgmental and accessible to those of all ages, levels of education and cultural backgrounds.

In Forum Theatre, the audience generates the scene or the facilitator can propose a scene that is recognizable to all. Participants become involved in the action through an invitation to provide commentary on what is witnessed. Scenes are replayed at the audience's request. The audience members act as 'spect-actors' in that they can replace any of the actors at any point, and they are invited to stop the action if they are of the opinion that what is being played out is incorrect or unrealistic.

Discussion is encouraged when an interruption occurs, thus creating an awareness of the different elements of the scenario. The scenario is then replayed, with the new suggested elements resulting in a different ending. The acting of and reacting to the scenario, with its alternative unfoldings, promote a deeper understanding of the issues involved and a platform for active creativity in collective determination of suitable solutions (Sliep and Meyer-Weitz 2003). As is the case with Forum Theatre, meaning is negotiated in NT between actors and the 'spect-actors' or audience. Unlike conventional drama, in which actors follow a script, NT becomes a democratic tool that can facilitate dialogue on many different levels. It cannot be delivered as a prepackaged message, which would imply that the voices of the members present, and therefore their specific contexts and situations, have not been included. NT attempts to raise levels of critical awareness so that situations can be examined collectively and appropriate solutions found; in turn, these solutions can be tried out to determine whether the desired outcome is feasible. NT highlights micro scenes from people's lives. By putting these scenes on centre stage, NT creates a space for reflection so that people can examine their problems. If they take on the role of observer and become less immersed in their circumstances, people are better able to see alternatives.

The spatial metaphor is further incorporated into the work by creating a literal physical space that can be used to focus a spotlight on what the community has found problematic. This can be under a tree, in the middle of the refugee camp or in a school or classroom, and it becomes a space where 'the potential' can become 'the actual' through experimentation.

A distinction is made between experiential and experimental spaces. In the former, there is an opportunity for people to gain greater awareness of marginalized or powerful others through embodiment of the patterns of action and speech they use. The scenario must resemble, to the extent possible, the 'truth' as described by the collective. In the experimental space, the theatre becomes a place to test different ways of reaching preferred outcomes. The first time the real scenario is acted out, the participants have an opportunity to witness what actually happened. During subsequent enactments of the same scene, participants are encouraged to experiment with different strategies to reach more preferred outcomes. The alternative strategies still have to be realistic within the described context, and the participants must continually realize that there are no magical solutions. It is a combination of local knowledge and the development of appropriate skills that creates the experimental space. During the workshop, the following true-life scenario was chosen to allow practice of the methodology:

> A man comes home drunk after being out all day. On arrival he expects food to be ready and waiting for him, but both the wife and the children know that he will find fault with the food. They also predict that the husband will use any excuse to beat up his wife. The abuse will happen in front of the children.

Theory and practice of Narrative Theatre

Importance of the wider sociopolitical context

NT draws on social constructionist paradigms according to which individual or group action derives from the social, historical and cultural processes within which it is embedded (Gergen 1994, 2001). Such a view understands individual action to be part of the social practices that operate in the local context. Social practices are communally defined, standard ways of doing things that structure and provide resources for action and relationships. NT seeks ways of enabling individuals and groups to come to an understanding of the broader contextual issues and processes that construct the meanings and effects of events in their lives.

NT also draws on Freire's idea of 'conscientization', central to which is an awareness of social, political and historical contexts (Freire 1970). Freire's work draws attention to the relationship of local context to the broader political context and webs of power within which communities function. Issues connected to globalization (Robertson 1992) and the history of colonialism and dependency (Frank et al. 1996) are examples of the ways in which webs of power construct local contexts. Freire argued for a collective critical analysis of personal circumstances to raise awareness of the operations of power at play in the social constructs and relationships within which one is daily engaged.

With these foundational theoretical ideas in mind, NT does not look at problems as though they are located within the individual, as some personal unchanging characteristic or personality trait; rather, NT views problems as emerging from the multiple relationships in which the individual is immersed. The approach, therefore, attempts to start with the direct relationships that exist within the household or family, which are then widened out to the community to address root causes of the problem. In this sense, the work attempts actively to involve the collective – the network of relationships and interpersonal processes that operate in particular activities and social practices.

Social practices provide the local knowledge that becomes the tacit means of living one's life. Such knowledge may provide a powerful resource for action, but, because of its tacit nature, it can also serve to make certain practices seem natural and inevitable. Moreover, it can silence and subjugate voices and positions. In the process of enabling people to understand contexts, NT also aims to make the tacit visible and the unspoken heard.

In the situation of the drunken, abusive man that was the primary scenario selected by the workshop participants, the woman tried to enlist the support of a male neighbour, but he indicated that he thought it was her husband's right to hit her if he wished to do so. Subsequently, in the enacted drama, the neighbour learned that the man had beaten his children. In the presence of the neighbour, the husband expressed regret that he had been violent. This led to a revisiting of the woman's position that the violence was not appropriate or acceptable. Ultimately, the woman made herself heard and seen, and the result was a revisiting of local values and the setting up of a structure of accountability on which all agreed. This created a platform for agreeing on future actions involving different members of the community if the abuse was repeated.

Management of intentionality

NT involves as an overall intent to promote social cohesion and social responsibility. This is particularly important in the case of disorganized and dislocated communities that have lost their access to a social structure that helps to control and make sense of general social practices. NT methodology, in moving from initial descriptions that highlight individual pathology to descriptions that clarify social structures, helps illuminate and form connections at the communal level.

The methodology of NT is tailored to meet the specific needs of the groups and communities in which the work is conducted. In the case of this community-based approach in the refugee setting, the fact that old social structures had collapsed and families had been torn apart was a central consideration. This had increased the sense of the refugees' and community workers' helplessness to deal with problems adequately. Thus, one of the intentions of the work was to increase social cohesion and stimulate the formation of social networks.

The term *intentions* is used here to capture the objectives and outcomes people have in mind when they are engaging in specific activities. Thus, facilitators may have intentions that are not understood, or even seen, by the people with whom they are working. Furthermore, when individuals work collectively, there is no necessary guarantee of a shared intention within the collective. This is especially the case if there are power differences and vested interests within the collective that do not have equal effects among everyone involved.

Work at a collective level, therefore, requires conscious management of intentions. We argue that this involves two levels of management. First, it requires that the facilitator and those participating in the workshop become aware of the intentions behind their own and other people's actions, including an understanding of intentions concerning their involvement in the social practices that are under the spotlight as well as their intentions in participating in the work itself. Second, it involves naming these intentions and then facilitating their collective understanding and coordination.

The skill of managing intentionality requires that the facilitator have a high level of reflexivity in relation to her or his intentions. Reflexivity here is understood to be more than reflective practice (Schon 1983) and includes a critical stance towards taken-for-granted assumptions that exist within specific contexts. Gergen captured this more active and contextual quality in his definition of reflexivity as 'the attempt to place one's premises into question, to suspend the "obvious," to listen to alternative framings of reality, and to grapple with the comparative outcomes of multiple standpoints' (Gergen 1999: 50). Reflexivity is a process that involves ongoing sensitivity to contexts as well as relationships, and it should lead the facilitator to be flexible in acting in relation to the multiple intentions that operate in local activities.

The issue of management of intentions came up in several ways during this work. At the start of the workshop, it turned out that participants had thought that the workshop would deal with HIV/AIDS only and that the outcome of the workshop would be that they had learned how to use drama as an educational tool. The facilitator clarified that creating a play for an audience to observe was not the aim of the workshop; rather, the goal was to collaboratively, through the use of interactive theatre, experience and develop strategies to deal with presenting problems.

HIV/AIDS might be the problem they wished to work with, but the workshop could also include a variety of other problems. The facilitator modelled and discussed that having reflexivity as a tool and skill to apply the NT methodology would directly increase the workers' capacity to deal with the presenting problems of their constituents, the refugees. This principle of action led to the workshop agenda being developed collaboratively rather than being pushed through by anyone from outside of the context and country. As it turned out, a domestic violence problem, not an HIV/AIDS problem, was selected as the content focus of the workshop.

Implementing intentions through the use of exercises

The experiential work done in NT by the participants is as valuable as the development of specific skills. NT creates the opportunity to refer back to actual examples during the workshop process to highlight meta-constructs that one wants to clarify. Exercises are built in as a process that is nonthreatening and involves an element of fun to help people relax and to stimulate group cohesion. The experiential exercises vary from expressions of nonverbal communication (e.g., the other members of the group have to guess a characteristic you aspire to by viewing an enactment of that characteristic) to expressing oneself around small familiar situations. As confidence grows, the enactments can begin to deal with experiences built on actual situations confronted by the community.

The exercise described in the following, used during the beginning of the workshop, demonstrates the utility of the initial exercises in terms of giving the facilitator an opportunity to use the 'here and now situation' to reflect on the strengths and abilities of the participants in having overcome many difficulties. In this way, the facilitator could demonstrate an intention to counteract the despair and sense of helplessness in the refugee camps.

Participants were asked, in the 'icebreaker exercise,' to share with the group the name they were given at birth and why they were given this name. If they now used a different 'call name,' the history of that name was also explored. This exercise was used with the knowledge that, in this part of Africa, children are given names to describe specific events and feelings at the time of birth. The exercise led to dynamic discussions about cultural context that highlighted the importance of gender and the circumstances, often including trauma or suffering, that surrounded the birth of the person now attending the workshop.

One of the participants shared that his name meant 'from the dead,' because his father had died during a conflict at the time of his birth. He then told how he had become a pillar of strength for his family and how, when he was a young adult, he had led them across the border, helping them relocate to Uganda. He was now the most educated man in his family, well respected by everyone, and his family still talks about how his father's spirit must have been transferred into him. It was clear how proud he felt of his own development. At a later stage in the training, when he spoke about feeling despondent and defeated by the endless problems he faced, the facilitator made reference back to the story of courage and leadership he had told and connected the past and current struggles to this story.

Participants had to be eased into using embodied communication rather than relying on verbal communication. The participants were not accustomed to experiential body and interactive work and expressed anxiety about having to demonstrate an ability to act to master the methodology successfully. The facilitator emphasized that the intention of the workshop was not for them to become adept at acting.

The facilitator further emphasized to the participants that they were the experts about their lives and not the facilitator, who came from outside. In like fashion, the psychosocial workers would not be expected to set themselves up as experts on the lives of the refugees with whom they worked; rather, they would learn to facilitate collaborative activities designed to understand and manage presenting problems. Working overtly through the concept of 'capacity building' became a useful way to implement this point (Labonte and Laverack 2001).

During the process, it was also necessary to clarify that although the facilitator was not an expert on the details of people's lives, she nevertheless had very clear and informed thoughts in regard to why the work should unfold in a specific way. It is not helpful to pretend that there is no power in place; working transparently at all times is the preferred style. For instance, the facilitator chooses when to interrupt the process to ask participants why a certain action is being taken or when to help them externalize a problem or feeling. Applications of different techniques at specific moments guide the process in desirable directions. This constitutes an appropriate use of power that the facilitator has to acknowledge while remaining sensitive to the ideas of others.

In the workshop, most of the initial work was done in small groups, and these groups then performed their particular scenario. Approaching the work in this way created a space where the participants and, indirectly, the communities in which they were working determined the content of the training. An example of a technique used in the process of acting out a scenario is a 'snapshot' created from a common experience of a problem. A scene is acted out of the experience of the problem and then stopped in a 'frozen' position, creating a sculpture on which all of the group members can 'work.' This creates an opportunity for the facilitator to bring in the local context and indirectly the voice of the absent community in which the participants are working. Discussing the sculpture as an image of 'the problem' and its effects further creates the possibility of determining the prevalence of the problem through review of the extent to which actors and 'spect-actors' see the problem as most prominent and most difficult to manage in their context.

A 'snapshot' from the workshop unfolded in the following manner. The facilitators were asked to make a 'snapshot' of a problem they encountered often. Four of the five groups depicted gender-based violence, with the man always being abusive. A group discussion that occurred among the men was 'overheard' by an outer circle of women. Follow-up discussion focused on what they had heard that was new and their thoughts regarding a preferred way of managing the problem.

Deconstruction and reconstruction

Deconstruction, used in an everyday sense, is about taking apart and disassembling objects or mechanisms. Deconstruction in a more philosophical context, based on the ideas of Derrida (1978), is about taking apart the meaning of things with the specific intention of revealing the hidden practices that construct how something comes to be understood in a particular way. Derrida concerned himself with 'decentring,' by which he meant unmasking the problematic nature of 'centres.' The centre refers to the pivot around which all meaning is constructed in a particular context, which, in terms of relationships, has to do with power and privilege. Decentring means rendering visible what is marginalized by the focus on the centre (i.e., making the unseen visible and the silenced heard).

In NT, this is actively done by bringing marginalized people, their experiences and the meanings they make of their experiences into the spotlight. This, then, explicitly gives them voice and makes their meanings visible and significant. Another means to this end is to place the powerful in a marginalized position so that they can experience the effects of power from a position of powerlessness. NT represents an experiential embodiment of powerlessness and powerfulness that goes beyond mere verbalization. A single experience may be deconstructed from many different points of view and social positions to increase awareness, clarify the effects of the scenario on oneself and others, develop a position in relation to the revealed effects and substantiate that position. The effects of such practices are to unmask the power hierarchy, subvert the centre and clarify the effect of power.

Following the deconstruction activities, reconstruction takes place toward a preferred scenario that is communally constructed by all of the participants. Such a reconstruction ensues from greater sensitivity in regard to how one's own and others' actions constructed the issue such that it became a manifest problem.

Whose knowledge and insight is valued and used is determined by the positions of power and privilege that operate in particular social practices. Within communities, this can result in the knowledge of marginalized groups being masked or denied. Engaging in different activities and occupying different positions in collective actions generate different knowledge.

For example, in communities where there is rapid change, the power of tradition may silence the voices of young people who are challenged by new social and technological demands. This subjugation can also occur in interactions of local community residents with outsiders. Thus, in development work, the power of the knowledge of external 'experts' can potentially silence local knowledge (Gilbert 1997). In NT, facilitators work to reveal such marginalizing processes, taking care that such action does not privilege their voices as the expert ones regarding local wisdom or dynamics. The deconstructive nature of NT provides an opportunity for expression of subjugated voices and forms of knowledge.

Foucault (1980) discussed challenging the constellation of power even if one cannot remove it. During NT, as in Forum Theatre, one preferentially works with the person on the receiving end of the display of power and not the perpetrator. The rationale is that it is difficult to change the perpetrator's position and easier to change the effect of such power. This process is about finding ways of working with power. An appropriate time to explore a more desired outcome is when there is both danger and opportunity, the commingling of which is represented by the character for crisis in the Chinese alphabet (Boal 1995). The facilitator works with situations that may depict danger but also have the potential for a different outcome if different strategies are adopted. In the scenario in which the woman is abused regularly by the same man, the pattern can be broken if a different action is taken by the woman individually and by the members of the community collectively.

In community work, it is important to represent and contextualize 'collective consciousness' and collective oppression and to work toward collective action. One of the ways in which 'collective consciousness' can be made more visible is to interview the characters involved and ask them their intentions. Alternatively, questions can be posed to the audience, such as, 'Why is it important to the man that the woman remains afraid of him and silent to outsiders about the abuse she suffers?'

In the 'drunken man' scenario, the woman who was going to be abused by her husband decided in her performance to remove herself from the dangerous situation, even though the children would be left in the house at the mercy of the man. This is a strategy that the facilitator would never have conceived of as an appropriate way of taking action. It was, however, enacted to experiment with what the outcome might be. The outcome in this example was that the husband did beat one of the children but was very remorseful about it, an emotion he had not shown toward his wife, because she always 'deserved' the beatings. In the structure of the ongoing theatre experience, this remorsefulness led to an opening in which 'the neighbours' had a conversation with the abusing man about preferred outcomes. The leader also became involved as part of the dialogue. Acting out what began, in the eyes of the facilitator, as a potentially negative outcome very clearly generated a collective solution rooted in local reality. During this process it became possible to address social norms, and it became clear that the facilitator, as an outsider, was not an expert on the lives of others.

The variety of techniques used in NT enabled the participants to express their understandings of the problem of domestic violence. What emerged in the workshop was their conviction that women and children are most informed about domestic violence. The psychosocial workers then made a decision to recruit the women and children onto their team as experts on the problem of domestic violence and to generate a collective strategy that would ultimately involve the voice of the overall collective. This reflection by the psychosocial workers became an example of promoting reflexivity at different levels during NT work.

Strength-based approach toward vision and hope

In NT, the spotlight has to be kept continuously on people's abilities and strengths. The entertaining nature of problems can seduce both the facilitator and the audience into letting them dominate the floor. It is in the nature of working with problems that energy is drawn to them, which becomes debilitating and demoralizing. The art of NT resides in juxtaposing the 'problem-saturated story' (White and Epston 1990) next to the strength-based story and continuously eliciting strength and hope.

It is useful to remember that one of the aims of NT is to facilitate the unseen, which can be contexts, marginalized individuals or groups, or strengths and abilities that have become camouflaged over time. This goal can be accomplished through a variety of techniques. One is bringing in relevant history in which specific abilities can be highlighted.

The refugees often have rich stories of courage demonstrated during their journeys of flight to countries of safety. These specific acts of courage have to be unpacked and retold by those who are currently captured by problems to bring them back in touch with the special abilities such acts required. Another way of facilitating a strength-based approach is to use circularity, such that the voices of others are brought in to highlight strengths. The aim is to move from a thin conclusion about people's lives in relation to their problems to a thick description focused on their abilities (White and Epston 1990).

Placing the focus on people's abilities and strengths rather than their difficulties had to be done many times in the course of training. During the workshop, while the psychosocial workers were acting out the scenario of the 'drunken father/husband,' one of the actors – 'the wife' involved in the domestic violence scene – said, 'I am not strong enough to deal with my drunk husband.' At this stage, the scene was stopped, and the main character – 'the wife' – was interviewed. Questions were directed at eliciting stories of strength and courage, and an opportunity was given for her to verbalize and experience those feelings again.

The woman was asked whether she had ever managed to persuade her husband to see something differently. She gave an example of letting him see that it was also important for their daughter to get an education. She told an elaborate story that had involved his mother and had led to satisfactory outcomes. Her knowledge about dealing with power relations and bringing about change was emphasized. The scenario was then allowed to continue. The next time it was stopped and the woman was interviewed, she said, 'If the enemy could not kill me and my children with their big numbers and their bombs and guns [referring to her flight to the refugee camp], then certainly one man is not going to kill us.' Immediately, a very different energy entered the room, and this energy then took the form of an experiential drama. This is an example of how eliciting stories of a past episode can give voice to subjugated knowledge with powerful effects.

Discussion

NT has the potential for surfacing and promoting strengths while working at the intersection of the individual, family and community. The conceptual framework of narrative therapy provides tools to work with issues of power, and the use of drama provides a method and space for such work, enabling greater reflexivity and creativity by participants. The creation of social and physical space to see one's own intentions and those of others allows an exploration of the effects of the problem and the dynamics of power that operate in relation to the problem. NT, however, does more than reveal what is often tacit or unspoken; it provides a base for moving forward through exploration of preferred options in a safe space.

There is, however, a very real challenge involved in sustaining the reflexivity that is a central part of NT in the ongoing activities of community workers. One of the ways in which this challenge manifests itself involves attitudes toward performance. NT harnesses the power of performative actions for the purpose of revealing problems and their effects rather than for the purpose of public entertainment. It is possible, however, to run with the thrill and power of performative work and use it simply to entertain or educate in a more didactic way, which greatly limits the potential of NT.

Community workers, in the approach described here, had an initial desire to gain performance skills so that they could establish drama competitions in their communities. Although public performance of scripted plays about social problems is a powerful educational tool in development work and can be used to mobilize certain sectors of the community (e.g., young people), NT attempts to intervene more directly in the lives of those engaged in the drama. Thus, community workers must establish a level of skill that moves beyond putting on community theatre presentations to educate or inform local residents.

Conclusion

This description of a workshop conducted in a refugee camp in Uganda illustrates NT as a vehicle for change. NT highlights the potential of this form to be participatory and transformative by making use of local knowledge. Although we have focused on a refugee setting that is far from the circumstances in which readers of this book may practice, the central philosophy of this chapter is consistent with the First World call for an orientation toward research and practice that centralizes community participation and links health care interventions to social change (Minkler and Wallerstein 2003). Furthermore, the NT approach may be directly applicable to learning about and collaborating on approaches to management of chronic illness in the first world.

We have described interactions for change aimed at four levels: the individual, the household/family, the community and society. Individual problems are often rooted in collective problems. Although one can start working with individuals to understand context, participation of the collective is more likely to maximize the possibility of sustained behaviour change. During the workshop, there was a progression from a focus on an individual to a focus on the household, the greater community, and, ultimately, the society. Entry can be made at any of the four levels and should be seen as an ongoing two-way spiral with the potential to yield collective conscience, collective efficacy and collective action.

This community-based approach makes capacity building an integral part of the process. Building capacity in this context is about acknowledging the skills, knowledge and resources of everyone involved in the process. It encourages building upon such abilities and linking others through coalitions and networks. Increasing a sense of social networks and social cohesion while moving towards collective action is an inherent part of such a capacity-building process (Sliep 2003a).

The dynamic interactive process of NT coupled with its highly relevant thematic content promotes increases in awareness and the bringing forth of local knowledge while permitting experimentation and practice with appropriate skills. It is a strength-based and nonjudgmental strategy that strongly encourages a shift from dependency on external agencies to reliance on the capacity of local contexts and communities. It does, however, need to be emphasized that the responsibility cannot stop at the local collective but has to be taken up by the institutions at the societal level that develop policy.

Sociopolitical and economic conditions will always have an influence on how effectively work can be done. The greater the support from the overall society, other organizations and government, the greater will be the ripples out of the work. Rather than pointing fingers at different stakeholders – from individuals and collectives affected by the problem to organizations and governments attempting to deal with the problem – a shift to shared responsibility that addresses the underlying causes of problems as well as their perpetuation needs to be made. The existing tacit knowledge of people, along with their historical strengths and abilities, needs to be brought forth in a way that generates energy and facilitates a belief in efficacy. Sustaining hope is a collective endeavour and activity, what Weingarten (2000, 2003) called 'doing hope.' This is crucial not only for those directly affected but also especially for the community workers who are continuously confronted with overwhelming problems. NT embraces this challenge with the full participation of all involved.

References

Ankrah, E. M., 'AIDS and the Social Side of Health,' *Social Science and Medicine,* 32 (1991), pp. 967–980.

Boal, A., *Games For Actors and Non-actors*, London: Butler & Tanner, 1992.

——, *Rainbow of Desire: The Boal Method of Theatre and Therapy*, New York: Routledge, 1995.

Coomaraswamy, R., *Violence Against Women in the Family: Report of the Special Rapporteur on Violence Against Women, Its Causes and Consequences*, Geneva, Switzerland: Office of the United Nations Commissioner for Human Rights, 1999.

de Guzman, A., 'Reducing Social Vulnerability to HIV/AIDS: Models of Care and Their Impact in Resource-poor Settings,' *AIDS Care,* 13 (2001), pp. 663–675.

Derrida, J., *Writing and Difference*, London: Routledge & Kegan Paul, 1978.

Dulwich Centre, *About Narrative Therapy,* http://www.dulwichcentre.com.au/homepage.html, 2003 (accessed April 2003).

Follette, V. M., Polusny, M. A., Bechtle, A. E., and Naugle, A. E., 'Cumulative Trauma: The Impact of Child Sexual Abuse, Adult Sexual Assault, and Spouse Abuse,' *Journal of Traumatic Stress,* 9 (1996), pp. 25–35.

Foucault, M., *Power/Knowledge: Selected Interviews and Other Writings*, New York: Pantheon Books, 1980.

Frank, A. G., Chew, S. C., and Denemark, R. A., *The Underdevelopment of Development: Essays in Honor of Andre Gunder Frank,* Thousand Oaks, CA: Sage, 1996.

Freire, P., *Pedagogy of the Oppressed*, New York: Herder & Herder, 1970.

Gergen, K. J., *Realities and Relationships*, Cambridge, MA: Harvard University Press, 1994.

——, *An Invitation to Social Construction*, London: Sage, 1999.

————, *Social Construction in Context*, Thousand Oaks, CA: Sage, 2001.

Gilbert, A. J., 'Small Voices Against the Wind: Local Knowledge and Social Transformation,' *Peace and Conflict: Journal of Peace Psychology*, 3 (1997), pp. 275–292.

Gilbert, A. J., and Rankin, J., 'Changing the Social Practices of Public Health Counsellors in the Eastern Cape: Tension, Uncertainties and Achievements,' in *Proceedings of the XIII International AIDS Conference*, pp. 287–293, Bologna, Italy: Monduzzi Editore, 2000.

Holzman, L., 'Performative Psychology: An Untapped Resource for Educators,' *Educational and Child Psychology*, 17 (2000), pp. 86–100.

Human Rights Watch, *Seeking Protection: Addressing Sexual and Domestic Violence in Tanzania's Refugee Camps*, New York: Author, 2000.

Jacobs, S., Jacobson, R., and Marchbank, J., *States of Conflict: Gender, Violence and Resistance*, London: Zed Books, 2000.

Koenig, M. A., Lutalo, T., Zhao, F., Wabwire-Mangen, F., Kiwanuka, N., Wagman, J., et al., 'Domestic Violence in Rural Uganda: Evidence from a Community-based Study,' *Bulletin of the World Health Organization*, 81 (2003), pp. 53–61.

Koss, M. P., Woodruff, W. J., and Koss, P. G., 'Criminal Victimization Among Primary Care Medical Patients: Prevalence, Incidence, and Physician Usage,' *Behavioral Sciences and the Law*, 9 (1991), pp. 85–96.

Krug, E. G., Dahlberg, L. L., Mercy, J. A., Zwi, A. B., and Lozano, R., *World Report on Violence and Health*, Geneva, Switzerland: World Health Organization, 2002.

Labonte, R., 'Health Promotion and Empowerment: Reflections on Professional Practice,' *Health Education Quarterly*, 21 (1994), pp. 253–268.

Labonte, R., and Laverack, G., 'Capacity Building in Health Promotion, Part 1: For Whom? And for What Purpose?' *Critical Public Health*, 11 (2001), pp. 111–127.

Majuga, J., *Uganda's Age Reforms: A Critical Overview*, rev. ed., Kampala, Uganda: Fountain, 1999.

Minkler, M., and Wallerstein, N., *Community Based Participatory Research for Health*, San Francisco: Jossey-Bass, 2003.

Nzita, R., and Niwampa, M., *People and Cultures of Uganda*, 3rd ed., Kampala, Uganda: Fountain, 1997.

Robertson, R., *Globalization Social Theory and Global Culture*, Newbury Park, CA: Sage, 1992.

Schon, D. A., *The Reflective Practitioner*, New York: Basic Books, 1983.

Sliep, Y., 'Malawi: A Case Study of an Integrated PHC/AIDS Programme,' *AIDS Bulletin*, 3:1 (1994), pp. 8–9.

————, 'CARE Counselling Model for AIDS Patients in Malawi,' unpublished thesis, Rand Afrikaans University, Johannesburg: South Africa, 1995.

————, *CARE Counseling Model – A Handbook*, Harare, Zimbabwe: SAFAIDS, 1996.

————, 'Working with Communities: Pang'ono pang'ono ndi mtolo – Little by Little We Make a Bundle,' in White, C., and Denborough, D. (eds.) *Introducing Narrative Therapy*, Adelaide: Dulwich, 1998, pp. 141–158.

————, 'Building Partnerships in Responding to Vulnerable Children: A Rural African Context,' *International Journal of Narrative Therapy and Community Work*, 2 (2003a), pp. 56–66.

————, 'Deconstructing Process Work in Community Context,' unpublished manuscript, 2003b.

———, *Report on Narrative Theatre Training: TPO Uganda*, Durban, South Africa: University of Durban Westville, 2003c.

Sliep, Y., and Meyer-Weitz, A., 'Strengthening Social Fabric Through Narrative Theatre,' *International Journal of Mental Health, Psychosocial Work and Counselling in Areas of Armed Conflict*, 1:3 (2003), pp. 46–55.

Transcultural Psychosocial Organization, *Transcultural Psychosocial Organization Uganda: Activity Report for the Year 2002*, http://www.xs4all.nl/!tpo/Publication_list.html, 2003 (accessed April 2003).

United Nations High Commission for Refugees, *Domestic Violence and Asylum*, http://www.uchastings.edu.cgrs/documents/media/unhcr_dv.htm, 1999 (accessed 20 July 2003).

United Nations Programme on HIV/AIDS, *Sexual Behavioural Change for HIV: Where Have the Theories Taken Us?* Geneva: Author, 1999.

Weingarten, K., 'Witnessing, Wonder, and Hope,' *Family Process*, 39 (2000), pp. 389–402.

———, *Common Shock – Witnessing Violence Every Day: How We are Harmed, How We Can Heal*, New York: Dutton, 2003.

———, 'Witnessing the Effects of Political Violence in Families: Mechanisms of Intergenerational Transmission and Clinical Interventions,' *Journal of Marital and Family Therapy*, 30 (2004), pp. 45–59.

White, M., 'The Narrative Perspective in Therapy,' in *Re-authoring Lives: Interviews and Essays*, Adelaide: Dulwich, 1995, pp. 11–40, .

White, M., and Epston, D., *Narrative Means to Therapeutic Ends*, New York: Norton, 1990.

World Health Organization, *Ottowa Charter for Health Promotion*, Ottowa: Author, 1986.

———, *Supportive Environments for Health: The Sundsvall Statement*, Geneva: Author, 1991.

———, *Building a Healthy City: A Practitioner's Guide*, Geneva: Author, 1995.

———, *Violence Against Women: A Priority Health Issue*, Geneva: Author, 1997.

Zimmerman, J. L., and Dickerson, V. C., *If Problems Talked: Narrative Therapy in Action*, New York: Guilford Press, 1996.

Note

1   The distinction between family and household is made as a corrective to the domination of the model of the nuclear family, which is often tacitly assumed to be the standard family context. In many developing contexts, the family lives in a household in which extended family and lodgers who are part of the wider social network are active members. Interventions at the household level must be inclusive of such people.

Chapter 6

Marketing Trauma and the Theatre of War in Northern Uganda

Laura Edmondson

The World Vision Children of War Rehabilitation Centre is located in Gulu, a town in northern Uganda that provides an oasis of relative stability in the midst of a 17-year-old civil war.[1] The centre itself provides a haven for children who have been abducted by the notorious Lord's Resistance Army (LRA) to serve as child soldiers, porters and/or so-called wives of the rebels.[2] A focal point of the centre is the counselling room, which is decorated with a series of paintings that condense the children's pasts into a single tale of terror, hardship and restoration. The story begins with an image entitled 'A Peaceful Acholi Home' which depicts children playing outside a circular, thatched-roof hut built according to local Acholi custom. Following an attack by the LRA rebels, signified as such through their trademark dreadlocks, the abducted children are marched to a rebel camp and trained to fight the Ugandan military (Uganda People's Defense Force, or UPDF). These same UPDF soldiers are transformed into liberators when they rescue the children and transport them to the World Vision Centre, where they receive medical treatment, counselling and job training. Following this humanitarian intervention, they are reunited with their families, and the archetypal Acholi home is restored.

During my research, I found that variations of this linear narrative repeatedly materialize in Ugandan representations of the LRA war. Its dominance excludes bewildering complexities such as the UPDF's pattern of killing abducted children as well as rescuing them, the LRA's practice of forcing children to murder their own relatives, the substitution of internally displaced people's (IDP) camps for the 'peaceful Acholi home' and the intensity of faith among some captives, who come to believe in the LRA movement and the spiritual powers of its leader, Joseph Kony.[3] In place of the 'epistemic murk' of terror-warfare (see Taussig 1986: 121), the linear sequence of serenity, suffering and terror, intervention, and restoration is laboriously sustained despite the chaos and confusion that surrounds its production.

To dismiss this tale as an inevitable effect of narrative's capacity to domesticate lived experience into a simplistic tale of good vs. evil would overlook the ways in which the narrative intersects with the politics of globalization. I suggest that its dominance resonates with local understandings of the global market – a market in which LRA rebels, international humanitarian organizations such as World Vision and Acholi civilians must all compete. I deliberately use the term 'market' in order to complicate its usual connotations in the popular discourse of globalization. Typically, the market plays a heroic role in a narrative of its own, one that tells a story of how multinational corporations and so-called free trade triumphs over the backward and recalcitrant Third World. Michel-Rolph Trouillot (2003: 48) cautions that the 'teleology of the market as the new master narrative of Western modernity' works to silence the effects of what he calls 'globalitarism' on millions of human beings excluded from the formation of its terms. This article marks an attempt to excavate the silencing of northern Uganda, which could too easily be categorized as an economic wasteland isolated from the transnational flow of corporate capital. For the Acholi people,[4] limited to the discourses of warfare and humanitarianism as means of entering the global market, narrative serves as one of the most crucial resources that they possess.

The concept of marketing provides a lens for exploring the roles of audiences and actors in the performance of war. In the first section, I focus mainly on the appropriation of arts therapy, specifically drama, in the World Vision rehabilitation centre as a method of self-promotion on the global stage. I go on to complicate the use of drama as a marketing tool in the second part, which delves into the overlap between the genre of realism and the reliance on linear narrative. As I address specific variations upon the narrative of war, I find that theoretical frameworks of globalization, either of the top-down, hegemonic model that emphasizes the domination of indigenous cultures or the grassroots paradigm that accentuates the process of indigenous transformation and hybridization (see, respectively, Robins and Webster 1999; Appadurai 2000) do not satisfactorily explain the fierce investment in a linear story and the trappings of realism. In the final section, I argue that former LRA captives use Acholi dance to carve out a space in which cultural memory and globalization intersect, allowing them to script alternative narratives of humanitarianism and terror-warfare in vivid displays of resilience and creativity.

The contours of audience, genre and narrative intermingle and overlap throughout this exploration of various theatres of war in northern Uganda. The audiences for which these performances play out include the former captives at World Vision, fellow Acholi, southern Uganda, the international aid community, and foreigners such as myself who come to Gulu, one of the few places where one can 'experience' the war in relative safety.[5] These multiple layers of spectatorship challenge and overturn the opposition of local and global upon which discourses of globalization continue to depend.

Humanitarian heroes and the global gaze

The war in Uganda, though rooted in the specific circumstances of Uganda's colonial and postcolonial history that divided the northern and southern regions,[6] is characteristic of what Mary Kaldor has called the 'new wars' of the late twentieth and early twenty-first centuries.[7] Under the terms of these wars, which increasingly target civilians instead of combatants,[8] the players seemingly try to outdo one another in the production of spectacles of atrocity. Mutilation, mass murder and the abduction of children are the methodologies *du jour* in Sudan, DR-Congo and Côte d'Ivoire as well as in Uganda.[9] Although regimes have long used torture and other forms of physical and emotional abuse as a weapon against perceived enemies in times of war, these traditional manifestations of state terror are typically concealed from the public eye. In contrast, practitioners of new wars openly perform their acts of violence. In her landmark study of the Mozambican civil war, anthropologist Carolyn Nordstrom (1997) has analysed these public displays of atrocity as a strategy meant to diminish local capacity for resistance.[10] Through forcing others to witness the atrocities carried out on neighbours and loved ones, the perpetrators succeed in 'unmaking the world' for victims and spectators alike,[11] clearing the way for eventual surrender and defeat.

This unmaking of the world, however, plays out before the world itself. The witnesses and victims relate their testimony to the international observers dotting the modern African warscape, who repackage this testimony for the global stage in the format of human rights reports, world news and international aid policy. This expanded audience provides crucial context for the ways in which terror-warfare is scripted and performed. Rebel armies have learned that the terrorizing of civilians on a massive scale ensures attention in the worldwide press, which inadvertently encourages additional acts through the process of reporting. Several LRA tactics denote careful study of the international scripts of terror-warfare; for example, their practice of cutting off the lips, ears and/or noses of civilians follows the example of the Mozambican RENAMO forces in the 1980s (Nordstrom 1997: 165). Interestingly, however, the LRA has not achieved the degree of notoriety of its fellow rebel armies found in Sudan, Angola and Somalia. The pressure to attract international attention might explain some of the LRA's improvisational tactics, such as padlocking the lips of civilians, which seems to be a phenomenon unique to northern Uganda.[12] My point is not to erase the historical and cultural specificity of these acts of violence but to emphasize the global context in which what is perceived as local acts of savagery are performed.[13]

In a study of the civil wars in Sierra Leone and Liberia, Danny Hoffman (2004: 211–226) identifies a particularly insidious intent behind these spectacles of violence, arguing that combatants purposefully target civilians in order to gain access to international aid money.[14] He found that the rebel soldiers of these West African countries were keenly interested in comparing their own atrocious acts to those of their predecessors in Mozambique, Angola, Sudan, DR-Congo and Somalia. He writes that '[o]ne tenet of this travelling knowledge of other African movements was that, when the international community responds to African crises, the more atrocious the conflict, the greater the level of aid' (Hoffman 2004: 216).[15] Although similar kinds of research have not been conducted among the LRA rebels, whose motives are undoubtedly as multifaceted as the causes of the war itself,[16] Hoffman's work helps to clarify how the politics of civil war and international aid intersect in African contexts. In the streets of Gulu, the allure of aid money was repeatedly displayed as Land Cruisers and Pajeros belonging to the World Food Programme, World Health Organization, Doctors without Borders, various branches of the United Nations, CARE International and World Vision drove past the locals who were on foot or, at best, on bicycles. These signifiers of wealth provide an impoverished population with tantalizing glimpses into the seemingly limitless Euro cash flow, affirming Michael Hardt and Antonio Negri's categorization of international humanitarian organizations as 'among the most powerful and prominent in the contemporary social order' (Hardt and Negri 2001: 313).

In the case of World Vision's rehabilitation centre, however, the Land Cruiser provided only a veneer of prosperity. Although the worldwide organization attracts considerable funds,[17] as reflected in its stately office in the capital city of Kampala in southern Uganda, the centre itself occupies a marginal status. Its facilities are run down, the children are crammed into battered UNICEF tents, and the counsellors' wages, though undoubtedly superior to those of many northern Ugandans, are still insubstantial. In their discussion of what they perceive as the considerable power of humanitarian organizations, which they associate with the supposedly apolitical aim of the organizations to '[meet] the needs of life itself' (Hardt and Negri 2001: 313), Hardt and Negri neglect to consider that some lives are worth more than others on the global market. Despite the UN's repeated declarations of northern Uganda as one of the worst humanitarian crises in the world,[18] the region, like World Vision, languishes in poverty due in part to the vagaries of global compassion that favour victims of 'natural' disasters over those of African civil wars.

The region's low status in the hierarchy of disaster means that World Vision, like the LRA, must cater to multiple audiences – albeit through the medium of humanitarianism rather than terror-warfare. As one of the largest rehabilitation centres for former child combatants in the country, they attract considerable attention. Every two to three days during my stay in Gulu, visitors ranging from US military officers, foreign ambassadors and church groups showed up at the centre, usually with little advance warning. Upon their arrival, scheduled activities invariably stopped as the staff rushed to provide the visitors with a tour, an assembly of the children in the common hall and a dance performance. Their behaviour conveyed a sense of anxiety to please these visitors and perhaps shore up their image as a worthy recipient of international funds. Nordstrom, who writes passionately and persuasively about the 'codes of creative worldbuilding' within a Mozambican civilian population decimated by war, coins the stirring phrase: 'It is in creativity, in the fashioning of self and world, that people find their most potent weapon against war' (Nordstrom 1997: 12, 4). In the LRA war zone, however, the codes of globalization ensure that this creativity is carefully circumscribed; the staff of World Vision seemed intent on *playing* to the world as well as rebuilding it.

Arts therapy played a critical role in World Vision's performances of humanitarianism. Although Westerners champion this methodology as an alternative to the 'talk therapy' model, in which the children are supposed to come to terms with their traumatic pasts through talking about their experiences with a counsellor, my research strongly suggested that arts therapy in northern Uganda was valued primarily as a means to market trauma. The staff members at World Vision, all of whom were from northern Uganda,[19] invariably began the tours at the counselling room which is decorated with the series of paintings mentioned at the outset of this chapter. After explaining that a former captive produced the paintings, and thus endowing them with a sense of authenticity, the counsellor who served as the guide used the series as a template for describing the children's collective experience of trauma followed by rehabilitation. The guide often invited the visitors to peruse the stacks of drawings scattered around the room, allowing the visitors to become voyeurs into the children's experiences of LRA brutality that many of the drawings depicted. These works did not function as personal expressions of trauma and healing; instead, they were assimilated into the master narrative of war. The counsellors used representations of life in captivity as evidence of suffering and light-hearted drawings as affirmations of World Vision's success at rehabilitation. Their value as a marketing tool exceeds the centre's walls, as replications of these drawings are found in the brochures that the visitors take as souvenirs and on World Vision's website in the pages devoted to northern Uganda.[20] The weight that these drawings carry helps to contextualize the ways in which the children's artistic expression was circumscribed. As the visitors examined the paintings and drawings, the counsellors did not mention their tendency to grade the children's work – a practice that seems antithetical to therapeutic discourse, which calls for traumatized victims to purge their painful memories in a space that is theoretically free of evaluation and judgment.[21] In the midst of personal and cultural destruction, private expressions of pain are a luxury that northern Uganda cannot afford.

For the remainder of this section, I address the cultural capital of drama in the economy of war. As part of the children's rehabilitation at World Vision, music, dance, and drama were supposed to be included on a regular basis. Every Thursday afternoon and Saturday morning were set aside for 'MDD,' an acronym for music, dance and drama. Despite the inclusiveness of this phrase, I found that drama was consistently omitted from the equation, passed over and even resisted in favour of Acholi dance.[22] An intriguing shift occurred, however, toward the end of my stay in Gulu – one that suggested that drama was deemed useful once representatives of power were watching.[23] The centre received two separate invitations to perform for diverse audiences that included government officials, representatives of NGOs, local schoolchildren and their teachers and European and US expatriates. In response to these prime opportunities for marketing and promotion, drama was abruptly rehabilitated as several members of the staff discarded their usual routines and devoted their energies to the creation of plays. Although the children themselves were the actors, the rehearsal process took place in an environment in which the counsellors determined all aspects of the text and staging. In my discussion of the two plays that were produced, I take the ethical risk of critiquing this approach. In doing so, however, my aim is to situate these constraints upon the children's creativity within a culture of war, which transforms representation into what Taussig calls a 'high-powered medium of domination' (Taussig 1986: 121).[24]

Ironically, both occasions were meant as celebrations of children's empowerment. For the first event, a group of about twelve children from World Vision joined a few hundred schoolchildren at Karo Abili Primary School to commemorate children's rights.[25] Under the 'VIP tent' erected in front of the clearing that served as the performance space, government officials, schoolmasters, staff from local NGOs and a few foreigners watched as groups of children who represented primary schools throughout the district performed songs, plays and dances related to the theme 'The African Child, Family, and HIV/AIDS.' Speakers and performers alike used the Acholi language, marking the event as a primarily local affair.

The second event took place at the prestigious venue of the Acholi Inn, an elite hotel where foreigners and national figures regularly stayed. The focal point of the occasion consisted of a photography exhibition called *Armed with Resilience*, a remarkable collection of photographs by war-affected girls of northern Uganda. In keeping with the theme of the exhibit, the invitation requested that former female captives staying at World Vision perform dance and drama related to the theme of female roles in building peace.[26] In addition to two other groups from local secondary schools, the World Vision girls performed for a select audience of about 50–60 spectators who included government officials and NGO representatives, and several Western foreigners. In reflection of the international tone of the event – the organizer of the exhibit herself was from the United States – a translator helped to ensure that all members of the audience understood the speeches, though not the plays themselves.

Despite the variations in context, the two plays that World Vision created were strikingly similar. For the children's rights festival, the play focused on a family living in an IDP camp. To the family's dismay, the older son spends his days drinking and carousing with girls. In the midst of this confusion, a World Vision counsellor escorts a former female captive home. Following a joyful reconciliation scene, the girl lectures her brother about the dangers of AIDS. She explains that she learned about such matters during her stay at the World Vision centre. The boy ignores her advice only to meet dire consequences, as he dies in the final scene. In keeping with the theme of building peace, the play performed at Acholi Inn assumed a more optimistic tone. Although it also depicted a confident former female captive returning from World Vision to a troubled family at the IDP camp, the problem consisted of excessive drinking on the part of the girl's father and brothers as opposed to sexual promiscuity. Like her counterpart in the AIDS play, she delivers a lecture about the folly of drinking; this time, the lecture produces the desired effect as the father and sons decide to give up drinking. The play ends on a note of harmony as the family gathers together for a celebratory meal.

Both plays strategically altered the typical narrative of war to place special emphasis on the role of humanitarian intervention. Anne Orford's (2003: 158–185) discussion of how the discourse of humanitarian intervention produces subjectivity through a classic, mainstream narrative helps to clarify the ways in which this discourse played out in the plots. She identifies a consistent narrative that recurs in the stories of intervention, in which a disruption of (Third World) order calls upon (First World) 'knights in white armour' to rescue the victims, who are uniformly cast as symbols of helplessness. On the one hand, the World Vision plays complicate this typical humanitarian narrative that depicts children as passive victims since the former female captives deliver their homilies about the dangers of drinking and AIDS from a position of authority and confidence. On the other hand, this strength does not stem from their experiences of war nor their Acholi identity; instead, it is credited to exposure to World Vision, and the girls become their emissaries of enlightenment. Although these characters expand the convention of white humanitarian heroes swooping down to save troubled Third World nations, they resonate with Orford's description of 'active, humane savior[s] intervening to help people in trouble spots, obscuring other sets of relations between those who identify with the international community and those targeted for intervention' (Orford 2003: 165). The quarrelsome families that serve as the recipients of World Vision's wisdom are isolated, and sociopolitical context concerning the cramped, often shocking conditions of IDP camps and the utter failure of the state to protect its citizens is erased. The families, lacking agency and cultural resources, simply wait for World Vision's guiding hand, which they ignore at their peril as the first play made abundantly clear through the brother's death.

I believe that a sense of anxiety pervaded these promotions of World Vision. Their use of the Acholi language ensured local representatives of power from the government and other NGOs received the messages of World Vision's worth.[27] The centre is not only dependent upon international charity but it also works with district authorities and the military in the children's transfer to the centre and their return to their families. The sympathies of high-ranking government officials – who served as guests of honour at both events – were vital to the centre's operations. Given the centre's dependence upon the generosity of other NGOs – for example, it relies upon donations of mattresses and food from UNICEF and the World Food Programme – the NGO representatives in the audience also served as potential targets.[28] Finally, the schoolchildren and teachers in the audiences might also have needed assurance of World Vision's ability to improve people's lives. World Vision prides itself on its close ties to local communities; for example, the centre has trained a few hundred volunteers in Gulu district to help keep track of the children's progress once they are reunited with their families. A reputation for excellence among all of the constituencies concerned was a key component of World Vision's success in negotiating these networks of interdependency.

These stakes help to contextualize the methods of staging that the staff employed. The counsellors conferred only with each other in the choice of topics, the casting and the dialogue. Once the rehearsals began, the counsellors exerted careful control over the words and delivery of the performers, emphatically telling them what to say and how to say it.[29] In a Western context, this approach would be relatively commonplace; in East Africa, where an atmosphere of collaboration and improvisation prevails in play rehearsals, I found it startling. In her analysis of the Mozambican war, Nordstrom (1997: 81–83) theorizes the prevalence of silence in cultures of terror as a refusal to speak in order to guard critical information; in other words, silence serves as a mode of survival in dangerous times. In the creation of the World Vision plays, the staging methods worked to silence the children's voices as their own ideas about children's rights or peacemaking were never solicited. Instead of speaking as commentators of war, they served as the mouthpiece of preordained messages. Although I found the rehearsals disturbing to watch, the situation in which the silencing occurred demands that I recognize the authoritarian approach to staging as, indeed, a mode of survival in dangerous times. In the charged atmosphere of Gulu, drama cannot assume the connotations of children's play but becomes caught in the politics of war. It was imperative that the linear narrative not be broken, disrupted or even complicated, lest the epistemic murk seep into these heroic tales.

Throughout this discussion, I have emphasized repression and domination at the risk of upholding the master narrative of globalization as a homogenizing and hegemonic force. In an analysis of how narratives of war overlap with the genre of realism, the next section begins to exceed this framework as it addresses issues of cultural memory and survival. Again, however, the children are caught in a web of interventionism, one that is constructed by Westerners intent upon the imposition of experimental theatrical techniques.

Circulations of realism and narratives of war

Anthropologists and theatre scholars alike typically disparage realism as a medium for the representation of violence because it integrates the violence into a seamless status quo resistant to social change and intervention.[30] Michael Taussig singles out realism for a harsh critique in the context of cultures of terror, calling it a kind of 'hermeneutic violence' that 'flatten[s] contradiction and systemitiz[es] chaos' (Taussig 1986: 132). Although scholars such as Vivian M. Patraka, who cautiously suggests that 'there are conditions [in the representation of violence] under which the traditional techniques of realistic identification may be useful' (Patraka 1999: 45)[31] complicate this line of argument, realism is generally understood as a conservative ideological weapon that domesticates and contains the destruction left in violence's wake. Since each of the dramatic and cinematic representations of the LRA war discussed in this chapter use conventions associated with realism, the overlap between war narrative and this distrusted, if not maligned, genre calls for closer examination.

Although an in-depth analysis of Ugandan theatre history and contemporary theatrical styles is well beyond the scope of this chapter,[32] a note of context will help to clarify the significance of the relatively stringent form of realism upon which representations of the LRA war depend. As in the case of other East African countries, spoken drama in the realistic vein was strongly encouraged, if not enforced, in the Ugandan colonial school system in the late nineteenth century and the first half of the twentieth century.[33] In the post-independence era, Ugandan playwrights such as Robert Serumaga, Rose Mbowa, and Byron Kawadwa sought to transform this colonialist style of theatre with one that drew upon Uganda's complex traditions of indigenous music, dance and folklore. Even in contemporary works that can be loosely categorized under the label of realism, meaning that they construct a dramatic narrative that adheres to a rational, causal sequence of events, performers regularly burst into song and/or speak directly to the audience. Such conventions both disrupt the veneer of illusionism and also demonstrate the well-theorized capacity of sub-Saharan Africa to transform Western ideas and conventions to suit local tastes and desires.[34]

In dramatizations of the LRA war, however, this expansive interpretation of realism yielded to a considerably more orthodox version that resisted any rupture in the linear narrative.[35] This shift in the politics of representation raises a crucial question, given the limitations of the form and its dependence upon a rational cause-to-effect progression of events. Why this preference for a form that belies, if not suppresses, the murk and mayhem of this war? At first glance, the indomitable force of globalization presents itself as a logical explanation for this pattern. In other words, the use of realism might be theorized as a capitulation to a global marketplace that uses the mirage of objectivity to convey the horror of the LRA war to fellow Acholi, southern Uganda and the world.

A 2004 film entitled *War Child: Abducted*, directed and produced by Robert E. Altman, a director based in New York City, serves as a classic example of how realism works to confine and domesticate atrocity. *War Child* relies upon a visceral level of realism to tell a story of the LRA's abduction and military training of an eight-year-old Acholi boy named Okello. After a lengthy introductory sequence that emphasizes the serenity of Okello's village in rural Gulu, LRA rebels kidnap him and his older brother from the local schoolhouse. Both boys, as well as their classmates, are marched to a rebel base in southern Sudan and provided with military training.[36] After being subjected to sustained trauma at the hands of a brutal rebel commander, who forces him to kill his best friend, Okello manages to escape along with one of his schoolmates. They make their way to Gulu, where a UN worker brings them to a rehabilitation centre that strongly resembles the one run by World Vision. In the final scene, his mother tracks him down at the centre, and the two are reunited in a joyful embrace. Although the murders of Okello's father and brother in the course of the film preclude a seamless restoration of the social order, the film still upholds a sense of reaffirmation since Okello's pre-war quality of innocence remains intact. The film, funded by Hallmark entertainment, was clearly aimed at a western audience and therefore constructed a classic example of 'an essentialized portrait of the universal sufferer, an image that can be commodified, sold, and (re)broadcast to global audiences who see their own potential trauma reflected in this simulation of the modern subject' (Hinton 2002: 26).[37] The mechanics of realism, which positioned Okello as the sympathetic protagonist in contrast to the otherness of the malevolent rebels, provided smooth terrain for this process of commodification and identification to occur.

Although the film was originally intended for US audiences, local investment in the trappings of realism played a key role in the film's conventions. On 21 May 2004, the film received its Uganda premiere at an international film festival in the capital city of Kampala, a thriving metropolitan centre where locals pride themselves on their cosmopolitan attitudes and practices.[38] Like most of the southern regions, Kampala is relatively indifferent towards the war; a visitor to the city could easily remain unaware of the war decimating the northern part of the country given the local media's focus on the political shenanigans of President Yoweri Museveni and the vagaries of cell phones.[39] Okello Kelo Sam and Milton Obote, two Acholi performers who participated in the filmmaking and actively contributed to the writing of the script, responded to questions from the audience after the showing of the film. One of the earliest questions, asked by an audience member whose accent and appearance conveyed a southern Ugandan identity, questioned the 'truth' of the film in a sceptical tone of voice. Sam responded immediately and firmly, 'This is not fiction. This is fact.' Sam, who is intimately acquainted with the paradoxes and ambiguities of this war,[40] elided this turmoil with a straightforward declaration that conflated realism with reality, or perhaps the reality that he wanted the spectator to believe, one that boiled down the inchoateness of war to the issue of an innocent child trying to survive. Both Sam and Obote then invoked their own experiences of having immediate family relatives abducted as a means of shoring up their authority to pronounce the veracity of the film. As early as the 1930s, Ernst Bloch (1990) called realism the 'cult of the immediately ascertainable fact,' a statement that foreshadows its unrelenting cross-cultural hold on contemporary consciousness. In Kampala in 2004, the medium of realism was conflated with reality in a collaborative effort to overcome the disbelief and indifference of southern Uganda.[41]

This investment in realism can be linked to the genealogy of a global trend that encompasses imperial, colonial and postcolonial cultures and states. In his exploration of the intersection between realism and personal narratives of violence in Northern Ireland, Allen Feldman calls attention to the impossibility of identifying singular origins for such a complex phenomenon:

> The molding of realistic modes of depiction into a hierarchy of credibility and fact-setting and as a public form of truth-claiming and depictive legitimation was a long and fragmented historical labor that emerged in a variety of discontinuous but overlapping social sites – and not all at one time if we consider the respective development of state archiving, juridical rules of evidence, popular media, optical experimentation, art movements, and the commodification of visual experience.[42]
>
> (Feldman 2000: 60)

In the specific social site of northern Uganda in 2004, I would add humanitarianism to Feldman's list of cultural, legal and artistic discourses as yet another influence in the privileging of the realism as a seemingly objective medium of representation. Although humanitarianism is perhaps more easily linked to examples of photorealism in which the images of suffering are meant to trigger a sense of moral outrage on the part of the viewer,[43] the master narrative of the LRA war intersects with the politics of identification in realistic drama, one that calls upon the spectator to imagine herself or himself in the role of the active humanitarian hero who will end the victims' suffering and restore the social order.

Although the globalization of realism can partly explain its dominance in northern Uganda, my experiences at the World Vision centre suggested that cultural issues were also at stake. I believe that the rationality of linear narrative becomes entangled in cultural memory as a mode to make things thinkable,[44] to render the senselessness of the war intelligible and remake the world however provisional and deceptive the result. In making this point, I do not intend to situate cultural memory and imagination as *internal* processes in opposition to the *external* demands of the global marketplace. As the therapeutic drawings in the World Vision counselling room reveal, private and public spheres become interchangeable in the economy of terror and war.

The role of Western intervention clarifies the intensity of local investment in realism. The Children As Peacebuilders (CAP) drama group, a children's theatre group in Gulu that includes several former captives, aims to raise awareness in the IDP camps about the harsh conditions that child combatants endure (Children As Peacebuilders 2004: 128–131).[45] For their first major production, which was created and performed in 2002, they adhered to the conventional war narrative of home life, abduction, escape and reintegration into their home communities. In an interview conducted with a Canadian journalist, they pointed to their ability to make the audiences cry as a sign of their success (Children As Peacebuilders 2004: 131). Instead of packaging this story for the international community and/or southern Uganda, the children used the techniques of realistic drama to provoke sympathy and identification with the plight of these children among fellow Acholi.

In 2003, foreigners deliberately challenged the children's reliance upon realism. Liesbeth Speelman, one of the few European expatriates who worked for World Vision in Uganda, contracted two Dutch acrobats, Djura Dame and Annemieke,[46] to teach CAP circus techniques such as acrobatics and juggling in order to expand their repertory of performance skills. The children strongly resisted the idea of incorporating circus techniques since they believed it would diminish the seriousness of the story they were telling. Speelman admitted that the children were more or less 'forced' to learn the techniques, and at the end of the month-long workshop, they produced a play in which the use of juggling, pyramid-building and plate-spinning was integrated into the usual tale of abduction.[47] For example, in a scene in which a female abductee frantically attempts to start a fire under the orders of an increasingly impatient rebel soldier, the performer used the technique of plate-spinning to help convey her sense of tension.[48] Although the resulting production provides a rare example of an experimental approach to the grim subject matter, it occurred only under Western duress.[49]

Issues of cultural imperialism and globalization intersect in this tale of culture clash, in which nonlinear techniques of representation confronted the monolith of realism. This particular tale, however, complicates the usual connotations of culture clash as the West versus Africa since Western theatrical practices are colliding against *other* Western practices on African terrain. On one hand, the reaction of the children refutes popular and academic discourses of globalization as an indefatigable Western force given their unwillingness to capitulate to the imported European experts and their updated performance techniques.[50] On the other hand, grassroots globalization also falters as a theoretical framework since this bottoms-up model depends upon the adaptation and transformation of dominant (Western) cultural forms. In this instance, the requisite transformation does not occur. Unlike the indigenized versions of realism that post-Independence Ugandan playwrights developed, the children's reliance on realism can be categorized more easily as a throwback to the colonial era than as an example of local creativity.

My own attempts to work with war-affected children also reveal limitations of these theoretical models. My husband, Robert Ajwang', and I were originally invited to the centre for the purpose of organizing theatre workshops for the children. Well-schooled in the academic distrust of realism, I, like the Dutch acrobats, was intent on introducing experimental theatrical techniques. I find it telling that on the two occasions when we did successfully organize a workshop,[51] the counsellor assigned to work with us responded with strong resistance. Although her reaction invites a variety of interpretations,[52] it is commensurate with the widespread preference for linear narrative and realistic representation that I saw throughout theatrical representations of war in Uganda. The insistency of this pattern leads me to speculate upon the possibility of a deep-seated cultural investment and to theorize this moment as an example of how genre plays out in the construction of cultural memory.

In consultation with the staff, we proposed working with a pre-existing script that a counsellor had composed based on the biblical story of the Prodigal Son. This parable contains layers of resonance for the former captives, who must confront complicated homecomings when they are reunited with their families since many of them, particularly the boys, have committed murder and other atrocities during their captivity. We suggested that we expand it using techniques that East African cultural nationalists have established as the hallmarks of an indigenous African theatre – storytelling and integration of music, dance and drama.[53] The intensity of the counsellor's resistance was, at the time, startling. She insisted that we would not be following the story if we used these techniques. She was particularly perturbed by my desire to introduce a flashback approach in which the story unfolded through the remembrances of the Son. While the children watched, much of our workshop consisted of our joint efforts to persuade her to let us try this approach. Although we finally convinced her, or so we thought, the Prodigal Son never made it home since we only succeeded in workshopping the first two scenes.

This encounter cannot be explained as another manifestation of the marketing of trauma. No powerful outside world was watching – just the children themselves. Still, we could not be left to our own experimental devices; instead, we were confronted with the absolutism of linearity in which the son is restored to the father's embrace through a series of causally related actions. It is particularly significant that this story manipulates the classic humanitarian tale of suffering followed by external intervention to emphasize the *internal* role of forgiveness. The closing scene of restoration in the parable, faithfully reproduced in the counsellor's script, allows the social order to be reasserted through the internal decision of the father. This narrative twist marginalizes, if not excludes, the role of humanitarianism, which depends upon the act of external intervention. In the 'local' context of this play, intended only for the children themselves, a suggestion of indigenous strength and resolve slipped through the cracks of humanitarian discourse. The counsellor's insistence upon this storyline suggests that the staff is invested in the terms of representation not only as employees of World Vision but also as Acholi who have endured considerable personal tragedies because of the war.

The formation of a narrative to make sense of traumatic events is not, in itself, surprising. Shoshana Felman and Dori Laub write that in order to come to terms with trauma and transform it into a relatively contained memory of the past, 'a therapeutic process – a process of constructing a narrative, of reconstructing a history and essentially, of *re-externalizing an event* has to be set in motion' (Felman and Laub 1992: 69). In her study of post-war reconstruction in Peru, Francine A'ness thoughtfully elaborates upon Felman and Laub's work, noting that the production of testimony requires an atmosphere of stability: 'In order to speak about the traumatic event a victim needs to feel safe. She needs to know that what happened in the past has come to an end and, moreover, that the listener before whom she testifies is someone who will listen and in whom she can trust' (A'ness 2004: 398). As children continue to be kidnapped and people massacred, and as the repeated claims of the Ugandan government that the war is ending appear increasingly ludicrous, these narratives play out in a region where the population is most assuredly *not* safe. The narrative itself, though, with its promise of restoration, holds out a cultural lifeline, one that places survival in local hands as opposed to those of the capricious and indifferent state, the United Nations and/or international charity.

The concept of local agency, however, should not be oversimplified as an inclusive space free of hierarchies and domination. As the three of us attempted and failed to come to an agreement about the dramatic interpretation of the Prodigal Son, the children simply watched our negotiations. They willingly, even enthusiastically, participated as requested, but their own interpretation of the biblical story is not known. Although I have called attention to instances of indigenous strength in the LRA theatre of war, the former captives have remained largely silent throughout this chapter. In the final section, I discuss how these children, particularly the girls, overcome these various modalities of oppression through expressions of Acholi dance. As they reclaim the murk of terror-warfare and re-script the humanitarian discourse that moulds them into traumatized victims, their resilience demonstrates the breadth of creativity and resources that were systematically suppressed.

Restoring the past

One of the demands of humanitarian discourse is to represent the traumatic past as a time of unrelenting terror and suffering. To complicate that image through hints of agency and inner strength is to run a considerable risk of diminishing the emotional response that theoretically generates charitable contributions. As children rights activist Jessica Lenz argues, however, these discursive moves negate the skills and resources that these victims cultivated during the trauma itself. Speaking specifically of the experience of female combatants in northern Uganda, she writes: 'During the process of reintegration and rehabilitation, far too often, we suppress and undermine skills and strengths that have enabled these girls to survive in the first place' (Lenz 2003: 6). An emphasis upon these strengths disrupts the seamless representation of trauma and begins to script an alternative narrative of war.

Lenz herself helped to produce such a rupture in her organization of the photography exhibit that showcased the work of former female captives of the LRA and other war-affected teenagers. The exhibit, which I previously mentioned in the context of the two World Vision plays, marked the culmination of a six-month-long project in which they were trained in photography and encouraged to take pictures that conveyed images of female strength. In addition to capturing a variety of powerful images, the photographers wrote brief commentaries about their role in peacebuilding that vividly illustrated their capacity for sociopolitical commentary as well as their desire to reclaim the complexity of their pasts. As one former captive who participated in the project writes, 'Sometimes they say "forget your past" to those who are formerly abducted [...] It is important to remember [these] times, the times that made you strong. Like me, I remember what is most important, my strength that kept me alive.'[54] This refusal to categorize herself as a helpless victim of LRA violence might not market well on the global stage, but it carves out a space in which the murk of this war, a war that requires children to find cultural resources even in the midst of terror, can be acknowledged rather than suppressed.

Lenz's ideas provide fresh theoretical space for understanding how the former female captives undermine the dominant narrative of war. Although the girls of World Vision did not participate in the photography project, they found other means to reclaim the complexities of their pasts. In the play that they performed at the exhibition, the girl who played the alcoholic father wore a rubber bracelet around her ankle. These bracelets, which are endowed with Kony's magic, are given to the girls as part of their indoctrination into the LRA. Several of the children at World Vision, particularly the child mothers, continued to wear them despite the staff's efforts to persuade them otherwise. This subtle visual cue in the performance conveyed a sustained belief in Kony's powers, a sign that World Vision's attempts at rehabilitation and intervention could not extinguish. Clearly, these bracelets confound attempts to classify them as symbols of resistance since they also serve as reminders of the brutally oppressive regime of the LRA; indeed, the girls' attachment to them is related to fear of harmful spiritual repercussions if they are removed. Nevertheless, these bracelets signify the formation of a counter-culture in the midst of humanitarian intervention, a space where the codes of creative world-building could be tested and explored.

Acholi dance provided rich terrain upon which the processes of world-building could occur. In contrast to the careful restraints in which drama and arts therapy operated, enthusiastic and impromptu performance of these dances flourished at the World Vision centre. Although the official timetable scheduled MDD only two times weekly, the children practiced dance steps and taught each other drumming rhythms on almost a daily basis. Artistic skill and Acholi identity coalesced in these spontaneous performances to produce a creative commentary on war.

The girls assumed a leading role in these productions. Although boys participated as musicians for official events or during the scheduled MDD activities, the older girls consistently initiated the informal performances. This distinction became especially prominent during a debate activity, which was scheduled every Monday afternoon.[55] For this particular debate, which addressed the value of formal schooling, the common hall that served as the nexus of the centre contained only boys. The debate provided a picture-perfect moment for the global gaze as a well-run rehabilitation activity in which the counsellors led the terms of the debate and guided their charges on the path to re-civilization. Meanwhile, a group of about fifteen girls blithely disregarded the formal schedule and performed a playful rendition of the *apiri* dance in front of the dormitories. Their display of enthusiasm and passion for their culture defied the tropes of humanitarian discourse that situated them as hapless victims. These parallel activities imply a classic dichotomy of official vs. unofficial cultures, in which male-dominated official culture was juxtaposed against a female counter-culture that played out on the margins.

The enthusiastic participation of three female counsellors in the dancing means, however, that this dichotomy cannot be sustained. Although this sanctioning gesture might be interpreted as an infiltration and co-option of the counter-culture, to do so would overlook the startling energy and passion of these performances, one that suggests the potentiality of tradition as a *resource* to produce new cultural meanings. The blurring of boundaries between staff and clients forged a democratic space that overturned the centre's conventional hierarchies. Instead of their usual authoritarian stance, the three counsellors simply danced alongside the girls, who clearly were in command. As was customary in these performances, one of the girls served as the dance captain, using her whistle to determine the shifts and rhythms of the choreography. Although a participatory, democratic atmosphere is hardly unique in the context of sub-Saharan African performance, it stood out in the context of World Vision where anxiety over the terms of representation tended to dominate artistic expression. This celebration of shared Acholi identity temporarily displaced the centre's hierarchical structures and challenged the classic narrative of war that situates not only the former captives but also the Acholi people themselves as victims of terror and oppression. In a moment of solidarity, female staff and former captives collectively displayed their resilience, performed their cultures and rebuilt their world.

This blurring of hierarchies and boundaries was not confined to the centre itself. For one of the scheduled MDD afternoons during our visit,[56] the dancers and musicians performed at the adult rehabilitation centre, which housed adult male LRA combatants who had surrendered to or were captured by the UPDF. Master narratives about the LRA war would characterize these men as the cruel oppressors who abduct the girls and force them into sexual slavery. As the testimony of hundreds of former female captives indicates, these narratives are the reality – girls regularly experience rape, beatings and deprivation as part of their indoctrination.[57] Given that an unspecified majority of the LRA soldiers were once abducted children themselves, however, the distinction between captive and rebel cannot be easily made. This zone of ambiguity provides critical context for the performance at the adult centre, which hinted at the nuances and complexities of the relationships between rebels and captives.

A particularly charged moment of the performance occurred during the *larakaraka*, a popular courting dance. As several Acholi enthusiastically explained to me, in the pre-war era, villages organized major performances of *larakaraka*, which allowed visitors from other villages to investigate potential marriage partners. Typically, male musicians and female dancers use the medium of dance as an opportunity to flirt and convey their interest.[58] In this particular performance at the adult centre, however, the young boys who served as musicians were not the objects of the girls' affection; instead, a sense of sexual tension played out between the adult male spectators and the dancers. In a classic example of how the LRA war confounds simplistic oppositions between good/evil and oppressor/victim, mutual relationships between rebels and captives occasionally develop in the camps.[59] Additional relationships also emerge during the rehabilitation phase; in order to sustain these ties, the girls are known to slip away to the adult centre to visit their boyfriends. The *larakaraka* produced a unique moment in which a sanctioned, formal activity provided a veil for this undercurrent of sexuality. Far from serving as a reification of tradition, these dances were adapted to serve a culture of crisis in which conventions of courtship occurred in war rehabilitation centres instead of rural villages.[60]

In addition to negotiating the demands of the present, these dances bear witness to the girls' experiences as LRA captives. Their assured confidence in executing the steps is a legacy of the rebel camps themselves, where the girls regularly performed the dances. These dances not only produce democratic, non-hierarchical spaces in which Acholi identity exceeds the limitations of war, but they also provide moments in which the girls reinscribe the past on their skilled, dancing bodies. Humanitarian discourse dictates that the life of LRA captivity must be represented as one of seamless oppression in which the innocent victims are subjected to relentless oppression and terror. While these tropes are perhaps necessary in order to raise international awareness, they also undermine the girls' memories of the times that made them strong, to rephrase the photographer quoted above, and the skills that they cultivated to survive. These dances expand the single tale of hardship and restoration into a discursive realm that encompasses complex pasts and complicated futures.

Even in the midst of these celebrations of resilience, however, the economy of marketing intrudes. The unending demand for resources insures that the dances become entangled in the politics of humanitarianism. As I explore the layers of commodification and appropriation in which the dances are enmeshed, I return to the ways in which globalization and the formation of cultural memory intersect and overlap. Again, theories of top-down or grassroots globalization falter in the face of these cultural productions that simultaneously embody both narratives.

On the one hand, the dances can be readily theorized as classic examples of appropriation. With their usual savvy comprehension of international aid politics, the staff skilfully incorporated these moments of counter-intervention into the narrative of rehabilitation. The dancers and musicians were regularly trotted out for the entertainment of official visitors, and their enthusiastic renditions of *larakaraka* and *bwola* were appropriated as spectacles for the global stage. Although the energy of the performances might prove a challenge to the visitors' preconceptions of oppressed and downtrodden LRA victims, the staff readily points to the children's high spirits as evidence of the success of rehabilitation. As a recent article in the Ugandan newspaper *The Monitor* relates, a journalist who expressed amazement at the happiness of the World Vision dancers was told that 'the joy we could see was after days and weeks of counselling by World Vision staff' (Mucunguzi 2004: n.p.). In other words, the considerable resilience of the dancers became repackaged as an 'after' picture in the makeover narrative of World Vision.

On the other hand, this interpretation adheres to the gendered tropes of scholarship on globalization and transnationalism that, as Carla Freeman argues, position the local as a feminine, disenfranchised space upon which the 'heavy [masculine] hand of the global makes its marks' (Freeman 2001: 1031). In this framework, the global eye commodifies the local dance, which passively submits to its penetrating gaze. I would not, however, characterize local attitudes toward these dances as passive.[61] In a workshop that we arranged at GUSCO, the other major rehabilitation centre in Gulu, we thought that our attempts at artistic intervention might be more productive if we focused on dance choreography instead of drama. In the renditions of *larakaraka* that we saw at both rehabilitation centres, the children employed a circular formation in which the male musicians surrounded the female dancers and effectively obstructed the spectators' view. Robert, who is trained in East African dance choreography, proposed that he help them create an alternative version of *larakaraka* for official performances, one that would open it up to the spectators' gaze. Both the GUSCO counsellor and the children themselves responded to his suggestion with a distinct lack of enthusiasm. Given the Acholi ability to adapt and reinvent their dances to suit the demands of the moment, this resistance cannot be chalked up to a reified notion of tradition as a museum piece to be protected from change. Instead, it suggests that even in the global economy of spectacularization, limits were placed upon the extent of commodification. Cultural definitions of what it meant to be Acholi were clarified among staff and children alike in response to external intervention.

Of course, to characterize these dances as the local force of resistance against the impact of globalization would sustain the local/global dichotomy. As numerous scholars of globalization have persuasively argued, global and local cannot be placed in opposition due to the intensity of mutual infiltration in the current historical moment. In his study of the Kabre people of northern Togo, a world characterized as one 'in which sacrifice and MTV, rainmakers and civil servants, fetishists and catechists exist side by side and co-author an uncontainably hybrid cultural landscape,' Charles Piot emphasizes the theoretical impossibility of separating tradition from modernity: 'Where does the "traditional" end and the "modern" begin? Where is there an "outside" to modernity's "inside"? Where is there a "local" that is not also "global"?' (Piot 1999: 173). In the uncontainably hybrid cultural landscape of northern Uganda, the dances serve as fodder for the imperialist international gaze and simultaneously nourish a vibrant subculture in which the children can commemorate their strength. Even after the official guests had departed, the dances frequently continued, constructing an alternative narrative that exceeds the representational frame of marketing trauma. In addition to demonstrating the impossibility of disentangling global forces and local customs, the dances pay tribute to the shrewdness of the children and staff. Like the soldiers throughout sub-Saharan Africa who manipulate the terms of globalization in order to gain access to international funds, the children use these dances to cater to a multi-layered audience that includes themselves, their counsellors and international guests.

One day when I was in the World Vision counselling room, I saw two girls, newly arrived at the centre, pointing at the paintings that circled the room and whispering.[62] Were they using the paintings to make sense out of their recent experiences? To flatten and homogenize them, perhaps, but also to make them bearable? Were they comparing the series of linear, causally related images to the disjointed reality that they lived? The girls were animated but hushed – even if I knew Acholi, I would not have understood their words. Their analysis of this particular representation of war was subdued, as if in awareness of the loaded context in which they spoke, in which a European-American foreigner was observing even a private conversation. It is tempting to position these girls as caught between Western and Acholi anxiety, each side intent on using artistic expression to realize their own particular agendas. This reductive opposition, of course, does not do justice to the complexities of globalization nor does it acknowledge their capacity to reclaim their pasts and the epistemic murk of war. To return to Nordstrom, creativity does indeed serve as 'their most potent weapon against war,' but it is a weapon coveted by a variety of players on the global stage of northern Uganda.

Postscript: Marketing post-conflict trauma

In 2007, two years after the original publication of 'Marketing Trauma,' the hostilities in northern Uganda between the LRA and the UPDF came to an official end. Joseph Kony and remnants of the LRA remain defiantly at large; at the time of this writing, it is believed that he is located in the Central African Republic.[63] Despite the LRA's continued presence in East and Central Africa, northern Uganda itself has achieved the status of 'post-conflict' – a deceptive term that sidesteps the ways in which structural and symbolic violence continue to permeate daily life in northern Uganda.

As I seek to understand the theatre of post-conflict Uganda, I have become increasingly interested in Didier Fassin and Richard Rechtman's concept of the 'empire of trauma' (2007), which I define as a neoliberal world order in which trauma serves as currency. Although Fassin and Rechtman do not specifically refer to Michael Hardt and Antonio Negri's influential work,[64] their provocative phrase invites an understanding of how the appropriation and consumption of trauma feed into the machinery of Empire. Hardt and Negri argue that Empire relies upon biopolitical methods of social control; following Foucault, they write that '[b]iopower is a form of power that *regulates social life from its interior*, following it, interpreting it, absorbing it, and rearticulating it' (Hardt and Negri 2001, 23–24, emphasis added). This concept of biopower resonates with Fassin's understanding that the empire of trauma permeates the articulation of testimony – a genre that is often privileged as a source of truth-knowing about marginalized and suffering populations.[65] Fassin argues that 'suffering beings' can become complicit in the process of 'essentializ[ing] the victim,' as 'these persons often willingly submit to the category assigned to them: they understand the logic of this construction, and they anticipate its potential benefits' (Fassin 2007: 512). In a post-national, post-postcolonial age in which the African state is increasingly diminished and international humanitarian NGOS and religious institutions have filled the gap of governance,[66] humanitarian narratives can serve as tantalizing points of access to cultural and material capital for resource-poor populations. Fassin explains further that 'the individuals in question tend to conform to this portrait [of suffering], knowing that it will have an impact on public opinion, and thus offer to the humanitarian agents the part of their experience that feeds the construction of them as human beings crushed by fate' (Fassin 2007: 517). Agency is realized through the manipulation of certain narratives as a means of gaining traction in the empire of trauma, negotiating what Fassin and Rechtman have called 'moral economies' of victimhood (2007).

Empire, which prefers its traumas to be alive and kicking, can be discerned in northern Uganda through a refusal to recognize the landscape as post–conflict. This tactic is perhaps most blatantly evident in the humanitarian rhetoric of Invisible Children,[67] a US-based activist organization devoted to raising consciousness about the plight of children in northern Uganda. Despite the cessation of hostilities in the region, the organization continues to portray northern Uganda in perpetual crisis. To call attention to the 'night commuters,' the children who poured into the town by the hundreds each night seeking protection from the LRA, the IC staged one of its most notorious media stunts, the Global Night Commute, in 2006 – when hostilities in northern Uganda were nearing an end. Indeed night commuters became so scarce that most of the shelters established for the children closed that same year. Mass rallies for the night commuters have continued to be held even as late as 2009,[68] three years after the commuters had ceased to exist. Such rhetoric keeps what Fassin calls the 'suffering beings' intact and negates the ongoing local effort to sustain a hard-won semblance of stability.

The fetishization of abductee status also provides a glimpse of the empire at work. Repeatedly I have observed foreigners in northern Uganda fixated on 'finding' former child soldiers and other abductees to the extent that other Ugandan youths are relatively ignored. Lest I come across as holier-than-they, I should explain that I find this behaviour disturbing partly because I'm painfully aware of my own tendencies toward sensationalization. It is hard for me to re-read 'Marketing Trauma and the Theatre of War in Northern Uganda' because I can clearly discern my own fascination with the idea of child soldiers and other abductees. Granted that my research focused on a rehabilitation centre located in Gulu for former LRA abductees, in hindsight, however, why did I not also seek out the children and youth in Gulu town since they undoubtedly had much to contribute to my understandings of the conflict? The reason, of course, is my single-minded focus on the more glamorous, even 'sexy' figure of the child soldier.

Given that inaccuracies and half-truths proliferate in conflict and post-conflict zones, one might ask why I should pick on earnest and well-intentioned foreigners traveling to northern Uganda as manifestations of the empire of trauma. The short answer is that the inflation of statistics and the sensationalization of African post-conflict realities have material consequences for northern Ugandans. Both Chris Dolan (2009) and the Survey of War-Affected Youth (SWAY) project found that a humanitarian emphasis on abducted children often triggered resentment and stigmatization across the wider population. Although the SWAY researchers estimate about 66,000 youth have been abducted (some for a few days, others for more than two years), they emphasize that these abductees represent a minority of northern Ugandan children and youth. As a 2007 SWAY report argues, 'abduction status is a crude and unreliable predictor of need; large numbers [of] non-abducted youth exhibit serious educational, economic, social and heath challenges, while significant numbers of abductees perform quite well relative to their peers.'[69] They argue against singling out former abductees for extra resources when the vast majority of northern Ugandans has suffered extensive trauma, violence and material and emotional loss. The fetishization of abductee status undoubtedly contributes to this sense of resentment and/or the manufacturing of testimonies.

As a provisional postscript, my findings suggest that the machinery of marketing trauma remains largely intact in the post-conflict era. I have repeatedly observed that nuance and complexity are blithely swept aside in the search for spectacles and narratives of suffering. People *hunger* for the image of a suffering northern Uganda. It is the sustenance upon which the empire feeds. In light of the recent news that the Ugandan government has designated four LRA massacre sites as tourist destinations,[70] these issues are especially timely. The state is clearly eager to take advantage of empire's appetites, and I can only look forward to additional fieldwork to learn how northern Ugandans legitimate their cultural resilience and strength on their own terms.

References

A'ness, F., 'Resisting Amnesia: Yuyachkani, Performance, and the Postwar Reconstruction of Peru,' *Theatre Journal*, 56 (2004), pp. 395–414.

Appadurai, A., 'Grassroots Globalization and the Research Imagination,' *Public Culture*, 12: 1 (2000), pp. 1–19.

Barber, K., 'Views of the Field: Introduction,' in K. Barber (ed.), *Readings in African Popular Culture,* Bloomington: Indiana University Press, 1997.

——, *The Generation of Plays: Yoruba Popular Life in the Theater*, Bloomington, IN: Indiana University Press, 2000.

Bloch, E., *Heritage of Our Times*, trans. Plaice, N., and Plaice, S., Berkeley: University of California Press, 1990.

Carlson, M., 'Antigone's Bodies: Performing Torture,' *Modern Drama*, 46: 3 (Fall 2003).

Children As Peacemakers, 'Reconciliation,' pp. 128–131, http:www//childrenaspeacebuilders.ca/resources/pdf/youth/26.pdf (accessed 9 December 2004).

Dolan, Chris, *Social Torture: The Case of Northern Uganda, 1986–2000*, New York: Berghahn Books, 2009.

Doom, R., and Vlassenroot, K., 'Kony's Message: A New Koine? The Lord's Resistance Army in Northern Uganda,' *African Affairs*, 98: 390 (1999), pp. 5–36

Fassin, Didier, 'Humanitarianism as a Politics of Life,' *Public Culture* 19: 3 (2007), pp. 499–520.

——, 'Heart of Humaneness: The Moral Economy of Humanitarian Intervention,' in Fassin, Didier, and Pandolfi, Mariella, *Contemporary States of Emergency: The Politics of Military and Humanitarian Interventions*, New York: Zone Books, 2010, pp. 269–294.

Fassin, Didier, and Rechtman, Richard, *The Empire of Trauma: An Inquiry into the Condition of Victimhood*, trans. Rachel Gomme, Princeton: Princeton University Press, 2007.

Feldman, A., 'Violence and Vision: The Prosthetics and Aesthetics of Terror,' in Das, V., Kleinman, A., Ramphele, M., and Reynolds, P. (eds.), *Violence and Subjectivity*, Berkeley: University of California Press, 2000, p. 71.

———, 'Memory Theaters, Virtual Witnessing, and the Trauma-Aesthetic,' *Biography* 27: 1 (2004), pp. 163–202.

Felman, S., and Laub, D., *Testimony: Crises of Witnessing in Literature, Psychoanalysis, and History*, New York: Routledge, 1992.

Freeman, C., 'Is Local: Global as Feminine: Masculine? Rethinking the Gender of Globalization,' *Signs*, 26: 4 (Summer 2001), pp. 1007–1037.

Hardt, M., and Negri, A., *Empire*, Cambridge, MA: Harvard University Press, 2001.

Hinton, A. L., 'The Dark Side of Modernity: Toward an Anthropology of Genocide,' in A. L. Hinton (ed.) *Annihilating Difference: The Anthropology of Genocide*, Berkeley: University of California, 2002, p. 26.

Hoffman, D., 'The Civilian Target in Sierra Leone and Liberia: Political Power, Military Strategy, and Humanitarian Intervention,' *African Affairs* 103 (2004), pp. 211–226.

Human Rights Watch, *Scars of Death: Children Abducted by the Lord's Resistance Army in Uganda*, New York: Human Rights Watch, 1997, available online at http://www.hrw.org.reports97/uganda/.

Lenz, J., 'Resiliency,' *AUP Magazine* (Fall 2003), p. 6.

Mucunguzi, J., 'A Visit to Uganda's War Children is Humbling,' *The Monitor*, 28 October, www.lexis-nexis.com, 2004 (accessed 10 December 2004).

Mutibwa, P., *Uganda since Independence: A Story of Unfulfilled Hopes*, Trenton, NJ: Africa World Press, 1992.

Nordstorm, C., *A Different Kind of War Story*, Philadelphia: University of Pennsylvania Press, 1997.

Orford, A., *Reading Humanitarian Intervention: Human Rights and the Use of Force in International Law*, Cambridge: Cambridge University Press, 2003.

Patraka, V. M., *Spectacular Suffering: Theatre, Fascism, and the Holocaust*, Bloomington: Indiana University Press, 1999.

Piot, C., *Remotely Global: Village Modernity in West Africa*, Chicago: University of Chicago Press, 1999.

Robins, K., and Webster, F., *Times of the Technoculture*, London: Routledge, 1999.

Survey of War Affected Youth (SWAY), 'Making Reintegration Work for Children in Northern Uganda,' Research brief (2007), available at www.SWAY-Uganda.org.

Taussig, M., *Shamanism, Colonialism, and the Wild Man: A Study in Terror and Healing*, Chicago, University of Chicago Press, 1986.

Trouillot, M-R., *Global Transformations: Anthropology and the Modern World*, New York City: Palgrave Macmillan, 2003.

Weber, A., Rone, J., and Saunders, J., *Abducted and Abused: Renewed Conflict in Northern Uganda*, New York: Human Rights Watch, p. 17, http://www.hrw.org/reports/2003/uganda0703/uganda0703.pdf, 2003.

Notes

1   Gulu town is located in Gulu region in the north-central part of the country; unless otherwise specified, Gulu refers to the town only in this article. The Children of War Centre, originally called The Gulu Traumatised Child Project, opened in 1995, a time when the number of abductions dramatically increased. At the time of our visit, it provided shelter, medical treatment, and counselling to approximately 400 former captives of the LRA, a number that constantly shifted due to the steady stream of arrivals and departures. Stays at the centre varied from a few weeks to a few months, depending on the length of captivity and the level of difficulty in tracing the child's relatives. It should also be noted that the term 'children of war' encompasses infants and toddlers born in captivity to older teenagers on the brink of adulthood. Some of the child mothers, the term used to describe the abducted girls who are pressed into sexual service and made to bear children of their own, have been in captivity for so many years they can be classified as young women at the time of their escape and/or surrender. Young men were housed in the adult rehabilitation centre discussed below.

2   At least 20,000 children have been abducted since the early 1990s; approximately 8,400 of these abductions occurred in the year of June 2002–May 2003 alone. See Weber et al. (2003) for a discussion of these statistics.

3   These statements are a compilation of various observations I gathered during two months of research in Uganda conducted from mid-May through mid-July, 2004, particularly the three weeks I spent in Gulu from 23 June to 14 July. Due to the sensitivity of these topics, much of this information was gathered through informal conversations with the staff and the children at the Children of War Centre; at no time did I record my interviews. Instead, I kept detailed field notes throughout my stay. Although I did not engage an official translator, the staff and some of the children spoke English; moreover, I was often able to communicate through my husband, a native speaker of Luo, which is closely related to the Acholi language. It should also be noted that with one exception, I have purposefully omitted names of the World Vision staff and children. Whenever possible, I have supplemented my observations with published scholarship on the LRA war. Unfortunately, this scholarship is extremely scarce, although Heike Behrend provides a useful discussion of the Holy Spirit Movement led by Alice Lakwena in 1986, from which Joseph Kony's movement emerged, in H. Behrend, *Alice Lakwena and the Holy Spirits: War in Northern Uganda, 1986–1997*, trans. M. Cohen (Oxford: James Currey, 1999). The last chapter and the epilogue summarizes the formation of the Lord's Resistance Army and includes descriptions of the various spirits that possess Kony and provide him with magical powers. Doom and Vlassenroot (1999) use secondary sources and interview material to provide an excellent analysis of the multiple cultural, political and economic factors that both culminated in the LRA war and that continue to sustain it. Finally, Human Rights Watch has also published highly useful sources on the Lord's Resistance Army based on the testimony of formerly abducted children. See Human Rights Watch (1997) , and Weber et al. (2003).

4   Although this article focuses exclusively on the Acholi since my research took place in what is known as Acholi-land, it should be noted that other ethnic groups, most notably the Langi, are also victimized in this war.

5   Because of safety concerns, my research was limited in scope. I did not leave the town limits throughout my stay, which prevented me from conducting research into World Vision's relationship with the Acholi living in the IDP camps and its role in reconciliation ceremonies. I must defer questions concerning these relationships to future research for my book, tentatively titled *Ugandan Theatre and the Performance of War*.

6   See R. R. Atkinson, *The Roots of Ethnicity: The Origins of the Acholi of Uganda Before 1800* (Philadelphia: University of Pennsylvania Press, 1994), pp. 2–7, for a discussion of how this division between the north and south partly stems from British colonial policies that favoured the Bantu ethnic groups of the south, particularly the Baganda, in terms of development and education. The British saw the northern Nilotic ethnic groups, who bore the stigma of seeming less 'civilized' than the Bantu, as primarily useful for military recruitment. As a result, northerners dominated the army at the time of independence. This pattern set the stage for a wave of military dictators (Milton Obote, Idi Amin and Tito Lutwa Okello) from the north. See Mutibwa (1992), for an overview of Uganda's postcolonial history that follows the extraordinarily complicated narrative of these successive regimes, in which Amin overthrew Obote's government in 1971, only to be eventually replaced by Obote again in 1980. After a bloody guerrilla war between Yoweri Museveni and his National Resistance Movement against the second Obote regime from 1981 to 1985, after which Lutwa Okello ruled for about six months, Museveni finally came to power in 1986 where he remains to this day. I am excluding mention of the struggle between Obote and King Mutesa of the Baganda in the months following independence in 1962, as well as other temporary heads of state who came to power after Amin's defeat in 1979. My main point is that because Amin and Obote, who spearheaded particularly brutal campaigns of mass human rights violations, both hailed from the north, their background helps to shore up the notion held by southern Ugandans that 'there has always existed more backwardness and perhaps a more disorganized and evil society' in the northern regions (Mutibwa 1992: 4).

7   Kaldor first uses this term in her introduction in M. Kaldor and B. Vashee (eds.), *New Wars* (London: Pinter, 1997). She expands on her ideas, which emphasize the role of globalization in so-called local wars, as well as the blurring of lines between protracted violence and formally declared war, in *New and Old Wars: Organized Violence in a Global Era* (Cambridge, Polity, 1999).

8   Although the LRA is ostensibly fighting to overthrow Museveni's government, the UPDF is seldom directly attacked. Instead, the LRA prefers to attack Acholi homesteads and, now that most homesteads are deserted, the IDP camps. The logic behind these attacks is difficult to determine given the lack of research, but the testimony of former captives and commanders indicate that Kony, who himself comes from a small village in Gulu region, justifies these attacks on his own people as a method to purge them of wrongdoers and thus pave the way for the creation of a new Acholi people who will rule Uganda. See Human Rights Watch (1997).

9   Armies in Liberia, Sierra Leone, Angola and Mozambique have also relied upon these techniques; fortunately, however, these conflicts have come to at least a temporary end.

10 Nordstrom is keenly aware of the thoroughly global aspect of African civil wars (see, for example, 1997: 36–73), but she conceptualizes the ultimate aim of these methodologies of terror within a local framework.

11 Nordstrom borrows this phrase from Elaine Scarry's famous work, *The Body in Pain: The Making and Unmaking of the World* (New York: Oxford University Press, 1985). Whereas Scarry conceptualizes the 'unmaking' to play out within the immediate social world of the torture victim, Nordstrom expands the notion to include the witnesses as well: 'In Mozambique, it is not the victim that is hauled off to an isolated room, but the torture that is hauled into the centre of home and community' (1997: 169).

12 I heard rumours that this practice has also spread to Sudan, which seems feasible given the links between the Sudanese government and the LRA (see note 39).

13 See Doom and Vlassenroot (1999: 27), for a discussion of cultural meanings behind the LRA's mutilations of civilians.

14 For similar studies of how international aid politics helps to facilitate atrocity, see P. Uvin, *Aiding Violence: The Development Enterprise in Rwanda* (West Hartford, CT: Kumarian Press, 1998), and J. Gundel, 'Assisting Structures of Violence?: Humanitarian Assistance in the Somali Conflict,' in D. Jung (ed.), *Shadow Globalization, Ethnic Conflicts and New Wars: A Political Economy of Intra-state War* (London, Routledge, 2003), pp. 163–183.

15 Interestingly, the LRA did not even register on the West African soldiers' scale of violence, despite the length of the war and the extremities of their tactics.

16 Material goods serve as a prime target of the rebels, who regularly conduct raids upon IDP camps. In their article on the LRA, Doom and Vlassenroot imply in their conclusion that impoverishment is a primary motive of the rebels: 'For the majority of the rank and file, [rebellion] is a survival strategy, a way to obtain things which are out of reach by all normal means: consummatory rewards as ideological drive' (1999: 36).

17 According to World Vision's 2004 annual report, it commanded revenues of $807 million. Available on-line at http://www.worldvision.org.

18 Most recently, Jan Egeland, the United Nations Under Secretary General for Humanitarian Affairs, called northern Uganda to the world's attention in a speech to the Security Council on 10 May 2005, which was widely discussed in the African press.

19 The only non-Acholi I met among the counsellors and other staff members such as the cooks and medical personnel was a Langi counsellor.

20 See, for example, the 2004 World Vision report, *Pawns of Politics: Children, Conflict and Peace in Northern Uganda*, available at http://www.worldvision.org/worldvision/imagelib. nsf/main/pawns/$file/Pawns_Of_Politics.pdf.

21 I am not suggesting that arts therapy in the West occurs in the space of 'pure' creativity. The politics of funding for such activities would ensure that its practitioners in the West must also find similar kinds of evidence of their usefulness.

22 Although Liesbeth Speelman, a Dutch expatriate working for World Vision, had invited my husband, Robert Ajwang', and I to the centre for the purpose of organizing drama workshops for the children, our attempts to organize these workshops were repeatedly turned aside. We would be told, for example, that the children were too tired for dramatic activities, only to find those same children spontaneously performing a vigorous Acholi dance a few minutes later. Although multiple interpretations of this reluctance, indifference and/or resistance are possible, this response suggests that drama was considered an insignificant activity in the context of daily life of the centre.

23 Although I signified power and wealth to individual Acholi, my lack of *organizational* trappings of wealth such as a Pajero bearing the name of an international non-governmental organization meant that I did not represent the kind of international power with which World Vision is accustomed to dealing.

24 My narrow focus on the World Vision rehabilitation centre means that I am addressing only a micro-level – perhaps mini-level is the more appropriate term – of the layers of domination that the LRA war contains. By targeting the counsellors, who, like most Acholi, are also victims of the LRA war, I risk negating the extremely important work of the centre and the dedication of the staff. It would of course be more legitimate to aim my criticism at the macro-forces that sustain this war, such as the politics of the US 'war on terror,' which allows President Museveni to label the LRA rebels as terrorists and thus shore up his friendly relations with the Bush administration despite the Ugandan government's seeming disinterest in ending the war. Even researchers such as myself who are allowed free access to the children with a modicum of supervision should be implicated in the forces of domination in which these children are caught. Alternatively, as a European-American academic, a less problematic approach would be to focus only on the instances of agency, resistance and/or resilience that my research revealed. To return to Taussig's concept of epistemic murk, however, I think that my work bears witness to the extraordinary complexities of terror-warfare by attending to the ways in which anxiety and economic desperation play out even among its victims.

25 This festival occurred on 9 July 2004.

26 The exhibition took place on 11 July 2004. The complete title of the exhibit was *Armed with Resilience: A Photographic Dialogue with Girls Affected by the Conflict in Northern Uganda*, funded in part by Save the Children in Uganda, Quakers Peace and Social Witness. Children's rights activist Jessica Lenz was the project leader who raised the funding and organized the training of the photographers. This fascinating exhibit is discussed in more detail in the final section of this article.

27 The use of Acholi was, of course, a practical issue as well, since most of the actors spoke little English. That said, I found it significant that the counsellors seemed unconcerned with making sure that the foreigners in the audience understood the plays.

28 The sponsor of the children's rights festival was Gulu Save the Children Organisation (GUSCO), which operated the other major children's rehabilitation centre in Gulu. Given the friendly rivalry between the two organizations, it is also possible that the World Vision staff was using the play to playfully affirm its superiority in the context of the festival.

29 This statement is based on my observations of the rehearsals of the two plays, which took place on 8 and 10 July, respectively.

30 Anthropologists such as Taussig, Nordstrom and Allen Feldman, all of whom are united in their distaste for realism as a method for representing violence, have engaged in insightful theoretical discussions of anti-realisms as useful alternatives. Taussig, for example, invokes Brecht's *Verfremdunseffekt* as a method for 'transmitting and transforming the hallucinatory reality of Putumayo terror' (Taussig 1986: 133). On her part, Nordstrom is intrigued at the possibilities of Bakhtin's theory of the grotesque as a means of resisting terror-warfare (Nordstrom 1997: 171–172), and Allen Feldman discusses dada and surrealism as means of

critiquing 'the festishized integration of realist aesthetics into warfare and the structure of everyday life' (Feldman 2000: 71).

31 See also E. Diamond, *Unmaking Mimesis: Essays on Feminism and Theater* (New York: Taylor and Francis, 1997), chapter 1, p. 38, for a discussion of the potentiality of what she calls 'contaminated realism, a realism-without-truth,' and Carlson (2003), in which she complicates the 'pornographic' connotations of theatrical representations of torture and violence, suggesting that 'even with psychological realism, the actor is perceived alongside the character' and therefore creates the potential for 'self-aware complicity for the spectator' (Carlson 2003: 392).

32 For a basic summary of developments and trends in Ugandan theatre, see M. Banham, E. Hill, and G. Woodyard (eds.), *The Cambridge Guide to African and Caribbean Theatre* (Cambridge, Cambridge University Press, 1994), pp. 121–126. Much of the scholarship on Ugandan theatre focuses on theatre for development; see, for example, E. Breitinger, *Theatre for Development* (Bayreuth, Germany: University of Bayreuth, 1994) and M. Frank, *AIDS Education Through Theatre: Case Studies from Uganda* (Bayreuth, Germany: University of Bayreuth, 1995). Recently, Jessica Atwooki Kaahwa published a dissertation on the use of theatre to educate the populace about democratization and human rights ('Theater and Human Rights in Uganda,' University of Maryland, 2001). For an intriguing examination of the history of theatre companies in Kampala, see S. von Fremd, 'Political Power and Urban Popular Theatre in Uganda,' Ph.D. dissertation, Northwestern University, 1995. For more in-depth discussions of Ugandan dramatic literature, see M. M. Ntangaare and E. Breitinger, 'Ugandan Drama in English,' in E. Breitinger (ed.), *Uganda: The Cultural Landscape* (Bayreuth, Germany: University of Bayreuth, 1999), pp. 247–272; and R. Mbowa, 'Luganda Theatre and Its Audience,' in E. Breitinger (ed.), *Uganda: The Cultural Landscape*, pp. 227–246.

33 Here I differ slightly from Karin Barber's historical account of African realism. She attributes the development of Nigerian realism in the colonial era as part of a 'general representational shift which took place across Africa' (Barber 2000: 352), implying that the shift was more of an organic response than an imposed style. Although I agree with her point that scholars cannot assume that European modes of representation were simply 'transferred wholesale to the rest of the world' (Barber 2000: 358), the anxiety of post-independence playwrights to counteract this style indicates that the violence of the colonial encounter played a key role in the East African context.

34 See Barber (1997: 1–12), for a useful summary of the various theoretical trends in theorizing African popular culture and its transformational capacity. See also Barber (2000: 352–361), for a thoughtful analysis of the incarnation of realism in Nigerian popular theatre, which manipulates European versions of realism in order to emphasize reflections of moral agency. As a representative example of the expansive conception of realism in Ugandan theatre, on 13 June, I attended a Luganda play by the group Afri-Talent at Bat Valley Theatre in Kampala entitled *Gogolimbo/The Intrigue*. At first, the play, which depicted the various shenanigans that play out among staff and guests in a hotel lobby, progressed in what my Western perspective characterized as a classic fourth-wall realistic style, both in terms of production style and script. As the play continued, however, the actors began to lip-sync

popular songs that were played over the sound system, and some of the more comic actors slipped in the occasional aside to the audience.

35 In addition to the examples of dramatization that I discuss in this article, I have also researched *The Aboke Girls*, a play developed by a Dutch children's theatre company called Het Waterhuis about a famous abduction of 132 girls from one of the most elite schools in northern Uganda. This play is decidedly nonrealistic, composed of a series of monologues written in lyric poetry. After performing it in the Netherlands in 2001, the company toured it in Uganda in 2002. According to Dragan Klaic, '[A]fter holding workshops for professional and semi professional actors, Het Waterhuis has handed over the production to a Ugandan cast who will perform the play in a local language' (2003: 33). My research, however, indicated that the play was not performed again once the Dutch performers returned to Europe. See Klaic (2003) for a discussion of this play.

36 Since the mid-1990s, the Sudanese government has provided a refuge for the LRA in exchange for its assistance in fighting the Sudanese People's Liberation Army/Movement (SPLA/M); in fact, returning child soldiers have reported spending more time fighting the SPLA/M than the UPDF.

37 Although Hinton is specifically referring to the representation of refugees in mass media, this passage can be easily applied to the univeralism of Okello's character. It should also be noted that although Hallmark sponsored the film, the network chose not to air it because of the violence of the subject matter (e-mail communication with Robert Altman, 15 December 2004).

38 The Amakula film festival took place primarily in the National Theatre from 21 May through 30 May 2004. I was in attendance at this particular premiere.

39 The 1980s civil war helps to contextualize the apathy of the south toward the LRA war. Even though the Acholi suffered greatly under the regime of Idi Amin in the 1970s, the massacres of Baganda and other Bantu groups by an army dominated by Acholi soldiers during the guerrilla war between Obote's government and Museveni's forces in the early 1980s remain a vivid memory in Kampala. In a passage that resonates with this sense of bitterness, Mutibwa, himself a member of the Baganda, writes: 'Much has been written about the "tribalism" and "apartness" of the southern people, about a "north-south divide syndrome". This is an unfortunately development, but we cannot unmake history; crimes were committed by one group of Ugandans against other groups' (Mutibwa 1992: 157).

40 Several informal conversations and formal interviews with Sam during a visit with us in Tallahassee, Florida, in October 2004, revealed that his experiences of war epitomize the complexities of war, which the film, in which he himself played the role of the rebel commander, belied.

41 Even though the presence of Altman, a New York director, might indicate that this realistic style was more his choice than that of the Ugandan actors, Sam has informed me that Altman relied heavily on the actors' participation in the shaping of the script. In fact, the few nonrealistic elements in the film, such as the incorporation of a soundtrack that juxtaposed scenes of horror with compelling, haunting Ugandan music, were clearly added after the filming and can be more safely classified as a Western choice.

42 To help illustrate the multiple manifestations of realism in colonial and postcolonial eras, Feldman also provides a useful summary of scholarship in this area (2000: 59–60), citing words such as E. Apter, 'Ethnographic Travesties: Colonial Realism, French Feminism and the Case of Eliss Rhais,' in G. Prakash (ed.) *After Colonialism: Imperial Histories and Postcolonial Displacements* (Princeton, Princeton University Press, 1995); T. Eagleton, *Heathcliff and the Great Hunger: Studies in Irish Culture* (London: Verso, 1995); A. Appadurai, *Modernity at Large: Cultural Dimensions of Globalization* (Minneapolis: University of Minnesota Press, 1996); J. Tagg, *The Burden of Representation: Essays on Photographies and Histories* (Amherst: University of Massachusetts Press, 1988), and A. Rabinbach, *The Human Motor: Energy, Fatigue, and the Origins of Modernity* (New York: Basic Books, 1990).

43 See Liisa Malkki, *Purity and Exile: Violence, Memory, and National Cosmology Among Hutu Refugees in Tanzania* (Chicago: University of Chicago Press, 1995), p. 11, for a discussion of dominant images used in humanitarian refugee discourse.

44 I am rephrasing Michel de Certeau here. The original quote is related to a more general discussion of historical work, which is 'organized as it is by the will to make all things thinkable.' See *The Writing of History*, trans. T. Conley (New York: Columbia University Press, 1988), p. 44.

45 Children as Peacebuilders, *Reconciliation* (accessed 9 December 2004), http://www. childrenaspeacebuilders.ca/resources/pdf/youth/26.pdf, pp. 128-131, 2004. The description of the 2002 project is based on this report.

46 Please note that I am still tracking down the complete names of these two performing artists.

47 Personal conversation with author, 7 July 2004.

48 I viewed a videotape of the performance that was filmed during its premiere on 29 May 2003 in Gulu.

49 Surprisingly, the children kept the play in their repertory and continued to perform it for at least a year following the workshop, which suggests that they shed some of their anxiety over this method of staging. The videotape of their premiere performance depicted a highly enthusiastic crowd, which might have lessened some of their concerns.

50 Although they yielded in the end, this compliance should be contextualized in their low-ranking position within a hierarchy of national and international organizations. Children as Peacebuilders is linked to a Canadian-based NGO that is sponsored by the Defense of Children International and funded by the Canadian International Development Agency. See the Children As Peacebuilders web page at http://www.childrenaspeacebuilders.ca/home.htm (accessed 9 December 2004).

51 This workshop took place on 1 and 2 July 2004.

52 An example of alternative interpretations includes that of authorial integrity; that is, the counsellor might have been reacting as a playwright to my rearrangement of her script. Although this explanation is certainly feasible, a strict adherence to notions of authorial integrity would be at odds with the majority of my experiences in East African theatre, where scripts tend to be treated as expressions of a collective voice. Another interpretation is that, as a devout Christian, the counsellor was uneasy with the rearrangement of the biblical version. She herself, however, had freely updated the parable by setting it in northern Uganda, which indicates that she was not beholden to strict, literal translations.

53 Tanzania and Uganda both serve as representative examples of former British colonies that sought to transform the colonialist style of theatre into one that reflected indigenous modes of performance. In addition to the sources listed in note 18, see Penina Mlama, *Culture and Development in Africa: The Popular Theatre Approach* (Sweden: Nordiska Afrikainstitutet, 1991), for a discussion of these issues in a Tanzanian context.

54 Caption on untitled photograph, *Armed with Resilience*.

55 This combination of debate and dancing occurred on 5 July 2004.

56 This visit occurred on 24 June 2004.

57 Human Rights Watch, *Scars of Death*.

58 See F. K. Girling, *The Acholi of Uganda*, Colonial Research Studies No. 30 (London: Her Majesty's Stationery Office, 1960), pp. 68–69, for a description of *larakaraka* in the late colonial era.

59 Following capture and/or surrender, former captives and their abductors have formalized their relationship through legal marriage, particularly in cases when children have been produced. One could easily argue that the former female captives have little choice given the social approbation they will face at home upon their release; however, to insist upon this perspective negates both the ambiguities of the situation and the agency of the former captives.

60 One might argue that the girls are serving as a spectacle for the men, who are watching rather than participating. In this particular performance, however, two of the men joined the drumming and displayed their skill. Their obvious delight in taking part disrupted what a Westerner might interpret as a conventional commodification of the female body.

61 This event occurred on 7 July 2004.

62 This incident occurred on 25 June 2004.

63 See Mareike Schomerus, Tim Allen and Koen Vlassenroot's article, 'Obama Takes on the LRA,' *Foreign Affairs*, 15 November 2011, for a detailed analysis of US President Barack Obama's announcement in October 2011 that he would be sending troops to Uganda to help track down Joseph Kony. In the article, they explain that '[a]t present, the LRA operates in an area as big as France, stretching from southern Darfur to parts of South Sudan and northern Congo.' They go on to specify, though, that '[g]reater numbers of surveillance flights over LRA-afflicted areas are said to have pinpointed Kony's position in the Central African Republic.' The article is available at www.foreignaffairs.com (accessed 12 December 2011).

64 A provisional definition of Empire is that of a 'new global form of sovereignty' composed of diffuse national and supranational institutions; Hardt and Negri add that '[i]t is a *decentered* and *deterritorializing* apparatus of rule that progressively incorporates the entire global realm within its open, expanding frontiers' (Hardt and Negri 2000: xii). Although NGOs and humanitarian organizations such as Amnesty International and Human Rights Watch merit only a brief discussion in this influential work, Hardt and Negri do not mince words regarding their level of influence: 'These NGOs extend far and wide in the humus of biopower; they are the capillary ends of the contemporary networks of power' (Hardt and Negri 2000: 313). In his article, 'Heart of Humaneness: The Moral Economy of Humanitarian Intervention,' Fassin's concept of 'humanitarian government' often intersects with Hardt and Negri's notions of empire although he stops short of citing or referring their work. For

example, he argues that humanitarianism is a pillar of modern governance (Fassin 2010: 272), and that humanitarianism has permeated the political sphere to the point that 'one could say that humanitarianism is nothing but the continuation of politics by other means' (Fassin 2010: 274).

65 As Allen Feldman explains in his critique of what he calls the 'trauma-aesthetic', in which testimony plays a key role: 'The testimony has a doubled density and gravitas due to its historiographic vocation and artefactual status; it is a window of historical visualization and also a historical object, midwifed from materialities of pain and suffering' (Feldman 2004, 164).

66 See Charles Piot's 2010, *Nostalgia for the Future: West Africa after the Cold War* (Chicago: The University of Chicago Press), for a spirited account about why 'postcolonial' no longer serves as a meaningful framework in a post-Cold War era given the continued effacement of the African state.

67 Invisible Children was conceived when three Californian university students 'went to Africa in search of a story' in 2003 and stumbled upon the plight of children of northern Uganda. IC's documentary film *Invisible Children: The Rough Cut* was the cornerstone of a massive awareness-raising campaign aimed primarily at US high school and college students.

68 An amusing example of one of these rallies (held at the University of Texas at Austin in April 2009) can be seen at this link: http://link.brightcove.com/services/player/bcpid1418565568?bctid=21094344001.

69 'Making Reintegration Work for Children in Northern Uganda', Research brief by the Survey of War Affected Youth, available at www.SWAY-Uganda.org.

70 See 'Government Gazettes Four IDP Camps for Tourism', *The Daily Monitor*, 21 June 2011, available at http://www.monitor.co.ug/News/National/-/688334/1186226/-/c08nmxz/-/index.html. Three of the IDP camps were the scenes of massacres; the fourth was the scene of one of the most famous LRA abductions, in which 150 girls (called the Aboke girls) were abducted from one of Uganda's most prestigious secondary schools. In a frank choice of words, Tourism State Minister Agnes Akiror called the package 'dark tourism'.

Chapter 7

Encounters in the Aida Refugee Camp in Palestine: Travel Notes on Attending Alrowwad Theatre's Production of *Handala* (2011)

Rand T. Hazou

Encountering my return

It has been about seven years since I was last in Palestine. The last time I was here I was recruited by the United Nations Development Program (UNDP) to run theatre workshops for the youth as part of The Hakwati Summer Camp. The camp was held in the northern town of Jenin and involved some one hundred youths from across Palestine participating in various artistic activities. Seven years is a long time. I am back in the country as part of a project supported by the Australia Council for the Arts through the Cultural Leadership Development Grant to develop theatre initiatives between Palestine and Australia. I am here to learn about current approaches to Palestinian theatre practice and to meet with Palestinian theatre makers and cultural producers. I am a bit anxious about how I will be received. My father is a Palestinian refugee who was born in Jerusalem. My grandfather began work at thirteen, transporting passengers in a horse-drawn cart the relatively short distance of nine kilometres along the old road between Jerusalem and Bethlehem. These days the Israeli occupation and the separation wall cut Bethlehem and the majority of the West Bank off from Jerusalem and Israel. I took a local 'Arab' bus from the East Jerusalem depot along a circuitous route through Wadi Al-Nar and via the village of Beit Jala. A trip stretched out to over an hour and a half as the bus wended its way through the eastern Judean hills, past Israeli military checkpoints, to finally arrive in Bethlehem. Although my grandfather in his youth traversed the road between Bethlehem and Jerusalem on a daily basis, and although my father spent much of his early school years living and studying in Bethlehem, the Israeli occupation, the checkpoints and the separation wall only served to instil a deep resentment and anger in me. This should feel like a homecoming. Instead I felt like I have been issued a visitor's pass for a temporary inspection of a large prison.

My simmering frustration was temporarily assuaged when a cousin of my father's picked me up in her car from the main Manger Square in Bethlehem. My 'Aunty'[1] was overjoyed to see me, asking questions about my father and enquiring after the health of various members of my extended family. My Aunty kindly offered to drive me to the Aida refugee camp. The Aida refugee camp was established in 1950 on land leased by the United Nations Relief and Works Agency (UNRWA) from the government of Jordan. The camp houses Palestinian refugees originating from seventeen different villages in the western Jerusalem and western Hebron areas. Today the camp houses over 4,700 registered refugees who are squeezed into an area of 0.71 square kilometres. Severe overcrowding, lack of infrastructure and utilities such as water and sewage and an unemployment rate of 43 per cent are some of the major problems faced by the camp inhabitants (UNRWA 2010).

My Aunty drove past the Jacir Palace, built in 1910 by a former mayor of Bethlehem and wealthy merchant, Suleiman Jacir, which was later transformed into a school in the 1950s. 'This was your father's school,' my Aunty said, pointing it out as we drove past the building that has been restored and is now the five-star Intercontinental Hotel. We took a side road past the beautifully restored stone architecture of Jacir Palace, and after asking directions from a bystander, proceeded into the Aida refugee camp where we were forced to navigate a maze of rough roads hemmed-in by cramped buildings made of cement and concrete-blocks. It was easy to get lost in there. Even for the inhabitants of the camp who know its labyrinthine roads by heart, the risk of being lost must take on a more daunting significance given the isolation and restrictions of the ongoing occupation and the need to contend with the lack of educational and employment opportunities.

Despite my Aunty's determination to get me to my intended destination I sensed a bit of trepidation. She asked me if I will be staying in the camp past nightfall and was worried about whether it would be safe and how I would get back. I noted her concern but assured her that I would be fine. I had been in contact with Dr. Abdelfattah Abusrour, founder and General Director of the Alrowwad Cultural and Theatre Training Society (ACTS). I had been invited to attend the new production that ACTS was presenting called *Handala*. The play assembles onstage a cast of characters inspired by the cartoons of Palestinian artist Naji Al-Ali. It traces the background of each of the characters, explores their significance in relation to the life of the artist and creator and provides commentary on the history of the Palestinian struggle. The production had recently returned from a four-week tour of France and Luxembourg and would be performed in the camp for residents and visitors.

Alrowwad, which means 'the pioneers' in Arabic, was established in 1998 and focuses on work with the children and women of the camp. Through theatre and artistic practice the company works to develop human capacity, enhance self-confidence and facilitate self-expression as a means to redress stereotypes of Palestinians.[2] ACTS is one of a series of youth centres and women's unions emerging out of refugee camps in Palestine operating at a community level. As important features of Palestinian civil society, these groups represent a grassroots and politicized network supporting the national liberation struggle and inalienable Palestinian rights (Wiles 2009: 21). Activities that ACTS provide include theatre and dance programmes for children, training programmes for adult theatre workers, employment projects for women, tutoring programmes for children, scholarship programmes supporting further education, language classes in English and French, video filming and editing workshops, photography, painting and music workshops and computer training. As a community-based and not-for-profit organization, these activities are supported through local and international donations and volunteers (Thompson et al. 2009: 57).

Encountering the wall

Conceding that we were lost, my Aunty called ACTS to ask for directions. We were told to find the separation wall that borders the camp and to follow the adjacent road. Regrettably, the separation wall was an easy landmark to find given the intimidating 8-meter-high concrete structure. The Israeli authorities justified construction of the 'security wall', which is connected by a system of observation towers, as a security measure to prevent would-be suicide bombers from entering Israel. However, the wall penetrates deep into areas beyond the borders of the 'Green Line',[3] annexing Palestinian land, denying Palestinian farmers access to fruit orchards and olive groves and severely restricting the rights of movement of local Palestinians. In 2004, Special Rapporteur to the UN Commission on Human Rights, Professor John Dugard, reported that the construction of the massive separation wall

[v]iolates the prohibition on the acquisition of territory by forcible means, and seriously undermines the right to self-determination of the Palestinian people by reducing the size of a future Palestinian State. Moreover, it violates important norms of international humanitarian law prohibiting the annexation of occupied territory, the establishment of settlements, the confiscation of private land and the forcible transfer of people. Human rights norms are likewise violated, particularly those affirming freedom of movement, the right to family life and the right to education and health care.

(UNHCR 2006)

On 4 July 2004, the separation wall and the ongoing Israeli settlements built on occupied Palestinian land were condemned as illegal by the International Court of Justice (ICJ) (Abu-Laban and Bakan 2009: 40). Yet despite international condemnation, the wall remains as an imposing barrier that has encroached into the already confined area of the Aida camp. According to Abusrour, General Director of Alrowwad, the wall adjoining the Aida camp was completed in 2005, and was erected 20 to 30 meters away from the UN run primary school. As a result, 'the camp is now isolated from the bit of green space where the children used to play' (Musleh 2011: 106).

As we followed the small road that ran adjacent to the separation wall, I noted the various murals, pictures and slogans scrawled in graffiti across the cement, turning the imposing barrier into a large canvas inscribed with messages of hope, support and defiance. Graffiti writing as a political act has a long history within the Palestinian-Israeli conflict, used in the 1980s and 1990s by Palestinians in the West Bank as part of the Intifada or general uprising, and understood as a popular form of political discourse (Hanauer 2011; Peteet 1996). As we drove past, I recognized the iconic image of Handala[4] that graced the cement façade: the famous cartoon created by cartoonist Naji Al-Ali of a Palestinian refugee child who stands with his hands clasped behind his back.

Figure 1: The iconic cartoon character of Handala by Naji Al-Ali. Reproduced with the kind permission of the Naji Al-Ali family.

Encountering Naji Al-Ali

Most probably born in 1937 in the village of Al-Shajara in the Galilee, Al-Ali was part of the Palestinian exodus of 1948 (Khalili 2005: 38). Forced to flee Palestine with his family at the age of ten, he settled with his family in Ain al-Hilweh refugee camp in southern Lebanon (Najjar 2007: 257). The Palestinian writer Ghassan Kanafani came across Al Ali's drawings on the walls of the refugee camp during a visit to Ain Al-Hilweh and published them in the *Al-Huriyya* newspaper that Kanafani edited at the time (Hamdi 2011: 25). Al-Ali's work gained popularity and notoriety for its uncompromising political commentary. He took up posts at several publications, contributing to *Al-Safir* and *Al-Taliah* in Kuwait, and *Al-Khalij* newspaper in the United Arab Emirates. In 1982, in the midst of the Israeli invasion of Lebanon, he witnessed the massacres of Palestinian refugees in the Sabra and Shatila refugee camps (Gandolfo 2010: 59). He eventually left Lebanon in 1983 for Kuwait, before being expelled and finally settling in London. Throughout his career, his work was routinely censored and he received numerous death threats. According to Gondolfo, 'Al-Ali's cartoons depicting Handala garnered him both notoriety as the highest-paid cartoonist in the Arab world – his cartoons graced publications from Abu Dhabi and Cairo to Paris and London – and as the most wanted man in the Middle East' (Gandolfo 2010: 60). On 22 July 1987, a lone gunman shot Al-Ali as he walked to the offices of *Al-Qabas International* newspaper in London. After five weeks in a coma, he died on 30 August, aged 51 (Gandolfo 2010: 60). Although questions about the identity of his assassin remain, Khalili suggests that both the Mossad (Israeli secret service) and Yasir Arafat's Force 17 have been linked to Al-Ali's assassination. Arafat's potential entanglement was attributed to his frustration with Ali's acerbic lampooning of him, while Mossad's involvement could have been a continuation of their entrenched policy of assassinating Palestinian political leaders, activists and intellectuals in Europe (Khalili 2005: 38).

Familiarity with Al-Ali's biographical details reveals the close affinity between Al-Ali and his artistic creation. As Hamdi notes, 'Handala is eternally ten years old in all of Al-Ali's cartoons, the same age Al Ali was when the 1948 Nakba, or catastrophe, befell the Palestinian people' (Hamdi 2011: 26). The significance of the Nakba will be explored in greater detail, yet it may be sufficient here to summarize its significance by citing Edward Said who observes, '[F]or Palestinians 1948 is remembered as the year of the Nakba, or catastrophe, when 750,000 of us who were living there – two thirds of the population – were driven out, our property taken, hundreds of villages destroyed, an entire society obliterated' (Said 2000: 185). As we drove past I stared at the powerful image of Handala painted on the separation wall. The titular character of the play I have been invited by ACTS to attend, Handala is most commonly depicted as a small barefoot child in tattered clothing with his hair standing on end and with his back always to the observer. The figure of Handala has become an international symbol of the Palestinian resistance and defiance (Hamdi 2011: 25). In souvenir shops throughout the West Bank, T-shirts of Handala compete with the images of Yasser Arafat, Hamas leaders and Che Guevara. On the Internet, you can also find key chains, T-shirts, posters and other paraphernalia featuring the iconic character (Najjar 2007: 259). Handala has also been appropriated as a mascot by the Marxist and an anti-Arafat faction, the Popular Front for the Liberation of Palestine (PFLP) (Khalili 2005: 39). A child witness of the refugee camps, Handala gets his name from an Arabic word for a bitter plant called *al-handal*[5] to represent the 'bitterness of the Palestinian experience' (Hamdi 2011: 26). Depicted with his back facing the observer, Handala turns his face from the onlooker's view 'in defiance of the international, historical forces opposing Palestinian liberation and of Arab complicity, lethargy and impotence' (ibid.).

Encountering Alrowwad

We finally arrived at a junction in the road and I noticed a sign identifying a three-storey building as the ACTS centre, which houses administration offices, training rooms, and a small hall on the ground floor used for performances and functions. A young man was standing outside, and after my Aunty received assurances that I would be given a lift after the evening's performance, I was led up the stairs to the second floor to the office of the General Director. Abusrour is a stocky man with kind eyes who welcomed me with a cup of strong black Arabic coffee. We sat and talked as his young daughter played a computer game at his desk. Abusrour was born in Aida camp and managed to secure a scholarship to pursue university studies abroad, eventually earning a doctorate in biological and medical engineering at Paris-Nord University in Paris. While he was studying science, he co-founded the Paris Nord Theatre Association where he pursued his love for writing, directing and acting, by producing several theatre productions. Upon returning to Palestine, he founded Alrowwad with a group of friends in 1998 in two rooms of his parent's house. Abusrour explains:

> When I finished my studies I came back from France after nine years thinking that Palestine was only waiting for me to save it. After working to earn my living in biology I thought I can do better with theatre than biology. So I quit my paying job in Biology.
>
> (Abusrour 2011b)[6]

From 2005 to 2007, Abusrour spent two years raising money to build permanent premises to house Alrowwad. He was eventually awarded the prestigious Ashoka Fellowship for social entrepreneurship, and after securing enough funds was finally able to pay himself an income as a general director and be officially 'employed' by Alrowwad in 2010. Abusrour's decision to pursue the financially precarious path of facilitating theatre instead of a relatively stable career in science is a tribute to the important emphasis he places on the transformative power of theatre to facilitate long-lasting social and cultural change. Sipping coffee in his office, Abusrour explained:

> I guess for me theatre is the most amazing, powerful, civilised, and non-violent means of self-expression – a way to build the peace within before talking about the peace with the others. Because its a way to tell your story – your version of your story and history without compromises, without trying to please others and tell them what they want to hear, but really what we want to say.
>
> (Abusrour 2011b)

Alrowwad is the first centre in the Aida camp to provide theatre training as a way of helping people tackle problems facing the community (Musleh 2011: 106). The members of Alrowwad's theatre group attend workshops weekly. In the summer months they spend up to four or five days a week in preparation for performances including international tours. The Alrowwad theatre group has performed in different European countries, as well as in Egypt and the United States. In 2007 they staged fifteen performances in refugee camps and cities across the occupied West Bank (Wiles 2009: 26). *The Children of the Camp* is probably their best-known production and has been performed in Sweden, Denmark, Egypt, France, Belgium and the United States (Abusrour 2006: 20). The play examined the complexities and struggles encountered by children growing up in the refugee camp and appeals to the international community to put an end to the daily suffering, and to compel Israel to comply with international law and UN resolutions on the right to return to their homes and villages in Palestine (for more information on the production, refer to Beadle 2006; Nassar 2006; Wiles 2009: 26; Thompson et al. 2009: 59–65).

As Abeer Musleh notes, it is important to emphasize that Alrowwad is 'not just a theatre organization; it is also a place that responds to various community needs' (Musleh 2011:

106). Alrowwad has always followed the approach that theatre activities can and should be integrated with the provision of urgently needed services. During Israeli invasions and curfews, the centre has served as a temporary health clinic. It has also provided much-needed educational opportunities for children with learning disabilities and for women in the camp. As Musleh explains:

> Alrowwad does not see these efforts as a diversion from the centre's main objective and neither does the community; on the contrary, this kind of integrated approach is seen as the best way to make a difference. Responding to people's immediate needs is not only a way of staying accountable to the community [...] but also a way of providing people with a sense of safety and support that is needed during difficult times.
>
> (Musleh 2011: 106)

Underpinning all the work that Alrowwad facilitates is a strategy of 'beautiful resistance' that informs all the various theatre, educational and creative activities that ACTS provide. According to Abusrour:

> Art, theatre, and education are some of the most amazing tools to reach and influence people. They are also very powerful vehicles of self-expression for children and adults. Starting from this concept, Alrowwad began its beautiful resistance against the ugly Israeli occupation and its devastating effects on the Palestinian population, especially its children. Art provided a 'safe' medium of expression and a beautiful alternative to the images continuously disseminated by the media about Palestinians.
>
> (Abusrour 2006: 19–20)

As Thompson, Hughes, and Balfour note, the concept of beautiful resistance 'teaches children that their daily experience of checkpoints, soldiers, incursions, explosions, as well as the generally overcrowded conditions are not normal or just,' and provides 'an opportunity to imagine and work towards the development of a different reality' (Thompson et al. 2009: 57). The strategy of beautiful resistance aims to empower youths by providing a safe environment that fosters their artistic imaginations, self-confidence and self-expression. As Musleh explains, '[T]hrough the creation and performance of plays, Alrowwad's students develop self-esteem, maturity, acceptance of others, dialogue skills, and the ability to work as part of a team' (Musleh 2011: 106).

In preparation for my visit, I have read about Alrowwad's strategy of beautiful resistance. An important aspect of Abusrour's concept of beautiful resistance that is absent from existing literature about Alrowwad is an uncompromising stance on refusing to 'normalize' relations with Israel. In an interview, Abusrour explained:

> My main interest [...] is not to make peace with Israelis for the moment. My focus is to build the peace within us, before being able to build it with anybody else. Because if

you don't have peace within you, how can you build peace with anybody else? And that's why I say I will not work with Israelis. [...] Israel still continues preventing people from circulating, continues building illegal colonies, continues extending this illegal wall of separation, continues violations of human rights, an apartheid system. How can anybody normalise with such an occupation?

(Abusrour 2011b)

Like other youth and women's centres emerging in refugee camps throughout the West Bank, ACTS follows principles entrenched in Palestinian society in defence of inalienable human rights, including refusing 'normalization' with Israeli organizations and funding or support from USAID (Wiles 2009: 29). Although anti-normalization with Israel has a long history, in recent years the strategy has become part of an international solidarity movement of Boycott, Divestment and Sanctions (BDS) against Israel. The BDS campaign began as an academic and cultural boycott following the decision of the International Court of Justice (ICJ) to condemn as illegal Israel's separation wall (Abu-Laban and Bakan 2009: 40). Coinciding with the ICJ ruling, the Palestinian Campaign for the Academic and Cultural Boycott of Israel (PACBI) issued a call urging the international community to boycott all Israeli academic and cultural institutions as a 'contribution to the struggle to end Israel's occupation, colonization and system of apartheid' (Barghouti 2011: 55–56).[7] A year later more than 170 Palestinian civil society organizations and unions, including the main political parties, issued the Call for BDS against Israel until it fully complied with international law (Barghouti 2011: 56). Inspired by the anti-apartheid struggle in South Africa, BDS adopts a rights-based and non-violent approach to pressure the Israeli state to comply with international law and respect the rights of Palestinians by ending its occupation and colonization of all Arab lands (occupied in 1967) and dismantling the separation wall; recognizing the fundamental rights of the Arab-Palestinian citizens of Israel to full equality; and respecting, protecting and promoting the rights of Palestinian refugees to return to their homes and properties, as stipulated in UN Resolution 194.[8]

As Abusrour launched into a well-rehearsed explanation of Alrowwad's approach to beautiful resistance, I sensed that this was an address he had been forced to give on numerous occasions to various delegations and potential partners. His commitment to Alrowwad's vision and uncompromising approach is a position that creates difficulties in securing funding:

I am not affiliated with any political party and Alrowwad's policy is also independent. Even if this means you will have no money from anyone here if you are independent. The important thing for me is to work with everybody but not under the umbrella or dictation of anybody. So that is why we do not change our programs to adapt to every funding that comes in or the dictation of donors. There are projects that I do not believe in so I will not be part of them. For example, the Ministry of Health asked us to do a play about Aids.

There are sixty declared cases of Aids in the whole of Palestine. Is this a priority for the country? Our priority would be teeth problems, for example, in children.

(Abusrour 2011b)

Perhaps due to the proximity of Aida to Bethlehem and the various religious charities that visit the camp, Abusrour also explained that the concept of beautiful resistance that drives Alrowwad ensures that ACTS is selective in the limited funding opportunities that arise. Abusrour explained that the concept of beautiful resistance was conceptualized after he perceived a shift in the way the Palestinian cause was being situated and transformed from a political cause into a humanitarian one:

We are not a humanitarian cause. People are not poor because they are lazy or because we don't have resources. We are put in poverty by an illegal occupation that prevents us from circulating freely, working, cultivating our land, importing, exporting, travelling, and so on. And so it is a political cause and not a humanitarian cause. We do not need charity or pity. This is more humiliating than the occupation itself.

(Abusrour 2011b)

Underlying the concept of beautiful resistance and Abusrour's opposition to humanitarian designations of the Palestinian struggle is an acknowledgement of how humanitarian regimes often work to depoliticize and dehistoricize refugee experience. As Malkki notes, the visual conventions for representing refugees and the language of raw human needs that accompany modes of humanitarianism act 'to trivialise and silence history and politics – a silencing that can legitimately be described as dehumanizing in most contexts' (Malkki 1996: 390).

While I sat in his office I began to appreciate that there was a deeper significance to Alrowwad's beautiful resistance, one that I was hoping to discern in the evening's performance. We descended the stairs to the small community hall where the performance would be staged. I left Abusrour to prepare for the performance and moved to stand outside near the entrance and chat with some of the smartly dressed youths who had volunteered as front-of-house staff for the evening. They chatted amiably, asking questions about where I was from, and displaying a genuine interest in my background. Despite my family connections to this place, I grew up in Jordan along with the feelings of dislocation that exile ultimately entails. Having a Kiwi mother and preferring to speak in English, which is my 'mother-tongue' after all, have served to compound even further the feelings of being 'out-of-place' that nearly all Palestinians living in the diaspora contend with. My background as a theatre academic also means I am a bit anxious about being perceived as a 'researcher' given the sensitivities surrounding cultural appropriation that necessarily emerge in a region experiencing the ongoing effects of occupation and Zionist-colonialism. My feelings of anxiety and of being an outsider were alleviated by the curiosity and amiability of the friendly young people around me. As we stood in the encroaching twilight, chatting and watching the younger children of the camp race up and down the narrow streets on foot and on bicycles, I recalled my Aunty's fears about my safety in the camp which seemed all the more unwarranted. Despite all the hardships that people here endure, there was a quiet confidence emanating from the group, a dignity in the faces of the youths, a sense of welcome, hospitality and generosity that I read as testament to the social and cultural work that Alrowwad is aiming to achieve and strengthen through its endeavours. I was comfortable, at ease, and privileged to be present. In the faces of the youths around me I sensed the embodiment of beautiful resistance.

Encountering re-presentations of refugee identity

Long after the performance was supposed to begin, and cued as if by some invisible consensus, the small group of audience members drifted inside the hall and took their seats. The lights dimmed to black as the play began. Naji Al-Ali (Abdelfattah Abusrour) enters and stands with his back facing the audience looking at a backdrop made of newspapers that frame the playing area. The stage is plunged into darkness. When the lights come back up, we see the child Handala (Kan'an Abusrour) standing with his hands clasped behind his back in the spot recently vacated by Naji. Darkness. When the lights return a second later, Naji stands adopting Handala's familiar stance, only to turn with a final meaningful glance at the wall of newspapers to directly addresses the audience and provide some background to the artist's life. In poetic language rich with symbolism, Naji exclaims:

> I was ten years old when the war broke out. I was forced to leave barefooted out of my village al-Shajarah. A storm erupted in my heart. The walls of our homes were destroyed and the aroma of the homeland evaporated like a summer cloud. It was replaced by the fog of exile and the camp fences. I lived the exile of hard bread and I translated my pain and longing into drawings on the sides of the tent sheltering us.
>
> (Abusrour 2011a)

The staging of the prologue eloquently enacts the creation of Handala, the character created by the artist, as a response to a wall of newspapers symbolizing a shroud of media propaganda against which Naji the artist is reacting. Similarly, countering negative stereotypes of Palestinians in the media is one of the essential aims underscoring the strategy of 'beautiful resistance' that Alrowwad espouses through its theatre work. Abusrour explains, 'Theatre is one of the most amazing tools of self-expression; it is a way to build bridges that can help people to understand the real stories behind the *mass media*. We express our rights through our work and the plays express a political message' (Wiles 2009: 26, emphasis added).

In an interview, Abusrour described a particular moment that concretized not only his ideas about 'beautiful resistance' and its role in countering media propaganda but also informed his decision to adapt Al-Ali's works and writings into a play. When he arrived in France to pursue his studies, he was forced to apply for his French residency card with an Israeli travel document that listed his nationality as 'Jordanian refugee under Israeli mandate.' Abusrour protested, arguing that 'I am not a Jordanian refugee who fled the dictatorship of Jordan to be in the beautiful democracy of Israel. I am a Palestinian refugee under Israeli occupation.' Eventually the French authorities acquiesced but changed his status to the equally unsatisfactory 'Nationality undetermined' (Abusrour 2011b).

Abusrour's experience demonstrates not only the denial of his Palestinian identity but also the construction of Palestinian refugee status through difference, ascriptions and labels. Rashid Khalidi elucidates this aspect of Palestinian identity:

> The quintessential Palestinian experience, which illustrates some of the most basic issues raised by Palestinian identity, takes place at a border, an airport, a checkpoint: in short, at any of those many modern barriers where identities are checked and verified. What happens to Palestinians at those crossing points brings home to them how much they share in common as people. For it is at these borders and barriers that the six million Palestinians are singled out for 'special treatment', and are forcefully reminded of their identity: of who they are, and why they are different than others. [...] As a result, at each of these barriers which most others take for granted, every Palestinian is exposed to the possibility of harassment, exclusion and sometimes worse simply because of his or her identity.
>
> (Khalidi 1997: 1)

As Kawash explains, borders are problematic sites for Palestinians because 'it is the function of such borders to put identity on trial' and it is at the non-place of the border that the negation of the Palestinian and their 'non-existence' comes most starkly into relief (Kawash 2003: 46). In his cartoons, Al-Ali explored the absence of travel documents common to the Palestinian experience and the negation of identity that ensues, by parodying the passport and replacing the 'official' text common in such documents with dark humorous commentary on the stark reality of Palestinian refugee 'travel' experiences, encouraging readers to recognize the absence of travel documents as a source of oppression and discrimination for refugees (for an example and an analysis of such a cartoon, see Najjar 2007: 267).

In the play, Abusrour enacts the very process where Palestinian identity is put on trial. In the next scene, Naji is being interrogated by an authority figure in military uniform. The guard Dahdool (Bassam Hasaneya) is a composite of various Al-Ali caricatures that Abdelfattah introduced into the play to symbolize various figures of authority, from the complacent Palestinian leadership, to corrupt Arab regimes and their henchmen. In the scene, the guard questions Naji while referring to a clipboard of 'official' documents in front of him.

GUARD:	Who are you?
NAJI:	A swallow looking for its nest, a space liberated and not mortgaged to any organization or regime.
GUARD:	Religion?
NAJI:	Unbeliever in sectarianism.
GUARD:	Age?
NAJI:	Short.
GUARD:	Eyes?
NAJI:	One eye on Ain al-Hilweh (a refugee camp in Lebanon) and the other eye on the enemy.
GUARD:	Hair?
NAJI:	Shaved in Arab prisons.
GUARD:	Head?
NAJI:	Held high.
GUARD:	Skin?
NAJI:	Flayed.
GUARD:	Hands?
NAJI:	Mine do not raise white or black flags.
GUARD:	Special indentifying features?
NAJI:	Marks from Arab daggers in the back, and Israeli bullets in the chest.
GUARD:	Your Occupation?
NAJI:	An engraver of the tragedies of our people from the Atlantic to the Gulf. Rubbish collector but I do not polish other people's shoes.
GUARD:	In short?
NAJI:	I draw.
GUARD:	And in what galleries do you display your works?
NAJI:	On the walls of our tent in the camp and on prison walls and the floor of my prison cell. I engraved them in the hearts of the poor and the minds of the fugitives and in the blood of the exiled and embroidered in the eyes of the grave dwellers.
GUARD:	What nonsense! Are you mad?
NAJI:	Maybe. I am one of the people.
GUARD:	I am the people!
NAJI:	Owls thinking they are nightingales
GUARD:	(threatening him with a gun): I will teach you a lesson you won't forget.
NAJI:	They raised their guns and I raised a flower.
GUARD:	You are making fun of me also? You shall rot in prison.
NAJI:	Better than to become a stupid consumer.

GUARD:	A filthy cheap rogue.
NAJI:	And my name is Naji Al-Ali.

(Abusrour 2011a)

The scene stages an encounter at an anonymous border site, where Naji is depicted resisting the power of authority that attempts to both negate and define his Palestinian identity. For Abusrour, whose own experience with the French authorities was a de-humanizing process, the mechanisms through which his identity and humanity were negated are firmly linked to the proliferation of negative stereotypes about Palestinians in the media:

> The media in France and other countries talked about Palestinians only as terrorists, and as human beings we did not exist. […] So I guess that was why I asked myself, how to show this other image of Palestine. How to say that we are human beings, we reclaim this humanity and we defend it. And we are not born to be just numbers, on a list of martyrs, or handicapped for the rest of our lives, or perishing in Israeli prisons. And we are not only capable of throwing stones and burning tyres as the media want to portray us. We are not born with genes of hatred or violence, because nobody is born with genes of hatred or violence. So how to show this other image… and I guess for me theatre was one of, and still is, the most amazing, powerful, civilised, and non-violent means of self-expression.

(Abusrour 2011b)

In the play, and in the absence of travel documents to legitimize his Palestinian identity, the authoritarian scrutiny directed at Naji in the last scene is counterposed with a scene that follows, where Naji reclaims the agency of creative self-expression to re-represent Palestinian identity as a radical and positive intervention. The scene begins with Naji drawing Handala as a cartoon on a screen. As the drawing finishes, Handala appears in person on the stage and turns his back to the audience with his hands joined behind his back. He wears a short shirt and shorts with patches and is barefooted:

NAJI:	You have come?
HANDALA:	I've come, bitter like 'al-handal' (Colocynth) I come.
NAJI:	You are bitter because of the poverty and debacle, but you are made of musk and frankincense.
HANDALA:	And my hair?
NAJI:	Rough like a hedgehog, a weapon against capitulation.
HANDALA:	Barefoot. Poor.
NAJI:	Son of Exile. You are the talisman that protects me from slipping. You are the drop of sweat on my forehead that will sting me if I contemplate retreat.

Figure 2: Naji Al-Ali (Abdelfattah Abusrour) talking to his cartoon creation Handala (Kan'an Abusrour) and describing what the Palestinian refugee child represents. Image reproduced courtesy of Alrowwad Cultural and Theatre Training Society (ACTS).

HANDALA:	And my hands?
NAJI:	Crossed behind your back until concessions, sales and cheap bargaining come to an end.
HANDALA:	I was born ten years old.
NAJI:	And you will stay ten. You are an exception because the loss of a homeland is an exception. You will not grow up until the mirage disappears. You are a flower in this autumn, an omen of hope, and you are the thorn that will puncture all balloons filled with false hopes and empty slogans.
HANDALA:	I am the scream.
NAJI:	The scream of those who pay the price and die in graves without shrouds and their corpses float in the seas of treachery and oblivion.
HANDALA:	The martyrs?
NAJI:	Yes, the martyrs from whose shrouds sandalwood trees grow and from their blood poppies bloom. Our people are the flower that embraces the cell bars and turns into a giant wrenching the bars apart.
HANDALA:	With their hands, they squeezed stones to water the poppies.
NAJI:	The water from the stones turn into a sea, into a giant with his hands planted in the sand of the shore, throwing sand up in the air like our dreams of return. Son, take a brush and draw a tree and decorate it with fruit, hearts and keys dangling from its branches.
HANDALA:	And the dove of peace?

NAJI: The dove in the moonlight turns into a woodpecker hard at work
                                    on the gallows in the squares. They have wrapped the moon with
                                    barbed wire that injured the dove, because the world sees the
                                    dove and the olive branch but ignores the right of nightingales
                                    to their homeland.

                                                                            (Abusrour 2011a)

Here the language of the scene is rich with the symbolism of Al-Ali's drawings but also
illustrates the agency that can come through the reclamation of the creative power of self-
expression. Here we also see the significance of 'beautiful resistance,' literally at play. Said
(1984) has called attention to the fact that Palestinians did not have 'permission to narrate' –
to tell their own histories, to make their own claims in mainstream media outlets (cited in
Feldman 2008: 498). As Feldman explains, the desire to highlight Palestinian visibility to an
'international community,' and to do so in a way that gives Palestinians an opportunity to
be agentive, not simply observed, has been part of the Palestinian struggle since the outset,
becoming a central concern in the years since their massive dispossession and displacement
in 1948 (498). For Abusrour, the importance of beautiful resistance as a strategy of creative
expression is ultimately bound up in the need to respond to the ongoing *invisibility* brought
about by the Nakba. Ultimately, what emerges from the need to respond to negative
stereotyping of Palestinians in the media, is an appreciation of creative self expression as a
form of 'visibility' practice, linked to the Palestinian struggle for human rights in the wake
of the cataclysm of the Nakba. According to Abusrour:

> Palestinians are no different from other people in their desire to share with the world their
> history and culture. They are like many other people in that they intend through their
> expressions to counter the images of themselves, their culture, and their history. Zionist
> propaganda has promulgated numerous fictions and stereotypes about the Palestinians
> and their history, such as the famous Zionist slogan 'a land without a people for a people
> without a land.'

>   (Abusrour 2006: 19)

Encountering remembrance

The year of the Nakba is a key date in the history of the Palestinian people, a year of 'dramatic
rupture in the continuity of historical space and time in Palestinian history' (Masalha 2008: 124).
In 1948 Israeli forces killed an estimated 13,000 Palestinians, 531 Palestinian villages were entirely
depopulated and destroyed, and almost three-quarters of a million Palestinians were made
refugees (PASSIA 2004: 1). Villagers fleeing their homes had their houses blown up or bulldozed,
the main objective to prevent the return of refugees and to help perpetuate the Zionist myth that
Palestine was 'a land without a people for a people without a land' (Masalha 2008: 130). Palestinian

geography and toponymy was subjected to a process involving the renaming, in Hebrew, of sites, places and events. Jewish settlements were established on the land of Palestinian villages. Naji Al-Ali's village of Al-Shajara (tree in Arabic) was re-named Moshav Elanit (tree in Hebrew) (Masalha 2008: 130–133). Importantly, as Masalha notes, 'the Nakba did not end in 1948. For Palestinians, […] al-Nakba is not just about remembering the "ethnic cleansing" of 1948; it is also about marking the *ongoing* dispossession and dislocation' (Masalha 2008: 149, emphasis added). Today the Nakba continues through the 'politics of denial.' According to Masalha,

> There are more than 5 million Palestinian refugees around the world, all of whom are denied their internationally recognised 'right of return' to their homes and land. The history, rights and needs of Palestinian refugees have been excluded from recent Middle East peacemaking efforts. The failure of both the Israeli state and the international community to acknowledge 1948 as an 'ethnic cleansing' continues to underpin the Palestine-Israel conflict.
>
> (Masalha 2008: 150)

While 'beautiful resistance' is implicated in the need to disseminate positive images of Palestinians to the international community on the outside, Abdelfattah believes that theatre also address a need within Palestinian society: 'A lot of people inside Palestine are not truly aware of the issues anymore. The new generations need to study the Nakba and refugee history again. During the first Intifada we lost so many people to Israeli prisons and this weakened education' (Wiles 2009: 26). Similarly, Abusrour explains some of the motivations in staging a play about Naji Al-Ali, suggesting:

> Not everybody knows his story and unfortunately even some of the young generations here don't know his story. […] And then I guess there is the appropriation of Naji Al Ali and Handala by the Popular Front. And of course he wasn't affiliated with any political party. He was critical of everybody. When they did something wrong he would put them under the spotlight. And because he became a symbol of the Popular Front and I wanted to liberate it also from this somehow. So the young people of the Popular Front would know Che Guvera and would know Handala and, maybe Naji Al-Ali. So it is also a struggle for the memory – to keep the memory of these integral people alive.
>
> (Abusrour 2011b)

In Alrowwad's production, the Nakba is highlighted in a scene involving the figure of Fatima. In Al-Ali's cartoons, the character Fatima represents a Palestinian farmwoman and signifies a particular attachment and belonging to the land as symbolized through her national embroidered dress. As Najjar explains,

> Each area of historic Palestine has a different type of dress, distinguished by the unique embroidered fauna and flora it carries. Women from areas with cypress trees, for example,

embroider cypresses in rows on the side panels and back of the dress. Particular flowers or birds may be seen in the costume of certain areas, but not in others. City women, who do not work in agriculture, have open long exotic sleeves that extend well beyond their wrists, while farmwomen like Fatima have shorter and narrower sleeves more practical for work. Thus, from her dress, the Palestinian interpretive community knows Fatima is a hardworking farmer from a specific geographic area of Palestine, suggesting that the place still exists in their memories despite the Israeli destruction of Palestinian villages in 1948.

(Najjar 2007: 269)

According to Hamdi, in Al-Ali's cartoons Fatima is not only a caregiver of the land of Palestine but is also enmeshed in her community's tribulations and not simply involved in her 'natural' role of mother and carer for her children. As Hamdi explains, 'the Palestinian peasant woman was never as cloistered or secluded in a domestic sphere' and 'many of Al Ali's cartoons show women totally involved in the thick of the struggle,' illustrating that 'without woman, there can be no liberation' (Hamdi 2011: 26). Moreover, these women represent:

more than the country, nation or *ummah*, which in Arabic comes from the same root or origin as the word *umm* meaning 'mother', they are active participants in the struggle, on the front lines, not reservists, so to speak, a far cry from the traditional, masculine, essentialised image of woman as merely representing the 'motherland.'

(27)

Importantly, Al-Ali's Fatima is usually portrayed carrying around her neck the key to the house left behind when the family fled in 1948. As Najjar explains, the key 'has symbolic significance because it articulates a major refugee claim: that "The Right of Return" has not been abandoned' (Najjar 2007: 269).

In the play we are introduced to Fatima (Hala Al-Yamani) as she sits alone listening to the radio. The radio programme is broadcasting messages of family members torn apart by the Nakba. She sits embroidering her dress with a key hanging from a chain around her neck, while various messages of regard and inquiry are overheard:

(Various voices): 'I am from Yarmouk camp, and I send my greetings to my mother and father in Hebron. I am from the south and I send my greetings to my beloved mother in Acre and to my sister Fatima in Aida camp. I am from Baqa'a camp, sending my greetings to my wife and my daughter Amal. Tell me your news.'

Eventually we hear Abu Saber, Fatima's husband who has been languishing in an Israeli jail: 'I am Abu Saber, in the prison of the occupation. I send my greetings to my wife Fatima and want her to know I am well' (Abusrour 2011a).

Figure 3: Fatima (Hala Al-Yamani) wearing a traditional Palestinian dress and with a key hanging around her neck. Image reproduced courtesy of Alrowwad Cultural and Theatre Training Society (ACTS).

This particular type of radio programme was a very popular daily half-hour programme broadcast in several Arab countries. Occasionally, an announcer may have taken a small tape recorder into a camp and recorded the greetings live to play on air, but most often family members would write letters to the station and an announcer would read the greetings on air. In an interview, Abusrour explained his intentions behind the scene:

> I wanted to revive this atmosphere of the waiting of Palestinians – this woman whose husband is imprisoned and finally it is his message that comes. So I guess its taking a part of this history that we had and putting it in the context of this Palestinian wife who is waiting fifteen years for her husband to be liberated while keeping her sincerity, faithfulness to the cause to her claim to the right of return to keep this key around her neck.

> (Abusrour 2011b)

In the scene, Abu Hussain (Mahmoud Noor) who has recently been released from an Israeli jail, visits Fatima.

ABU HUSSAIN:	Salam Fatima.
FATIMA:	Welcome Abu Hussain. Thank God you're well.
ABU HUSSAIN:	Trustworthy Fatima. You're still holding the key to your home in Jaffa.
FATIMA:	I'm still holding it. What news?
ABU HUSSAIN:	The sun has set in an ocean of tears, the sparrow is a prisoner of screams, and we are prisoners of exile.
FATIMA:	We are prisoners of waiting, prisoners of news and greetings.

They talk while Fatima prepares some tea and pours a glass for her guest.

FATIMA: Abu Hussain, you know when I listen to the messages on the radio between mother and son, wife and husband and all the others, my heart aches. I recall how they told us 'wait for a week or two and you will return to smell the thyme and mint in your gardens'. Weeks passed, then months followed by year after year. The lemon blossom withered and its fragrance changed, and the walls of our homes were transformed into the canvasses of tents.

The pair sit and discuss the impotence of Arab regimes to effect change and the resilience of Abu Hussain's deceased wife, who never once removed the house-key from around her neck during the entire period her husband was in jail, and Abu Hussain's regret that he could not burry his wife in the soil of their land in Jaffa. Abu Hussain's regret is met by Fatima's determination:

FATIMA: If we don't return today we will tomorrow. If not tomorrow, the day after, or the one after that… God willing, after one hundred years… If not us then our children… or their children's, children's children…

(Abusrour 2011a)

The scene movingly enacts the struggle to remain resilient amidst the bereavement and hardships of exile. The significance of the scene resonates in Schulz and Hammer's eloquent description of the significance of 'return' in Palestinian experience, when they explain that, 'bereavement of both land and time suggests a loss of orientation in life, and therefore of meaning. Only a return can change present turmoil and non-existence. In a liminal condition, it is only the constant wish and hope of returning which is meaningful' (Schulz and Hammer 2003: 207). Feldman describes the importance of certain objects such as flags and keys as visibility practices which feature as part of 'a dense landscape of memorialisation' in Palestinian refugee experience. This memorialization has been focused inward as much as outward; as much concerned with making and keeping the Palestinian past and future possibility visible to the Palestinian community as with making outsiders aware of Palestinian claims. As Feldman notes, 'while these practices have an internal voice, the refusal to forget the past has also been one of the crucial mechanisms through which Palestinians have promoted their visibility to an international audience (Feldman 2008: 504). According to Assmann and Czaplicka (1995), cultural memory blends memory, culture and society to not only enable the concretion of identity but also imbue individuals with the capacity to reconstruct and formulate identities and nurture a sense of obligation to the values and differentiations inherent within existing cultural knowledge and symbols (cited in Gandolfo

2010: 49). As Gandolfo explains, in the context of Palestinian identity, 'the concretion of identity is essential to the process of sustaining the sense of "being Palestinian" and the task of keeping Palestine alive' (Gandolfo 2010: 50). Masalha argues that remembering, as a work of mourning and commemorating, opens up new possibilities for attending to the rights of the victims of the Nakba. 'In English, "re-membering" means reuniting things and putting the wreckage of a painful past together in ways which helps end suffering and helps the process of healing (Masalha 2008: 151)

As I sat watching the performance, I took in the audience sitting around me. People were wandering in to sit; others left only to return a few minutes later. Parents leaned in to whisper an explanation of a significant reference to their children that had resonated with the rest of the crowd. There was laughter, titters, restlessness and quiet. Some were texting on their mobile phones, perhaps checking on friends or family that had not made it through Israeli checkpoints to attend the show. Some were taking pictures; others were recording the events on mobile video cameras, perhaps to be uploaded on YouTube to the Internet. This was not a subdued collection of passive spectators, but as is common in applied theatre contexts, a congregation of active participants (Watt and Pitts 1991). My attention turned to the sounds of the camp around me. I could hear the younger children playing outside in the narrow streets, and riding up and down the alleyways on their bicycles. Someone set off a firecracker up the street and there was laughter quickly followed by the admonishments of an adult from a nearby house. I could hear a goat bleating in a house close by. Suddenly the call to prayer rang out from a nearby mosque. They say memories live in everything; in tastes, smells and sounds. The melodic echoes from the mosque and the sounds of life in the camp reinforce the site-specific qualities of the performance and made me feel that I had arrived, that I was *there*, present and in-place. I was 're-membered', to use Masalha's term, in the sense of feeling re-united and whole. In contrast to the sense of being 'out of place' that I have become accustomed to, the feeling carried a sense of being 'home'. It was a strange revelation given that for all the other people who surrounded me, the inhabitants who lived there, the camp is a constant reminder of homes left behind. Like the keys of return, Feldman argues that refugee camps also 'operate as forms of visible commemoration.' They are visible reminders not only of 'Palestinian losses,' but also of 'their claims to their homes' left behind: 'The fact of the camps means that the very conditions of people's daily lives articulate both displacement and desire to return to their homes. Living in a camp is one way for people to "authentically" embody the experience of being Palestinian' (Feldman 2008: 507–509).

Encountering beautiful resistance and *Sumud*

In an interview, Absrour tells me, 'I was born in this refugee camp. I still keep the old rusty keys for doors that do or do not exist anymore, reclaiming my right to return' (Abusrour 2011b). He tells me his family are originally from Beit Natif one of villages occupied and destroyed after 1947. His family stayed in the fields near the village of Beit Ummar making futile attempts to return home while being shot at by Israeli soldiers. Eventually the family rented a room in Beit Sahoor for around a year before the UN started renting lands and establishing refugee camps. Moving to Aida camp, his family lived in a tent for six years until what was supposed to be their 'temporary' predicament was transformed by necessity and they started building more permanent shelters. Southwest to Jerusalem, Beit Natif is only 17 kilometres from where we sat talking, but given the Israeli occupation, the wall and the refusal of Israel to accept his internationally sanctioned rights to return to his family home, his village might have been a continent away. But Abusrour is patiently insistent:

> Eighty-seven per cent of these destroyed villages are still empty. Nothing is built on them. So when the Israeli or the international community say it is not realistic to go back or to reclaim … why is it not realistic? And what do I care about what is realistic and what is not realistic. Since when do realities on the ground erase the rights of people? Since when do realities on the ground dictate to you what you can do and what you cannot do?
>
> (Abusrour 2011)

Underscoring the importance of the right of return, I ask him if the production of *Handala* is about 'acting for human rights.' He replies, 'Yes. It is mainly an act against forgetfulness. Keeping memory, the values of human beings, and the rights of people alive' (Abusrour 2011b).

While I appreciate the significance of beautiful resistance as a means of self-expression, a way to counter the 'ugliness of occupation' and the negative stereotypes of Palestinians, and as a method to build confidence and enhance capacity of participants, my reading of the play and the analysis that has been informed by discussions with Abusrour has alerted me to a deeper significance of beautiful resistance that I have attempted to trace throughout this chapter. This significance is intimately linked to the history of the Palestinian non-violent struggle, and informed by the collective experience of the Nakba, Palestinian refugee identity, and the right of return which penetrate deep within the fabric of life in the refugee camp. It is a significance also felt in the cartoons of Naji Al-Ali. As Hamdi notes, 'the truth that Handala communicates to the Palestinian collective consciousness revolves around rootedness and resistance. Many of Al Ali's cartoons tell the story of *sumud* or steadfastness under the most difficult of conditions' (Hamdi 2011: 26). The Palestinian lawyer, author and rights-activist Raja Shehadeh described sumud as a non-violent attitude of life or 'steadfastness.' For Shehadeh, *sumud* denoted a third way that lies between, the opposing paths of accepting the occupation and opting for a violent struggle:

> *Sumud* is watching your home turn into a prison. You, samid, choose to stay in that prison, because it is your home, and because you fear if you leave, your jailer will not allow you to return. Living like this you must constantly resist the twin temptations of either acquiescing in the jailer's plan in numb despair, or becoming crazed by consuming hatred for your jailer and yourself, the prisoner.
>
> (Shehadeh 1984: viii)

As Musleh explains, *sumud* implies a kind of patient strength, an active commitment to righteousness, and a firm nonviolence, 'this is sumud, often translated as "resilience": the act of carrying on despite suffering, of insisting upon your rights without hating your oppressor. This is empowerment' (Musleh 2011: 98). As an artistic practice epitomized in beautiful resistance, *sumud* 'helps us to transform our identities from that of the victim to that of the *samed* – one who practices or embodies sumud' (Musleh 2011: 100). By linking Alrowwad's work and strategy of beautiful resistance to the Palestinian concept of sumud, Musleh clarifies the kind of resistance that the non-violent approach engenders:

> While people from outside might understand 'resistance' solely as an armed process, for Palestinians it also refers to the process of building healthy and effective individuals and communities, maintaining a rich culture, and developing the social, political and economic infrastructure required for independent statehood – all in the face of forces that seek to thwart these efforts. For many Palestinians, an important part of resisting the injustices they face is educating their own people, particularly the youth, by building their self-esteem and helping them to see themselves not as passive victims but as active citizens.
>
> (Musleh 2011: 98)

As I stood in the street outside the theatre waiting for Abusrour to give me a lift, I chatted with a small girl who was proudly displaying her bicycle. Hanan was about eight years old and was confidently chatting and showing-off her prized possession. The absence of street lighting meant that it was dark, and I asked her whether she would be able to get a small light for her bike. She explained that she could get a bike-light from town, one for the front and one for the back; a light to illuminate her way and another red one to warn people behind her. As Abusrour locked the door to ACTS building, I told Hanan to look after herself. My parting comment took on a more meaningful quality, when Abusrour paused to say, 'Did you hear Hanan what Uncle said, "take care of yourself". In Abusrour's delivery the phrase resonated with the powerful message of self-reliance and self-determination underscoring the theatre and creative work that Alrowwad has been engaging in. There was pride, dignity and *sumud* in that message, and as we drove away I glimpsed a final view of Hanan in the car's side-mirror, sitting astride her precious bicycle, smiling, confident, hopeful and waving good-bye.

Acknowledgements

I would like to thank the wonderful staff and volunteers at Alrowwad for inviting me to the Aida camp and making me feel welcome. I would also like to acknowledge the time and generosity of Dr. Abdelfattah Abusrour whose feedback and comments on the writing of this chapter have been invaluable. I would also like to thank the Naji Al-Ali family for permission to publish the image of Handala that appears in this chapter. Finally, I would like to acknowledge the assistance of my father, Tuma Hazou, who helped in translating the script of *Handala* from Arabic into English.

References

Abu-Laban, Y., and Bakan, A., 'Palestinian Resistance and International Solidarity: The BDS Campaign,' *Race and Class* 51: 1 (2009), pp. 29–54.

Abusrour, A., 'Beautiful Resistance, Revolting Memory,' *Al-Majdal* 29 (Spring 2006), pp. 19–20.

———, *Handala* (unpublished script), trans. Tuma Hazou, Aida Refugee Camp, Bethlehem: Alrowwad Cultural and Theatre Society (ACTS), 2011a.

———, 'Interview with the Author on 9 October 2011,' The Alrowwad Cultural and Theatre Society offices, Aida Refugee Camp, Palestine, 2011b.

Assmann, J., and Czaplicka J., 'Collective Memory and Cultural Identity,' *New German Critique*, 65 (1995), pp. 125–133.

Barghouti, O., *BDS: Boycott, Divestment, Sanctions – the Global Struggle for Palestinian Rights*, Chicago: Haymarket Books, 2011.

Beadle, D., 'Al-Rowwad Theatre Community: Children Surviving in the Rubble of the Palestinian-Israeli Conflict,' *Youth Theatre Journal* 20: 1 (2006), pp. 94–109.

Feldman, I., 'Refusing Invisibility: Documentation and Memorialization in Palestinian Refugee Claims,' *Journal of Refugee Studies* 21: 4 (2008), pp. 498–516.

Gandolfo, L., 'Representations of Conflict: Images of War, Resistance, and Identity in Palestinian Art,' *Radical History Review* 106 (2010), pp. 47–69.

Hamdi, T., 'Bearing Witness in Palestinian Resistance Literature,' *Race & Class* 52: 3 (2011), pp. 21–42.

Hanauer, D., 'The Discursive Construction of the Separation Wall at Abu Dis: Graffiti as Political Discourse,' *Journal of Language and Politics* 10: 3 (2011), pp. 301–321.

Kawash, S., 'Nation, Place, and Placelessness: Identity, Body, and Geography in the Case of Palestine,' *Nar.umjet* 40: 1 (2003), pp. 37–48.

Khalidi, R., *Palestinian Identity: The Construction of Modern National Consciousness*, New York: Columbia University Press, 1997.

Khalili, L., 'Places of Memory and Mourning: Palestinian Commemoration in the Refugee Camps of Lebanon,' *Comparative Studies of South Asia, Africa and the Middle East*, 25: 1 (2005), pp. 30–45.

Malkki, L., 'Speechless Emissaries: Refugees, Humanitarianism, and Dehistoricization,' *Cultural Anthropology*, 11: 3 (1996), pp. 377–404.

Masalha, N., 'Remembering the Palestinian Nakba: Commemoration, Oral History and Narratives of Memory,' *Holy Land Studies: A Multidisciplinary Journal*, 7: 2 (2008), pp. 123–156.

Musleh, A., 'Theatre, Resistance, and Peace Building in Palestine,' in Cohen, C., Varea, R. G., and Walker, P. (eds), *Acting Together: Performance and the Creative Transformation of Conflict. Volume I: Resistance and Reconciliation in Regions of Violence*, pp. 97–122, Oakland, CA: New Village Press, 2011.

Najjar, O., 'Cartoons as a Site for the Construction of Palestinian Refugee Identity: An Exploratory Study of Cartoonist Naji Al-Ali,' *Journal of Communication Inquiry*, 31: 3 (2007), pp. 255–285.

Nassar, H., 'Stories from under Occupation: Performing the Palestinian Experience,' *Theatre Journal*, 58 (2006), pp. 15–37.

PASSIA, 'Palestinian Refugees', in *PASSIA (Palestinian Academic Society for the Study of International Affairs) Special Bulletin* (May 2004): 1–15. http://www.youblisher.com/p/30388-PALESTINIAN-REFUGEES/.

Peteet, J., 'The Writing on the Walls: The Graffiti of the Intifada', *Cultural Anthropology*, 11: 2 (1996), pp. 139–159.

Said, E., 'Invention, Memory, and Place', *Critical Inquiry*, 2 (Winter 2000), pp. 175–192.

———, 'Permission to Narrate', *London Review of Books*, 3: 3 (1984), pp. 27–48.

Schulz, H., and Hammer, J., *The Palestinian Diaspora: Formation of Identities and Politics of Homeland*, London and New York: Routledge, 2003.

Shehadeh, R., Samed: *Journal of a West Bank Palestinian*, New York, Adama Books, 1984.

Thompson, J., Hughes, J., and Balfour, M., *Performance in Place of War*, London and New York: Seagull, 2009.

UNHCR, 'UN Commission on Human Rights, Report of the Special Rapporteur of the Commission on Human Rights, John Dugard, on the Situation of Human Rights in the Palestinian Territories Occupied by Israel since 1967' (2006), pp. 1–21, http://www.unhcr.org/refworld/docid/441182050.html (accessed 18 December 2011).

UNRWA, 'Aida Refugee Camp', *West Bank Camp Profiles*, 31 December (2010). http://www.unrwa.org/etemplate.php?id=104 (accessed 15 December 2011).

Watt, D., and Pitts, G., 'Community Theatre as Political Activism: Some Thoughts on Practice in the Australian Context', In Binns, V. (ed.) *Community and the Arts: History, Theory, Practice*, pp. 119–133, Leichhardt: Pluto Press, 1991.

Wiles, R., 'The Art of Resistance: Education through Grassroots Arts and Culture in Bethlehem's Refugee Camps', *Al-Majdal*, 42 (Autumn 2009), pp. 21–27.

Notes

1 As is common custom in tribal societies, the terms 'Aunty' (Áama) and 'Uncle' (Ámo) in Arab society are honorific terms of deference used to refer to elders regardless of immediate family relation.

2 Alrowwad Cultural and Theatre Society Website: http://www.alrowwad-acts.ps/etemplate.php?id=44.

3 The internationally recognized border separating Israel from the Occupied Palestinian Territories created following the ceasefire in 1949.

4 The Arabic name of the iconic cartoon figure that has come to symbolize the Palestinian struggle is translated into English as 'Handala', 'Hanthala' or 'Hanzala'. For consistency and personal preference, I have opted to use Handala throughout this chapter.

5 The bitter *al-handal* plant or Colocynth is commonly referred to as the bitter apple in English.

6 Note on the interview and transcription process: I have generally attempted to transcribe the interview by being faithful to the respondent's intended meaning in order to mitigate problems of misrepresentation and allow Abusrour to have his work and his ideas presented in his own words. However, I have taken the decision to occasionally reword the respondent's

grammar or vocabulary to facilitate accessibility to his ideas while also attempting to maintain the authenticity and integrity of his voice.

7   By characterizing Israel's system of bestowing rights and privileges according to ethnic and religious identity as apartheid, BDS advocates draw on the UN definition of the term as enshrined in the 1973 *International Convention on the Suppression and Punishment of the Crime of Apartheid*. The Convention defines Apartheid as 'inhumane acts … committed in the context of an institutionalized regime of systematic oppression and domination by one racial group over any other racial group or groups and committed with the intention of maintaining that regime' (17). Refer to United Nations, 'International Convention on the Suppression and Punishment of the Crime of *Apartheid*,' Article II (30 November 1973), available at http://web.archive.org/web/20061001200717/http://www.unhchr.ch/html/menu3/b/11.htm.

8   The UN General Assembly set forth the legal framework for resolving the Palestinian refugee issue in UN Resolution 194 which demands repatriation for those refugees wishing to return to their homes and live in peace with their neighbours, or compensation for those choosing not to return. This has become commonly referred to as the 'right of return.'

Chapter 8

Rape as War Strategy: A Drama from Croatia

Sanja Nikčević

I met Lydia Scheuermann Hodak several years ago while I was working as theatre adviser for the Ministry of Culture where I was also in charge of the play contest the Ministry organizes every year. She had sent in a play with a funny title (*I Must Rush, My Masseuse Is Coming*) that happened to be a very good war comedy. The Awards committee said that although it was very good play, she was too unknown to be given an award. So, I did something unusual: I phoned her to relate that the committee had good things to say about her play and that I personally liked it. She sent me another one, *Maria's Pictures*.

It was 1995, and war was still in our country. I was surprised – an unknown playwright, translator and computer expert has written such a powerful play. Where was she hiding, why is she not staged all over Croatia? I started to offer this play around to people as a revelation, but the doors were shut tight, for reasons which I will explain later. The play is based on a true story. Hodak lives in Osijek, capital of Slavonia, one of the most destroyed parts of Croatia during the war. Although it was shelled itself (some parts of the city were completely destroyed and even the Croatian National Theatre was targeted by two bombs), Osijek was big enough to function properly so everybody came there – to the hospital, as the first refugee station, and in spite of bombing, because it was a safer place than many other smaller towns nearby that were taken by the Yugoslav Army or Chetniks, the Serbian paramilitary forces.[1]

The story of two women who come to Osijek from an occupied town after being chased through mine fields – two raped women, a mother who eventually miscarries and a daughter who gives birth to a child and then dies – was told to Hodak by an old woman who escaped with them. But not just the main story, every story, every experience, in the play is true. The old diabetic woman in the play, living on scraps in the occupied small town, was really a midwife who had delivered the boys now chasing her through mine fields; one of them told the women where to walk to avoid them. The character of the Psychologist who left her home and lost her life's research papers actually went through the experiences dramatized. Not only her story but her energy and strength are in the play. When her cancer was diagnosed, she was given six months to live. She is still alive. She is a friend of the playwright who changed her name in the play.

The idea of a 'true story' is interesting for theatre historians but not important for the quality of the play. These kinds of stories were occurring all the time in this or slightly different forms. Men who were cruel soldiers now threatening their former teachers (that was the playwright's own experience), neighbours who were yesterday's friends now paramilitary forces, atrocities that happened to innocent people because of their nationality or place of birth, the death of friends and family, bombing of civilian targets, churches, theatres (Osijek), hospitals (Vukovar), death and concentration camps. We grew accustomed to the fact that Serbian media and paramilitary forces called every Croat 'Ustache', the fascist term for military forces in World War II, and considered everyone of us an enemy, regardless of age or political orientation.

There are refugee stories about those who left 'for a few days' and than never returned home, leaving everything behind – documents, clothes, photos, books, lives. There were more than two million refugees from Croatia and Bosnia at that time. We could recognize refugees in Zagreb for a long time afterwards because *other people's clothes* on them were so obvious. Individual tragedies, collective tragedies (people from whole small towns chased from their homes with just plastic bags in their hands) dominated the media, so, to tell another common story is not a reason enough for a play.[2]

In *Maria's Pictures*, Hodak shifted the focal point of the drama to the grandmother who survives the tragic story, rather than the daughter. But, this is not at all a play about war atrocities or death; there is no direct explanation of events, no mention of the word 'rape.' It is about life and acceptance, even after terrible things that have occurred without any logical reason. It is also about denial and acceptance of terrible things you yourself did to someone you love: Maria not being there for her own daughter because she did not want to accept the truth of the rape. Finally, it is a story about forgiving yourself in order to get on with your life. The Psychologist encourages Maria: 'Paint, that's the best solution. And be happy that you can express yourself in your pictures. You are lucky, you don't have to search for words, you recognize yourself in the painting, and you find yourself there [...] We all carry our life's painting inside ourselves. You just have to call it up, to express it. Everything seems less terrible when it comes out into the open, when we finally come face to face with our own feelings and thoughts.'

Her memories start with an image of a Slavonian girl with ripe dark red cherries at the railway station. Later she recalls the peaceful life in her small Slavonian town: a garden and flowers and fruits, warm sunny days, the Assumption Day feast that brings people together. Such pictures evoke Thornton Wilder's *Our Town* which celebrates the meaning of life in everyday things, or as Maria's father would say, sitting with a little granddaughter on the porch: 'There is nothing nicer on this earth than being a grandfather, sitting with a little granddaughter on this porch, telling fairy tales.' But these pictures are always open doors for war memories. The juxtaposition of pictures of harmony with pictures of war allows us to 'swallow' easier the pictures of war, or to rest from them, but also to feel them stronger, in comparison with the harmony of before.

Hodak has had an interesting fate as a writer. The first part of her war novels about Osijek and the love of two people in the middle of the war, *A Snake Around the Neck*, was published in Croatia in 1999, and the second part in 2000, the same year when it was published in Germany. A well-known Hungarian playwright saw it and translated it into Hungarian, and it awaits publication in Hungary. Her last book, which collects her experiences as a playwright, was written in German under the title *A Woman Wearing a Silk Blouse*. As a playwright, Hodak has not been so lucky. She has some very interesting unpublished and unperformed plays (*Ana or the Bird in the Tree-Top*; *Herr Hermann Reads 'Spiegel'*; *The Cormorants in Kopacki Rit Are Sad Too*; *Eve is not Adam*).

Maria's Pictures is her only published play – in Osijek's literary journal in 1996: In the meantime a book of Hodak's five plays has been published (*Women, Love and Wars*, Osijek, 2009). But in Germany there are two published editions. The play had been performed at the 1999 International Theatre Festival Border on River (Grenze im Fluss-meja na reki) in Radkersburg, Austria, by Vlasta Knezovic. At the 2000 festival entitled Who Wants To Be a Woman Tomorrow held in Braunschweig, Germany, the author conducted a workshop after readings of the play. Some of the participants of the festival liked it so much that the play is now translated into Spanish and Russian. It was staged in Persian in Tehran in 2000 under the title *Marija Without a Name* by Theatre Moasar, and performed by Narges Hashempour. In Croatia, the play was staged in 1999 through the individual effort of the esteemed Croatian actress Vlasta Knezovic, as a private, one-woman show, and without an official opening night in Zagreb. Hodak's war comedy (*I Must Rush, My Masseuse Is Coming*), referred to above, was staged by an amateur theatre in a small town, Bjelovar, in 1998. But, for several reasons, *Maria's Pictures* has largely been rejected by Croatian theatres, as I noted above.

Croatian theatre, as is the case in European theatre, in general, disdains emotional plays, preferring intellectual and political ones. European mainstream theatre likes thesis plays not ordinary stories, a tendency rooted in the power of the European director who dominates theatre.[3] This play is all about feelings – feelings of fear and despair and of denial and guilt as very intimate, emotional responses to the war situation. This is not something theatre directors want to deal with. The strong emotions that pour from *Maria's Pictures,* based as it is on actual events, and with its final affirmation of life, touches the audience on the emotional level. This is a dramatic style that goes counter to the current dominant trend of so-called New European Drama (exemplified by Mark Ravenhill and Sarah Kane) on continental stages. Such plays offer violent pictures of human relations but without any emotion or affirmation of the meaning of life, and they are mostly set in undefined space and time.

Another reason for the lack of attention to a play like *Maria's Pictures* is specific to Croatian theatre politics. Croatian theatres don't like to stage war plays. Theatre managers and directors are very clear: during the war they said that audiences did not want to look at war on the stage while it exists for them in reality. After the war they said people want to forget it. It is true from one point of view, but there are many more reasons for this particular refusal.[4]

There are some specific reasons for not staging this play. Those who had hoped to expose atrocities made by Serbian paramilitary forces and the Yugoslav army did not like the reconciliation at the end of the play and the women's side of the story (it was missing any historical explanation of the conflict and a clear political attitude about guilt). How can they seek revenge or prosecution of the people who committed crimes when the grandmother in the play accepts a baby that is the fruit of such a terrible act as rape? Those of another political perspective wanted to forget the war as soon as possible: they loved the reconciliation at the end of the play but did not like the exposition of life in a small, occupied town. Although it is very subtle and nowhere is it said what nationality the soldiers were, we knew that they were Serbs, some of them from outside and others from this very town. So how could our politicians work toward the return of the Serbs to these towns with proof – as detailed in the events of the play – of their atrocities, in spite of the reconciliation at the end? Thus, neither political position was open to this war drama.

Although enthusiastic about *Maria's Pictures*, I myself avoided writing about it until now. Not only are there the strong feelings that pour from every page, but it is a very rare play that speaks directly to me as a woman. It could be my story, very easily. I was only a hundred kilometers away from that region. In this war, for the first time in history, the tactic of rape became a monstrous strategy. Soldiers took women from their homes, from UN or Red Cross or refugee convoys, and put them in the so-called 'rape camps.' These were young girls, daughters taken from mothers, mothers taken with their daughters. They were systematically raped until they got pregnant; then they were released from the camps, but in a late stage of pregnancy when it is too late for a legal abortion. These women came to Zagreb, the Croatian capital and second refugee stop. Newspapers were filled with their stories: what to do with the unborn conceived in such terrible circumstances. The word 'children' was avoided. The 'fruit of evil' became a substitute phrase. Women who decided to abort or give away the babies explained their decision in newspapers, searching for public support. Though victims, they also felt guilty at the same time, which is the biggest victory of their torturers. The women who decided to keep the babies were silently disappearing, caring for them in some other place where nobody knew them and believing that somewhere else they could forget how the child was conceived, because it was still their child. Like Maria. That is why Hodak could not find Maria and her granddaughter, although she tried. She discovered that they went away with the help of the Red Cross to try to start a new life.

Notes

1 War in Croatia started in 1991, after Croatia declared its succession from the former Yugoslavia. As one of the republics, Croatia had a right to do so but Serbs, as an ethnic minority in Croatia but majority in Yugoslavia, started the rebellion. Croat Serbs were helped by paramilitary forces coming from Serbia (so-called Chetniks) and by the heavily armed Yugoslav People's Army. The Croats had only a police force, and started to build their own army, initially called Guardsmen. War lasted for nearly six years and during that time, some parts of Croatia were heavily destroyed and others occupied by Serbian forces. After the Croatian military action called 'Storm' (1995) the occupied territories were regained and the war in Croatia ended.
2 A wonderful Bosnian movie was made recently on that topic, about using the 'real war stories' by the Western film industry – *Remake*, written by Zlatko Topčić and directed by Dino

Mustapic. There is also an English example – the play *Treatment* by Martin Crimp, about the fate of a true story used by Hollywood for its own purposes.

3 Nikčević, S., 'British Brutalism, the "New European Drama", and the Role of the Director', *New Theatre Quarterly,* Cambridge University Press, 83 (2005), pp. 255–272.

4 Nikčević, S., 'Croatian Theatre and War,' *Slavic and East European Performance,* New York, 23:2 (2003), pp. 49–67.

Chapter 9

Far Away, So Close: Psychosocial and Theatre Activities
with Serbian Refugees[1]

Guglielmo Schininà

The Theatre [...] is the craft and art of transforming what one looks at into something that regards us. Its raw material is relationships. [...] I have never believed in a theatre that claims to transform a number of individuals into a communion. Collective identity may perhaps have had positive aspects in social communities characterized by small numbers. But mass civilization has produced such monstrous surrogates of this fabled unity that we have no nostalgia for them. The image of theatre that guides me is not that of an action that unifies, but that of a circle of encounters and barters. Various people gather around an action that binds them and allows them to debate, to discover a territory, a time, in which to exchange something. It is the very fact that each one can deepen his knowledge of his own specificity that creates the solidarity between them. [...] The fact that today cohabitation with the different is often felt like a dramatic historical situation must not make us forget that it is the matter on which the theatre has always worked, on which those who make theatre their profession must know how to work [...].

(Barba 2001: n.p.)

Introduction

S ince April 1999, I have been living in the Balkans where I have worked as a workshop facilitator, trainer, and supervisor with psychosocial and cultural integration projects. These efforts are a part of the emergency relief services that focus on the persistent problems caused by the recent wars. All of the projects have included theatrical components and some were centred on the communication and relationship-building logic of a 'theatre game.'

It is impossible to summarize a professional and human experience that is now over four years old and includes various projects within which I played a number of different roles. Therefore, I have decided to concentrate only on my experience in Serbia in 1999. This choice has been made primarily for two reasons. The first is technical: my experience in Serbia led to the emergence of some convictions that have become fundamental to my overall approach. The second can be defined as political: in the Kosovo crisis, the international intervention (first and foremost the military and journalistic one) was centred on the victim/perpetrator/saviour structure (Losi 2002). Within this framework, the victims were the Albanians, the perpetrators were the Serbian population as a whole, and the saviours were the NATO forces and international humanitarian workers. Writing about the experiences of some of the people considered to be the 'perpetrators' enables us to understand the groundlessness of this simplistic schema/classification and, perhaps, to understand the groundlessness of any 'humanitarian' or 'anti-terrorist' military attack.

Serbia, August–December 1999

I arrived in southern Serbia on 4 August 1999, two months after the end of the war in Kosovo. Places and people showed clear signs of the effects of the NATO bombings; at that time, one would still run into groups of Serbs escaping from Kosovo following the end of the 'humanitarian war.' In unfinished buildings, and in the mud under bridges there were groups of Roma who were also fleeing from Kosovo but were by no means welcome in Serbia. In total, during this period, there were some 180,000 people living in these conditions. When I entered Serbia, hundreds of refugees from Bosnia and Croatia were arriving daily. Previously, they were sheltered in collective centres in Kosovo but after the war there, they had to flee to Serbia as 'double refugees' – refugees for the second time. My task was to create a psychosocial project consisting of creative activities for children, adolescents and elderly refugees living in the collective centres in southern Serbia.

When I arrived in 1999, a total of 400,000 refugees from Bosnia and Croatia who fled from their own countries following the previous wars in the Balkans lived in Serbia, where roughly the same number remain today. The most unfortunate among them, around 40,000 people, had spent the last six to ten years of their lives in hundreds of collective centres scattered around the country, living sometimes with up to 30 people per large room. They were accommodated in what were once hotels, motels, schools or former construction yards located many kilometres from the nearest small villages, without any public transportation. There was only one bus per day to take the children to and from school – but often the children did not go at all. They survived thanks to the assistance given by the national Red Cross, but even that became unavailable as each war and economic crisis meant that feeding the army became the top priority. Only a few were able to work and earn the average wage for local underpaid jobs (about 40 Euros – US $40 at that time – per month for ten hours of work a day, six days a week). Alcoholism and depression were rampant among adults and adolescents who did not see any prospect for the future.

Unfortunately, from a bureaucratic point of view, the Serbians that had just come from Kosovo, except for the 'double refugees,' could not be defined as refugees and instead were classified as IDPs (Internally Displaced People), because Kosovo was formally still part of the Yugoslavian federation. For this reason, they could not officially be included in the project. These are the kinds of political contradictions and constraints one often faces when working in emergency relief services. Therefore, our project had to focus on the actual and double refugees, trying to involve the IDPs as much as possible without being too obvious about it, because this would have caused political problems with the local government.

The deep poverty of southern Serbia was intensified by the embargo and became intolerable during the war. In contrast to what was happening at the same time in Kosovo, due to the international perception of the Serbians as the 'perpetrators,' there were very few international humanitarian agencies and NGOs in Serbia. My car was the first one in many months to visit the collective centres in the southern part of the country.

Immediately upon our arrival, the staff and I were barraged with questions, requests and demands regarding the problems that had been brewing for a long time and for which we had no answers. Worse still, the IDPs from Kosovo, who we encountered during our trips, had basic, urgent needs to be satisfied before turning to the psychosocial ones. In a context in which the beneficiaries had primary needs that no person or agency was able to satisfy, it was very difficult to concentrate solely on a creative programme. Additionally, I felt the pressure of limited time: given the political situation it was likely that I would have to abandon the country and the project in a short while.

Theoretical background

This type of project is tightly bound to practical and urgent action and leaves little time for theoretical elaboration. In this case, I was guided by my previous experience, four main ideas, and by a simple ritual model. I would be lying if I said that all the theoretical implications were clear to me before designing the project. It was, as it always is in these cases, a trial-and-error experience. What theory exists has been derived from my experiences.

Sustainability and community-needs sensitivity vs. pre-packaged models

I do not believe in international 'saviours' who take action according to a predetermined model, think they can 'save' a group with a one- or two-month workshop and then disappear or maintain only feeble contact. Unfortunately, this harmful approach is very common in emergency relief services. But to improve what is no longer a short-term crisis but rather an endemic emergency, efforts must be made to ensure that the community takes its destiny into its own hands according to its own models. Therefore, it should not be 'fed' coping tools or, even worse, helped to cope with a situation that is unacceptable. Instead, one first asks the community what its priorities are in order to understand its resources. Then one must adapt one's competencies to meet those needs. Simultaneously, one tries to ensure that the expectations, which will emerge as a consequence, can in fact be met, at least to some extent.

Therefore, I do not impose theatre. My experience and my know-how are in the area of using theatre in the process of community-building, but I always try to respect peoples' existing abilities and goals. In this case, the communities living in the collective centres were more interested in sport and handicraft activities than in creative arts; and even then, only a few of the creative arts involved the theatre. I respected these choices and tried to take advantage of the existing resources. Theatrical activities remained only an informing logic, a communicative reference model, and my way of passing that model on in the training.

Individual vs. group in the construction of roles in war-torn communities

While visiting the centres, I realized that regardless of their very strong common history, the inhabitants' sense of community was destroyed to such an extent that the refugees were unable to collectively claim their rights. Community-building needed to be one of the first aims of the project.

Psychosocial activity aimed at community-building in difficult circumstances has to focus on three components: relationships, communication and creativity. The objective is to reconstruct *roles* – on the individual, group and community level. However, when we work on reconstructing a sense of community in conflict situations, we must always keep in mind certain implications, which I often encounter in my experiences in war-torn societies. An example illustrates the point. Working during and just after the war among groups of Kosovar Albanians interested in the creative arts, it was necessary to interact with an incredibly compact community/communion that never doubted its nationalistic values and seemed to reduce its existence only to such values. All the international trainers with whom I talked were frustrated with the workshops since they found themselves interacting with a collective body that responded collectively. This led to rhetorical and standardized results but also made dialogue between the trainer and the group and, above all, between members of the group impossible. In my opinion, the emergence of this dynamic had two causes:

(1) *Political* – The war in Kosovo was called 'humanitarian' so it implied a relational triangle: victim/perpetrator/saviour, and this had an effect on the relationships between individuals. Every person, when relating with someone else, had to follow a precise narrative, according to the group-identity to which s/he belonged. The workshops were run by international trainers (the 'saviours') for Albanian groups (the 'victims'). Within this triangular frame, it was impossible to raise multiple voices.

(2) *Technical* – The trainers were used to working in Western countries where the creation of a group and an emphasis on rituals are the prerequisites of any workshop. Therefore, they did not understand that in these situations, deconstruction of the group's rhetoric, the *empowerment* of individual differences, and criticism of the rituals of war would be the only actions that could lay the foundations for long-term intercultural and interethnic processes. Happily, these actions are also effective in the very short term. However, in a war-torn situation, there is no free expression of multiple voices, and differences within the same ethnic group tend to be suppressed in a process of self-censorship. Thus, the group must be given the opportunity from

the very beginning to experience its own limits. This is done in order to counteract the fact that anger or nationalistic feelings, reactive racism, justification of hate, and self-victimization often become the only prerequisites for belonging to the group in these circumstances.

In an endemic situation, like the one involving refugees in Serbia, even this 'negative' sense of community no longer existed. In fact, building their sense of community from the wrong perspective might throw them back into a situation similar to the one just described. More likely in this case, the arrogance of the winning group would perhaps be replaced by the depression and anger of the group defeated and recognized internationally as perpetrators not victims. For these reasons, the process must be understood, as indicated by Barba, as a circle of encounters and barters and not as a search for communion. The first act of a workshop or a creative process was therefore to bring people back to an awareness of their individual value and their own means of expression.

Creative communication/social communication vs. coping mechanism

In situations where social problems and discrimination have strong political implications, artistic activities and especially theatre are of special value because they create a relationship between creative communication in the group and social communication in the more political sense. In this specific case even if we could have recreated a sense of community among those living in the centres, this would not have solved their problems. It would have only improved an unacceptable objective situation. Once a process of creative communication had been initiated, leading to the reformulation of individual and group roles, we had to help the people develop this into a larger social communication exercise connecting effectively with the society outside the centres.

The first objective was information. Most Serbs did not know of the existence of the collective centres. The Milosevic government had used the media to focus on the refugees in order to enhance nationalistic feelings and the acceptance of suffering inflicted upon the common enemy. However, the media had hidden the conditions these individuals lived in to avoid the dramatic evidence of political contradictions. Consequently, exhibitions, shows, concerts, photographic displays, ritual tales and so forth produced in the centres and presented outside were designed to lead to the recognition of the existence of the centres and of an 'other' Serbian history. This we hoped would also help to overcome some of the prejudices and stigma that had put additional weight on the refugees.

The second objective was political. Publicizing the creative identity of the refugees and displaying the conditions in which they lived were both in themselves acts of opposition to the regime and agitation for change.

Therefore, in this case, the creative arts were chosen not only as one of the privileged tools for the development of *coping mechanisms* (see Dokter 1998; Jennings 1999) but rather for their 'performative' and 'eventual' possibility: the possibility of initiating processes within the group that would establish them on the basis of individual difference with the ability also to communicate this to a wider social arena.

The Complex Circle Model

For the Serbian project, I used the ritual model of a complex circle (Schininà 2002). Its basic principle is to consider theatre as a means of communication, which, regardless of the activity undertaken, brings about a circle of barters and encounters and is also able to present these barters and encounters to a reality outside the circle. The ultimate goal is to begin to change perceptions of certain problems and to include multiple voices and narrations in a collective act of communication.

Technically, everything starts with a group of individuals, each of whom has his/her own characteristics. To form the circle, they construct relationships according to the inset model:

A						
A	B					
A	B	C				
A	B	C	D			
A	B	C	D	E		
A	B	C	D	E	F	
A	B	C	D	E	F	G

The individual (A) is always himself/herself and free but his/her actions interact with the actions of others (B, C, D, E,…); thus, they change and are changed by one another in a linear relationship. This continues until the line contains the entire group. At this point, a ritual circle is created, in which each person retains his/her individuality and his/her own characteristics but also develops personal relationships, and expresses feelings and questions that are shared with the entire group.

IN THE GROUP

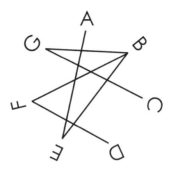

The group becomes the place in which diversity is respected and personal or collective relationships are recognized by everyone in the group. The process develops with problems being pluralized and the resources of every individual member being shared. The same circular mechanism can also be established among groups and institutions.

In the Serbian project, this model can be applied within each group of children, adolescents and elderly people living in the centres. Each letter is an individual, while the lines represent some of the possible creative relationships. The circle is the symbolic structure of the group and the setting. The same model applies to the other centres.

IN THE CENTER

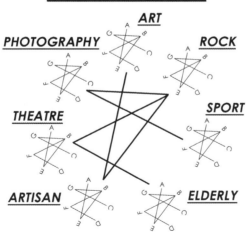

The various groups of activities build the circle; they develop their linear relationships through creative exchanges and the display of their creative results.

Additionally, the same process is valid for the entire community of refugees living in the various collective centres. The different groups involved in the same activities – for example, sports or art – in the centres create a circle, with the lines representing their possible creative encounters (or sports clashes, as we will see).

AMONG THE CENTERS

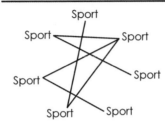

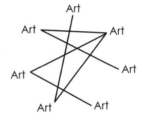

The circle is a symbolic but also practical space in which to create relationships and a sense of identity. This led to the idea of utilizing a large room in a social centre in Nis (the largest city in the area) as the common room for events. This way, whenever one of the centres' groups wanted to present something, there would be enough space to invite all the other centres. But the circular relationship had to be expanded within the region of Nis. The Nis common room had to become a significant point in the dynamic between the associations, the formal and informal groups, and the region's political bodies.

IN THE COMMON ROOM

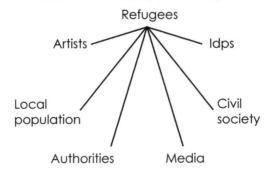

Implementation

Assessment: selection of the centres and identification of which creative activities to run

In the first weeks, I repeatedly visited twenty centres, which were selected because they had the highest degree of vulnerability among the hundreds located in the area. In addition, without being too obvious about it, we included in the activities two spontaneous centres (the name given to those structures used for refuge by the IDPs from Kosovo) and three Roma communities.

Initially, I wanted the people living in the centres to identify their own needs and address them, but I had to be very precise about the limits of what I could offer through the existing guidelines of the project. I did not want to create false expectations and subsequent frustration. The only way I could accomplish this was by going and talking with people and developing close relationships, without which the entire process would have been impossible.

In all the centres, I gathered the adolescents, the women, and the elderly and started by trying to understand what activities the residents were organizing themselves. This included finding possible trainers within the community and trying to help young people identify their creative interests. Bringing people together, due to long-standing tensions, was not always easy and took time. What I found most surprising was that very often the adolescents, when asked to identify which activities they would like to do, were not able to understand the concept of choice. My collaborators and I tried to find different words and metaphors, but in some cases we never succeeded. It took us a while to make the painful discovery that for people whose wishes had never been granted, the act of making choices and identifying desires was foreign. Sometimes we had to make proposals ourselves. Other times we asked the most responsive adolescents and elderly people to identify the groups' interests and prepare lists of activities with the names of the people who had expressed those choices.

The staff

In all of the centres, we tried to identify refugee intellectuals, artists and artisans so that we could train them to work with children, thus giving them a social role while at the same time allowing them to recuperate interests that often had been neglected for years. In addition, we offered facilitator roles in the project assisting our experts to the adolescents who were helping compile the lists. Some, but not all of them, accepted.

It was also necessary to find outside expertise to facilitate the activities skilfully. As soon as I arrived in the country, I began to look for artists, actors, animators, intellectuals, musicians, teachers, instructors, psychologists of the arts (a discipline that once existed in the former Yugoslavia) and anyone else with previous experience in community work. We spread the word in bars, cultural centres, associations, scout groups and so on. We put up notices in theatres, in newspapers, in front of cinemas and at the university.

In order to start, I needed to identify what resources were available. I needed to know that the technical terms I had to use were understood. I needed to learn about the existing approaches to creativity and working with communities. Then, I needed to locate professionals who were among the best in their fields, with an attitude conducive to community and group work. Finally, I wanted people who belonged to different segments of society but were all creative and, above all, committed to social communication. In this way, they could facilitate the social communication process, even if this was not their specific task, disseminating the work they were going to do in their respective communities. The selected team consisted of photographers, playwrights (from alternative theatre, commercial theatre, and television), local rock stars, members of NGOs in visible opposition to the regime, a doctor, a movie animator, some scouts and graduates of the Sports Academy. Although the group included refugees and IDPs, the majority was from the local population. This group became what we referred to as the 'central team.'

Training

I trained the central team, asking them to pass along the model that emerged from this process to the adult refugees living in the community centres who were willing to work with us. As soon as young facilitators in the centres were identified, each began training in a programme specifically designed for them. I asked an experienced local NGO specializing in youth development to train the young facilitators.

The first time the central team came together, even before talking about their contracts, I decided to test them. I explained the terrible situation in which some Roma IDPs were living. I asked them to go, without me, to these Roma settlements. The objective was to carry out creative activities with the children that had as their objective the prevention of skin infections, which were caused by the insect bites that were ravaging their faces. A doctor provided the content and we prepared a programme built around the story of a bird without water, which was presented through songs, stories, drawings and a workshop offered advice to the children as well as to the adults. We came up with the idea of leaving a birdcage in the camp, along with bird food and hygiene instructions. Our assumption was that if the children could take care of the birds, they would take care of themselves. I knew the squalor the team was likely to find and its political implications. The Roma were kept in terrible conditions so that they would return to Kosovo rather than stay in Serbia – even if at that time it meant certain death. I knew that in this context such a programme would not have significant results, but I needed to evaluate the team's reactions. When they came back, they were shocked and offended by the conditions in the settlements but already they were thinking about how to improve the programme. I realized that through this test of fire, we now had a team. Later, Roma activists themselves facilitated the activities in their settlements.

I will not dwell on the various aspects of what amounted to on-the-job training. This training was loose, taking place in variable settings and groups, including long conversations in the car and at dinner. However, I would like to emphasize a great richness that this form of training has in emergency situations. The lack of a specific structure and thus the informality, leads to a less rigid border between professionalism and the human experience of a group, even while the professional objective remains steadfast. Interpersonal bonds are strengthened by all that is learned. Each discussion and each achievement has an immediate effect on the work and on the group. The urgency forces you as a trainer to quickly come up with and transmit a reproducible tool that can be used by the trainees in their field work, and can coincidentally present examples of more general processes. This leads to a circularity that, I can say from experience, brings more benefits than confusion.

The activities

As mentioned previously, after some weeks we had lists of activities that the different groups wanted to engage in the collective centres. They varied from hairdressing to percussion, from theatre to rock music and photography, from football to volleyball and basketball. Many mothers asked us to run activities for very small children so that they could have some time for themselves.

The actual plan of activities tried to balance the requests made by the communities, the theoretical assumptions behind the project, the logistical implications of each activity, and the expertise and personal attitudes of the staff. We attempted to put into practice the model of the complex circle – creating safe spaces in the centres for creative expression and exchanges between individuals who had differences. We tried to create events that fostered mutual exchanges between the different creative groups within the centres, between the individual centres, and between all the centres and the wider Serbian society. The process and the results are outlined in the short description below.

Creative corners

In twenty collective centres, two informal IDP centres and three Roma settlements we created safe spaces for children, adolescents and elderly refugees. A space would be created in a room, when possible, or otherwise in a corner next to a wall or, in the worst case, such as in the Roma settlements, in a tent. These spaces were rehabilitated and equipped in order to run the different activities. They had to look nice; the community had to take care of them. In these spaces, the children and adolescents found a way of expressing their feelings and abilities by painting, singing, playing instruments, performing in plays, participating in photography and video workshops and any other activity they selected. Each was carried out for an hour and a half, twice a week. At least two activities were held in each 'corner' according to the specific requests of the centres' inhabitants. In some of the centres, adult refugees with artistic or artisan skills led workshops for the youngest in addition to the weekly programme. These included icon carving, painting, piano classes and crocheting.

Adolescents and young people carried out activities for the younger children on a voluntary basis. They had been trained to do so and worked with the central team. The adolescents participating in a creative activity during the week and organized the same activity for younger groups, thus improving their sense of responsibility.

'What a Fucking Place'

The common room in Nis became the space where the results of the activities from the various corners of the different collective centres were performed for the public. It was also the place where young and old refugees and the IDPs, even those not involved in our project, could show, perform and meet each other (by organizing concerts, parties, solo exhibits, fairs, etc.). It was the place where the different stages of the project were presented and discussed. Each time an event was organized, the inhabitants of the centres were invited to attend (with financed transportation), helping to establish a circle of creative communication. The media, journalists, politicians and other townspeople were invited as well, thus enlarging the circle to the level of social communication.

The beneficiaries, through a written questionnaire following informal discussions, chose the name of the common room. The name created some problems with our donors and with the local authorities, but we were able to keep it. 'What a Fucking Place' opened in October 1999 with a concert by a refugee rock band and the exhibition of paintings and photographs produced in the corners. Adolescents and their families from all the centres were invited, as well as representatives from local youth authorities, organizations and the media. It was a great party.

Memory

Embroidery and sewing activities for elderly women as well as card and chess tournaments for elderly men were organized in the centres. A memory activity was carried out in seven centres. During the sewing and card tournaments (daily rituals for the Serbian community) our animators encouraged the elderly who were so inclined to tell their stories and express their feelings. They used affective memory games and an autobiographical method, partially inspired by Duccio Demetrio (Demetrio 1997). A dramatist, involved in all phases of the process, wrote each story into a short story or monologue in the third person. The short story or monologue was then given as a gift to the person involved. If s/he agreed, this person could tell her or his story or have it told by an actor during a special storytelling evening that took place once a month in each community centre.

All the stories told throughout the month were presented during a special memory night that was held every month in the common room of Nis. The elderly 'owners' of the stories and their communities were invited to Nis for the event. They could tell their stories or listen to them being told, or could also decide not to present the story. The memory project created stronger relations between adults, as well as between the elderly and youngsters in the centres, reaffirming the role of the elderly within their communities. More generally, the memory evenings held in the common room of Nis, in front of a mixed audience of refugees from the centres and the local population, including artists, the authorities and media, were of political as well as social relevance.

After several weeks, it became clear that in some centres – not surprisingly the ones with the worst living conditions – the memory sessions provoked collective outcries, even though the programme tended to work on positive memories and avoided the subject of the war and loss. Because of this, a special programme was developed for these centres, where the activities of the memory programme were accompanied by psychological support, and a psychologist was added to every team.

Health education

In the Roma settlement a team of animators, directed by Doctor Nebojsa Brankovic and Nejsha (a marionette doctor), carried out a special health education programme. The purpose was to explain, using games and marionette shows, how to maintain a minimum level of hygiene given the terrible conditions in which they lived. Of course, the children paid much more attention to Nejsha, who had the same facial features as Doctor Brankovic. Later, the programme focused on sex education, mother-child relationships, HIV/AIDS prevention and contraception.

We received immediate feedback on the project: each time our car appeared in a Roma settlement, the children would run around the vehicle to greet us; after a while they did so with the palms of the hands completely open and still. It was to show us that they had washed their hands. This education programme was closed when the national health authorities were finally allowed to take care of the health situation in the Roma settlements and the IDPs were included in the national healthcare plan.

Soccer and basketball leagues

In each centre we organized one or two sports teams.

Adults as well as youths participated, and the teams ultimately included a very large number of players of all ages. There were two leagues between all community centres, one for children and one for adolescents and adults. It was a huge success, except for some organizational problems (for example, some players received their shoes too late and demanded to replay all the games!). On every day of the league, all the teams and their fans would arrive in Nis to play in various combinations. Teams from the town also participated. After the games, recreational activities were organized in the common room. These sports activities were based on the model of the complex circle, and we tried to have a very performative approach to the leagues—creating events and exchanges. After the first year, the leagues were no longer organized. The teams were incorporated into the different leagues being organized in the municipalities where their centres were located. Mutual matches between the teams of the various collective centres were and are organized directly by them.

Cinema club

A movie club was organized in the common room of Nis. A children's film was shown every other Friday afternoon, while a film for everyone else was shown in the evenings. Experimental films for students and adolescents were shown on the last Saturday of the month. On all occasions, a debate followed the film. The programmes were also shown in eight remote centres, in a kind of travelling cinema that also included post-film discussions as well as organized games. The films were selected according to their subjects. Two participants, Sasa Stefanovic and Srdjan Vresnik, were involved with the games, as well as with choosing the videos and facilitating the debates. Vresnik was a refugee from Croatia living in one of the collective centres. He began as an adolescent volunteer and is today a creative facilitator and a student of psychology.

2000

The Classic Theatre, a private theatre company associated with the government, started a programme focused on children's visions of the end of the millennium. Twenty-five workshop-rehearsals were held in various community centres. The children were supposed to direct the rehearsals and create the drama. The result was presented in the common room of Nis in January 2000. All the children involved and their families were invited to participate. Unfortunately, because the Classic Theatre was not trained for this type of work, instead of a process, the result was a prepackaged product. The theme for 2000 inexplicably focused on *Cinderella*.

But if the free and creative communication mechanism failed, the social communication mechanism worked well. When I arrived in Kosovo in May 2000, I was invited to attend the same show in the Serbian enclave of Gracanica. The Classic Theatre, though not paid to do so, continued to present the show, and also provided material assistance in the Serbian enclaves in Kosovo and to refugee centres throughout the federation. This part of the project ended after the first year, however, while the centres involved continue to host community theatre workshops for children.

Three and a half years later

Three and a half years later, Serbian society has undergone great changes. In 2001, after a very heavy electoral defeat, Milosevic became a prisoner in The Hague and the embargo of Serbia ended. Refugees and their plight were among the top priorities on the new government's agenda (at least until the new Prime Minister was assassinated). The project is still alive because the centres still exist, even if the new government has begun to close some of them and resettle the refugees in private homes. The government wanted to close all of the centres by the end of 2003. Indeed almost all the hotels have been privatized in the meantime and the new owners are lobbying for new solutions for the remaining refugees. Those who still live in the centres are now suffering hardship due to increases in the cost of living.

I completed the final training and the last supervision with the team in December 1999. Two other internationals and then the Serbian staff itself managed the project after I left. The core of the team remains in place even though some left because the project was not given proper support and others because they were just worn out. There were moments of extreme poverty in which the group worked on a voluntary basis and other phases in which the project received substantial funds. In the first few months of 2000, a lack of funds meant no opportunities to improve the programme. This was followed by a phase in which, for logistical reasons and by choice of the international manager, the work inside the centres got done but the transition to the subsequent circles stopped (Segre 1999/2000). Therefore the common room was used more as a safe place for the refugees being hosted in and around Nis than as a place for building relationships between the various centres and making connections with the outside world. The sports activities continued but without any leagues. The memory project continued successfully in the centres but no more memory evenings were held in the common room. The itinerant Cinema Club turned out to be the most popular activity.

From October 2000 to the spring of 2002, the social communication component was again established as the essential part of the process, but there was no further analysis or training on the psychosocial component of the work. Finally, in the spring of 2002, the project was handed over to a group of local NGOs, many involving the former central team and some including former adolescents who had been part of the activities over the years. Overall, the project continues to reach its beneficiaries through its model of intervention. For instance, the rock groups of the creative corners of some centres recently released their first CD. All this can be considered as a positive and important achievement for the group.

However, what are truly surprising to me are the facts:

(1) The group did not receive any training or any form of supervision about the content of the work and their experiences for two years. Psychosocial and creative activities are not like other types of work; they keep you constantly involved, burning energies and capacities. I am firmly convinced that the priorities of this type of project must include some structured exchanges, supervision and training of the staff, not only at the beginning, but throughout the project.

(2) The project has been duplicated almost identically every year. Some activities were shifted from one centre to another, and new centres have been involved, but the structure and the activities remained the same, even when the reality outside has developed and changed radically. I believe that a project has to be linked to its social and historical context and should be reevaluated and redesigned constantly because the needs of the beneficiaries keep changing.

Conclusions

Working on rituals, on the construction and reconstruction of individual, group and collective roles, on community building, on the creative reelaboration of mourning and anger should all be vital activities for war-torn and war-displaced communities. It is also essential to support the empowerment of internal differences and work on the collective limits and borders of each of the communities involved in war. This is from the perspective of strengthening individuals, increasing the diversity of their experiences, and for long-term intercultural goals. Theatre and theatrical actions are able to satisfy these needs. Theatre has to be understood here as a means of developing relationships, communication and expression that concentrates on the construction of roles. It contains the possibility of creating a circle of barters and encounters between differences and a real ability to work on the 'borders' – to forge passages and relationships between individuals, groups and communities.

This opportunity is the proper domain of the theatre because theatre's natural outcome is social communication. This process is fundamental when working with communities in war-torn situations, but it is also fundamental when, in order to change the status of a group or wider society's perception of a group, it is necessary to introduce its problems and ethics into the circle of communication between political subjects and decision-making powers. This process, starting with individuals and arriving at institutions, facilitates the construction of plural communities that contain extreme differences among members. This process has the capacity to reveal differences even in closed social systems that are characterized by an intense cohesion forged in the name of 'compulsory' values/non-values.

The above-mentioned process is linked directly to ritual. Theatrical ritual has always had a capacity to create a collective space for peaceful confrontation and dialogue among differences. The modern practice of theatre and psychosocial animation in war-torn situations is therefore nothing new. Theatre has always dealt with confronting the limits of human experience.

References

Barba, E., 'Theatre, Cohabitation of the Different', in *Armadilla 2001*, Milano: EDT, 2001.

Demetrio, D., *Il gioco della vita. Kit Autobiografico. Trenta proposte per raccontarsi*, Milano: Guerini ed associati, 1997.

Dokter, D. (ed.), *Arts Therapists, Refugees and Migrants: Reaching Across Borders*, London: Jessica Kingsley Publishers, 1998.

Jennings, S. (ed.), *Dramatherapy: Theory and Practice III*, London: Routledge, 1999.

Losi, N., 'Some Assumptions on Psychological Trauma Intervention in Post-Conflict Communities', in Papadopoulos, R. K. (ed.), *Therapeutic Care for Refugees: No Place Like Home*, London: Karnac Books, 2002, pp. 110–135.

Schininà, G., 'Cosí lontano, cosí vicino. Interventi di animazione psicosociale e creativa insituazioni d'emergenza e di conflitto nell'area dei Balcani', *Comunicazioni Sociali*, 23: 3 (2001), pp. 234–255.

———, 'Arts and the Theatre: A Circle of Barters and Encounters – A Training Module on Community Needs', *IOM Psychosocial Notebook*, 3: 3 (2002), pp. 67–104.

Segre, A., *La comunicazione sociale negli interventi di solidarietá internazionale. Il caso del consorzio italiano di solidarietá, tesi di laurea*, Padova: Universita' Di Padova, 1999/2000.

Note

1   This article is a translated, updated and summarized version of the article 'Così Lontano, Così Vicino', which appeared in *Comunicazioni Sociali* (Schininà 2001).

Chapter 10

Play Extract: *Refugees*

Zlatko Topčić
Translated into English by Davor Diklić

ROLES:	*Jester/Asim*, acted by the same actor. They are very strange and different.
	Almasa, a noble mature beauty.
	Adem, a Highlander who lost his left arm in war.
	Aziz, got away at the beginning, but he has been contributing from afar.
	Abaz, He is a toady, who got away at the beginning and has been contributing from afar.
	[...]

Light changes on Jester. During his speech the set changes into a bar with two men sitting at the table. They are motionless, looking into their glasses. Jester introduces them and, with a touch of his hand, they become 'alive.'

JESTER:	[...] As in life, everything changes with a twinkle – twinkle after twinkle. The place of the action is a bar called 'The Golden Lily', somewhere in the world where they fell like pollen brought by the wind. Home is far away. Sometimes I think: 'These people deserve disdain!', and then I admire them. They are coming from the world where people are made of extremes: a dog and a man in the same skin! They should disappear, I think sometimes: Mohammedians, they really don't belong to our world; they don't drink wine, they don't eat pork, they are circumcised – as if the smallest piece of that part of body was not precious! There aren't many of them, but they are good and proud with clear eyes and with the look clean and straight like the look of a ram. They fell somewhere from the sky down between two crosses, as if God sent them to make the world more colorful. They have a great role trapped between the hammer and the nail...... someone could even laugh if this was not made for crying. I wouldn't like to be an actor in this play. But nobody chooses his path and everybody's path is given...... different, only words that explain it are the same. Ah, misery, suffering...... love is known. About that they sing, talk...... it being so rare...... they create sonnets about it because love is their treasure. Shhhh...... *(exits)*

AZIZ:	*(Wrapped in the Bosnian flag with fleur de lis, drunk.)* There is nothing I wouldn't give for my Bosnia. Do you want my head? Or, you want my heart? Here it is.
ABAZ:	But … it's not … that Bosnia any more. That Bosnia … doesn't exist.
AZIZ:	What do you mean 'doesn't exist'? Where could it be, then?
ABAZ:	A bit of it in Croatia, much more in Serbia … you open the window in Sarajevo to take a deep breath, and look at the mountains, you see … a miracle. A miracle that the world hasn't seen yet. The mount Trebević disappeared over night and Šumadjja, somewhere from Serbia turned up here.
AZIZ:	Never! Never, as long as we live, until the last Bosnian heart is still beating. Never! We should be organized, send help. Do you see these people here? They take care of theirs and look at us! One cares for oneself!
ABAZ:	Right you are. Only together we can stop Serbs.
AZIZ:	Bridle!
ABAZ:	Curb!
AZIZ:	Fold!
ABAZ:	Shhhh … *(together)* Shhhh …
AZIZ:	We have to organize our artists, to have concerts for Bosnia. We have talents. We need only bass and drums … I am going, mother, to defend Bosnia myself. When we pay for the hall, electricity, insurance, publicity, tickets, printing, and food … everything left over we are going to send to Bosnia.
ABAZ:	I am writing a poem. Something like a monument: not made of stone, but of words, It's too fragile, to last forever. My beaten-up Bosnia …! Something heavy, angry, bitter eye-opening …

Adem enters. He sits at another table.

ADEM:	… if you add some pepper, you'll have soup.
AZIZ:	Let's not talk about politics today, Adem.
ABAZ:	You know the politics have brought us here, where we are.
AZIZ:	Let s not speak about merits, either.
ABAZ:	Nobody's. Neither yours, nor mine!
AZIZ:	I will constrain myself too!

Aziz, ashamed, takes the flag off, folds it and puts into his pocket

AZIZ:	Do you know that another hero has come from Bosnia? He is crippled too … not like you that could be seen from far away … but he says that his wounds are serious and deep in his soul.
ABAZ:	Now, Adem, you are not the only hero around here any more.
ADEM:	I wish we all were, Abaz and Aziz.
ABAZ:	God didn't make everybody a hero. Someone a hero, someone a weakling. God knows what's better. I know what hurts less. I am also going to Bosnia, as soon as my back gets better.
AZIZ:	His name is Asim. He says he was a warrior and he sent a hundred of Chetniks to hell to burn there.
ADEM:	Good warrior. I hope that's true.
ABAZ:	He comes here every night to talk. We buy him drinks and he tells us stories. We listen to him with our mouths open. It's unbelievable!
AZIZ:	It's strange that he hasn't come yet.
ABAZ:	I wish he were here.
AZIZ:	And he is not here as for spite.

Silence. *Abaz and Aziz are whispering.*

AZIZ:	It's not a good time, Adem. It's actually very bad.
ADEM:	It's not good.
ABAZ:	Everything's very expensive … it will be better …, I hope.
ADEM:	It will be. It couldn't be worse.
AZIZ:	Do your wounds hurt … from last summer when you leveled a bunch of Chetniks and they leveled you, too?
ADEM:	No, one's wounds don't hurt, but the soul suffers when one sees … and it wasn't a bunch of Chetniks, there were only three.
AZIZ:	Ours are doing well there.
ADEM:	Yes, they are. It would be better if they had more weapons and if there were more of us there.
ABAZ:	Chetniks are nasty people.
ADEM:	Very nasty, there aren't worse then them … and they are not human beings, they are just Chetniks.
AZIZ:	Why did it happen to us!? We don't deserve it.
ADEM:	We did, because we forgot God. Now he is trying us, calling us and warning us.

Aziz and Abaz come very close to Adem.

AZIZ:	Do you think, Adem, that it is true what everyone speaks around here that every human being was an animal before and will, after death, become an animal again, or something even worse…
ABAZ:	People are afraid of becoming… Chetniks.
AZIZ:	People are dying a lot these days, so, Adem, they are very concerned.
ADEM:	(*Stands up suddenly obviously upset*) God knows that, not people.

Silence.

AZIZ:	Have you found it out?
ABAZ:	It would be right if you knew.
ADEM:	Know what?
ABAZ:	That … where is she from?
ADEM:	Who …?
AZIZ:	Almasa.
ABAZ:	Your Almasa.
ADEM:	Oh, my Almasa.
AZIZ:	Almasa. Yours. Where is she from?
ADEM:	From nowhere, she says, and I believe her.
AZIZ:	From nowhere. Well, that's where she is from.
ABAZ:	Nowhere. Where is that?
AZIZ:	Fine!
ABAZ:	We will believe her if she says so and if you believe that she is from nowhere.
AZIZ:	Do you know, at least, whose she is?
ADEM:	Her mother's and father's. And mine, she says. But mostly herself's.
ABAZ:	Herself's?
AZIZ:	She's on her own.
ABAZ:	What do you mean: 'Herself's?' A woman must be somebody's.
AZIZ:	Yours.
ADEM:	She is herself's and mine and I am hers.
AZIZ:	O.K., then we will believe her if you believe that she is from nowhere and nobody's.
ADEM:	Good.
AZIZ:	It's not good … but it's O.K.
ABAZ:	O.K. but not quite good.
AZIZ:	Bad.
ABAZ:	Very bad.

ADEM: Well, O.K., let's say it is bad …

[…]

Darkness. Light on Jester.

JESTER: The story, like a river, flows in its course. There are hundreds of
                          possibilities for one who sings it to find oneself in front of a delta.
                          There is always only one ending. If you want a happy ending it's
                          time to end it now and everyone should go home: once upon a
                          time there was she … once upon a time there was he … they lived
                          long lives together in happiness and joy. But who looks for the
                          truth must look in the darkness with us for that precious stone …
                          shhhh …

Aziz and Abaz are at 'The Golden Lilly.'

AZIZ: It's going to be a concert for Bosnia … about Bosnia … for the
                          sake of Bosnia … from Bosnia …
ABAZ: In Bosnia!?
AZIZ: Here, you fool!
ABAZ: Of course, not over there!
AZIZ: We can do much more here for Bosnia.
ABAZ: Sometimes I am really stupid … In Bosnia…
AZIZ: You can see further and better from here.
ABAZ: When you move far away, you can see the entire field
AZIZ: Here, we will sing with music and my poem. Let people hear it.
ABAZ: They will listen to it with their mouths open *(opens his mouth)* …
                          they will wonder how it is possible to have such a great poet over
                          there. Such a great one, here in front of their nose. So great and
                          right here among them.
AZIZ: I wonder if anyone after all this, will come to us and say: 'Thank
                          you.'
ABAZ: … one simple, the simplest possible, warm, human 'Thank you.'
AZIZ: And 'Thank you, brothers, for the suffering you went through. We
                          can count on you in the worst misfortune, as well as in celebration
                          … you, when it was the hardest, the most bitter, you gave us …
                          brother Aziz!'
ABAZ: 'We will never forget, brother Abaz!'

They start crying together touched by their own goodness. Suddenly, Aziz jumps.

AZIZ:	But, maybe they won't!
ABAZ:	*(Surprised and disappointed)* Do you really think they could be the way you suspect!?
AZIZ:	Them there … they are like that!
ABAZ:	*(With anger)* Like that! Well, brothers, that's the case with you!
AZIZ:	They will look at us differently.
ABAZ:	Then they don't deserve us moving our little finger for them.
AZIZ:	Tomorrow, they won't be able to breathe from their own merits.
ABAZ:	*(Imitating)* 'I was hungry … I was thirsty … It was cold … It was bitter …'
AZIZ:	Only when they deserve us, they will get us … maybe … maybe …
ABAZ:	Just when my back gets better. As if it was easy for us here? What about home sickness? What about longing? What about adaptation?
AZIZ:	But, we are better than them, and we don't need anything in return, not even 'Thank you.'
ABAZ:	Goodness for the goodness sake … Concert … A net income. It's obvious.
AZIZ:	At the concert … a poem … for Bosnia … about Bosnia … because of Bosnia …
ABAZ:	In Bosnia?
AZIZ:	Here, you fool!

Almasa and Adem enter and listen for some time to Abaz and Aziz. At the end of their conversation, Almasa gives them the presents she was holding. She walks around looking like a queen and gets very excited.

ALMASA:	Let's dance, Adem. I want to dance so often … dance … the whole night and the next day. When I dance it looks like I am flying far away, far away … and I am light like a bird, without weight, with feathers on my skin and with air in my bones …

They start dancing. Adem doesn't know how to waltz and drags his feet like a bear. She leads him, turns him, enjoying herself tremendously and going faster and faster. Aziz and Abaz start dancing, too, drinking brandy from the bottle that Almasa gave them – they look silly. Then they notice that Almasa and Adem are dancing more and more in harmony and beautifully. They stop and watch, puzzled.

ADEM:	I never danced, you won't believe me, but you have many times before, haven't you?

ALMASA:	Dance carries me and my feet go on their own … and you, you dance like it's the hundredth time. Look at you … how you are dancing.
AZIZ:	How could he learn so fast? He couldn't dance a moment ago.
ABAZ:	There are people who are born like that – they don't need much …
AZIZ:	The same like me, more or less.
ABAZ:	Sometimes, can manage, too.

Almasa and Adem dance faster with more passion. Asim, the warrior, is already there, watching. When they stop, Almasa sees Asim and Adem doesn't. Almasa is obviously afraid of Asim.

ADEM:	I am so happy now, Almasa. I was never so happy, not even in the trenches. It's so beautiful I would like more …
ALMASA:	It's getting late, Adem. Some other time. It's time to go.
ADEM:	We have just come. And we are happy … Look, here is Asim who owes us a dream.
ASIM:	Two. Tonight, for the lady, because of the lady, two…
ADEM:	Do it fast, Asim, our child is waiting for us at home.
ASIM:	I am glad to meet you. I will give you two dreams. First the second one, and then the first, because we will keep the better one for the end.
AZIZ:	Nice of you. Tell us the second one in a word or two so we can get to the main thing.
ABAZ:	You are generous.
AZIZ:	Let's listen to the second one. Tell it in a word or two and then come to the point.
ABAZ:	I am as impatient as a soldier with a woman …
ASIM:	I had a bad dream: I am a Chetnik and everything that I am not. I walk over the corpses: it feels like walking on pebbles and it feels like I am not a human being, I as if were not alive; I don't feel fear or disgust. I step with one foot on somebody's head, with another on somebody else's shoulder. Then I move my right foot to a child's arm with a clenched hand – threatening sign to someone – to me? – with my left I step on somebody else's breasts, big, motherly full of milk with a colorful sweater over them; I push myself and stumble over somebody's slippery legs, slippery of mass. I have a couple of marbles in my hands – somebody's eyes. A river, wide, shallow, without a name and an edge… above the river there is dense fog, dense and thick, through which birds without wings fly … the song of a peacock is heard from somewhere, bringing wet wind over the endless and lifeless river. How do I know these

are tears that I walk through? – I don't feel neither wetness not bitterness. I hear a voice telling me "Back to life, dead regions – that's the way you will be brought back to life." I am alone – there is nobody here except me, yet I feel someone's presence and a glance the color of chamomile on me. There are no secret talks among the three unless He is the fourth, or among the five, unless He is the sixth one. No matter if their number goes up or down – He is always with them. I walk while water doesn't make any noise as if its tears were made solely of misery. Black and blue heads like blown balloons float among swollen bodies, giving a strong support for my steps. Where am I coming from and where am I going? I keep walking over naked dolls with pink, glassy eyes… it smells like heavy sweat… I feel joy. How easy it is to be without soul; state of bliss, a sort of freedom! This way I could even be happy. Then something suddenly happens: in the mud, in the slimy mud, I step on my own head.

Aziz and Abaz are bored, yawning and waiting for the next dream.

AZIZ:	Yes, yes, that's very … without any doubt … a very powerful dream … educational, good and very powerful. A bit too long, though, but you have to be satisfied with every gift you get …
ABAZ:	It passed in a jiffy for me … can we hear the first one now?
ALMASA:	For today, for us, this one is enough … it's time to go home.
ASIM:	It will take a blink of an eye, maybe even less …
ADEM:	Let's hear it … we are already here anyway.
ASIM:	It is morning. Every picture is clearly seen. Morning … bright … vehement … with clear shapes so you can remember longer, as long as you live. Dolidi Donji, that's the name of my village not far away from Bijeljine. My village is calm and gentle in the valley between two mountains an inch from the sky. My village. Our village. It's a little paradise. It's full of people. But the world is so small, and if you go on a desert island and further still, your village will follow you step by step and you will hear a voice from it … suddenly everything starts spinning around … the ground is trembling! How did it happen? That everything turns into a hell? When the Chetniks come … when they burn the village … when they engrave crosses into my skin with knives … when they slaughter all the members of Hakrja's household. When they bind with a wire all of Ekrem's when hundreds end

194

up in the bloody river Drina … when they, my Almasa, rape you in front of your father, brother, in front of the entire village … ten of them … twenty of them … rape you … *(Asim opens his eyes as if he just woke up, comes up to Almasa and looks closely in her eyes)*

Do you remember me, my Almasa, we grew up together … you should remember me, it wasn't so long ago … do you remember, Almasa, I was lying down all in blood as if I was dead but I stayed alive … my eyes were alive, my poor Almasa.

Almasa goes out Adem approaches Asim.

ASIM: You must know this. It's for your own good. You live your life with many lies already … that child, brother, has many bearded fathers!

ADEM: *(Holding Asim's neck with his only hand)* Liar, dog! Do you want to destroy even this dream of mine!?

ASIM: *(Without resisting)* I am guilty, Yes, I am, I am destroying your dream … lie, deceit could bring it, and already did, into heavens … but, do you think it was easy for me to tell the truth? Do I have the right to a lie, if you don't give me the right to truth?

ADEM: This is not the truth, this is a lie!

ASIM: Almasa is not guilty in God's eyes – poor she, she is good and unhappy. The child she gave birth to is not guilty in God's eyes. I am giving you the truth and I don't know if I put a burden on your soul or not, if I committed a crime or not … I said it, and you have to decide what to do with it … I thought for a long time about what to do: 'Am I going to destroy everything or not?' But now, you know … she is not guilty in God's eyes … but, for you … is she pure, brother?

Adem hits the table with his fist and exits. Lights on Jester.

JESTER: The story is coming to its terrible end. What kind of advice can it give to us? Now, I am standing in front of you as a guilty man, as a criminal. Nobody is innocent here. I had a dream and that's my crime. There are hundreds of possibilities, and only one end: those who did it, those who suffered it, those who told it, and those who watched in silence like you did – we are all parts of the chain of victimization? Well, let it be then!? But the suffering that exists in someone's life is tremendous, why is it then a sin to throw some light on it? Let it be known: 'The truth, the whole truth and nothing but the truth.' So help us God.

Darkness. Light on Almasa and Adem in their room.

ALMASA: You can kill me, the guilty one … that would be easy. Why have we been coming to each other like a bear to honey … anyway, this misery would find its way into our lives like a foal into the grass field. It happened … there is nothing we can do to erase the past. But, where are we … *(pause)* They made me filthy forever, with filth under my skin; all the rivers of the world couldn't wash it off. They infested me with pus, so I can hate myself and everything that's mine: Alma is mine … came from me and someone … one of them …

My father spat on me, my brother rejected me, and the other one would have done the same if he had stayed alive … what are you waiting for? You have even more right to do so, you are my husband. What are you guilty for? To suffer my wounds? You have enough of your own … I must not ask from anyone to be a part of my misery!

No matter what, I know, there will be a silent question, I can see it on your lips … 'They are filthy, drunk, greasy, evil, and they were inside you, there, where I, in love, was too? They spilled the semen at the same place … or pus!?' From the pus in me grew, in my womb, a baby … I gave birth to … Alma! A human being without a sin.

My Alma! I say that in full voice, with all my strength, only now.

Isn't she going to stand between us and remind you forever, of the picture: long line of men. They exchanged me when it was too late. Isn't she carrying, little as she is, a birdie still, the seed of her father's evil … he is the father even though I am the mother. The seed is waiting… hiding in the corner and waiting to explode. Isn't that sin aimed at me, at you!? No! God knows how much I love you, how much I trembled over us. To love you meant to enlarge my sin. 'Is that a "thank you" for goodness?' – you ask, I see that, hear that, know that. Was that the way to find out the truth – from someone else. Everything is the cruelest game – we are played with and everyone knows the score! You returned me to life. Maybe that's your sin. If it was different, would it hurt less? Maybe there is some justice in it? Soot is black, without a sin, but it really is black! My Alma. My destiny. I don't have the strength to look into your eyes. That voice came to destroy the secret, everything. Maybe to make it easier for me because it is the hardest to wait in fear for the evil to come. When it comes somehow, it's easier. That's happening to me. My God, how light and naked I am.

Was I supposed to tell you the truth? I think it's good that I didn't. This way, until recently, we had love and a lie, now, with the truth, nothing is left. God is the witness that I am innocent in front of people and in front of Him, but I know I am not innocent in front of you. I don't ask for forgiveness because I didn't get it from my father or my brother, and why should you, my husband, who took someone else's child as his own. And she is not the only one who stands between us … only God knows what I would be capable of doing … I love you so much … I wanted to throw her… the part of her that is not mine, but I didn't know how to recognize which one is that, and I threw all of her, away once, long time ago … she started crying as if she was calling me, saying: 'My mother.' I had to take her back, and now she is with me to love … and hate her at the **same** time.

Thus, last night the end has come. Luckily we are all dead by now. They killed us finally. My God, let it be better the next time. In the future life, don't give us human shapes, and if it is human, please don't let me be a woman … let them kill me like a dog or crush me like a fly … my God! My Almighty God!

Darkness, Light on Jester.

JESTER: What happened to them in the end? I don't know much about that myself. They said Adem went to Bosnia and there entered that winter dream of Asim's. Almasa lived for a while; nobody never saw Alma in her lap anymore. When they were so drunk to gain the courage to enter the refugee shelter, Aziz and Abaz didn't find anyone except this dove which looked at them from the edge of the table with its glassy eyes and without anything human in them.

He lets the dove out of his hand. The end.

Chapter 11

'Politics Begins as Ethics': Levinasian Ethics and Australian Performance Concerning Refugees

Tom Burvill

T his chapter discusses a selection of the diverse Australian theatre and performance work concerning refugees and asylum seekers in the light of Emmanuel Levinas's radical concept of ethics. Levinas invokes an unconditional responsibility for the other, signalled by the epiphany of the encounter with 'the face of the other.'[1] For Levinas this traumatic encounter with alterity founds ethical subjectivity *as* responsibility. Especially during the period from late 2001 to 2004, Australian theatre produced an extraordinary array of performance responses to the refusal of generosity and hospitality, the denial of ethical responsibility, inherent in the Howard Government's policy towards asylum seekers. The extreme 'border protection' regime put in place by the State encouraged a widespread xenophobic 'border panic' at the same time it effectively removed asylum seekers from national space. Louis Joinet, of the United Nations Working Group on Arbitrary Detention declared that 'a system [such as practised in Australia] combining mandatory, automatic, indiscriminate and indefinite detention [of asylum seekers] without real access to court challenge is not practised by any other country in the world' (Joinet 2002: 18).

The productions created in response to this situation adopted a variety of performance strategies, but in explicit ways attempted to articulate an ethical approach to those who present themselves at our borders seeking asylum. The productions I will discuss present different tactics for approaching two major issues that have been the subject of ethical political performance work in this area: the human consequences of the anti-ethical policy of 'hide-away' detention and the tragic sinking of the *SIEV X*, which drowned hundreds of asylum seekers. Sidetrack Performance Group's *Citizen X: Letters from Refugees* (2002) and Shahin Shafaei's solo piece *Refugitive* (2003) probe the first issue; the second is at the heart of Hannie Rayson's *Two Brothers* (2005b) and *CMI (A Certain Maritime Incident)* (2004) by Sydney company version 1.0.

However diverse in form, I see the majority of the Australian shows on the topic of asylum as interventions impelled by ethical outrage at what was being done 'in our name' by the Howard Government. They are attempts to assume the 'responsibility for the other' denied by the Government's cynical policies and to provoke that assumption of responsibility in their audiences. These works were not so much concerned therefore with ideological as with affective transformations in their audiences and constituted a performance of ethics in themselves; they were forms of ethical practice.

Levinasian ethics

Dissatisfied with philosophy's preoccupation with being and essence – its occlusion of our relation with others – Levinas argues that ethics must be fundamental to philosophy and that ethics involves an openness to the face of the other and a responsibility for the other. Indeed he speaks of this responsibility as the essential, primary and fundamental structure of subjectivity. In Levinas's words, 'Positively we will say that since the Other looks at me, I am responsible for him, without even having *taken on* responsibilities in his regard; his responsibility is *incumbent on me*' (Levinas 1985: 96; original emphasis). He continues:

> I analyze the inter-human relationship as if, in proximity with the Other – beyond the image I myself make of the other man – his face, the expressive in the Other (and the whole human body is in this sense more or less face) were what *ordains* me to serve him. I employ this extreme formulation. The face orders and ordains me.
>
> (Levinas 1985: 97; original emphasis)

In this simple gesture of individual response-ability to the face of the other, the ethical relation is born. Ethics for Levinas involves 'the putting into question of the self by the infinitising mode of the face of the other' (Robbins 1999: xiii). Levinas is fond of reinforcing the absolute character of this responsibility, quoting Dostoyevsky's formulation in *The Brothers Karamazov* that 'We are all responsible for all men before all, and I more than all the others' (Ettinger 1997: 22). The concept of ethics elaborated by Levinas is a radical one, and not only in the sense of claiming a foundational place in the concept of the self, of subjectivity. However, it is also important that it is through our response to the other that we are connected to what Levinas calls the 'third', to society itself. In Levinas's formulation ethics therefore is inextricably bound up with the political. The epiphany of the face and the discourse to which it gives rise 'attests to the presence of the third party, of humanity as a whole, in the eyes that look at me': 'It is my responsibility before a face looking at me as absolutely foreign ... that constitutes the original fact of fraternity' (Levinas 1979: 213). In Simon Critchley's words, 'The ethical relation does not take place in an a-political space outside the public realm; rather, ethics is always already political, the relation to the face is always already a relation to humanity as a whole' (Critchley 1992: 226). It is in this sense, at least, that politics begins as ethics.

Levinas says that it is in the encounter with the 'face' of the other that we experience infinite and transcendent alterity. He invokes this experience as a way to express the immediacy, the non-negotiable radicality of the ethical encounter with the other, the way that experience in fact actually calls us into existence as subjects, interpellates us *as* ethical subjects, collapsing the scales of the infinite and the intimate. The 'face' can also refer to 'speech (or any other typically human aspect that reveals the other)' (Peperzak et al. 1996: xi).

Even more effectively than the asylum seekers detained onshore in Australia, those sent to Nauru and other island gulags as part of the so-called Pacific Solution to unauthorized immigration have been deliberately placed 'out of sight, out of mind.' All those in detention were effectively rendered faceless and voiceless to the majority of the Australian population, their actual faces and voices as well as images of them systematically hidden from us by Government edict even as they were slandered continually by Government ministers. In a highly visual and mediatized society, not to have media images of 'newsworthy' subjects renders them not quite real. We have had ominous media images of the camps at a distance, of guards and barbed wire, all signifying imprisonment and implying criminality in those interned therein, but no access to the faces of the detainees.

I believe we may take Levinas's injunction to assume the 'unassumable responsibility' for the other, for all others, to enjoin a state of mind, a readiness of openness to alterity. We may take it as indicating a basic affect, a 'comportment' towards the other, almost literally an embodied habit of openness. This becomes significant when we begin to look for the trace of the Levinasian ethical in specific work. It is not so much the characters' struggle with moral dilemmas, so central to the traditions of serious European drama, that is the issue here. It is more a matter of how the experience of 'being there' interpellates the audience, what it 'does to you' to be present at the event of the performance, in terms of the encounter with alterity.

Levinas: Art as substitution versus 'the saying and the said'

Jill Robbins points out that at various points Levinas expresses an objection to art, understood as mimetic representation or what he calls 'substitution.' In his early work he sees the attempt to 'represent' the face of the other as fundamentally an obstacle to the embodied response to the other which initiates the ethical encounter. He thus casts art as a dangerous substitution of an image for the face itself. This substitution is a form of sovereign knowing of the other which does not call my own subjectivity into question and which puts an image in place of the face-to-face encounter. Robbins claims that the theoretical stance in the early essay, 'Reality and its Shadow,' is that art is by nature unethical: 'art is a kind of irresponsibility, that it is a kind of death, an idolatry' (Robbins 1999: 83). Indeed Robbins cites Levinas as writing even in the major later work *Totality and Infinity* that '[t]he whole possibility, indeed the very temptation, of violence is inscribed in the face's presentation as form or image' (Levinas cited in Robbins 1999: 84).

However, there is another side to this question. Performance, as an embodied and interactive *event*, as processual practice unfolding within the co-presence of its spectators and actors in real time, need not be subject to Levinas's objection here. This type of performance, perhaps performance qua performance, may be thought of as interactive human discourse, a form of what Levinas calls 'the saying' rather than the more purely representational 'said.' In *The Ethics of Deconstruction*, Critchley explains that in Levinas,

the Saying is my exposure – corporeal, sensible – to the Other, my inability to refuse the Other's approach. It is the performative stating, proposing, or expressive position of myself facing the Other. It is a verbal or non-verbal ethical performance whose essence cannot be caught in constative propositions. It is a performative doing.

(Critchley 1992: 7)

Critchley continues: 'The saying is the sheer radicality of human speaking, of the event of being in relation to an Other; it is the non-thematisable ethical residue of language that escapes comprehension [and] interrupts philosophy' (Critchley 1992: 7). Critchley's articulation of performative nature of 'the saying,' I believe, helps to identify the way performance practice may be ethical in the Levinasian sense, particularly his reference to the 'sheer radicality of human speaking' as the event of being in relation to another, a relation which itself constitutes an ethical enactment.

Levinas's insistence on the 'event' of the ethical encounter suggests something embodied, something that happens, something, in that sense, performative. What we might call a truly Levinasian performance then might not be so much simply a staging of ethical or unethical behaviour or situations (although it could certainly include those things) as it would be a provocation to an experience of the ethical encounter with alterity, embodying the enactment of that 'unassumable responsibility.' This is again not necessarily so much about knowledge of the other, or information about their situation (although in the refugee context this may be necessary to make possible the ethical encounter) as it is about the ethical quality of the experience itself, about a certain kind of affect. It is not perhaps even about, in the first instance, empathy or sympathy with the other, as these forms of relationship may be more about seeing in the other what is like oneself (what Levinas calls the Same). It is perhaps something more purely embodied than that, less explicit. We might be able to suggest that at least some modes or moments of performance have some of this character. These might be forms or instances of performance in which the face of the other is not simply represented or imaged but where a relationship or connection with the other or perhaps with otherness as such is transitively created.

Australian interventions

I want to indicate how a sample of productions from different genres dealt with the ethical challenge of the refugee issue. To sketch the range of responses, I will confine my discussion to particular aspects and/or brief moments of the shows concerned. In each case the dramaturgical solution was deeply conditioned by the specific context of performance. I believe this is consistent with the productions as pieces designed to encourage that genuine engagement with asylum seekers.

In a very interesting essay in *Borderlands*, Paul Miller (2004) applies a Levinasian perspective to the lies told by the Australian Government over the supposed 'children overboard' incident (see David Williams's essay for details; Williams 2008). Miller asks, 'How might the discourse around the children overboard affair have been different if one adopted a Levinasian understanding of ethics and the logic of hospitality and un-assumable responsibility?' In response to this question, he proposes that

> Levinas's philosophy demands a primacy be given to the recognition of the other as an absolute Other calling for hospitality. In relation to the asylum seekers, this change in affect would have totally resituated the problematic, not so much by telling us what we should have done, but by ruling out any response that came totally from a position of sovereign self interest whether individually or as a nation. At a minimum it would have required a genuine engagement with these asylum seekers as people rather than as simply invaders.
>
> (Miller 2004)

In what follows, I argue that a number of Australian productions demonstrated a broadly Levinasian ethical approach to the possibilities of performance as a form of response to the asylum seekers, albeit in quite different ways.

Refugitive is a one-man show written and performed by Iranian refugee playwright and actor Shahin Shafaei (discussed at more length by Rand Hazou; Hazou 2008). The piece is a recreation and reflection on the surreal quality of the refugee in detention and the often cruel absurdity of the actions of immigration officials and of detention camp life in general. There is a pervasive sense of melancholy in the piece that speaks of a very general condition and a sadness borne of direct experience. The performance is poetic in form and in diction, and strongly physical, with rapid transformations between characters, drawing on Shafaei's performance training and Iranian traditions of storytelling. Using only a single blanket, he transforms into different detainee figures and into two figures of authority, the official from the Department of Immigration and Multicultural and Indigenous Affairs (DIMIA) and the Homer Simpson-like Australian Correctional Management (ACM) overseer. *Refugitive* is set in a cell in the isolation wing of the Curtin detention centre, the 'India' compound, which the central detainee character known as The Man addresses as 'lovely India Compound, cave of loneliness' (Shafaei 2003). The performance ends with The Man reciting directly to the audience a poem in eight stanzas. As the light fades, he holds out his hands to the audience and recites: 'I dreamed I saw a building with one thousand floors, / One thousand windows and one thousand doors, / Not one of them was ours, my dear, not one of them was ours' (Shafaei 2003).

As a portable one-man show, *Refugitive* could be performed in any hall or meeting room requiring only a small amount of available floor as the playing area. This portability meant that Shafaei was invited to perform in scores of theatre and non-theatre community settings to all kinds of audiences including in many rural settings with initially hostile or sceptical audiences. Shafaei (2006) has pointed out that some of these hostile audiences provided good opportunities to debate the issues – and make vital contact with people who were in fact responding face to face, albeit at times with anger. It seems to me that this form of encounter, not simply with the represented conditions of detention and its psychological consequences for detainees but also with the responsive and interactive intelligent maker of the show, willing to answer and respond in turn to responses, inherently increases the likelihood of the audience's ethical engagement with the issue of hospitality to the refugee. In Levinasian terms, even an angry response is a response, an encounter with alterity, much better than a refusal to engage. After-show discussion was always integrated into the presentation. This Shafaei regarded as a crucial part of the efficacy of the performance.

The eloquent presence of the actual body of the former detainee grounds the performance strongly not only in personal testimony but also in the corporeal face-to-face encounter. In moments of comedy, Shafaei's physical adaptations to the grotesques of the DIMIA and ACM buffoons enacts the resilience of his sense that in a surreal world he still sees what is absurd and has not become the abject figure, the victim of the authoritarian situation. The performer's own melancholy dignity and physical grace – the image of dignity in a solitary confinement cell – evokes pity and anger in the audience certainly, but is filtered through a renewed sense of the immanence of human value, the value of the human itself.

Citizen X by Sydney's Sidetrack Performance Group also focuses on the condition of detention in ways that call for an ethical response. The script was woven together from letters from a number of unnamed incarcerated asylum seekers, thereby continuing that quiet ethical form of activism involved in establishing correspondence with the particular detainees. In 'making public' the letters as part of a new text, *Citizen X* perhaps creates a third kind of space, a space in which the directness of testimony, of 'bearing witness' in that direct and interpersonal way, is reclaimed for an audience representing not the original personal addressee, but the social collectivity. The dramaturgy the Sidetrack show adopted did not try to turn the material from letters into narrative but rather took a haunting poetic form, as voices and themes rose and fell. The three actors did not attempt to impersonate the letter writers but, as it were, to deliver their message, often an imploring one, very often a sad and desperate one, usually couched in imperfect English that betrayed the signs of laborious work with a dictionary. Amazingly, few of the letters are angry and accusatory, and many are eloquent in surprisingly lyrical ways. Perhaps because of this lack of aggression in the letters, the show also included the extremely confronting and accusatory verbatim testimony of a female Australian nurse who served in the detention centres, delivered straight to the audience with painful force.

In the original Sidetrack production in 2002, each of the actors presented in body and voice their non-Anglo ethnicity, not 'representing' particular ethnicities in detention, but certainly displaying via accent and skin colour, some of the 'unassimilable' embodiments (African, 'Middle Eastern,' Indian) many Australians still have trouble fully embracing as part of the national 'we.' The effect was to suggest that these performers had experience, if not of the kind of oppression peculiar to detention centres, of the way some people in Australia treat the visibly 'other.' The absence of a dramatic narrative allowed the refugee voices – transmitted via their own words in the letters – their full force as a form of contact with them. Even in the variety of their responses to the circumstances of detention, as well as in the underlying similarities in their situation as sensate humans subjected to massive deprivation of normal sociality, let alone given access to visible justice or hospitality, the play of voices embodied alterity in itself. In this sense, the production was able to assist the Australian public to bear witness to the cruel workings of the asylum system, as many of the individual writers expressly wished in their letters.

Whereas *Citizen X* invites multiple instances of ethical witnessing as each of the detainees' letters is given voice, *CMI (A Certain Maritime Incident)* turns on two Levinasian moments to position audiences in relation to its exploration of the Government handling of the 'children overboard' affair (see Williams 2008). In the production, the re-contextualized verbatim replay of the constative and authoritative 'Said' of the deadeningly formal evidence of military men and bureaucrats to the Senate inquiry was framed by two passages of performance which had essentially a metaphorical and poetic mode of interpellating the spectator. These were, first, the way that the audience entering the performance space was forced to negotiate a path over and between the naked bodies of the performers laid out mute and corpse-like on the floor of the entry way. This could not be clearly thematized or interpreted by audience members at that moment. The situation had first of all to be physically negotiated: one wanted to go in, one did not want to step on the performers nor really invade their privacy by looking at them, but it was necessary to look down to get through. The passage of experience involved was obscure and mysterious in terms of signification (who? why?) but directly affecting in terms of a chilling confrontation with images of watery death. By the time we got to the closing passage of the overall performance we could give this horror a name – the tragic sinking of the *SIEV X* with its human cargo of asylum seekers. Testimony at the CMI Senate enquiry raised the question of a link between this tragedy and the Government's policy of using the navy to repulse (turn back from Australian territorial waters) refugee vessels while still on the high seas.

The *CMI* audience's encounter with this horror was constructed of three elements. The personal narration of several survivors of the sinking ship, including the testimony of a surviving mother who had seen her husband and children taken by sharks and drowned, was presented through the medium of a flat computer conditioned voice, with uncanny effect. At the same time we saw continuous projections of a featureless and endless ocean while a single male actor's naked body, not representing a specific person's body but suggesting a corpse, was positioned on stage then cleaned and prepared for burial. Perhaps in this case not seeing an imitation, a representation in any literal sense, of the face of that infinitely suffering other was nevertheless more like an encounter with its alterity.

By framing the surreal banality of the interminable Senate inquiry process itself – the transcript takes up many thousands of pages – with these direct and unsettling moments, the show attempted to reconnect us with an atrocity that the formal process of the actual inquiry itself desperately insisted on pushing to the margins or out of sight altogether. Williams's essay (2008) clearly describes the numbing effect of the 'professional' approach to his narration by senior naval witness Rear Admiral Geoffrey Smith. Smith's language in evidence exemplifies that form of speech Levinas calls 'the Said,' which in this case enacts a violence to the other it refuses to encounter as other, reducing the other to the known and controllable, to 'the Same'. This repeats that other feature of the governmental language around asylum seekers, the use of distancing terms ('these people') and acronyms (SIEV, SUNC, UA[2]) that work to keep the reality of refugee lives at arms length and embody a refusal to engage ethical responsibility.

Hannie Rayson's fictional political thriller *Two Brothers* also examines a fundamental failure of ethical engagement. The play, staged in mainstream theatre venues in Melbourne and Sydney in 2005, created a major controversy based on the alleged similarity of its contrast between one (idealistic/progressive) brother and another (political/ruthless) one and then Federal Treasurer Peter Costello and his clergyman and charity CEO brother Tim. Rayson's play is 'political' in staging a conflict of value positions around the refugee issue somewhat parallel to the differences in politics between the actual two brothers. It is traditional in form in that respect and also in focusing on a melodramatically heightened moral conflict with the drama depending on the outcome of choices by central characters. The moral conflict drama is about the sinking of a fictional vessel, the *Kelepasan*, which clearly alludes to the *SIEV X*. Also at the heart of the play is the son of the politician character, a young officer in the Royal Australian Navy; his moral dilemma concerns his complicity as a serving officer in the tragedy. The substance of the naval involvement is obscure in the play, perhaps because the facts are indeed as yet unknown, but there is a strong sense of something to answer for conveyed in the young man's crippling sense of guilt. This element of deliberate ambiguity in the details of the (fictional) sinking in the play was not registered, however, by some of the media commentators, who accused Rayson point-blank of indicting the Navy of mass homicide by inaction.

In *Two Brothers* the encounter with the other is violently refused. In the opening moments of the performance the 'political' brother, later to become Prime Minister, violently knifes Hazem, the sole surviving refugee from the *Kelepesan*. The shock of this scene resonates throughout our experience of the rest of the play, a disturbing emblem of the negation of the other inherent in Government policy towards refugees and asylum seekers. Act One shows how we arrived at this place. The denouement in Act Two I found particularly devastating as, one by one, the characters whom we might have expected to act ethically and expose the Prime Minister-in-waiting cave in for a variety of reasons – expedient, pragmatic and personal (a desire to keep a son out of jail, reluctance to betray a father, and so forth). In this dystopian drama set in a not too far distant future, there is a total refusal of Levinasian ethics; everyone in the play is compromised. It is perhaps only the audience who is offered a place to respond ethically to the other so violently negated in the opening. The single most shocking incident in this parable of the thuggery of Australia's border protection regime remains. The callousness of the initial murder challenges the audience to consider the violence of Government asylum policy, the violence of its results on the lives of refugees, including perhaps the deaths of hundreds of people. The murder of Hazem is a powerful metaphor of brutality and evokes the complicity of the bystander – that is, us.

Two Brothers attracted large and appreciative mainstream audiences in both Melbourne and Sydney but struck a raw nerve with some more closely connected with the structures of political power. The play and the author himself were savaged by right-wing columnists. Andrew Bolt in the *Herald Sun* called the show a 'vomit of smug hate.' The play, he writes, 'endorses the vile conspiracy theory that *SIEV X* sank as our sailors watched' (Bolt 2005a). Two days later in a further piece titled 'Hannie's Evil Brew' he elaborated his attack, stressing Rayson's 'tax-payer-supported' career: 'It took a hot spa-full of your money to produce Hannie Rayson' (Bolt 2005b). If there is an affect here, it would appear to be shame and guilt, leading to an otherwise unaccountable vehemence of denunciation. According to David Marr, 'so stung was the [Howard] government by *Two Brothers* that debate began among senior ministers about abolishing the Australia Council' (Marr 2005). In the Sydney press, Gerard Henderson contented himself with calling the play 'trite and clichéd and pointing out that 'the assertion that the navy allowed asylum seekers to drown was emphatically denied by the navy's former maritime commander, Rear-Admiral G. F. Smith' (Henderson 2005). Admiral Smith, as we have seen, also figures largely in *CMI (A Certain Maritime Incident)*. The pro-Howard commentators take it as read that the play applies directly and literally to the Costello brothers and to the real events of the *SIEV X* sinking, against Rayson's insistence on the play's fictionality as 'a thriller about power and evil' and a 'dystopian vision of what could happen if our political culture becomes debased by a lack of public accountability and by the suppression of compassion and tolerance' (Rayson 2005a).

Conclusion

According to Levinasian ethics, it is not even their existence as destitute and their situation as appealing for asylum which enjoins upon us to provide for refugees seeking asylum, and indeed to provide for them decently, whatever their 'character' or compatibility with us or our culture. Prime Minister Howard claimed in 2001 that refugees who went on hunger strike were attempting to 'intimidate us with our own decency' (cited in Marr and Wilkinson 2003: 63). For Levinas, we are always already 'hostage' to the other, for whom we have an infinite and therefore 'unassumable' responsibility, which we must nevertheless strive to assume. I am suggesting that a Levinasian dramaturgy might be one that strives to keep open the space of indeterminacy in order to stand against the closed 'Said' of the Government's language. Certain strategies of narrativization may tend to provide an audience with a sense of secure knowing, which is less 'productive' of the affect that is essential to the Levinasian ethical encounter. In Levinasian terms, comprehension or knowing about a human situation can militate against openness and response-ability. Perhaps the Levinasian encounter can only occur fleetingly, in powerfully affecting moments.

In *Ethics and Infinity* Levinas puts the embodied nature of the saying as exemplifying the human necessity of response to the face:

> … the saying is the fact that before the face I do not simply remain there contemplating it, I respond to it. The saying is a way of greeting the Other, but to greet the Other

is already to answer for him. It is difficult to be silent in someone's presence; this difficulty has its ultimate foundation in this signification proper to the saying, whatever is the said.

(Levinas 1985: 88)

It is Levinas's idea of the active, responsive, corporeal encounter with alterity that is so pertinent to ethical responsibility. Performance is uniquely situated to embody and facilitate this.

References

Bolt, A., 'Shameful Saga of Hate', *Herald Sun*, 13 February 2005(a), http://www.news.com.au/heraldsun/story/0,21985,12835373-25717,00.html (accessed 21 February 2008).

———, 'Hannie's Evil Brew', *Herald Sun*, 15 February 2005(b) (accessed 21 February 2008).

Critchley, S., *The Ethics of Deconstruction*, Oxford: Blackwell, 1992.

Ettinger, B., *Qui Dirait Eurydice? What Would Eurydice say?*, *Brache Lichtenberg Ettinger in Conversation with Emmanuel Levinas*, Paris: BLE Atelier, 1997.

Hazou, R., '*Refugitive* and the Theatre of Dys-appearance', *Research in Drama Education*, 13: 2 (2008), pp. 181–186.

Henderson, G., 'Left Intelligentsia Misses Right Turn', *Sydney Morning Herald*, 28 June 2005, http://www.smh.com.au/news/opinion/left-intelligentsia-misses-right-turn/2005/06/27/1119724576696.html (accessed 21 February 2008).

Joinet, L., 'Report of the Working Group on Arbitrary Detention on its Visit to Australia', *United Nations Commission on Human Rights*, E/CN.4/2003/8/Add.2, 18, 2002.

Levinas, E., *Totality and Infinity*, translated by Lingis, A., The Hague: Martinus Nijhoff, 1979.

———, *Ethics and Infinity*, translated by Cohen, R. A., Pittsburg, PA: Duquesne University Press, 1985.

Marr, D., 'A Wallet Full of Censorship', paper presented at the *2005 Philip Parsons Memorial Lecture*, 9 October 2005, Sydney: Seymour Centre, http://www.currencyhouse.org.au/pages/downloads.html (accessed 21 February 2008).

Marr, D., and Wilkinson, M., *Dark Victory*, Sydney: Allen and Unwin, 2003.

Miller, P., 'Truth Overboard: What Does It Mean for Politicians and Statesmen to Assume Responsibility for Their Words of Mass Destruction', *Borderlands e-journal* 3: 1 (2004) http://www.borderlands.net.au/issues/vol3no1.html (accessed 4 January 2008).

Peperzak, A. T., Critchley, S., and Bernasconi, R. (eds.) *Emmanuel Levinas – Basic Philosophical Writing*, Bloomington and Indianapolis: Indiana University Press, 1996.

Rayson, H., Writer's Note, theatre programme for *Two Brothers*, Sydney: Sydney Theatre Company, 2005a.

———, *Two Brothers*, Sydney: Currency Press, 2005b.

Robbins, J., *Altered Reading: Levinas and Literature*, Chicago: Chicago University Press, 1999.

Shafaei, S., *Refugitive*, Sydney: Old Fitzroy Hotel Theatre, 7 January 2003.

———, Untitled public talk given at Performance and Asylum Symposium, Sydney University, Department of Performance Studies, 10 September 2006.

Williams, D., 'Performing Refugee Policy in Politics and Theatre,' *Research in Drama Education*, 13: 2 (2008), pp. 199–204.

Notes

1 Levinas capitalizes the word(s) he uses for 'the Other/other' in the original French texts somewhat inconsistently. Scholars and translators adopt various solutions. I will use lowercase 'the other' to refer both to the other human being and more generally to that which is not the Same, that which is other than the self. See the Preface to Peperzak, Critchley and Bernasconi (1996), for a concise discussion of this topic (p. xiv).

2 These acronyms indicate Suspected Illegal Entry Vessel, Suspected Unauthorized Non-Citizens and Unauthorized Arrivals.

Chapter 12

Refugee Performance: Encounters with Alterity

Michael Balfour

Figure 1: Copyright Wendy Ewald, *Towards a Promised Land*, reprinted with kind permission.

Introduction

Conquergood's (2002) discussion of de Certeau's adage 'what the map cuts up, the story cuts across' (1984: 129) highlights the transgressive boundaries between formalized ways of knowing, 'the map' and the subaltern, embodied knowing of 'the story.' In the context of refugee performance, in which individuals and groups in a new 'host' country attempt to survive, remake homes, make sense of traumatic past experiences and locate themselves in new cultures, the story can become a site of both negotiation and resilience.

In this chapter I will discuss two projects, one based in Logan, Australia, that works with new humanitarian entrants from Africa, and the other a multi-ethnic project, Exodus, which used participatory photography, performance and a combustible sculpture to explore the impact of migration in Margate, a seaside town in the United Kingdom. The examples offer different tactics in how to elude the apparently inescapable antimony of refugee theatre practice, and suggest how arts practice can respond to issues of refugee representation, bi-cultural adjustment and social integration.

The Multilink project manages this because of the focus on acculturation issues and the centrality of the target audience (refugees performing for refugees). However, the project also had limitations particularly in regard to its aesthetic efficacy, and its potential as a piece of performance for a more general audience. The Exodus project tackles the victimhood issue by prioritizing the aesthetic experience and contextualizing the refugee experience within a broader more generalized frame. The emphasis on a sensual, non-verbal, aesthetic experience relates to Burvill's ecology of hope, via Levinas, in terms of performance as an encounter with the other in which we experience 'infinite and transcendent alterity' (2008: 235).

The Multilink project

In October 2007 I was invited by a community organization, Multilink, to develop a theatre project with newly arrived humanitarian entrants from Burundi and Ethiopia. Multilink are based in Logan City, Queensland (Australia), and are a respected service provider of multicultural services whose aim is to assist new migrants and refugees in settling in Australian communities. The Department of Immigration and Citizenship (DIAC) funded the pilot project that aimed to use the arts to disseminate experiences about Australia's culture to the Burundian and Ethiopian humanitarian communities in Logan City.

The project's steering group, representatives from Burundi and Ethiopia, signalled that there were significant settlement problems within their community groups. With each group of new arrivals similar difficulties emerged, ranging from pragmatic domestic issues (learning to cook with a gas cooker, understanding how to use an ATM, etc.) to the more complex negotiation of understanding new cultural paradigms and values. The community representatives suggested that beyond the initial 'honeymoon' period of arrival, individuals and groups encountered considerable stress and anxiety in dealing with the acculturation process. This observation is supported by researchers working with other communities. For example, Askland (2005), drawing on Giddens' (1991) work, found that many young Timorese refugees living in Australia suffered from a loss of ontological security: a loss that undermines their sense of control, trust and power. Within school and community settings, this lack of security and identity led to adjustment issues including delinquent behaviour, attention problems, aggressive behaviour or withdrawal (Allwood et al. 2002).

The first stage of the Multilink project was to gather stories and experiences from Burundian and Ethiopian community members who had been here for four to five years, complemented with interviews with community elders/leaders, and other community organizations. There was a deliberate request for a broad range of stories, not just issue-based experiences but funny, surprising and unusual observations about living in Australia. The collated material from these responses provided a rich resource of anecdotes, reflections and moving accounts of difficulties in adjustment. The stories also signalled the considerable pragmatism and resilience needed in the process of making and unmaking 'home.' As one of the participants in the project defined it:

Here is where I am living, because I came from that home, where I call home. I've seen there's no home there. There's nothing, completely nothing. So, I am still alive and I've found somewhere to call home. Now I am at home, where I am living in peace. I am doing everything, so it's home for me.

(Personal notes, 2008)

Using the collected stories as a starting point, the project team sought volunteers from a mixed group of Burundian and Ethiopian volunteer participants to attend a workshop and perform the material. The response was beautifully anarchic. The participants came from diverse cultural and linguistic backgrounds (Ethiopia alone has over 80 different linguistic groups) as well as countries (Ethiopia, Burundi, Sudan) and had an age range between six months and 55 years. The rehearsals were a chaotic mixture of different performance levels, ethnic languages and English comprehension, and involved developing and refining three stories that would highlight common areas of experience. What (finally) emerged was a composite portrait of a newly arrived African family, told from the different perspectives of each family member.

The first scenario started with a dream and the excitement of arrival. This was followed by the mother's (Ajok) growing frustration in finding work because of her lack of English knowledge and transferable qualifications. The second scenario concerns the father (Baheza) of the family. This scenario was based on community concerns about the high incidence of domestic violence and child abuse among refugee families. The scenario shows how Baheza is dealing with his dramatic change in status within the family and socially. The third scene focuses on one of the daughters – and highlights a common issue in which the younger generation picks up English faster and become more adept at negotiating a new culture. The relative speed of adaption, and in particular the 'rights' that they see other Australian children having, exist in tension with more traditional family values.

The structure of the performance event was simple. It was introduced by a Multilink presenter (translated by an interpreter), and the invited audience was offered a brief outline and background to 'the family' and a plot summary for each scenario. Each scenario ends in a dilemma, a problem that is not resolved within the drama, on which the audience are invited to comment. In the presentation, the action was stopped after each scene. The facilitator checked with the audience to see whether the story had been clear, and then asked for suggestions from the audience to help advise the characters on what they could do.

The performance was rudimentary; it had a 'job to do' and reflected the need to communicate experiences clearly using basic language. The show was performed for three different audiences, with diverse responses. The Burundian audience responded with a high level of enthusiasm, demanding the actors come onstage to explain themselves (in character). In classic Boalian style, advice, scorn and observations flowed with ease. The second performance was to a group of Afghani women who had asked to see the play. Culturally they provided a very different response. The women were generally quiet when asked for questions or comments, but there was considerable whispered debate between them. The third group was dominated by two to three members of the audience: one was a man who had been separated from his family due to a domestic violence order, and became fixated on trying to solve the problem for the character; the others were young and old members engaged in a rich discussion (conducted in four languages) about the merits of 'traditional values.'

The Multilink facilitator encouraged these debates and also guided the audience to support networks. In this way the specific needs of the audience were identified through the focus of the discussion. Following the performance, a large feast was prepared for audience members. The discussions flowed with considerable enthusiasm out of the theatre space and into the eating space.

The audience responses and questions recognized the extent of the difficulties of acculturation. One woman in the audience explained that the concept of 'social security' or any form of government support was impossible for her to understand. Another response was the difficulties of budgeting and managing money after a long period in a camp: a significant issue for the audiences was that of landlords, who after the first six months (in which rents are paid directly to them via social security) terminate the contract, leaving individuals and families to move at short notice. The intergenerational issue also attracted considerable response. The discussion in the Ethiopian group reflected on how in newly arrived families, the older children are offered places in schools, and both their English and cultural awareness develop quickly. The mother and father (if they are both in the country) feel more isolated by having to look after younger children and/or being unemployed and therefore have little opportunity to gain confidence in the language and culture.

Despite the limited scale of the project, the nature and richness of the stories from the process highlighted important issues. The stories aimed to enable a peer group of performers to communicate experiences of settlement to an audience of new humanitarian arrivals, and focus on resilience in the context of raising what problems might occur, and what pragmatic support strategies might be available. In working with a specific community and developing a performance with a strong aim (communicating strategies for resilience) the project usefully avoids some of the difficulties encountered with other refugee performance practice.

The Multilink project deliberately eschewed 'public' performance, in preference for an invited and specifically targeted audience. The centrality of the audience governed the content of the event. It led to a focus on survival strategies and tactics of resilience, with attention to the pragmatic present and the possibilities of the future. The practice stemmed from a strong analysis of the needs of new humanitarian groups, as articulated by community organizations, community representatives and the volunteer performers. The project emphasized 'ownership' of the material and the stories were constantly aligned to the priorities of the community in terms of what community members felt was important to represent. The narratives were generalized fiction, based on personal accounts, but rendered universal by the process. The emphasis was not on who was telling the story (or whose story it was) but on the pragmatic 'what' of the story, in terms of offering strategies to deal with specific issues. The aesthetics were straightforward and functional, perhaps a little neglected, in the rush to encompass all the other objectives of the project. Certainly there was no 'cultural specificity' in the style and the form, and this was perhaps its greatest weakness.

The Multilink project seems, on the face of it, to effectively avoid being enmeshed in the paradox of refugee performance. It might be tempting to leave it there, and develop this as a 'model' approach. However, within the refugee performance group there was always a frustration that having created the work, they wanted to demonstrate their own issues by performing it to a wider audience who might therefore 'get' what kinds of settlement issues refugees face. This raised a dilemma for the performance, as it had been tightly conceived within a particular context (refugees performing for refugees). Changing the nature of the audience would make it susceptible to other interpretations and connotations. The performance's ability to sidestep the problematic of refugee theatre arose not from the content, but from the restricted identity of the target audience. Out of its original context, the performance would likely produce the kinds of secure knowing that Burvill (2008) notes as being less productive than other encounters with alterity.

In searching for other examples of theatre that might respond to these issues, specifically those that feature refugee performers acting for a general audience, it is possible to trace fleeting moments of transcendence that escape the 'personal narrative' paradox (the demonstration of victimhood, etc.). Jeffers highlights how in *A Letter from Home* the central character is 'momentarily elevated' (Jeffers 2008: 220) from her victim status through moving from testimonial dialogue to a sudden 'rowdy, adversarial dance' (Jeffers 2008: 219) in which she reveals a provocative demonstration of her internal rage. The abrupt switch between the realism and the fantastical breaks the audience's sense of secure knowing. Dennis also appreciates that the act of improvising testimony in playback theatre is a fine synthesis between authenticity and essence:

> Far from bringing a script to life or presenting a transcript or testimony, the playback theatre actor is responding to a real-life story, in the presence of the (real-life) teller. In this distinctive form, efficacy is somehow tied up in the negotiable nature of the improvised aspect.
>
> (Dennis 2008: 214)

These examples, while useful, break the audiences' sense of secure knowing only partially. The performances are still deeply embroiled in the quagmire of personal narratives and victimhood discourse. They offer a hint at some possible devices, in the ways that they momentarily destabilize audience expectations through disrupting the mode of performance or rephrasing familiar stories. Another example offers a little more scope. The Margate Exodus project suggests, in certain areas of its practice, feasible tactics that respond to both the paradox of refugee performance and the Levinas mode of interpolating the spectator in powerfully affecting moments.

'I am not a social worker': The Margate Exodus project

In 2005–2006 a new arts project called the Exodus project was developed by Artangel in Margate, United Kingdom. The project had three strands, Penny Woolcock's Exodus play, a day-long experimental film/performance version of the Biblical fable; Wendy Ewald's *Towards a Promised Land*, a participatory photography project; and Anthony Gormley's 25-metre *Waste Man* sculpture. I want to concentrate on Ewald and Gormley's sub-projects, as I think they offer pertinent strategies for examining how refugee experiences can be brought into dialogue with general audiences, while avoiding, or at least eliding, some of the paradoxes associated with refugee performance.

Margate is a small seaside town, an hour from London, with a highly transient population. One of the local primary schools has a 40 per cent turnover of pupils (Aitch 2006). The town provides a temporary home for many of the asylum seekers who arrive at Dover every year. Will Self describes Margate in the following terms:

> Next to the station stands the enormous, wrinkled digit of Arlington House, a Brutalist 20-storey block of flats that seems to waggle a warning at all asylum seekers: 'Enter this land of promise, and you'll be banged up in here forever.' Or worse, in the decaying terrace of the Nayland Rock refugee hostel. Once this was a luxury hotel, now it houses Roma on the run from central Europe, Congolese fleeing the meltdown of central Africa, Iraqis evading the maelstrom of the Middle East. Strange, that so many people escaping the dread gravity of these landmasses, should find themselves clinging on to the very tip of the Isle of Thanet, which in turn is like a cold sore on the Kentish lip of old England.
>
> (Self 2006)

The imperative of the Exodus project is drawn from delivering an aesthetic project, rather than responding to the needs of a specific community (refugee or otherwise). Unlike the Multilink project, there is no specified social objective, other than producing a show or series of events. The difference in intentionality between the two projects is marked. Engagement with non-actors was part of the process, but the makers were keen to distance themselves from 'bad' community art. Woolcock, the director of the theatre show, asserted, 'I am not a social worker' (Durrant 2006). Perhaps to exaggerate this, Woolcock is dismissive in quite maverick terms about the notion of 'community'. When asked about the choice of Margate to host the project, she simply states, 'random' (Woolcock 2008). Therefore, unlike community art (good or bad), the needs of the community were not the starting point, nor the foundation of the project.

The development of a large-scale project exploring the theme of exodus and exile in a town simmering with tensions and disharmony may be perceived as an ambitious, rather unethical undertaking. Particularly troubling, from an applied/community theatre perspective, is the disavowing of identifying and attempting to understand the complex needs of the community, before shaping a performative response. If Exodus had operated under more traditional community/applied theatre orthodoxies, surely a more responsive entanglement with the complexities of different community values and perspectives would have been central to its process?

Interestingly, it is the very antagonism to the 'social' imperative that enables the project, at times, to subvert, if not completely elide, contradiction. Chiefly, it is the prioritizing of an aesthetic task in governing the participatory relationship between artist and non-actors, community members. The form, quality and substance of the 'art/performance' work were markedly in the control of a professional 'creative team'. Woolcock directed; she did not facilitate. Gormley designed and built the giant sculpture without community involvement. Ewald's photographic portraits were her work, not those of the children. Aside from the accidental and anecdotal moments of social encounter, how then did the project deepen the moments of alterity between individuals from a refugee background and the local community?

The *Waste Man*

Because of the profile of the artists, and the fact that the performance was due to be screened on national television, the project attracted considerable attention from the press. A. A. Gill likened the project to 'offering missionary art to the natives' (2006: 46). Will Self approached the project with the same level of scepticism, until he saw the giant sculpture in context:

> I have to say, the stated aims of Exodus – to call attention both to foreign incomers and the internal exile of Margate's disadvantaged – struck me as just a little patronising when I heard about them. It hardly seemed likely that the furious – often quasi-fascistic – denizens of Thanet were going to respond to the art-house filmic conceit by throwing their arms around the inmates of Nayland Rock in a gesture of human solidarity. Nor could I envision the burning of a lot of old chairs becoming the fire from which the phoenix of Margate's civic beauty would be reborn. But that was before I saw Waste Man in all his fleshly, wooden glory, towering up above the defunct rollercoasters of Margate's Dreamland Funfair. His peculiar, 3D collage of a body was reminiscent of a giant Arcimboldo, devised to remind us all that all is vanity.
>
> (Self 2006)

The sculpture was created over six weeks with over 30 tonnes of waste materials collected by Thanet council and local people. The debris was deposited in 'Dreamland,' an empty wasteland next to the sea that had been the former site of a vast funfair. Gormley's sculpture was part of Woolcock's promenade retelling of the biblical Exodus fable, and for Gormley was 'a sign of those who had been dispossessed or refused a place, standing up defiantly to be recognised' (2008: 62).

The process of constructing the *Waste Man* enabled a wide range of people to engage at whatever level they wanted. The work was a collective body made from the raw materials of people's home lives: beds, tables, dining chairs, toilet seats, desks, pianos and rubbish (all the limiting baggage of the householder), 'transformed into energy' (Gormley 2008: 62).

Figure 2: Copyright Anthony Gormley, *Waste Man*, reprinted with kind permission.

Figure 3: Copyright Anthony Gormley,
Waste Man, reprinted with kind permission.

Volunteers donated waste from the bottom of their gardens, the contents of their sheds and old furniture, as well as documents, photos and mementos they wanted – for whatever reason – to see ignited.

The Exodus project approached the issue of exile not by specifically engaging with community politics, but by taking a universalist stance, in which the enforced movement of people is portrayed as the result of larger socio-economic, political and historical interplays. It avoids specific ethnographic stories and experiences, by representing displacement as a broad generalized human happening. Like the popular theatre of the medieval morality plays, the tale is a lesson about the vicissitudes of political leaders, and their manipulation of prejudice. Given the lack of interest in the social imperative, the generalized approach to exploring the issues was probably the most appropriate one. While Woolcock's performance/ film resided in this moral paradigm, it was not until the audience encountered Gormley's *Waste Man* sculpture that there was any sense of a Levinas connection or comportment towards the other. The explicit morality of Woolcock's performance/film returns us not to the problems of victimhood narratives, but to Burvill's (2008) 'secure knowing' in which morality is not discovered or revealed by the representations, but is merely reconfirmed as a general social value. Gormley's burning *Waste Man*, on the other hand, approaches the thematic of exile 'crabwise,' as Hamlet might put it. The (somewhat limited) process of local residents helping to build the *Waste Man* meant that the sculpture was filled with the town's debris purged from attics, sheds and furtive hiding places. The expunging of unwanted objects and mementos, piled up into a beautiful and awe-inspiring structure that was then burned to the ground, seems to literally embody Margate's secrets and material secretions. The depositing of the waste had been an individual act. The residents had turned up with stuff in the boots of their cars, from wheelbarrows pushed across the town, and in large transit vans. The depositors were asylum seekers, refugees, employed and unemployed; the full range of the town's inhabitants. The contents of the structure were implicated into the town's identity. The statue was not a representation of Margate or its community politics; it was an embodied performance of the town. The audience for the burning represented a full and varied demographic of Margate town. It was unusual to have such a range of people present for a single event. The 'burning' became an odd form of communion – more than a collective response to something like a council-funded firework display, it was imbued with a certain wordless significance. The transition from following the play's promenade through the town to the 'Dreamland' site moved from a performance about the morality of exile to a performance that created an embodied symbolism – a moment of shared collective emotion.

> [...] with a sudden 'crack', smoke began to pour from his belly and lick up his chest. He was on fire – and so were we. I have no paradigm for what it's like to watch an enormous wooden figure burn – save perhaps the film of the Wicker Man. But without fear of hyperbole, let me tell you, it was a beautiful sight. The silence of the crowd transformed from being surly, to being awed, and we were all moved. Perhaps that was the mystery of the Margate Exodus? A voluntary exile, away from the quotidian ills of the early 21st century, and towards some deeper, darker, more chthonic place and time.
>
> (Self 2006)

The *Waste Man* offers a possible instance of how an exposure to the other might be most effectively created as indirect experience, an 'ethical performance whose essence cannot be caught in constative propositions. It is a performative doing' (Critchely 1992: 7).

As Burvill (2008) argues, these types of ethical performative encounters with the other often appear fleetingly. The openness and responsiveness to alterity are bounded by the more constant fixed ways of knowing. Performance might seek to dislodge or destablize, but often these tactics fall short. In escaping the paradox of victimhood narrative and understanding refugee experiences, Exodus seems to set up a fresh contradiction, in that the meaningful, corporeal encounter with alterity is often accidental and momentary; therefore, the closer the art moves to trying to create a comportment towards the other, the faster the meaningful experience disperses.

The other part of the Exodus project was Wendy Ewald's *Towards a Promised Land*, and this offers yet further tactics of how to explore this issue.

Figure 4: Copyright Anthony Gormley, *Waste Man*, reprinted with kind permission.

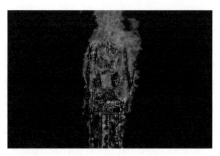

Figure 5: Copyright Anthony Gormley,
Waste Man, reprinted with kind permission.

Towards a Promised Land

In *Towards a Promised Land*, Wendy Ewald worked with 22 young people who had arrived in the area from diverse locations, including Iraq, Belarus, Egypt, the Congo, London, Derby, Belfast and Germany. Ewald is an experienced 'participatory' photographer. She strives to develop close working relationships with her co-photographers, helping them develop camera skills and a strong sense of ownership over the material. Her portraits are of the children taken from locations of their choosing around Margate as well as images of their possessions, selected from belongings brought with them. The possessions are designed to evoke memories of home and lives left behind. As well as being used for an exhibition in the local library, the photographs were made into large-scale banner images displayed along Margate's seawall, as well as smaller images shown in Dreamland Amusement Arcade, a cinema, a pub, a fish-and-chip shop, and a domestic home. A downloaded audio 'banner trail' around the multisite gallery was created, which included interviews and moving testimonies by the young people. Visitors followed a map and were guided by the stories of the children and the places and possessions they had chosen.

In her approach and process, Ewald seems to be able to bridge the seeming disparities between Woolcock's disregard for participatory processes and the significance of the aesthetic. The intimacy created in Ewald's longer-term work between artist and co-artist in which both work together in the shared understanding of the artistry is a governing element in the process.

Ewald's project seems to have constructed a useful process and an engaging and important ethical encounter with the other. The process enabled the development of skills and reflection on the new situation in which the young people found themselves. The negotiation of the portrait, and the selection of possessions, neatly encompassed the link between two versions of home: one lost, the other in transition. The visitor/gallery experience brought into relief the different experiences and feelings associated with the exodus theme: the children's excitement, sadness, longing and anxiety of displacement. While some of the children disclosed the background to their exile, others did not. Within this ambiguity, the categories of refugee, migrant, asylum seeker

Figure 6: Copyright Thiery Bal, 2006, reprinted with kind permission.

and transient became superfluous. The project deliberately explored the theme of exodus from the children's different experiences of enforced as well as economic and circumstantial relocation. The diversity of cultural backgrounds of the 'exiles', ranging from Middle Eastern to Belfast, also helped to loosen expectations of what or who a refugee might be. It splintered the 'secure knowing' of the listener/viewer, and interpolated it in the stories as broad human experiences, away from categories and victim narratives.

The process of walking through the town, with the headphones, searching for the next image, also brought the context of the town into play. The children's commentaries talked about their favourite places in the town, or first impressions of arriving, as well as aspects about themselves. However, the listener/viewer following the map and audio commentary was involved in an active and dynamic way with the town, as he or she inevitably had to navigate unexpected changes and encounters. Myers (2008), who has used similar site-specific modes of walking tours with refugee participants, describes the process, drawing on Ingold, as 'wayfaring'. Ingold distinguishes the ways in which wayfaring is neither 'placeless nor place-bound, but place making' (cited in Myers 2008: 174). Myers states that '[t]hese contexts and environments of enactment can be understood as relative and as developing, coming into being through a process of discovery and attunement of attention and perception rather than through a mental construction' (Myers 2008: 176).

Figure 7: Wendy Ewald, *Towards a Promised Land*,
reprinted with kind permission.

The process that the viewer/listener undertakes while wayfaring his or her way to view the photographs around Margate, and listening to the children's commentaries, emplaces him or her in the contextual layers of the town. *Towards a Promised Land* demonstrated how the children have contributed to the formation of place, made accessible the ways in which their lives coexist and co-inhabit the other identities of the town, and articulate 'a plurality of forms of place and provide mechanisms for passing on knowledge and experience to others in similar situations' (Myers 2008: 177).

Ewald's project seems to offer another tactic for dealing with the unwavering paradox of refugee performance. Although the children do discuss personal stories related to exile, the stories are contextualized within a complex set of frames that serve to disorientate a viewer/listener from secure knowing. The selection of stories from a broad cultural base, for example Belfast, London, Iraq and the Congo, sets up questions about who or what is an exile. The content of the children's contributions ranges from discussions about special possessions, to favourite places in Margate, and episodic accounts of home and the journey to the United Kingdom. These stories surprise, and extend any fixed notion of refugee. The diverse location of the images around the town (from the seawall to a fish-and-chip shop) force the viewer/listener to engage with and at times actively negotiate the plurality of place. The viewer/listener is therefore able to encounter the ways in which the children's stories and lives interpolate with other experiences and perspectives.

The examples of refugee performance in this chapter demonstrate an effort to avoid the victimhood narrative – a common problematic in refugee performance (Jeffers 2008). The Multilink project deliberately sidestepped the issue by focusing on the needs of a specific audience to develop present-day and future strategies for surviving and adjusting to relocation. The stories provide a basic outline to adjusting to the 'other' from the perspective of experience. The actors are all from the same region and have similar backgrounds, and the material has been generated from research, interviews and the actors' own experiences of the first few years. The 'otherness' (Australianness) is presented through the dilemmas and disruptions the fictional family experience – the cautionary stories that might lie ahead, but underlined with a discussion about strategies and support networks that are available.

With the Margate performances there is a deliberate displacing of victimhood from ethnic-specific experiences. Refugee narratives are framed as part of a wider historical and political context (we are all subject to history). In Ewald's work, the narratives of the children offer a collage of impressions of the town, likes and dislikes, favourite objects, reflections on different ways of being at home. In Gormley's work, narratives are displaced into objects, ritual and the non-verbal. The paradox of refugee performance is that it can imply the production of a secure map of experience, by fixing testimonial points and coordinates, which make an encounter with alterity more elusive. These examples offer tactics on how to 'sneak up' on the paradox, by exploring 'the other' in different ways:

> This is […] not necessarily so much about knowledge of the other, or information about their situation […] as [it] is about the ethical quality of the experience itself, about a certain kind of affect. It is not perhaps even about, in the first instance, empathy or sympathy with the other, as these forms of relationship may be more about seeing in the other what is like oneself (what Levinas calls the Same). It is perhaps something more purely embodied than that, less explicit.
>
> (Burvill 2008: 236)

The alternative to the map may be some form of wayfaring that suggests 'a more temporal, embodied, and sensorial relation within the world, a movement along a trajectory through the world and through memory' (Myers 2008: 175).

Perhaps, as Conquergood affirms, the potential promise of performance and story lies in the 'promiscuous traffic' between different ways of knowing (1998: 145). These ways of knowing involve engaging the arts to help transcend the process of mapping secure forms of knowledge onto others, through avoiding victimhood narratives, and foregrounding the importance of listening for stories that emerge in their own time and their own ways.

References

Aitch, I. 'Plagues of frogs and lice,' *The Guardian*, 26 September 2006, http://www.guardian.co.uk/artanddesign/2006/sep/26/art?INTCMP=SRCH (accessed 31 March 2011), p. 22.

Allwood, M., Bell-Dolan, D., and Husain, S., 'Children's trauma and adjustment reactions to violent and nonviolent war experiences,' *Journal of the American Academy of Child & Adolescent Psychiatry*, 41: 4 (2002), pp. 450–457.

Askland, H., 'Young Timorese in Australia: Becoming part of a new culture and the impact of refugee experiences on identity and belonging,' unpublished dissertation, University of Newcastle, NSW, 2005.

Burvill, T., '"Politics begins as ethics": Levinasian ethics and Australian performances concerning refugees,' *Research in Drama Education: The Journal of Applied Theatre and Performance*, 13: 2 (2008), pp. 233–243.

Conquergood, D., 'Health theatre in a Hmong refugee camp,' *The Drama Review*, 32: 3 (1998), pp. 174–208.

———, 'Performance studies interventions and radical research,' *The Drama Review*, 46: 2 (2002), pp. 145–153.

Critchely, S., *The Ethics of Deconstruction*, Oxford: Blackwell, 1992.

Dennis, R., 'Refugee performance: Aesthetic representation and accountability in playback theatre,' *Research in Drama Education: The Journal of Applied Theatre and Performance*, 13: 2 (2008), pp. 211–215.

Giddens, A., *Modernity and Self-Identity: Self and Society in the Modern Age*, Cambridge: Polity Press, 1991.

Gill, A. A., 'The Exodus Project,' *The Times*, 10 September 2006, p. 35.

Gormley, A., 'The Waste Man,' http://www.antonygormley.com/viewproject.php?projectid=62&page=1 (accessed 14 December 2010).

Jeffers, A., 'Dirty truth: Personal narrative, victimhood and participatory theatre work with people seeking asylum,' *Research in Drama Education: The Journal of Applied Theatre and Performance*, 13: 2 (2008), pp. 217–221.

Myers, M., 'Situations for living: Performing emplacement,' *Research in Drama Education: The Journal of Applied Theatre and Performance*, 13: 2 (2008), pp. 171–180.

Self, W., 'Psychogeography. The wicker chair man,' *The Independent*, 14 October, http://www.independent.co.uk/opinion/columnists/will-self/will-self-psychogeography-419792.html (accessed 2 December 2010), p. 14.

Woolcock, P., 'Interview about Exodus,' http://www.channel4.com/fourdocs/papers/penny_int.html (accessed 19 December 2010).

Chapter 13

Repeat Performance: Dancing DiDinga with the Lost Boys
of Southern Sudan

Felecia Faye McMahon

In this chapter, I focus on transnationality and the cultural effects of global processes on emerging traditions of refugees from southern Sudan now living in New York state. I explore the gap between understanding expressions of transnational identity as it relates to the lived experiences of refugees, who are more concerned with maintaining cultural authenticity and less concerned with their relationship to hegemonic American society. Central to this inquiry is the performance of tradition in a new context, resulting from the forced migration of refugee children who have lost connection with their parents and elders. In today's world, folklorists are coming in contact with more and more diasporic groups whose cultural identities are transnational; that is, they maintain dual identities that can be said to involve both the globalization and the localization of culture (Safran 1991; Basch, Schiller and Blanc 1994). Folklorists have long understood the performance of tradition to be a dynamic process that is emergent and not static (Hymes 1975; Bauman 1978, 1986; Glassie 1995). Because historical periods can never be replicated, even if outward expression appears unchanged, the meanings of traditions have changed. Emergent traditions, selected and reformulated as representative of a group's identity, serve as a means of identifying, affirming and valuing uniqueness and personal history. In my research with Sudanese 'Lost Boys,' I found that understanding their re-contextualized dance song tradition was complicated by their life circumstances: they had lived for more than ten years with no contact with adult members of their DiDinga tribe. Further, because their culture is based largely on orality, there are few published sources and no official orthography for their language.

Before suggesting a theoretical model for understanding the emergence of tradition, I will ground it in a discussion of my fieldwork as well as a description of the inductive methodology I used to document the danced song traditions of the Lost Boys. It is not enough to say that the traditions of this small group are emergent. Comparisons over time of the videotaped danced songs and taped conversations with the Lost Boys about their performances reveal several forces acting on these traditions performed outside of their original context. It becomes apparent that diasporic authenticity can be defined when we recognize that, like all tradition, it involves a to-and-fro movement between culturally shared knowledge and group negotiation, ever affected by changing internal and external tensions.

My work with Sudanese refugees was one of those proverbial life coincidences with profound personal consequences. Like many people in other American cities to which the Lost Boys of southern Sudan had immigrated, I was at first only vaguely aware of this small community of young and parentless male refugees living in Syracuse, New York. I did not seek them out, nor they me. Less than a year after these Sudanese refugees arrived here, I contacted the local Refugee Resettlement Services to invite recently relocated people of any origin to my university class to share some of their traditions. That is when their amazing story of survival began to unfold for me. They were enthusiastic about performing for my American students, but there were programming limitations that would affect their presentations. Although traditional artists should be encouraged to self-present for new audiences, the mediating role of the public folklorist helps to ensure that traditions are adequately and appropriately re-contextualized. As Robert Baron (following Dan Sheehy) has noted, 'Folk artists should be adequately prepared in order to appropriately and effectively adapt their repertoires and performance styles and rhetoric of performance' (Baron 1999:192). Therefore, the primary responsibility of introducing traditional performers through new frames falls squarely on the shoulders of the presenting folklorist.

Documenting re-contextualized tradition

The compelling stories of all the Sudanese refugees are tragic, but none more so than those of the Lost Boys.[1] In the late 1980s, after decades of civil war in their native land, thousands of Sudanese children, some as young as six and seven years of age, fled their burning villages and trekked to Ethiopia. Many of the survivors remained in camps in Ethiopia until, in 1991, a newly elected government there expelled them. Finding themselves back in Sudan with civil war again threatening, in 1992 the boys continued walking more than 600 kilometres into northwest Kenya, where the Ka-kuma camp was established to protect them. Some were imprisoned by officials at the Kenyan border; many others died in a war they did not understand and for which they were not responsible (Zutt 1994: 2). Dinka, as well as the smaller group of DiDinga men, now comprise the total of 75 Sudanese Lost Boys who arrived in Syracuse in 2001 after the United States offered 3,000 young men safe haven in several cities throughout the United States. Until they volunteered stories about their traditional village lives prior to the war, I had not fully comprehended how different life is for the many refugees who come to the United States from rural, remote regions of the world such as southern Sudan (Pipher 2002: 63). I marvel at the resilience of this group of young, shy men who have manoeuvered their way in the United States with no parents or elders here to advise them. With the help of a few dedicated volunteers of Catholic Charities and other local parishes, they adjusted quickly to a Western way of life: the Lost Boys work, pay rent, buy cars, go to school, talk on cell phones and surf the Internet on donated computers.[2] Most Americans who come in contact with them are struck by their exuberant friendliness and adaptability. The young men are cheerful, bright and genuinely playful. They feel privileged to be in the United States, but when asked about their families in Sudan, their voices become serious: 'We don't know.'

My documentation of the traditions of the DiDinga young men began incidentally. As a freelance public folklorist, I had wanted to find an appropriate venue where I could introduce Americans to the rich culture of refugees now living in the city. I had already decided it was important to honour the living traditions of the newest residents in the neighbourhood surrounding our university by inviting folk artists from Bosnia, Burma (Myanmar) and Ukraine to my classroom. But in my first interview with them to prepare for the classroom visit, I began to ask directly about dit, the Dinka word for the traditional male bull song; they said they did not know the word. When I asked about the colourful beaded vests for which the Dinka are renowned, they said they did not know about such things either. I suspected that their lack of knowledge resulted from separation from their families at such an early age. When I overheard the young men speaking among themselves, I asked if they were speaking Dinka. It was then that I heard the word DiDinga, which they described as an 'entirely different language.' The difference, they explained, was so great that the two groups communicated in Arabic or, in the United States, in English. They reassured me that I had made a common mistake, which was not 'too bad,' because both DiDinga and Dinka were cattle herders and sang bull songs, which the DiDinga called olé (also oli). After apologizing for my ignorance, I used the opportunity to ask them if they would teach me what I needed to know before they came to my classroom (Briggs 1986).

After meeting this small group of DiDinga Lost Boys, I also recognized the importance of documenting their traditions as they continue to evolve in a new context and, in this case, a new country, while at the same time finding new outlets for their cultural expressions. A part of this inquiry was to elucidate the ways a group comes to consensus about appropriate and meaningful traditions performed outside of their natural cultural context. This process involved re-contextualization and transnationalism, both of which affected the young men's performance of identity. Focusing on the negotiation process related to aesthetics and identity, it soon became clear that the young DiDinga men selected, omitted or recombined traditions learned as children in their remote rural villages, as refugees in Kenyan camps, as students in Nairobi missionary schools, and as residents in an urban American environment. The young men told me that they had sung together in a Dominican missionary school in Nairobi under the leadership of Charles, now about 21 years of age, because he was the oldest. In Nairobi they had learned to harmonize in the Western choral tradition. It was at the University of Nairobi that the DiDinga had competed with the Dinka in a dance competition in which they won first place 'over the Dinka.'

In general, there are few publications to guide folklore research with the many refugee groups in the United States. Although I have had many opportunities to observe firsthand the Lost Boys' traditions as they continue to evolve here, my dilemma as a folklorist is how to collaborate with the young men in order to adequately present and interpret these traditions now being performed outside of their natural context in Sudan. It was two years before I had the good fortune to observe DiDinga traditional dance in its original context, and that opportunity was limited to a home video made by a DiDinga elder who returned from a refugee camp in Sudan. But eventually I witnessed and documented the first full-scale DiDinga dance performed in the United States when DiDinga elders drove en masse from distant states to Auburn, New York, for a public performance with the Lost Boys.

There can be no accurate discussion of the performances of these young men without an understanding of how war has disrupted the lives of every man, woman and child in southern Sudan. As the U.S. Committee on Refugees (USCR) reports, the Sudanese have suffered more war-related deaths during the past fifteen years than any single population in the world. The current phases of the war began in 1983, pitting the Sudanese Peoples Liberation Army (SPLA) and its allies against the government of Sudan and its military and allies. Since 1983, the SPLA has been fighting for the rights of the largely Christian south against domination by the Arabic-speaking Islamic government in the north. This war has cost the lives of more than two million people, the death toll greater than all the fatalities in Bosnia, Kosovo, Afghanistan, Chechnya, Somalia and Algeria combined. Today there are still four million Sudanese internally displaced within their own country, and the young DiDinga men whom I know are only a few of the 350,000 refugees who fled to neighbouring countries, unable to return to their war-ravaged homes. In July 2002, the Sudanese government and southern rebels reached an agreement to hold a referendum that will give the south the option to secede from the north after a six-year interim period. Because the Arab League wants to see a unified Sudan, during the first round of talks the government will exempt the southern Christian and animistic Sudanese from Islamic sharia law.

But the war in Sudan is more complicated than a simple north-south territorial conflict. The conflict has now spread to western Sudan, where the mostly black Muslim populations are engaged in armed conflict with the Islamic Khartoum government military that is engaging in 'ethnic cleansing.' As Francis Mading Deng (1995) and others have shown, many deaths have also resulted from infighting among southern Sudanese rebel armies. Among both DiDinga and Dinka young men in our city, there are some who have witnessed the murders of their own families by neighbouring rebel soldiers. In Syracuse, the majority of the young male Sudanese refugees are Dinka, who insist that the killing of civilians is a misunderstanding among brothers and not an issue for international concern. From the DiDinga perspective, however, it is more than mere misunderstanding. Because of the domination of the DiDinga by not only the northern Islamic government but also Christian and animistic groups like the Dinka and Nuer in the south who make up these rebel armies, what might appear to be a traditional danced song about warriors and cattle-raiding of long ago between DiDinga and their neighbours like the Toposa can be sung as a protest against the atrocities committed by Islamic government soldiers from the north as well as by southern Sudanese rebel armies against southern Sudanese civilians:

Etedia toliti
Nalimaya tuhui hadim nak hasina bee shinang Naleimaya tuhui
Ero ero ero
Nalimaya tuhui hadim nake hasina bee shingang Nalimaya tuhui
[The tolit fruit has detached itself from the tolit tree.
We would like to see Mt. Nalimaya overturn.
Ero, ero, ero,
We would really like to see Mt. Nalimaya turn over.][3]

According to the group, tolit is DiDinga for a special kind of tree that is 'very, very big' and has very big 'plums.' When I later found tolit in Rosato's dictionary, I learned that it is DiDinga for the sausage tree (kigelia pinnata). It was no exaggeration when they said that the 'plums' were very large. The fruit of the tolit, which is in the bignonia family, is two feet long and can weigh as much as fifteen pounds. As a matter of fact, the fruit hangs on long ropelike stalks and resembles giant sausages. I thought it was strange that a song about a sausage tree would be sung with such emotion until I learned that 'Eetedia tolit' means 'the tree dropped its fruit,' an ode to the tree that killed a group of invaders when it dropped its fruit on the invaders sitting under it. The singers, therefore, request the tolit to 'do it again' and further invoke Mt. Nalimaya to 'turn over' to evict the invaders. Eventually, the DiDinga told me that songs like tolit have 'hidden meanings.' As Lino told me, 'This song means the DiDinga are a hospitable people and the SPLA who are Dinka rebel soldiers came to our land, but then they would not leave and we are asking the tolit tree to drop its fruit to kill them' (Interview, Syracuse, 10 March 2004).

'Really DiDinga'

The DiDinga have two traditional dances: gyrikot and nyakorot.[4] Although there are many kinds of songs for healing, weddings, funerals and so forth, the songs the Lost Boys performed for American audiences include only three types: political songs, mocking songs and warrior songs. Mocking songs are sung during gyrikot, impromptu social dances, in which singers form a stationary semicircle and then sway as they sing. Story songs can also be sung during this spontaneous gyrikot, or during nyakorot, the formal full-scale celebratory dance, which often lasts twelve hours or more. Nyakorot opens formally with lilia, a very slow procession that is also performed to signal the end of nyakorot. Political songs and warrior songs are usually sung during nyakorot, while olé, the bull song, can be sung, usually by the creator of the song, anytime and anywhere. If the singer is a renowned bull singer, he will be encouraged by the others to perform his song during the full-scale nyakorot. If the song is considered exceptional, it may be sung by others even when the song's creator is not in their presence. The DiDinga I interviewed all told me that nyakorot is based on padan and ngothi, two dance steps unique to them, and that nyakorot is 'really DiDinga.' By contrast, gyrikot is said to have been adopted from neighbouring groups in Uganda and, in some ways, demonstrates creolization, the combining of cultural elements from two or more distinct aesthetic systems that give rise to a new expressive behaviour (Szwed 2004).

I first heard the DiDinga sing Ichayo, which translates simply to 'fighting,' during a public performance in the nearby city of Auburn, New York. The programme was sponsored by the Schweinfurth Memorial Art Center, which had contracted me to coordinate their public folk arts programme. I saw this as an opportune time to introduce Americans to the Lost Boys and convinced the director to provide the venue – the parking lot of the Thompson Memorial AME Zion Church in Auburn. The audience for the performance was mainly

African American with no prior exposure to DiDinga language or culture. Although a printed programme with historical information and translations by the young men was distributed, the ensuing questions after the performance demonstrated the audience's strong desire to connect with an African heritage and, at the same time, exposed the audience's unfamiliarity with Dinka or DiDinga cultures. When the young men attempted to explain the cultural differences between DiDinga and Dinka, both of whom were performing that day, several audience members insisted, 'But don't you think at one time you were one people?' The DiDinga and Dinka, who are linguistically and culturally distinct and do not intermarry, merely stood still – and blinked in amazement. Both Dinka and DiDinga repeated, 'We are different tribes.' Although it would have been impossible for me to step in and explain the debate over the usage of the word 'tribe,' I did try to clarify the cultural differences between the two groups who, according to extant archaeological evidence, originally migrated to southern Sudan from very different parts of Africa. For the American audience that observed the performances, however, the Dinka and DiDinga remained simply a 'Sudanese tribe.'

After the performance, all of the dancers seemed surprised by the degree of American unfamiliarity with Sudan and its numerous 'tribes.' Indeed, because the audience was made up of mainly African-American Christians, most had giggled when the DiDinga mentioned their continued tradition of polygamy, still practised by many Christian Dinka and DiDinga and other groups in southern Sudan. Despite the audience's general unfamiliarity with Sudanese cultures, the young men expertly demonstrated their traditional artistic virtuosity with coordinated rhythmic movements and vocal agility through quickly changing musical modes. The audience was stunned. After the programme, one American expressed what many of us were thinking: 'They [the dancers] appeared to transport themselves back to Sudan – and at one point, I too felt they took us with them.'

The power of this performance could never be properly captured on video or in print because, as John Miles Foley has so aptly noted, 'The play's the thing (and not the script)' (2002: 184). When I later met with the young men to review the videotapes in my home, their comments supported Foley's statement in a literal way that even Foley may not have expected: when I asked why they had been laughing during some of the songs, they explained that a playful teasing exchange between Fortunato and Lino had been taking place during the dance. Fortunato had substituted Lino's name in a song, a change that made Lino a cuckolded husband whose masculinity is in question when his wife receives a love letter from another man. In addition to missing these playful substitutions, in this re-contextualized performance, the traditional critique by the audience was nonexistent. In spite of limitations, the audience's enjoyment of the men's rhythms and movements and the experience of being transported to Sudan indicated a degree of aesthetic appreciation beyond the spoken word. As I later worked on the translations for these danced songs with the singers, however, it became increasingly clear that outsiders could never fully appreciate culture-specific, oral-poetic language such as that used by the performers. It is extremely difficult for English-speaking DiDinga to render the meaning of the songs into English. For example, some of the words have been adopted from their traditional enemies, the Toposa.

One DiDinga elder admitted that DiDinga do not know the meanings of these words, but the Toposa words nevertheless contribute to DiDinga aesthetics. I relied mostly on Charles's translations and then checked them with Paul Atanya, a Canadian DiDinga musician who had taken a three-day bus trip to perform with the young men on 17 August 2003. Earlier, I had contacted Atanya by e-mail and later by telephone after hearing a cassette tape of his Canadian band, Kojo, which the young men had given to me. After speaking several times with Atanya, I realized the subtlety that existed in what I thought were relatively straightforward texts:

Ichayo hotongutho lota
Ichayo hotongutho lota
Ichaya gore baoko nyao
Ichaya hotongutho lota
Ichaya loholia hotonguthu lota
[They fought a gun battle until they lay on the ground.
They fought a gun battle until they lay on the ground.
They fought a gun battle during the war of Nyao.
They fought a gun battle until they lay on the ground.
The children fought a gun battle until they lay on the ground.][4]

The repetition of this song is characteristic of all DiDinga songs. The refrain is repeated unless the lead singer inserts another line and changes the octave. When the soloist returns to the original octave, it indicates that the song is about to end. The reference to 'they' in this song is intentionally vague. According to Atanya and the young men, the song describes one particular historic battle between the DiDinga and their traditional enemies, the Toposa (whom the DiDinga claim to this day are hostile to them). Battles often relate to the cattle-raiding that occurs among many of the ethnic groups. The use of the word 'children' (loholia) for 'warriors' is an example of special language; and like the repetition and the parallelism of most DiDinga songs, it is fundamental to the song's meaning as well as to its inherent power (see Foley 2002: 184).

Although the DiDinga word for children is used, the song is sung by villagers to encourage young men to continue the hereditary fight. When I asked the performers to comment on the meaning of the text, they merely described it as 'a nice song.' Another DiDinga explained that the song was about a tribal war and DiDinga men 'who really fought and didn't give in.' They suggested to me pride not only in the bravery of the DiDinga warriors, but also in the cultural acceptance of cattle-raiding, which traditionally has been the root of almost all intertribal warfare. Yet, they admitted on several occasions that cattle-raiding is 'destructive.' The DiDinga word for children is essentially facetious in this context, because this song is praise for young adult males who have already been initiated and granted warrior status. It is also ironic because modern Sudanese armies on all sides have conscripted male children to fight in an adult war.

The word 'fighting' refers to ethnic conflicts over cattle-raiding as well as to the killing of DiDinga civilians during the current civil war. Many of the songs (e.g., Ichayo) that the DiDinga identify as old ones, can also be new; that is, such songs may imply both recent wars and political events in addition to the original historical battles. When sung for American audiences, the commingling of old and new meanings may in fact produce a hybrid – two distinct reference points forging a new identity for the performers, not as warriors, but as refugees of that war. None of the young men explained the song in this way, but because of their new life experiences and education, the word 'warrior' for them has perhaps taken on new meaning.

Other songs, however, were designated as new, because they may be transitory. For example, during one performance, they sang 'Tinga Tinga Lobulingiro,' a strangely upbeat tune that praises Peter Lorot (whose bullname is Lobulingiro), commander of a DiDinga rebel army. One young man explained that they sang the song to honour Lobulingiro because he killed another commander and that it was 'a new one':

Enek Sadiq Lugo icia
Gerengi anyaha guwa ci hauna kicaya Kapuata ma kicaya Kapuata tel hotia Tororita lahadi
Juba ci ngati hengera huwanya iwir Sadiqi uha Khatiba
Nakeny hichayo
Muksasa ereyo icia
Khatiba Ghazali nica anyaha guwa ci Sudani
[Tell Sadik to leave (the South).[5]
Garang is coming, bringing (military) force.
That we intend to bombard and liberate Kapoeta.
After we have liberated Kapoeta, we march on Torit until Juba (whereupon) we divide (munitions).
Nakeng Battalion, let us fight!
Broom Battalion, wait (for us!)
Gazelle Battalion is coming, bringing Sudan's force.][6]

In the mid-1980s, John Garang, commander-in-chief of the SPLA/M (Sudanese People's Liberation Army and Movement), scored many military victories when he liberated strategic towns in southern Sudan from the control of Arabic soldiers. The southern rebel soldiers in this song are warning Sadik, who was Prime Minister at that time, to leave southern Sudan because Garang was bringing his military forces to liberate the cities of Torit and Juba. Charles later explained, 'We are telling Sadik to move out [of] that place [Kapuata] and leave southerners alone to have peace as other people do. We will move from Kapuata, Torit, and Juba if you [Sadik] will not move' (Interview, Syracuse, 20 June 2002). The young men smiled broadly as they sang this military song and the soloist later added that there was a positive 'feel' to the song, telling me that Sadik should move out of Kapuata before the 'team came for reinforcement to overthrow,' indicating the young men's boast that their DiDinga 'team' will ultimately prevail.

Unlike traditional (old) songs, this new song was not highly repetitious, and examples of parallelism and special language seemed to be absent (see Foley 2002). Dancers formed the traditional dance circle of nyakorot but remained motionless until the song was finished. At that point, they resumed their clockwise movement using a traditional dance step called ngothi, in which the feet are only slightly tapped before a jump. Also, unlike the old song in which nuance is subtle, this one is specifically tied to a particular event and person; anyone familiar with the history and politics of Sudan can understand the message.

Prior to the performance, I observed that the inclusion of this song had been heatedly debated by the DiDinga on several occasions. By consensus, both songs were eventually included, although initially the soloist had argued that the song about Sadik was not a traditional (old) song but rather a new (political) one and should not be performed for Americans. Once the decision was made to include these two songs, however, I was surprised when the DiDinga also sang 'Ee Uket Nohoni'/'Why Are You Torturing Us Like This?':

Ee uket nohoni
Ee longo cik gang dekererik i horoma ho
Uket nohoni
Ee uki hati koruma iin meder
[Why are you torturing us like this? Yes, you guys on the hill above? Why are you torturing us? Yes, it will one day become a vendetta.][7]

This song is about oppression of the DiDinga by the Islamic majority. Although the groups are not named, they sing that one day the situation will be reversed. 'Guys on the hill' is a reference to the police post built near Mount Lotukei, close to the Ugandan border, by Muslims from the north. The song is actually a protest about police brutality against the DiDinga, who were powerless to resist. Instead they taunted their enemies with songs like this one recalled from their childhood. Unlike the other political songs, however, Ee Uket Nohoni is sung in the traditional DiDinga proverbial style; that is, the text is a symbolically dense narrative that relies heavily on contextual information for the audience to grasp its meaning. Like most traditional DiDinga songs, its specificity is only recognizable to DiDinga, and, without an intimate knowledge of DiDinga oral history, the meaning is entirely lost.

By contrast, 'new' songs like 'Tinga Tinga Lobulingiro' incorporate specific references to people and current events. Yet both old and new songs are sung to the same kind of traditional melody, with a soloist taking the lead and the chorus replying in a sort of call and response. In other words, whether the texts were traditional or new, the melody and the delivery remained old. In essence, all DiDinga songs are both old and new because the DiDinga often express themselves in a traditional proverbial manner without naming specific people or places. I also came to realize that 'nice songs,' however militant, expressed bravery, resistance and a positive outcome for the DiDinga. Sometimes it was only the soloist, the eldest in the group, who knew the songs and introduced them to the group, demonstrating how an individual's repertoire can increase that of the group. The fact that only the soloist understood the references did not seem to hamper this process. 'Proverb' is the word used by the DiDinga to explain that, in the original village context, their succinct songs serve as a newspaper: referring back to specific incidents or specific people, but always in flux. It is 'generative theory', rather than Albert Lord's oral-formulaic theory, that I believe best explains the nature of these mutable songs, an approach described by Bruce A. Rosenberg in his work on black sermons: 'Lord ties the creation of new formulas (metrically governed utterances) to the singer's recollection of the commonest ones. Actually, the singer is freed from such memory and such hydraulic reliance. He has at his command not several score or even several hundred formulas which can be altered by a word or phrase substitution but rather a metrical deep structure enabling the generation of an infinite number of sentences or utterances in the metre of his native language' (1990: 147). The DiDinga singers also demonstrated a similar facility with 'metrical deep structures', and, even if they did not know the words, they responded to the call of the soloist, who strung together several songs. The following texts elucidate a subtle negotiation process occurring during re-contextualized performances.

[...] In this way, the young men had preserved a shared tradition. Because of the continuing civil war in Sudan, it was impossible for me to visit DiDingaland to learn more about these traditions. It was necessary, therefore, that I rely on these young men's descriptive memories about DiDinga dance traditions and honor their traditions as they were emerging in a new context. [...] Some of the versions sung by the Lost Boys did not change even after DiDinga elders pointed out that their songs were not 'good' – that is, the young men did not fully understand the traditional meaning. It was then I realized that the Lost Boys had created their own nostalgic repertoire: as 'immature' as some of the songs might appear to the elders, these traditions were the ones the young men shared and continued to perform after the elders' departure from our region.

Gyrikot: It's all about love stuff

On the surface, none of the DiDinga young men's songs appeared complex enough to warrant an in-depth text-centred approach. While applying Dennis Tedlock's microanalysis to the DiDinga songs gives the impression that an oral performance can be adequately represented in print (Tedlock 1983), I found a more useful approach in inviting the singers' commentaries as they reviewed a videotape or listened to a cassette tape after the performances. Similarly, capturing the danced songs in print is not easy. The lively and highly repetitive antiphonal melodies of this group, based on the pentatonic scale, are composed spontaneously even when performed in Sudanese villages – hence, no two melodies are ever performed in exactly the same way. DiDinga songs possess unique musical characteristics, such as frequently changing keys, stringing different songs together with little or no break and changing melody or rhythm. Musical accompaniment is unique because, unlike other neighbouring Surmic-speaking groups, the DiDinga, until recent contact with other African groups, did not use the drum. For the most part, songs are unaccompanied by instruments, except for a tooeri (reed trumpet), occasional hedemeta (hand-held rattles made from dried gourds), or chugurena (small bells worn on the forearms and thighs). Percussion is produced by stomping the feet while clapping and standing in a line; when females are present, a male-female formation called padan is formed. During nyakorot, the movements also include ngothi, jumping in rapid sequence.

All the young men in Syracuse knew padan and ngothi. Even without instruments such as hedemeta, the young men improvised the sound by using aluminium pans and tin trays with forks and knives from their kitchen. When I offered them wooden instruments, which I had bought at a store specializing in African wares, they politely accepted the instruments but still performed on the next occasion with the aluminium pans. I thought that perhaps they had misplaced the wooden instruments, but they clearly preferred metal whistles, knives and forks as accompaniment for their songs; however, when I purchased two horse- and cow-tail fly-whips and community members donated African thumb pianos, they did use these additions. It is interesting to note that the DiDinga tell me their word for the fly-whip is nyalado, a word borrowed from the hostile Toposa. Thus, their incorporation of cultural objects from the Toposa, and from countries like Kenya and the United States, demonstrates the creativity that occurs during cultural contact. Although nyakorot was danced and sung in the 'truly DiDinga' way, the musical instruments had been hybridized. And soon after performing with Africans from Ghana, the young men requested that I provide a drum for their next public performance.

Like many other East African groups, in addition to political songs the men most frequently danced and sang mocking songs like 'Mariah,' during which the tempo increases until it culminates in an insult or reprimand. Other songs included references to love relationships between young men and women, and therefore gyrikot is the genre favoured by DiDinga youth in Sudan. In the United States, gyrikot lent itself to many performance opportunities because it is a vigorous dance tradition that could be appreciated by non-DiDinga speakers. One young DiDinga explained a young man's preference for this tradition because 'gyrikot is all based in love stuff.' The most obvious example of 'love stuff' follows:

SOLOIST: Ai Mariah hanyaki thong Ai Mariah hanyaki thong
CHORUS: Ai Mariah hanyaki thong Ai Mariah hanyaki thong
SOLOIST: Ee tira thiga da Chorus: Arita hina gi ci ereketa Ee Ai Mariah hanyaki thong
[SOLOIST: Maria says, I'm pregnant. Yes, Maria says, I'm pregnant.
CHORUS: Maria says, I'm pregnant. Yes, Maria says, I'm pregnant.
SOLOIST: Yes, so let us see you give birth.
CHORUS: Instead she is giving birth to it (something we do not know).
Yes, Maria says, I'm pregnant.][8]

This kind of repetition, according to Foley (2002), is connotatively explosive. Like repetition, omissions can also be part of the art of performance. Based in DiDinga tradition, the repetition in the song may be for effect, but the humour also conveys a serious warning about premarital sex: outside the institution of marriage, sex has its consequences. Among the DiDinga, sometimes an unmarried woman, like an unmarried man, might have multiple relationships. In this song, Maria tells her lover that she is pregnant, but DiDinga society has no way to determine fatherhood scientifically. This poses difficulties for many men and judges, who rely on physical similarity of the child to determine the father, a process that takes time. In this song, Maria claims she is pregnant by one of her lovers whom she believes is definitely the father of her child. But she is chided that she could be giving birth to something we do not know, because the father's identity, human or not, is uncertain. The insult might go unnoticed even by linguists because of the subtlety of DiDinga verbal play. As the young men explained, in Maria's case, the insult is 'something we do not know,' which implies not only that Maria is promiscuous, but also that perhaps her offspring is not even human. Although few words are sung, each is loaded with meaning encapsulated in this shorthand form. It was difficult to interpret the pithy humour of these songs for an American audience. The songs were not exactly hybrid or creole, nor were they exactly incomplete, combined or recombined. The young men were preserving their DiDinga tradition as they had understood it when forced to flee their villages at a very young age.

Retheorizing tradition

When I began this study of the Lost Boys' performances, a theoretical model to interpret re-contextualized tradition was lacking. I needed to know who decides which traditions are tied to this group and how that might be decided, with issues of identity at stake. To address these questions, it was critical to note that the dance songs represented the young men's memories, their cultural values as DiDinga males, their experiences as refugees from Sudan, and their lives as educated young men living in the United States.

Because of their life circumstances, nostalgia and childhood memory acted on their traditions (McMahon 2002). Their lives as displaced people, the new audiences, and my role as a presenter when they performed were all external forces that affected the aesthetics of their traditions. For example, when sung for American audiences, the commingling of old and new meanings produced a hybrid where two distinct reference points forged a new identity for the performers – not as warriors, but as refugees of a war. None of the young men explained the song in this way, but because of their new life experiences and education, the warrior role for them may have taken on new meaning.

For the Lost Boys, the opportunities to perform in the United States could be both liberating and constraining. Performing their traditional songs enabled them to express a group identity and their musical talents were honoured as something unique to share with American audiences. Here they had no cattle, however, so the songs became nostalgic and sometimes playful expressions of a lost childhood and a former way of life rather than songs of bravery. Conversely, in Sudan it would be incomprehensible for lower status males to perform these songs during nyakorot and certainly never apart from specific community celebrations. In the United States, free of adult DiDinga censure and strict traditional rules, they enjoyed the licence to perform the traditions that they favoured. Here was a 'safe space'; the traditions became a way through which their urban western identity was integrated with their DiDinga heritage.

More important, over time I learned that for this parentless group of youths, the strongest variable affecting their traditions was the play phenomenon. Their traditions were based on childhood games. Much of their performance was like adolescent teasing or mock fighting in a way reminiscent of children imitating adults. When I met Marino, a DiDinga refugee who newly joined the group in Syracuse in February 2004, he described songs and dances that he too recalled as a child in Sudan: 'When it is evening and the moon comes up, they are playing [a] gourd and when others come they are singing then. It is like a kind of practice about what they hear the adults singing. One of the ways to learn our culture is to just imitate it' (Interview, Syracuse, 19 March 2004). It was this combination of children's games and warrior songs that had resulted in the Lost Boys' repertoire.

Conclusion

In the preceding pages, I proposed a theoretical model to elucidate how tradition emerges in a new context, a theory arising from intensive fieldwork and documentation of one small group of refugee youth. I believe it is applicable, however, for understanding the traditions of diasporic communities everywhere. When I began working with the DiDinga Lost Boys, it had been less than six months after their immigration to the United States. Although they were still experiencing culture shock and I knew little about DiDinga culture, I believed this was a critical period for researching their traditions and for finding new cultural outlets. Globalization has created a global commons, a performance space where there are few guidelines to help facilitate interaction. But folklorists today are in a unique position to make valuable contributions with long-term effects. Public folklorists, in particular, are in a critical position to facilitate ways for newcomers to maintain cultural identities and thus avoid being overwhelmed by American culture.

As Greg Gow suggests, traditions for diasporic communities are articulated within the present. When a ritual is performed in a new context, there is 'a series of alignments and lived conjunctions that do not represent a hidden real but are the real. They constitute the individual and collective reality of being [...] in exile' (2002: 3). Likewise, the performances of the Lost Boys are 'real' and 'authentic', not incomplete or invented. The Lost Boys engage in a kind of compartmentalization, a latent state, which enables them to 'travel' back and forth across cultures. This is a process they had engaged in before coming to the United States: while in Africa, they had had to adjust in a short time from rural village life to refugee camp life, and then to urban life when they were given the chance to attend a boarding school in Nairobi. Philip Mayer discusses the tension between the accommodation and preservation of traditions occurring within new contexts: 'In town as in country these two "localities," the local and the "tribal," are interwoven. They maintain and reinforce each other' (1971: 291). We can extend Mayer's observation to transnational communities as well.

To define an authentic diasporic identity, it is necessary to recognize that every group has a shared cultural memory, a cooperative 'vault,' but equally important are the players involved in consensus. We need to know whether those involved in the negotiation process are insiders or whether decisions are being dominated by outsiders. In the United States, the Lost Boys negotiate among themselves to create a combination of children's songs and warrior songs that result in playful, powerful performances. This improvisational ability has enabled the Lost Boys to take control of their past and to present themselves not as refugees, but as DiDinga warriors in a new land. In this way, the young men are both preservers of DiDinga culture and harbingers of social change. Because those involved in the negotiation stage are all Lost Boys, consensus has been possible.

At the same time, it is important to remember that every consensus has a 'history,' made from a collection of differing opinions that do not just disappear once a tradition is negotiated. Under new circumstances, when new variables act on tradition, earlier opinions of group members may resurface. Thus, the dynamic process of tradition is set in motion. Each time, there remains the need to identify new variables and conditions that play a central role in the production and reproduction of the collective identities of diasporic communities.

References

Baron, Robert, *Theorizing Public Folklore Practice: Documentation, Genres of Representation, and Everyday Competencies*, Journal of Folklore Research 36: 2–3 (1999), pp. 185–201.
Basch, Linda, Nina Glick Schiller, and Cristina Szanton Blanc, *Nations Unbound: Transnational Projects, Postcolonial Predicaments and Deterritorialized Nation-States*, Basel: Gordon & Bread, 1994.
Bauman, Richard, *Verbal Art as Performance*, Rowley, MA: Newbury House, 1978.
——, *Story, Performance and Event: Contextual Studies of Oral Narrative*, Cambridge: Cambridge University Press, 1986.
Briggs, Charles, *Learning How to Ask: A Sociolinguist Appraisal of the Role of the Interview in Social Science Research*, Cambridge: Cambridge University Press, 1986.
——, *War of Visions: Conflicts of Identities in the Sudan*, London: Brookings Institution, 1995.
Foley, John Miles, *How to Read an Oral Poem*, Urbana: University of Illinois Press, 2002.
Glassie, Henry, 'Tradition,' *Journal of American Folklore* 108: 430 (1995), pp. 395–412.
Gow, Greg, *The Oromo in Exile: From the Horn of Africa to the Suburbs of Australia*, Victoria: Melbourne University Press, 2002.
Hymes, Dell, 'Breakthrough into performance,' in *Folklore: Performance and Communication*, Dan Ben-Amos and Kenneth S. Goldstein (eds), pp. 1–74. The Hague: Mouton, 1975.

Mayer, Philip, *Townsmen or Tribesmen: Conservatism and the Process of Urbanization in a South African City*, London: Oxford University Press, 1971.

Pipher, Mary, *The Middle of Everywhere: The World's Refugees Come to Our Town*, New York: Harcourt, 2002.

Rosenberg, Neil V., 'Repetition, Innovation and Representation in Don Messer's Repertoire,' *Journal of American Folklore* 115: 456 (2002), pp. 191–208.

Safran, William, 'Diasporas in Modern Societies: Myths of Homeland and Return,' *Diaspora* 1: 1 (1991), pp. 83–99.

Szwed, John F., 'Metaphors of Incommensurability,' *Journal of American Folklore,* 116: 459 (2004), pp. 9–18.

Tedlock, Dennis, *The Spoken Word and the Work of Interpretation*, Philadelphia: University of Pennsylvania Press, 1983.

Zutt, Johannes, *Children of War: Wandering Alone in Southern Sudan*, New York: UNICEF, 1994.

Notes

I wish to thank Lee Haring, Brian Sutton-Smith and Robert Baron, for reading earlier drafts of this chapter. A special thanks to Eric Holzwarth, Assistant Dean, College of Arts and Sciences at Syracuse University, for institutional support of the initial performance that enabled me to introduce my students to the Lost Boys. Thanks also to Robert Rubinstein, director of the Program on the Analysis and Resolution of Conflicts at the Maxwell School, for providing office space and secretarial support. I am also indebted to Elaine Lawless, Sw. Anand Prahlad and the JAF reviewers, for their insightful comments and encouragement.

1   According to folklore, refugee workers named this group of boys, who arrived en masse to refugee camps, the 'Lost Boys' after the unaccompanied group of male children in the story of Peter Pan. Of the 75 Lost Boys in Syracuse, the majority are Dinka, but a few DiDinga also arrived in 2001. The Dinka and DiDinga do not record birthdates; thus, for immigration purposes, the young men's ages had to be estimated. There were nine DiDinga youth who initially arrived in Syracuse and with whom I worked on public performances: Charles (21); George (17); Dominic L. (16); Joseph (16); Dominic R. (21); James K. (21); Lino T. (21); Fortunato (21); and Simon (21). Peter (14) arrived in 2003; in 2004, Marino (21), Benjamin (20) and a few other DiDinga arrived whom I did not interview. In this article, to ensure their privacy, I use only their first names and no details about their social lives.

2   This small group of nine had been resettled in Syracuse by Catholic Charities and the Refugee Resettlement Services, which had found apartments for the young men, who lived in groups of four or five to an apartment and secured factory or service-industry night jobs so that they could be financially independent when their three-month federally funded subsidies ended. The youth who were teenagers were placed with foster families and attended local high schools. All of the other men attended a local community college, education being a high priority for

them. Their complex culture and tragic stories remained unknown to most Americans. Even now, some two years after national media coverage (e.g., on CBS's *60 Minutes II*), the remarkable narrative of these young men, who have lost fathers and mothers, brothers and sisters, and who for all intents and purposes are now orphans, still waits to be told to those outside their group.

3   Translation by Marino.
4   Translation by Paul Atanya.
5   Sadik was the former Sudanese Prime Minister who was deposed in 1989 by Omar Beshir, the current military ruler.
6   Translation by Paul Atanya.
7   Translation by Charles.
8   Translation by Charles.

Chapter 14

Theatre as a Healing Space: Ping Chong's *Children of War*

Yuko Kurahashi

M any theatre practitioners and scholars have investigated 'theatre as psychotherapy'. Such people encourage participants to recognize and reevaluate their position and subjectivity in the full context of theatre's history, and, more importantly, to reframe their participation by describing in their own words their experiences. For example, together with hospitalized children who have psychiatric problems related to trauma, the Children's Therapeutic Puppet Theater project (at Children's Theater in Chicago) has co-created fantasy stories that have allowed those children to recognize and articulate deeply rooted emotions and ideas.[1] Examining the methods and approaches that the Children's Therapeutic Puppet Theater uses, Linnea Carlson-Sabelli (a specialist in the use of action methods in psychotherapy) argues that the process of collaborating in those puppet plays helps the children 'release the power of imagination, story, and cocreative adventure' (Carlson-Sabelli 1998: 93). Through the 'activity of cocreating stories,' which involves 'action' (that is, energy or a forward flow in time), the children go through 'the complexity of the process of change through experience' (Carlson-Sabelli 1998: 95). That process generates what Peter Elsass, a chief psychologist at the Psychiatric Hospital in Aarhus, Denmark, calls a 'good performance' (Elsass 1992: 334). Examining similarities between psychotherapy and theatre, Elsass clarifies that both produce a 'life and insight' that promotes 'effective healing,' which, in the world of theatre, is simply called a 'good performance.' That 'effective healing' (in other words, that therapeutic experience) takes place in a 'healing space' that is not the consulting room or psychiatrist's office (Elsass 1992: 333, 342). In a psychotherapeutic theatrical realm, that 'healing space' is created through the process of participating in the theatre as an active agent to speak about and share one's experience.

The act of re-examining problems and searching for possible solutions often entails incorporating non-traditional therapeutic strategies, including 'narrative therapy'. When considered from the perspective of post-structuralist analysis of language and its power, narrative therapy can be described as being 'premised upon the idea that the lives and the relationships of persons are shaped by the knowledges and stories that communities of persons negotiate and engage in to give meaning to their experiences' (Besley 2002: 127). Reshaping and reclaiming 'knowledges' and 'stories' helps to re-examine the existing views and values attached to a specific history, and then to investigate the space of, in Foucault's terms, non-hierarchical relationships between the individual and authority.[2] Narrative therapy challenges traditional 'compliance' methods in which the patient blindly follows the practitioner's orders. Instead of constructing a traditional therapeutic dialogue where the patient is rendered as a passive recipient of caring and treatment, the therapist of narrative therapy decentres her position and encourages her client to resolve problems by questioning the ways of life that subjugate and oppress him or her. In the process, the client is able to 're-author' his or her own life through conversations with the therapist, who is considered his or her collaborator (Besley 2002: 127).

Narrative therapy tactics and methods have been used by various therapy-theatre projects. One exemplary project in contemporary theatre is *Children of War*, co-produced by Ping Chong & Company and the Center for Multicultural Human Services (CMHS) in Falls Church, Virginia in 2002. As Elsass argues, it is a collaborative work that demonstrates new insights for effective healing by incorporating two of narrative therapy's therapeutic processes: 'complementarity' (which means that participants with similar experiences are grouped together) and 'congruency' (which means that participants with varied experiences are grouped together and are helped to understand the differences among them) (Elsass 1992: 334).

Children of War is one of the installments of *Undesirable Elements*, the community-based oral history series that is the result of collaboration between Chong and various adults and children. *Undesirable Elements* has been in development since 1992 when Chong produced it while he was in residency at Artist Space in New York City. Since then, *Undesirable Elements* has been staged in numerous cities, among them Charleston, Cleveland, Minneapolis, Seattle, Washington DC, Chicago, Rotterdam and Tokyo. *Children of War* started with Chong working closely, through the autumn of 2002, with five young refugees (from Somalia, Sierra Leone, El Salvador, Afghanistan and Kurdistan) who now live in Northern Virginia, and with a therapist (who is herself a refugee from Iran) at the Center for Multicultural Human Services (CMHS). The resulting play comments on both the past and current political conflicts in each of the participants' homelands, and on the effects such conflicts have had on their individual lives. Through monologues and dialogues, the play evolves as a woven tapestry of their family histories and of the violence, torture, mutilations and massacres they escaped.

My aim in this chapter is to examine how *Children of War* creates a 'healing space' (and thus a therapeutic opportunity) for the participants to reflect on their experiences, to articulate their memories, negotiate many of their unresolved feelings, and consequently to arrive at a deeper insight into the trauma in their lives. My goal is, by no means, to evaluate the production in psychotherapeutic and medical terms. Rather, I intend to show that the performance of *Children of War* creates a site for expressing the 'unspeakable,' and for symbiotically creating a kind of communal healing, a kind of understanding, that allows for both the participants and audiences to re-author horrific experiences.

Ping Chong's initial introduction to the CMHS dates back to 2000 when the Gala Hispanic Theater in Washington DC presented *Undesirable Elements* with various community artists and activists – from Mexico, Costa Rica, Guatemala, Vietnam and Liberia – in the community of Columbia Heights and Mount Pleasant in DC. Chong created a piece that illustrates the history of their transnational journeys as well as the familial 'stories' handed down over generations. Ricarda Dowling, Director of Development at CMHS, who attended a performance at the Gala Hispanic Theatre in DC, was so intrigued that she asked the

Gala to stage the play in Northern Virginia. With Rebecca Medrano, Managing Director at the Gala Hispanic Theatre, Dowling staged *Undesirable Elements* at the Northern Virginia Community College in December 2000, and again in Arlington, Virginia in October 2001. Dowling and CMHS invited Chong, and subsequently Dr Dennis Hunt (Executive Director of CMHS and a licensed clinical psychologist specializing in work with traumatized refugee children) asked Chong to create a new play that would focus on local refugee children and the psychological damage they have suffered.

The processes of selecting 'actors' and of script-making for what became *Children of War* were unconventional. The CMHS pre-screened more than 80 children and selected 25 (due to liability issues, the Center eliminated its own clients), out of which Chong chose five children – Fatu Sankoh (age 15), Abdul Hakeem Paigir (age 13), Dereen Pasha (age 15), Yarvin Cuchilla (age 18) and Awa Nur (age 15).[3] Chong interviewed each child in two-hour segments totaling six hours. All of the children were eager to talk about their stories, and Chong, who has always valued the participants' need to express themselves, found this interview process extremely therapeutic for them and himself. He began to realize that the children were opening up often 'with tears and smiles,' and that the process was helping them to re-see their experiences through a more detailed perspective. Chong also interviewed the children's parents in order to get more accurate and detailed information. The original 'script' was revised a number of times during the rehearsal period. The CMHS staff also worked with Chong to help him understand trauma-related matters that particularly pertain to children. Although every piece of their stories was invaluable, Chong had to edit them in order to make the performance just an hour and 20 minutes long.

Like many other pieces of *Undesirable Elements*, *Children of War* follows a staged-reading format. Seven chairs are arranged in a semi-circle. Six participants sit on six chairs; one chair remains unoccupied throughout the performance. Certain areas of the world are projected in blue on the back wall. The projected shapes suggest the maps of different countries that are not necessarily spoken about in the piece. This visual marker of the unspecified countries symbolizes how the world can be perceived both macrocosmically and microcosmically. It also illustrates the tension and balance between generalizations and personalization – the very threads that create the fabric of this theatrical piece.

Although conventional theatricality is not a prominent part of the production, Chong accentuates the beginning, as well as the transitions, with music, costumes and intentionally choreographed poses. As the music plays, the performers appear and sit on their respective chairs. They wear traditional costumes, which reflect their cultural heritages and native languages, thus highlighting the individuality of each culture and specific history, and simultaneously transforming them into a vital collective, a new multicultural community. Between certain segments, the performers clap their hands ten times, which is yet another way to emphasize the collective's energy and power. Then Yarvin begins: 'Let's get started, please sit. Mi nombre es Yarvin Cuchilla. Yo naci en el llano Los Patos, departamento de la union El Salvador.'

By intricately embedding the personal histories of each child into the accounts of their countries' history, Chong creates a tapestry of polyphonic voices that echo both on the microcosmic and macrocosmic levels. The children trace the history of colonization and occupation from 1492 when Pedro da Sintra, a Portuguese explorer, 'map[s] a mountainous peninsula and calls it Serra Lyon, or Lion Mountain' (*Children of War* 2002b: 6). The action is propelled by Dereen, a fifteen-year-old boy from Kurdistan, who defines himself as a person 'without a homeland' (*Children of War* 2002b: 9); then the children recount representative historical events which describe the series of invasions, colonizations, corruptions and destructions that took place in their countries. The participants sweep the audience into an overview of major colonial, postcolonial and diasporic historical events: the Ottoman Turks' systematic destruction of the Kurds in the nineteenth century, the British colonization of Sierra Leone in 1895, the division of Kurdistan by France and Britain in 1921, the independence of Somalia in 1960, and of Sierra Leone in 1961, followed by a coup d'état in 1964, the assassination of Khala Shahab (a member of the Patriotic Union of Kurdistan) by the Iraqi government in 1976, the Iranian revolution in 1978, followed by the new regime of the Ayatollah Ruhollah Khomeini in 1979, the Soviet invasion of Afghanistan in December 1979, the outbreak of the Iraq/Iran war in 1980, the civil war in El Salvador in 1988, the Gulf War in 1991, the outbreak of the civil war in Somalia in 1991, the beginning of the civil war in Sierra Leone in 1992 and then the attacks of 11 September 2001 in the United States.

Those historical and political events and tragedies are entwined with the individual and very personal histories of each child: Awa's grandfather takes a trip to England as one of the first Somalians to receive a Western education; Farinaz Amirsehi (the Center's therapist and the only adult in the play) reminisces about her grandfather, Rahmat Sheybani, who, in spite of his high social status, treated everyone – including servants and their children – equally. She also remembers her father who courageously refused to cooperate with the corrupt Iranian government. Dereen's father, Dillshad, a nephew of Khala Shahab, tells about joining the independent movement of the Kurdish people. Dillshad later fell in love with a young college girl, Shayan, and married her. Likewise, Abdul recounts how his parents met during the war in Afghanistan when he was a soldier and she a nurse.

As the play proceeds, each performer's story becomes more personal, urgent, and dire. In 1981, Farinaz was sentenced to ten years in prison in Tehran for her involvement with the underground political movement against the Khomeini regime. In 1986, because of her fellow prisoners' futile attempt at uprising, she was blindfolded and put in a small space, which was 'just wide enough to sit up in,' for nine months (*Children of War* 2002b: 19). More than seven members of Yarvin's mother's family were killed in the civil war in El Salvador in 1988. In 1991 Awa's baby sister was killed when guerrillas attacked a bus filled with refugees. When Dereen was five, he witnessed his father being shot by Iraqi soldiers. In Sierra Leone, Fatu escaped killings and mutilations by covering her face with ash and wearing old clothes to look like a crazy person. Amazingly, all of the atrocities recounted by the participants are extremely specific but never gratuitously graphic or sentimental. The tone of their voices is calm, yet with so much 'hidden' emotion. Yarvin quietly says: 'I dream that one day I will find a place [where] nobody will beat us again, and people will be kind to us' (*Children of War* 2002b: 29). Like Yarvin, many other participants share their painful stories without tears and screams – they do so as if simply reporting 'facts' to the audience. Yet, all the more so, the audience is led to realize how, behind their tranquil appearances, there is an endless trail of tears and blood connecting agonising nights and days. By their matter-of-factness, the audience is constantly reminded that the graphic images are for ever marked in each consciousness – a place the audience can never touch deeply enough to erase each of their scars.

One of the common tragedies recounted is the continual separation each participant experienced. All of them had separated from parents, siblings, relatives and/or friends. Each of their stories has at least one heartbreaking severance caused by violent and inhuman conduct. Helene Berman, a professor and career scientist in the School of Nursing at the University of Western Ontario, writes about such circumstances. Her research has found that forced and violent separations are more distressing to children than air raids and bombings.[4] Berman writes that children of war are more likely to have enduring trauma when they are also separated from their loved ones: 'depressive symptoms were more evident among children who had experienced separation from their parents than those who remained with their parents' (Berman 2001: 245). She argues that one of the most important treatments for this type of suffering is the (re)building of solid family and community ties (Berman 2001: 244). Active dialogue in the family and community, she writes, helps to create and strengthen new and positive relationships. The very process of 'voicing' and 'sharing' traumatic experiences is one significant way for those relationships to be established, and yet that is often one of the most difficult things for those children to do, since the natural tendency is to suppress agonising memories. As Berman writes, a 'common response to a trauma is to deny and repress painful memories, rather than confront them. Although this type of response tentatively enables young people to cope with disturbing events, it does not allow them to heal' (Berman 2001: 249). Therefore, Berman concludes, such children need to have opportunities to talk openly and safely about their histories; they need to talk to their families and loved ones, as well as to their homes and countries.

Children of War functions as just such an occasion. This play provides the participants with a place and reason to name and articulate their memories, first with Chong, then with each other, and later with the audience. This developing 'communal' and co-participating process is reinforced in their polyphonic voicing of specific events. For example, when Fatu talks about the death of her friend, all of the participants join the telling of her story:

Following the transcultural 'call-response' form, this individual's story is changed into the story of many communities. In reframing her story as part of a community, Fatu (as well as the other participants and the audience) finds solace and companionship.

The subtext in each of the children's accounts reveals the complexity of war's violence, abuse and neglect. The repercussions of war echo in multiple ways. One of the participants is not only a victim of war but of domestic violence. Her grandmother and aunt beat Yarvin and her siblings. After Yarvin herself emigrates to the United States to live with her mother, the beating begins again, this time, by her own mother. Her mother eventually 'sells' her to a man when she is fourteen years old. When she escapes that situation, she starts living with her boyfriend, and then becomes pregnant. Eventually, Yarvin ends up in a foster home, where she finally finds love and security. Yarvin's story exemplifies how political and social unrest impacts on both adults and children, and how it robs individuals and communities of their ability to give and receive protection and nurturance; it also shows how the vicious cycle of violence is perpetrated – and, in Yarvin's case, ended.

This theatre production is amazing, partly because the hope and energy that each participant generates is palpable. They exude resilience, a willingness to confront any hardship and true excitement about their new life in the United States. That is inspiring and healing for the audience as well. For example, the audience laughs uproariously at the children's genuine enthusiasm for pizza, and it chuckles at Fatu from Sierra Leone who tries to keep snow to show it to her friends back home. Chong's deliberate attempt to reveal the indomitable child's spirit of each participant is successful; that provides a balance with the litany of atrocities they describe, and it creates a safe space for both the children and the audience to think about what they are experiencing. Some of the most poignant scenes centre on children who have memories of a life before the wars. Toward the end of the play they ask each other: 'What do you think of when you hear the words "El Salvador" or "Sierra Leone?"' Then they ask: 'What do you think of when I say the word "War"?' Along with gruesome memories, the children remember food and nature most vividly. Yarvin thinks of 'carne asada', 'Pupusas' (those delicious corn-flour *empanadas* filled with savoury meat and cheese), all of the games they used to play and the warm weather. Fatu remembers 'peanut-butter cake, cassava-leaf sauce, and fufu' (a cassava porridge). Awa reminisces about 'blue skies', and Farinaz melancholically describes 'climbing cherry trees in the summer and the Caspian Sea.' Abdul remembers his grandparents and the smell of roses. Dereen thinks of Alab, a valley in Kurdistan. In articulating and exchanging these memories, the participants and the audience recreate the desolation of their pasts, but they also recreate 'imaginary homelands,' as each child hopes it can be: that in itself is a very healing process.

Having traversed multiple geographical and psychological boundaries that deprived them of so many of their loved ones, in this play the children are able to cross yet another demarcation: they are able to think deeply and self-reflexively about the role of war in their lives. For Awa, war symbolizes 'how people should want peace more than they want war.' For Fatu, 'war' is the result of quarrels among selfish adults who do not know how to cohabit with others; she asserts that 'whoever is fighting should put us on a plane and let us go, and when they finish fighting bring us back.' Abdul thinks of 'wives without husbands, children without parents.' These astonishing visualizations and 'theorizations' also help the participants and audience to ponder on the futility of war.

Children of War was conceived with the aim to affect participants, primarily, in very positive and healing ways. And indeed, participants' testimonies confirm that they found the project to be life altering. Prior to participating in the play, many of the participants suffered severe symptoms of Post-Traumatic Stress Disorder (PTSD). That is not unusual. For instance, a study on PTSD and grief among the children of Kuwait reports that when exposed to military fighting, children consequently have nightmares, bouts of terror when confronted with reminders (e.g., planes, helicopters, soldiers or police), reduced self-esteem and increased depression. They often regress (e.g., start wetting their beds), become disobedient, aggressive and have trouble falling asleep (Nader et al. 1993: 408). Studies on children with PTSD confirm that it is imperative for them to articulate their feelings. Researchers such as Kathi Nader and Robert Pynoos assert that teachers should 'help to validate and normalize children's responses as well as permit the open expression of concerns' (Nader and Pynoos 1993: 311).

Unfortunately, the reality is that usually these children do not feel safe to tell their stories. In the play, Fatu embodies that reality. She describes how, when she talked about her experience in her class at school, nobody believed her. As a result, she stopped talking about what had happened to her, her friends and her family in Sierra Leone. That is one reason why healing spaces such as this play are very important. It was during rehearsals that Fatu finally felt affirmed enough to express herself. Farinaz Amirsehi notes that Fatu 'totally depends on the setting and environment she is in when she talks about her experience' (Amirsehi 2003). But that changed after participating in this play, since it provided Fatu and the other children with a safe haven for externalizing, without being judged, memories that in usual circumstances are unutterable and often, to the listener, totally incredible.

Plays like *Children of War* point to the power of theatre in our society. Theatre is more than mere entertainment. It is a place, an occasion, a reason, for exploring and defining our inner selves, our pasts, our future, our roles in the multiple societies and communities we inhabit across geographies and psychologies. Eugenio Barba, an internationally acclaimed theatre educator and director, and also the founder of ISTA (International School of Theatre Anthropology), attests that, 'In theatre we have the possibility of defining ourselves in relation to others, and it is of the utmost importance to have a precise point of departure' (Barba 1985: 44). That pertains to all of us, whatever our life circumstances. And for those who have been deprived of a trauma-free life, the place of theatre is even more crucial. When children, especially, are dispossessed of safety, family and friends, when they are uprooted from home, they lose their point of departure, the anchor in their lives. Therapeutic theatre, like that which Chong creates in *Children of War*, can become the catalyst for finding a new point of departure – for recognizing and rebuilding a new anchor.

The central method used in this project – telling stories – is the very core strategy that is used in narrative therapy. Farinaz Amirsehi explains that in this play 'telling stories is very similar to narrative therapy – which is the modality of treatment,' and that is crucial in helping a child to heal, because, as research has shown, and Amirsehi contends, 'by narrating your own stories over and over and over, you are able to desensitize the original trauma' (Amirsehi 2003).

There are other therapeutic modalities used in *Children of War*: although it may seem paradoxical, silence is also a vital component. Traumatized children cannot be pushed to verbalize; they must be given the space and safety to do so, and until they are ready, their silence has to be respected. It is important to realize that, as political theorist Hannah Arendt observes, some experiences – especially 'the experience of great bodily pain' – are the most private and least communicable, and cannot 'withstand the implacable, bright light of the constant presence of others on the public scene' (Arendt 1958: 50–51). As in therapy, in this play Chong honours the silence of those participants who are not yet able to speak. That is evident in the symbolic empty chair on the stage, which in addition stands in for the millions of children who did not survive, or who were not participants in the play. This acknowledged and created space for 'silence' also functions as visible reassurance that no one is being coerced in this theatrical healing space. And hence, silence becomes part of a continuum in communication, just another step in the process of healing. In this play Chong strikes a sensitive balance between the stories that are told and those that are left untold. His stand on silence echoes many therapists and theoreticians who acknowledge the need for and value of not forcing people to speak. Cultural theorist Foucault, for one, writes that 'silence and secrecy are a shelter for power, anchoring its prohibitions,' yet loosening its hold and providing for 'relatively obscure areas of tolerance' (Foucault 1980: 101). Those 'areas of tolerance' include sites in which people can suspend their immediate reactions to others, and where they can reflect on their positions and power relations. Susan Sontag asserts[5] that 'the highest good for the artist is to reach the point' that allows him or her to be 'satisfied by being silent,' as opposed to feeling compelled (by others and circumstances) to find 'a voice in art' (Sontag 1990: 364).

While Chong works actively to help each participant to articulate, he also creates a safe zone for silence and meditation. Farinaz Amirsehi embodies one of those zones. She plays dual roles in this project: she is a former 'child' of war, and a professional therapist for 'children of war' – and she holds on to silence as her right. In a personal interview Amirsehi revealed that she was working in Iran as a nurses' aide in 1981 when she became involved with the underground movement. One night, when she was delivering anti-government flyers, she was caught, tortured and put in prison. In the play she explains how she was thrown into what her captors called 'graves,' a space that was just wide enough for her to sit up in, and where she lived for nine months. But Amirsehi remains completely silent about everything else. She does not describe the details of her torture, nor how she felt then or now. Nonetheless, her silence communicated reams to the audience, and to the other participants. At the very least, her silence communicates that what she experienced is beyond words, and that her pain is so deep, and perhaps her apprehension so intense, that she dares not share herself with strangers. Her silence is powerful: it is what caught my attention when I watched the performance. Of course, there could be other explanations for why she remains silent and why Chong did not prompt her to speak further. Perhaps Chong wants to protect participants from voyeurism, or perhaps Amirsehi has chosen to reinscribe her experiences and pains in her own terms. Whatever the reasons, she embodies a silence that communicates more than words could ever convey.

Whether or not they fully realize it, participants in the making and staging of *Children of War* were provided with an opportunity to re-author their memories. And in re-authoring their personal (his/her) stories, the participants created what Jean François Leotard calls 'micro-narratives,' which convey not only 'verifiable statements about reality but also notions of competence, images of how to do things, how to live, how to care for one another, how to be happy' (quoted in Singh, Skerrett and Hogan 1996: 19). Those micro-narratives help 'the process of re-visioning that is essential to gaining control over one's life and future' (Singh, Skerrett and Hogan 1996: 19). In retrieving whatever the participants had consciously or unconsciously erased, they began to reaffirm, at the very least, their own unique transnational identities. That, in turn, as their post-production comments indicate, has become the fuel for them to continue re-inscribing and negotiating their complex and mutilayered sense of self. Collaborating in this theatrical piece allowed the participants to begin re-examining, for instance, their fixed identities as 'refugees,' and to reposition themselves as strong and determined survivors in a new adopted homeland, the United States.

One can discover his or her own identity, says Stuart Hall (a Jamaican cultural theorist), by acknowledging the 'ruptures and discontinuities' in one's history, by identifying the 'unstable points of identification,' and by understanding that, contrary to essentialist notions about the forming of selfhood, identities are always in 'constant transformation' (Hall 1990: 225–226). Two months after the play closed, Fatu spoke about that very phenomenon at the Grant Makers' Conference (where part of *Children of War* was staged again). With a broad smile, Fatu explained that after participating in *Children of War* she began to feel vindicated and empowered, partly because the veracity and value of her stories were recognized. She told the Grant Makers' audience that after the play was discussed in newspapers, her schoolmates were more willing to listen to her: 'the girl who had not believed my story in our geography class came up to me [and said] "Oh, my God, I didn't know, why didn't you tell me more?" She and I are now best friends.' Fatu's sense of empowerment and positive view of herself and her friend stem from her acknowledgement of 'ruptures and discontinuities' in her history – an acknowledgement gained by participating in the creative process of *Children of War*. And in this very process one witnesses the therapeutic power of a theatre that functions as a 'healing space' where identities and positions of the participants are constantly questioned and negotiated.

References

Amirsehi, Farinaz, telephone interview, 21 January 2003.

Arendt, Hannah, *The Human Condition*, Chicago: University of Chicago Press, 1958.

Barba, Eugenio, *Beyond the Floating Islands,* J. Barba, R. Fowler, J.C. Rodesch and S. Shapiro (trans.), New York: PAJ Publications, 1985.

Berman, Helene, 'Children and war, current understandings and future directions,' *Public Health Nursing*, 18: 4 (2001), pp. 243–252.

Besley, A. C., 'Foucault and the turn to narrative therapy,' *British Journal of Guidance and Counselling*, 30: 2 (2002), pp. 125–143.

Carlson-Sabelli, Linnea, 'Children's Therapeutic Puppet Theatre – action, interaction, and cocreation,' *International Journal of Action Methods*, 51: 3 (1998), pp. 91–112.

Children of War, performance by Ping Chong & Company, George Mason University, Virginia, 15 December 2002a.

Children of War, unpublished manuscript, Ping Chong & Company, New York, 2002b.

Chong, Ping, telephone interview, 20 January 2003.

Dowling, Ricarda, telephone interview, 8 January 2003a.

——, e-mail interview, 15 November 2003b.

Dreyfus, Hubert L., and Rabinow, Paul, *Michel Foucault: Beyond Structuralism and Hermeneutics*, 2nd edn., Chicago: University of Chicago Press, 1982.

Elsass, Peter, 'The healing space in psychotherapy and theatre,' *New Theatre Quarterly*, 32 (1992), pp. 333–342.

Eth, Spencer, and Pynoos, Robert S., 'Interaction of trauma and grief in childhood,' in Spencer Eth and Robert S. Pynoos (eds), *Post-Traumatic Stress Disorder in Children*, Washington, DC, American Psychiatric Press, 1985, pp. 171–183.

Foucault, Michel, *The History of Sexuality*, vol. 1, Robert Hurley (trans.), New York: Vintage, 1980.

Gere, Anne Ruggles, 'Revealing silence: rethinking personal writing,' *College Composition and Communication*, 53: 2 (2001), pp. 203–223.

Hall, Stuart, 'Cultural identity and diaspora,' in J. Rutherford (ed.), *Identity: Community, Culture, Difference*, London: Lawrence & Wishart, 1990.

Nader, Kathi, and Pynoos, Robert, 'School disaster: planning and initial interventions,' *Journal of Social Behavior and Personality*, 8: 5 (1993), pp. 299–320.

Nader, Kathleen, Pynoos, Robert, Fairbanks, Lynn A., Al-Ajeel, Manal, and Al-Asfoud, Al-Abdulrahman, 'A preliminary study of PTSD and grief among the children of Kuwait following the Gulf Crisis,' *British Journal of Clinical Psychology*, 32: 4, (1993), pp. 407–416.

Rutter, Michael, *Maternal Deprivation Reassessed*, 2nd edn., New York: Penguin, 1981.

Sankoh, Fatu, Questions and Answers on *Children of War*, breakout session at the Grantmakers in Health Conference, Los Angeles, 21 February 2003.

Singh, Amritjit, Skerrett, Jr., Joseph T., and Hogan, R. E. (eds.) *Memory and Cultural Politics: New Approaches to American Ethnic Literatures*, Boston, MA: Northeastern University Press, 1996.

Sontag, Susan, 'The Aesthetics of Silence,' in Pat C. Hoy II, Esther H. Schor and Robert DiYanni (eds.), *Women's Voices: Visions and Perspectives*, New York: McGraw-Hill, 1990, pp. 363–81.

Notes

1 The Children's Theater was established in 1986 at Rush Presbyterian-St. Luke's Medical Center in Chicago, Illinois. Since then, it has evolved through many forms. The Children's Therapeutic Puppet Theaters were introduced into the Children's Theater in January 1991. Participants are young children aged between four to nine years. Most of them are between placements, such as foster families or group homes, and they are hospitalized because they have tried to injure themselves or have attempted suicide (see Carlson-Sabelli 1998: 91–2).

2 Foucault discusses how various forms of resistance against different forms of power are exerted in a post-structuralist society. He investigates a power relation rooted deep in the social nexus and argues that to live in modern society it is imperative to maintain a 'reciprocal appeal' between a human and a governing institution. See his 'The Subject and Power' which is included in Dreyfus and Rabinow (1982: 208–226).

3   The CMHS did not include their own clients among the cast in order to avoid any possible perception of exploitation of the children or conflict of interest. Their therapists feared that if they asked any of their child clients to participate, there might be undue influence involved. For instance, the child might agree to participate in order to please the therapist. Moreover, since the first set of performances were held as a fund-raising event for the CMHS, they particularly preferred to separate the project from their current or recent clients. See Dowling 2003b.

4   See Berman (2001: 244). Effects of parent-child separation have been researched by such scholars as J. Bowlby, H. R. Schaffer, M. D. Ainsworth and Michael Rutter. In *Maternal Deprivation Reassessed* (1981), Rutter comparatively assessed various studies (done in the 1950s, 1960s and the 1970s) of the adverse effects of early deprivation of maternal care. More recently, Spencer Eth and Robert S. Pynoos (1985) have investigated the interplay of children's trauma (experienced through such traumatic experiences as parental suicide and homicide) and the subsequent bereaving process.

5   Indeed, this realization has become a topic of discussion even in writing pedagogy; composition theorist Anne Ruggles Gere, for instance, comments that in the last thirty years, teachers of writing have privileged 'articulation over withholding, fluency over reticence'; and that, she says, has been stifling and probably hegemonic for many students. See Gere (2001: 206).

Chapter 15

Drama and Citizenship Education: Tensions of Creativity, Content and Cash

Sarah Woodland and Rob Lachowicz

This chapter explores the key tensions of an applied theatre project, *The Good Citizen Ship*, designed to assist refugees in passing the Australian citizenship test. The project aimed to explore in an interactive and dynamic way the key values, privileges and responsibilities underpinning Australian citizenship, as well as other more factual details contained within the test. The project was instigated by the Refugee and Immigration Legal Service (RAILS), a community legal centre, in partnership with Griffith University's Applied Theatre programme (Brisbane, Australia) and funded by the Department of Immigration and Citizenship (DIAC) in 2008–2009. Tension is an inherent and key quality in our respective fields of law and applied theatre, and we hope that by discussing the tensions within our project, we might illuminate some of the challenges that face such interdisciplinary approaches, and explore the project's position in the context of contemporary applied theatre theory.

Background

The Good Citizen Ship manifested as a two-hour theatre piece which incorporated performance, workshop activities and facilitator-in-role. The project was framed around the story of two refugees at very different stages of their journey, who discuss the experiences of arriving and living in Australia, and learn about its history, values and laws. They meet in transit. Emmanuel is an Australian citizen on his way back to Burundi to visit friends and family after five years. Destha is just arriving in Australia – seeking a new life from a troubled home in Ethiopia and determined to become a citizen. This pretext was then used to extrapolate the content and concepts of the test and citizenship in Australia – involving the audience in various interactive workshop activities including sharing stories in small groups, participating in a mock election and forming frozen images. It was delivered in traverse formation to between 30 and 100 participants, and it invited a gradual building of participation from audience members as the piece progressed. The cast and facilitator team was made up of two refugee actors, three staff members from RAILS and Griffith, and two Griffith applied theatre students on voluntary placement.

The Good Citizen Ship performance and workshop toured to eight refugee communities in South East Queensland.

Political contexts

Australia can be said to have 'one of the largest refugee resettlement programmes in the world,' with over 13,000 refugees annually settled permanently under its Humanitarian Programme (McKay et al. 2011: 2, citing 2007–2010 figures from DIAC). Yet these authors note, 'while Australia's acceptance of refugees has contributed to its humanitarian reputation, the policies towards, and treatment of, asylum seekers have caused widespread national and international criticism' (2). From the 1990s mass international movements of migrants and refugees have had a significant impact on Australia. The treatment of 'boat people' attempting to land on Australian soil and the imprisonment and punitive treatment of asylum seekers have been contentious and divisive subjects: the Tampa Crisis in 2001 (when a boatload of 433 mostly Afghan asylum seekers were refused entry to the Australian mainland); the 'Pacific Solution' where refugees were transported to Naaru for 'offshore processing'; the children overboard situation (again in 2001) in which the government claimed parents were throwing their children off the boats to ensure they would receive help, and the ongoing protests over conditions and overcrowding in detention camps.

McKay et al. point out that the September 11 terrorist attacks in 2001 served to intensify negative community attitudes towards asylum seekers (see also Dennis 2007 and McPherson 2010) and within this climate, the conservative government under John Howard began enacting a range of policies that emphasized not only strong border protection, but the protection of 'Australian Values' (see McPherson 2010). At this time, the government also made rhetorical links between terrorism and asylum seekers, leading to increased community hostility towards them (McKay et al. 2011: 3). This hostility continues today, fuelled by political bickering and intense media focus on asylum seekers.

In October 2007, the Howard Government introduced the citizenship test that required applicants to demonstrate an understanding of Australian values, history and traditional and national symbols, as well as a reasonable grasp of the English language. McPherson (2011) asserts that this test emphasized conformity 'as pivotal to social cohesion' and that 'desirable Australian character traits [were] exemplified by Anglo-Celtic male figures [...] conservative Anglo-Australian political leaders and Anglo-Australian sporting heroes' (553). At the time, there was a great deal of debate over the test and its content, particularly the requirement to know seemingly trivial facts about Australia's history (see Cassin 2007). Writing in the context of the UK, Jeffers (2007) echoes the scepticism that opponents to the test in Australia felt, fuelled by the conviction that the average existing Australian citizen would not be capable of passing it. In November 2007 the Liberal Government was replaced by Kevin Rudd's Labor, who were committed to retaining the test, but in a changed form. A new trimmed down version was eventually developed, eliminating much of the unnecessary detail, and it commenced in October 2009. Having to develop and deliver *The Good Citizen Ship* during this stormy period in Australia's political and social history created a key tension for the project.

Commissioning *The Good Citizen Ship*

It was during this transitional time that the Department of Immigration and Citizenship made funding available through a pilot Citizenship Support Grants Program (DIAC 2008). The programme emerged out of concern over the high proportion of mainly humanitarian entrants failing the test, and RAILS was one of 32 organizations from across Australia that applied for and obtained funding. The 'primary objective' of the funding was 'helping clients to prepare to sit for the citizenship test' (DIAC 2008: 3) and the funding guidelines emphasized the need for a wide range of services that would:

> Cater for the specific needs of the clients which include low English proficiency, a lack of formal education, difficulty performing within a formal testing regime and little or no experience with computers.
>
> (DIAC 2008: 3)

RAILS is a community legal centre specializing in refugee and immigration law casework and also develops innovative community legal education programmes often incorporating role-play, music and video. After community consultation around whether theatre would be appropriate for citizenship training, RAILS approached Griffith University's Applied Theatre Program to partner in the project.[1] In its application to DIAC, RAILS described its aim to create a 'dynamic, participatory programme using drama to promote the key modes of learning (visual, auditory and kinaesthetic)' (RAILS 2008). *The Good Citizen Ship* was commissioned.

Naming the ship

The name *Good Citizen Ship* emerged rather innocently from a play on words. Yet it could be said that, in the eyes of the public, the road to redemption for refugees relies upon them becoming 'good citizens' in their host countries. Yap et al. (2010) observe that 'discourses about "good" and "bad" citizenship are disseminated through government policies, which then shapes our conduct as citizens. Such norms create and reinforce in our minds, standards of desirable behaviour within society' (Yap et al. 2010: 161; see also McPherson 2010: 547). In the Yap et al. UK study, this 'good citizen' was in fact constructed by refugee participants themselves as possessing concern for others and a respect for the law and making a contribution to the economy and community (Yap et al. 2010: 161–162) – the latter producing what the authors describe as a 'good value citizen' – one who is economically productive. Similar ideals about 'good citizenship' appear to reside in parts of the Australian consciousness, reinforced through government policy and the media. Full acceptance of refugees here is often conditional upon them learning the language, making a contribution to the economy and *integrating* with the social fabric of the nation. While these benchmarks can be honourable in themselves, and are certainly aspired to by the majority of refugees we have encountered, *The Good Citizen Ship* project aimed to move beyond these discourses of 'good' and 'bad' citizenship to explore ideas of equality, inclusive democracy and active citizenship.

Citizenship education and applied theatre

The very nature of Applied Theatre forms as participatory, educative and democratically political means that they are inexorably linked with ideas of citizenship. For Haedicke and Nellhaus (2001), examples of community-based theatre from across the globe are conceived as 'performances of democracy.' Nicholson (2005) sees both drama and citizenship as creative practices: 'Both are concerned with the values, needs and aspirations of individuals, communities and societies' (Nicholson 2005: 33). Winston (2007) suggests that applied drama 'has readily allied itself with the educational and above all the emancipatory, aspirations of citizenship and human rights' (Winston 2007: 270). O'Connor (2010) describes the link in terms of drama education, which he suggests reflects how we live, relate to each other and act in the world (O'Connor 2010: xiii). In this particular work, O'Connor frames the drama education work of Jonothan Neelands as being a catalyst to create democratic citizenship. Williams (2008) views the ceremonies and rituals associated with citizenship through the lens of performance theory. Nicholson (2005) suggests, 'in whatever way it is construed, an interest in questions of citizenship remains a central tenet of many aspects of applied drama' (Nicholson 2005: 20). While hers is not an argument for theatre and drama to be put 'at the service' of citizenship education (33), she recognizes the potential for theories of social citizenship to inform applied drama theory and practice (33).

All of these theories promote a view of citizenship that moves beyond legal status, and into ideas of participation and engagement – or as Nicholson describes, a 'participant,' or 'social' citizenship that is based on collectivism, community and contribution to social change. Nicholson also sees it as a 'fluid and pliable set of social practices' (Nicholson 2005: 22), a view that is shared by Delanty (2003) who also advocates 'a more dynamic view of citizenship' that involves 'developmental processes of learning' (600). For Nicholson, drama has the potential to bridge the division between citizenship as legal status and a more social citizenship (Nicholson 2005: 32). Shaw and Martin (2005) hold a view of citizenship in its 'holistic sense of association and membership' (86). They assert that 'democracy is sustained by the critical and creative citizen, not the conformist citizen' (85), citing the views on pedagogy put forward by Dewey in suggesting that 'learning citizenship is as much about feeling empathy as it is about knowledge and understanding' (86). For them, this ideal is engaged through the imagination in both cognitive and affective terms. Acknowledging the widespread acceptance of drama education as an avenue to engage participants on both of these levels, McNaughton (2010) suggests that citizenship education through drama can 'provide a balance of the rational and aesthetic' (291).

In the United Kingdom, drama and theatre has been increasingly used directly in citizenship education (see McNaughton 2010), or as a means to question and explore ideas of citizenship (see Deeney 2007; and Winston 2007). This has been in part due to an increased focus on citizenship within government policy and subsequently the school curriculum (see McNaughton 2010; Nicholson 2005; and Winston 2007). While much of this literature has been focused on children and young people, some parallel analysis has appeared from within the field of adult education (see Delanty 2003; Martin 2003; and Tobias 2000) – albeit outside of the realm of applied theatre. Alongside this, the exploration of theatre forms by, for and about refugee and asylum seeker groups is receiving increased attention, as is evidenced by publications such as this one, and the special edition of *Research in Drama Education* (2008).

The Good Citizen Ship appears to have held a unique position at the intersection of all of these areas: a drama-based citizenship education project for adult refugees. This position was characterized by a range of tensions for us as artists and educators, not the least of which were the ethical tensions of sailing *The Good Citizen Ship* under the ultimate command of a federal government, and at the mercy of its citizenship agenda.

Figure 1: *The Good Citizen Ship.*

Ethical tensions

Nicholson expresses unease over the idea of applied drama being used to promote 'officially sanctioned versions of citizenship education' (Nicholson 2005: 20). Indeed, scholarship from across the applied theatre field continuously maintains a reflexively critical eye to practices that may reinforce the dominant hegemony (see Prentki and Preston 2009). Winston (2007) describes this process more specifically in relation to citizenship education and drama: 'When a subject becomes institutionalized within an education curriculum, as it has done within the UK, we can expect coercion as well as enlightenment and a particular ethical/political vision to be strongly in play' (Winston 2007: 269). As Shaw and Martin (2005) suggest, 'the context of democratic citizenship today is often best understood as the tension between the top-down, imposed imperatives of policy and bottom-up, popular aspirations of politics' (89). For Martin (2003), the central purpose of adult education is to develop agency (575): 'Any government seriously interested in citizenship education has a primary role and duty to create the educative conditions in which citizens learn to be informed and active' (571–572). Following Nicholson (2005), applied theatre's potential may lie in its ability to create space for some of this agency – to deeply explore and perhaps challenge prevailing ideals and discourses relating to citizenship, rather than reinforcing the dominant ideal of the 'good citizen' as imposed by a 'top-down' agenda.

But, of course, organizations such as RAILS, and practitioners of applied theatre, often find themselves in a double bind: hoping to create bottom-up, emancipatory and participatory projects within the constraints of top-down government funding guidelines and social policy. However, refugee participants have come from countries where genocide, corruption, persecution and inequality are the order of the day. To them, gaining an understanding, albeit a glossy one, about the laws and values within a democratic and relatively peaceful country, may not be seen as problematic. While a government-supported citizenship education process may induce tension in us as practitioners, for participants it may signify a welcome opportunity to learn something about their new home and finally put down anchor in a place of peace.

As described earlier, one of the ways that *The Good Citizen Ship* addressed these tensions was through a commitment to use the drama as a way to promote inclusive democracy, human rights and active citizenship. We also wished to avoid glossing over the reality of how rights and privileges under the law, which do exist and are enjoyed by some, do not always flow equally to all. RAILS was clear in these objectives from the outset, which were articulated in their project proposal to DIAC, alongside content that addressed the more functional aspects of doing the test. In its proposal, RAILS stated that the project also aimed to 'explore realities, provide practical pathways and engage participants in establishing a deeper connection to Australia and its people' (RAILS 2008). Yet these multiple layers of meaning and content presented significant challenges and further tensions in creating the project, sometimes prompting heated debate between us as collaborators in attempting to achieve such aims within a range of constraints. Whether or not *The Good Citizen Ship* project did achieve these aims is explored a little more below, however the ethical tension described here could be seen as the 'meta-tension' that underscored and at times precipitated a range of other tensions within the process of developing the piece, the content covered and its delivery.

Tensions within process

Operating from the ethical position described above, RAILS was committed to a robust process of community consultation and refugee participation in all stages of the project. As mentioned earlier, there had been initial consultation with refugee community leaders and representatives around whether a Theatre in Education (TIE) approach would be an appropriate and effective way to approach citizenship education. Consultations yielded a positive response, which gave the project its initial green light. However, as funding timelines bore down, along with other logistical demands, it became clear we would not be able to accommodate the level of ongoing consultation we would have liked in the scripting and workshop development. On the other hand, the inclusion of refugee actors during the devising process provided some integrity, and the post-performance discussions and surveys from our early presentations informed subsequent shaping of the piece, which was essentially being developed on-the-hop, again due to time and logistical demands.

The timelines and logistics of delivering *The Good Citizen Ship* had a huge impact on how it manifested as an example of Theatre in (Citizenship) Education. One of the key tensions of working in a community context in Australia is that service organizations are often funded project-by-project, and are pressed to deliver complex outcomes on the smell of an oily rag. There is a constant sense of juggling projects, short-term contracts and consultancy work in an effort to keep the wolves from the door – whether that is the door of the not-for-profit organization or the freelance individual's home. The logistics of bringing together for rehearsals the project team of three workers, two refugee community actors and two student volunteers was extremely difficult given everybody's other work, study and family commitments.

Within this tension, the RAILS/Griffith facilitator team held some brief discussions and exchange of documents and ideas, before an initial draft outline of *The Good Citizen Ship* was put together and then edited into a working script. This more insulated process took us away from our initial hopes for an inclusive and participatory approach to the project's development. With limited time until the first delivery was due, the rehearsal process began, and became a site for further script and structure changes. However throughout this process, we each had strong and often conflicting opinions about creative workshop exercises, scripting material and dramatic metaphors to hold the educational content of the piece. 'Too many cooks' was not a luxury that we could afford in the time we had available.

Indeed, the rehearsal and devising process for *The Good Citizen Ship* continued right through our first delivery of the programme in a community organization in Brisbane's south, and continued through several more presentations. Given this frustrating set of circumstances, we decided to deliver the project in stages, adding sections of the drama each delivery, rather than presenting it in its entirety from the outset. Although it was useful at times to get feedback on an ongoing basis through what was essentially Action Research, it transpired that we only ever really had one shot at getting the whole fully completed project right, with DIAC's pilot funding being pulled the following year, and no foreseeable opportunity to repeat the programme in its live form. The limited scope for sustainability around such pilot projects is another key issue facing practitioners and organizations in Australia, where the pilot often only seems to get off the ground once. Applied theatre and participatory arts processes can be labour-intensive and logistically challenging and to address this, they often become adapted to video or website format so that their lives can at least continue in some form.

Tensions within content

Developing the content for *The Good Citizen Ship* became a significant challenge; not only in terms of our ethical position, our holistic view of citizenship and the time constraints and pressures described above, but also with the very specific and prescribed outcomes required by the funding, that more humanitarian entrants would pass the citizenship test. In addition, we held a commitment to highlight the traditional Indigenous ownership of the country of arrival and settlement. The desire to pack all of this into a two-hour performance and workshop format essentially manifested as a tension between content and form, and subsequently a tension between the two of us as members of the creative team, each trying to reach our educational and aesthetic goals, yet both keenly aware of the need for an elegant combination of the two. Additionally, the project commenced in May 2008, with knowledge that the change in government would eventually bring about changes to the citizenship process and test, thereby affecting the content of the piece.

The foundational content came from a five-page summary that was developed by RAILS from the then citizenship test handbook (Commonwealth of Australia 2007). This covered a range of topics about Australia: privileges, responsibilities, values, Indigenous Australians, facts about Australia (including population demographics, geography, religion, economy and national symbols) the country's history (including explorers, colonial settlement, world wars and multiculturalism) and the structure of Australia's government. We immediately saw that all this material would need to be cut down to a manageable size and negotiations among the project team to synthesize this content, as well as ideas about inclusive democracy into a two-hour workshop were sometimes strained. From a TIE perspective, it felt important for participants to have a meaningful experience of the drama whereby they would be emotionally engaged in the stories of the characters and the issues being explored. The piece would need strong recurring motifs, a through-line and a coherence of style that could carry participants along through the material. On the other hand, the imperatives of the project meant that RAILS wished to include as much useful information from the five-page summary as possible that might assist participants in passing the test. RAILS also recognized that inclusion of such material would be a strong drawcard for community participation and support.

The content evolved throughout the project, but ultimately was sequenced into four sections, each focusing on a different element of Australian citizenship. The first focused on the more basic facts about Australia, with the character Emmanuel's photo album being used as a vehicle to engage participants in an exercise of matching photos to facts. This exercise demanded a reasonably low level of engagement from participants, with actor/facilitators working with them to look at facts such as states and capital cities, climate, floral and faunal symbols and so on. This exercise broke the ice and got people chatting, swapping photos and allowed the actor/facilitators to build rapport with the participants.

The second section focused on the timeline of Australia's colonial history. After a brief conversation between the two refugee characters, the drama was cut and the remaining actor/facilitators each spoke about a significant moment in Australia's history, relating it to a particular object that was then placed on a physical timeline on the floor. For example, an admiral's hat signified Captain Cook's arrival; some gold nuggets corresponded to the gold rush and so on. Once this was complete, the actor/facilitators each took an object to the participants and had a discussion in small groups about the story that had been told, and also encouraging the sharing of similar stories from their diverse homelands.

The third section focused on the privileges and responsibilities of Australian citizenship. Here, participants were invited to participate in a mock election in which two parties were represented: The Privilege Party, whose platform was the free attainment of privilege without any responsibility, and the Privilege and Responsibility Party, who advocated for the same privileges, but with the condition that responsibilities would be upheld in return. After the voting, participants were introduced to the system of Australian government and given ideas about how they themselves could participate in democracy.

The final section of the programme introduced values of peace, respect, freedom of speech, freedom of association and freedom of religion. This section also focused on the fact that values are not always upheld in Australian society. Here, the character of Emmanuel replayed a scene from his past in which a discriminatory landlord refused him access to housing. A facilitator then explained that this was illegal and offered options for participants to pursue if something similar should happen to them. This last part of this section demanded the most interaction from participants, inviting them to create frozen images of the various Australian values being challenged or upheld. A facilitator then debriefed each image with the whole group.

The target groups for the project were those who were more marginalized through their refugee status and limited English-language knowledge, and RAILS made use of its strong networks with community service organizations, as well as Technical and Further Education (TAFE) colleges where English is taught, to reach as many individuals as possible. Despite our efforts to cut the content down, we certainly dealt with a great deal of material in the two-hour time frame. The programme also held within it a range of different purposes – to educate about the content of the test, to educate about the reality of what it means to be a citizen, to encourage participation in democratic processes and to provide education and advocacy about issues of discrimination. Aside from some translation from interpreters who were briefed beforehand, the drama was presented in English, as were the handouts and the posters that listed privileges, responsibilities and values. This, combined with its delivery in partnership with TAFE, meant that a further benefit of the drama was to enhance English literacy.

We also felt it was necessary to honour the Indigenous history of Australia, but with a completely non-Indigenous cast and little time and resources, this had to be compromised also. Again, the short time frame meant that only a cursory glance at 40,000 plus years of Australian Aboriginal history was allowed for. The initial aim was to have the *Good Ship* presentation introduced by an Indigenous elder of the area, with a 'Welcome to country' address.

But as time and resources ran out, we settled on making a recording of two leaders from the Aboriginal and Torres Strait Islander communities describing pre-colonial Australia, Indigenous connection to country, the injustices and losses suffered through colonization and the ongoing strength and hope for the future. This was played at the beginning of the historical timeline section of the drama. The team was fully aware that this was not an ideal way to address Indigenous issues, but as it stood, each section of the drama could have been a two-hour process in itself: one of the central tensions of putting it together.

In April 2008 it was announced that the Labor Government would undertake a review of the citizenship test to identify barriers to citizenship. The number of applicants had decreased considerably since the test was established and around 20 per cent of humanitarian applicants had failed on their first or subsequent attempts. The prospect of changes to the test, particularly the more factual details, meant that we now felt more justified in focusing on more foundational content such as privileges, responsibilities and values. Yet we still did not know what the final outcome of the review would be, and whether our project would ultimately have any relevance at all.

Despite these tensions within creating content for the piece, it ultimately worked reasonably well in trying to integrate the avalanche of necessary and unnecessary information contained in the citizenship test booklet as it stood. Participants were able to engage with a range of relevant citizenship test content, and begin to reflect on ideas of inclusive democracy and Indigenous heritage.

Tensions within delivery

As described, the one-off two-hour workshop time limit felt like a very small space in which to cram a great deal of content, while attempting to maintain some elegance of dramatic form. The decision to combine performance and workshop processes into a TIE structure was considered by all of us as a logical way to deal with this, however, in practice there were some significant challenges to this structure. We had hoped that the through-line or coherence of the piece would come from the refugee characters of Emmanuel and Destha who introduced each section with an exchange of dialogue and at times were directly involved in other dramatic scenes. The character of Emmanuel took the 'let me show you how it works…' or expert position, introducing the different concepts to Destha (the newcomer). On paper, this structure seemed to work well, tied together by transition music played live on a wooden flute. However, in reality, limited rehearsal time meant that the transitions between scenes and in and out of workshop activities could not be tightened up sufficiently. This was not helped by constant personnel changes, particularly the character of Destha who was played by four different actors through the project.

Some of the coherence was also lost through the involvement of interpreters whom we found difficulty integrating effectively into the structure of the drama – not knowing who, or how many (if any) would be present at each presentation, and which parts of the piece they would be translating. Participant numbers sometimes reached up to 100, often from a diverse range of countries, and with limited English-language ability. Interpreters would therefore translate the performance and workshop content in situ – sometimes up to five of them, each speaking to a different pocket of participants during the performance. There was also the challenge of staging the piece in community centres, where people came and went during the presentation, brought with them babies and small children and often rearranged the traverse seating to suit their social (and possibly spatial) needs. These most practical of concerns also contributed to the difficulty in achieving focus and clarity in the presentation. With the benefit of hindsight, we now recognize that a far less complicated dramatic structure may have been more realistic given the challenges described above.

Outcomes

It is certainly not our wish to leave the reader with the impression that *The Good Citizen Ship* was irredeemably beset by tensions and challenges. The project was delivered in various forms to eight participant groups in Brisbane and nearby regional centres of Ipswich, Toowoomba and the Gold Coast. Participant responses to the project were very positive from the beginning, as were the observations of support workers and staff from the target community organizations and colleges. Our own observations as well as verbal and survey responses from participants after each delivery suggested that they were positively engaged by the interactive, drama-based approach. During the presentations, we observed a considerable amount of participant engagement with both the dramatic and educational elements of the piece. Evaluation of the project involved post-presentation multiple-choice surveys and informal post-presentation discussions with participants over food and drink. Close to 100 per cent of survey respondents found the piece to be 'enjoyable,' 'helpful' and 'informative,' however, we were not able to gauge which workshop exercises and dramatic elements were particularly effective or valuable. Our discussions with participants were often very positive after sessions, with people most often reporting that they enjoyed the piece overall.

Over 90 per cent of RAILS clients who sat the citizenship test passed at first attempt. Some of these also undertook other parts of the suite of projects that RAILS offered under the DIAC pilot. We do not know what proportion of this outcome can be attributed to the drama, however, we were able to make some useful observations about its structure and efficacy. We noted that the opening sequence between the refugee characters Emmanuel and Destha was dramatically engaging. The actors moved in slow motion to the sound of the flute, carrying suitcases, waving goodbye to their loved ones. This image in itself drew the participants in, quieting the room and preparing them for what was to follow. The participants also seemed to respond very well to the timeline of Australia's history, as well as to the mock election, laughing and showing keen interest and participating in the vote with gusto. The final image-making exercise that was focused on Australian values was an interesting and somewhat unresolved element to the piece. Here, we hoped that the progression of participation throughout the drama would eventually warm the group up to be able to create their own frozen images of Australian values, first being challenged, and then being upheld. This was to be done in small groups and then shared with each other. When we finally did bring this section into the presentation, participants responded very well, yet somewhat nervously. Some groups needed encouragement from facilitators to create and show their images, and there was a sense that we were only now getting into the level of participation and meaning-making that would really create connections to the more complex ideas of citizenship beyond the test, and beyond what it means to be a 'good citizen.'

As is the case with many community projects, a range of ancillary outcomes was also achieved through the networks and partnerships that were established in creating *The Good Citizen Ship*. The project was able to employ two refugee actors in paid work, which supplemented their modest welfare benefits and factory wages. Both of these actors had been involved in a previous Griffith project and are now highly valued members of Griffith's applied theatre network. The project deliveries also resulted in referrals for participants who required additional support with their settlement and citizenship issues, some of whom may not have been aware of services offered by RAILS. At presentations, participants were able to ask direct questions of RAILS staff, who were in turn able to engage the host organization in follow-up support. The project also developed a strong partnership between Griffith applied theatre and RAILS, furthering the possibilities for such projects to be initiated in the future. The production of a DVD and learning resource based on the drama was another outcome that RAILS was able to dovetail into the project with surplus funding. This is currently evolving into a more comprehensive tool that addresses settlement as well as citizenship, while incorporating more integrated engagement with the story of Australia's Indigenous peoples.

It was certainly a privilege to be funded to experiment with this mode of citizenship education, and we hope that there will one day be an opportunity to refine our approach. It is true that the project although seemingly simple on paper, became progressively more complex as time went on, influenced by national political events, funding imperatives, and the diversity of creative and educative approaches within the project team. All of this was taking place within the context of what most of the team saw as a deeply flawed model for citizenship induction in Australia. Yet despite these tensions, the project yielded some positive outcomes in terms of its initial aim: to provide an interactive and dynamic learning experience for participants. Hopefully, it can help pave the way for more inclusive, creative and participatory form of citizenship education for refugees in this country.

Conclusion

This project was a huge challenge, yet filled with valuable lessons about how to manage and negotiate through the tensions we faced and still achieve a positive outcome. We have discovered that applied drama approaches in this context may need to be less complicated in terms of structure, allowing for the chaos that will undoubtedly be present through both the development and delivery, yet they present some significant possibilities in terms of engaging this very specialized target group with ideas of social citizenship and inclusive democracy. The project may also be a useful model for facilitating much needed peer education and mentoring between already settled refugees and those who are newly arrived.

For us there is a sense that *The Good Citizen Ship* was a very effective pilot and we worked well together as a multidisciplinary, multicultural team. Maintaining our nautical metaphors, the tensions within this project were like the levels of tension needed to operate the lines on a sailing ship. Sometimes those tensions became too taut, causing *The Good Citizen Ship* to steer off course, but the team was invariably able to pull together and bring her back around. As is the case with many one-off community-based applied theatre projects, now that it is over, we are certain that we could create something *really* great!

References

Cassin, R., 'All You Need to Know,' *The Age* Newspaper, 3 October 2007, http://www.theage.com.au (accessed 2 November 2011).

Commonwealth of Australia, *Becoming an Australian Citizen: Citizenship, Your Commitment to Australia.* Australian Government, 2007.

Deeney, J. F., 'National causes/moral clauses?: the National Theatre, young people and citizenship,' *Research in Drama Education: The Journal of Applied Theatre and Performance*, 123 (2007), 331–344.

Delanty, G., 'Citizenship as a learning process: disciplinary citizenship versus cultural citizenship,' *International Journal of Lifelong Education*, 22: 6 (2003), 597–605.

Dennis, R., 'Inclusive democracy: a consideration of playback theatre with refugee and asylum seekers in Australia,' *Research in Drama Education: The Journal of Applied Theatre and Performance*, 123 (2007), 355–370.

Department of Immigration & Citizenship, *Citizenship Support Grants Program: Service Provider Guidelines*, Australian Government, 2008.

Haedicke, S. C., and Nellhaus, T., *Performing Democracy: International Perspectives on Urban Community-based Performance,* Michigan: University of Michigan Press, 2001.

Jeffers, A., 'Half-hearted promises or wrapping ourselves in the flag: two approaches to the pedagogy of citizenship', *Research in Drama Education: The Journal of Applied Theatre and Performance,* 123 (2007), 371–381.

McKay, F., Thomas, S. L., and Kneebone, S., 'It would be okay if they came through the proper channels: community perceptions and attitudes toward asylum seekers in Australia', *Journal of Refugee Studies* 25 (2) (2011), 1–21.

Martin, I., 'Adult education, lifelong learning and citizenship: some ifs and buts', *International Journal of Lifelong Education,* 226 (2003), 566–579.

McNaughton, M. J., 'Educational drama in education for sustainable development: ecopedagogy in action', *Pedagogy, Culture & Society,* 183 (2010), 289–308.

McPherson, M., 'I integrate, therefore I am: contesting the normalizing discourse of integrationism through conversations with refugee women', *Journal of Refugee Studies,* 234 (2010), 546–570.

Nicholson, H., *Applied Drama: The Gift of Theatre,* Basingstoke UK: Palgrave Macmillan, 2005.

O'Connor, P. (ed.), *Creating Democratic Citizenship Through Drama Education: The Writings of Jonothan Neelands,* Stoke-on-Trent, UK: Trentham Books, 2010.

Prentki, T., and Preston, S., *The Applied Theatre Reader,* Abingdon, UK: Routledge, 2009.

Refugee & Immigration Legal Service, DIAC Citizenship Support Grants Program, Proposal for Funding 2008–09, 2008.

Shaw, M., and Martin, I., 'Translating the art of citizenship', *Convergence,* 384 (2005), 85–100, National Institute of Adult Continuing Education.

Tobias, R., 'The boundaries of adult education for active citizenship? Institutional and community contexts', *International Journal of Lifelong Education,* 195 (2000), 418–429.

Williams, D., 'Performing refugee policy in politics and theatre', *Research in Drama Education: The Journal of Applied Theatre and Performance,* 132 (2008), 199–204.

Winston, J., 'Citizenship, human rights and applied drama', *Research in Drama Education: The Journal of Applied Theatre and Performance,* 123 (2007), 269–274.

Yap S. Y., Byrne, A., and Davidson, S., 'From refugee to good citizen: a discourse analysis of volunteering', *Journal of Refugee Studies,* 241 (2010), 157–170.

Note

We would like to acknowledge the following members of the team who helped create *The Good Citizen Ship*:

Amy Bradney-George
Kuddus Abera Ferede
Jackie Huggins
Kate Lee

Bill Lowah
Venuste Nyandwi
Ashleigh Slader
Natasha Veselinovic
Nikki Wynne
Sylvia Niyonsaba

1   While the drama project was a key focus there was much more that RAILS had to do under the funding contract. RAILS also: established volunteer local citizenship mentors; provided other more conventional-style citizenship test workshops to large and small groups, as well as high-need individuals at flexible times; and also provided legal advice about gaining citizenship and test waivers. The project operated in city and close regional areas of South East Queensland.

Chapter 16

Inclusive Democracy: A Consideration of Playback Theatre with Refugee and Asylum Seekers in Australia

Rea Dennis

Community-based performance finds frequent application in contexts where asymmetrical issues of power, authority and involvement predominate. There has been recent consideration of the value of performance practices employing participation and personal story as civic dialogue as an opportunity to *perform* democracy (Haedicke and Nellhaus 2001). This has had a natural progression into work with asylum-seeker groups in detention centres and refugee groups forced to congregate in an uncertain territory as holders of temporary protection visas (TPVs). The interactive dimension to these theatre practices tends to see them positioned as democratic and interprets them as empowering. The place of personal story is often extrapolated as a chance to reclaim *voice* and as such enable the participants to establish legitimacy in the spirit of democracy. In the refugee sector there is also scope to reinforce the promise within such events for an encounter with difference and for inclusion in civil society.

This chapter is an attempt to grapple with my aspirations as an artist and citizen within this framework. It questions the assumptions implicit in the community-based performance event – playback theatre – that a kind of democratic citizenship is enabled. Through the lens of a specific event within the Australian refugee context, the sociopolitical context of the performance and the ritual momentum within the playback form are investigated as an avenue for inclusive democracy through the momentary disruptions of social control. The chapter includes a discussion of how the central elements of personal storytelling and public performance might actively collude with the global maltreatment of refugees.

Inclusive democracy and personal storytelling

The idea that a community-based performance fosters experiences of belonging and collective community reflexivity is not uncommon. The practice of including *voices* through the telling of personal stories is a principle avenue for participation in community-based performance. Telling a story sheds light on a perspective and can move it from a personal marginalized place towards a collective centre. Political action is embedded in the personal. Cohen-Cruz (2005: 135) claims storytelling provides a way for participants to become political: not with 'political theory but with political experiences' and to be included in the production of big ideas and social action. The personal dimension to storytelling provides participants with an organic and genuine opportunity to be involved in creative activity and to communicate what is important to them. Such ideas are regularly used to promote and justify the playback theatre method.[1] Playback is often spoken of in terms of its inclusive nature and the way it can liberate the disenfranchised voice. Such ideas are synonymous with many of the political and social resistance theatres of the 1950s and 1960s; a time when the value of theatre shifted away from the aesthetic judgement of performance product towards recognition of the value intrinsic in the *making*. Heddon and Milling (2006) acknowledge this as a time of social (self)-reflexivity in theatre, where audience attention was drawn to the process of making the performance. Playback theatre takes account of this transparency through the aesthetic elements of audience participation and improvised performance.

Co-founder Jo Salas describes the playback method thus:

> audience members [...] are invited to [tell a story] [...] guided by the director or 'Conductor,' [the teller] casts his or her story from the row of actors. The chosen performers, supported by music and lighting, transform the story into a theatrical scene, using boxes and pieces of cloth as props.
>
> (Salas cited in Feldhendler 1994: 101)

Haedicke (2003) differentiates participatory theatre practice from other theatre by the way in which active involvement rather than spectatorship is at the core of the event. Salas' comment suggests that notions of participation and spectatorship are highly defined within the playback theatre framework and that opportunities for participation are linked to an audience member's decision to tell a personal story. This implies that the audience member has some form of agency. But as Salas' remark indicates, the process of making the performance is transferred to the playback ensemble; 'the chosen performers,'[2] which raises questions about how power, authorship and consent are negotiated throughout the performance and whether the participatory nature of the method and the central place of personal storytelling within the framework of a collective public event can equate to a forum for inclusive democracy.

Calling for a democracy that 'refuses exclusive sovereign boundaries' and seeks to be effective 'beyond membership and voting rights,' Iris Marion Young (2002: 9–10) claims 'inclusive democracy enables participation and voice for all those affected by problems and their proposed solutions.' In highlighting participation and voice, Young could be claiming that community-based performance enacts inclusive democracy. It seems ironic to use concepts like 'community,' 'rights' and 'democracy' in resettlement contexts when people are experiencing disenfranchisement, the cessation of their rights, and an associated kind of civic invisibility and impotence. For refugee and asylum seekers, aspirations of citizenship and agency must appear as futile mirages on a horizon of tenuous occupancy. That community-based performance practice finds regular application with refugees and asylum seekers is possibly linked in part to a genuine desire (by the non-government organization, the funding body and the theatre practitioner) to shore up hope for people. Yet the personal story in the refugee context represents a complex cultural, political and social currency. Salverson (2001) cautions that 'innocent listening' to such stories undermines the great complexity of the lives of the tellers and the purpose of the telling. Playback theatre's history as one of working with people not used to telling stories – or who may have been excluded from telling – and its blend of participation and personal (local) story has seen it find favour on the margins.[3] It is necessary, therefore, to question how the method translates to the refugee context where people are *required* to tell their stories – over and over and over again. *Who is listening?* In order to interrogate this I wish now to turn to Brisbane, Australia, and to the specific event produced in Refugee Week, October 2002.

Local context: 'Children overboard,'[4] Australia (un)welcomes you

All community-based performance such as playback theatre is immersed within a broader circumstance, and in this section I begin by evoking the political climate in Australia at the time. The twelve months leading up to the performance at the centre of this discussion were a watershed in Australian history. In the wake of September 11, the conservative Australian Prime Minister undertook an unprecedented action in response to claims for entry and asylum by refugees from Afghanistan. A now iconic representation of the changing landscape of Australian foreign policy in the early twenty-first century, 'the children overboard affair' marks the time when refugees who had 'previously been referred to as "boat people" [were] now routinely described as "illegals"' (Marr and Wilkinson 2003: 178) and where significant numbers of Australians were demanding that the government turn boats away. In promoting the 'other as dangerous' and thus in opposition to the Australian nation state, Prime Minister Howard had somehow justified the unjust treatment of refugees and asylum seekers. Sheer (2007) claims that the Howard Administration has been the least ethical Australian government in living memory. Thus, this period is a watershed because it illuminates the disintegration of the Australian multicultural identity under Howard; disintegration embedded in the growing contemporary fear of The Other (Ahmed, 2000).

Multiculturalism has been the dominant community-building discourse in contemporary Australia. Ahmed links the breakdown of Australian multicultural society to the surge in the preoccupation with stranger-danger discourse[5] in social and educational policy. Stranger-danger discourse competes with the more traditional discourse of multiculturalism as a way of thinking about Australian society. For the purpose of this chapter, it is useful to consider Ahmed's argument, that 'stranger-danger' discourse promotes a community where the stranger is expelled 'as the *origin of danger*, whereas the multicultural discourse [operates] by welcoming the stranger as the *origin of difference*' (Ahmed 2000: 79, original emphasis). Both discourses have acted against one another in the past two decades. By juxtaposing the two, Ahmed illustrates how an essentially colonial discourse like 'stranger danger' – premised on the idea that another will invade territory and threaten person and property – serves to undermine the promotion of communities of inclusion and diversity (values promoted in the multicultural discourse). This was something of the spin used by Prime Minister John Howard, in his claims against the asylum seekers arriving on the *Tampa* in 2001. Indeed he 'crudely linked boat people with terrorists ...' (Marr and Wilkinson 2003: 280).

Introducing the event: Refugee stories and public performance

The performance was produced as part of a United Nations Refugee Week[6] calendar of events, compiled by peak bodies and service agencies. In response to the radically changed landscape outlined above, organizers sought to create an experience embodying the principles of multiculturalism so that refugee participants might feel *welcomed*.[7] It could be argued that the vision for the event was an alternative kind of democracy; one that could be considered in the spirit of Anne Phillips' (1996: 144) description of democracy as 'an exciting engagement with difference: the challenge of "the other"; the disruption of certainties; the recognition of ambiguities within one's self as well as one's differences with others.'

The decision was taken to commission the Brisbane Playback Theatre Company,[8] and I was asked to conduct. I was immediately aware of the danger for the organizer of contriving an event for all the right reasons without paying due attention to the colonizing potential of the process. I was not at all sure whether playback theatre was an appropriate form. In a bid to address this, we discussed the purpose(s) of the event, strategies to ensure diverse composition in the audience,[9] the importance of ensuring inclusive participation without expectation and of showing refugee and asylum seekers that there were Australians who were 'on their side.' Attending to audience composition meant that the playback performance met some of the preconditions for the kind of radical democracy that Phillips identifies above. On the night of the performance there were 57 audience members,[10] almost all of whom had no prior experience of playback theatre. Of the audience, approximately half were refugees and asylum seekers; ten were professionals associated with the relevant agencies within the local community sector; and there were a handful of government sector workers. The remainder of the audience members were a form of 'general public' connected to the broader Brisbane Playback Theatre Company network or to a range of social justice networks in Brisbane.

I now wish to turn to the playback performance itself by first of all recounting the stories. This account is compiled from my perspective as conductor and includes reference to my actions.[11]

The organisers introduce the performing ensemble and we take the stage in a chorus of eagerness. As conductor I invite the first contributions – they are brief: a government official states, '[I]t is nice to be invited to something outside of the ordinary'; a worker from the sector says she is interested in seeing something different; a third woman refers directly to the theme announcing that she is 'keen to be celebrating our colourful community.'

Stories turn to belonging and feeling *at home*: someone has recently moved back to Brisbane after living away, '[I]t's home but it's not really home.' A man speaks of migrating from England: '[T]his is my new home.' A woman who migrated from Korea expresses that 'it doesn't feel like home yet.' A Japanese woman speaks of how she now feels more at home but is still homesick. A young woman from El Salvador reflects on the opportunities she has in Australia and wonders what it would be like for her if she had stayed 'home,' in El Salvador.

In my role as conductor, I am aware that this story signals a shift; while previous tellers have spoken as migrants, this young woman has experience as a refugee. I acknowledge this and state that it is necessary to include the diverse range of experiences that are here. This also signals a shift in the ritual that involves participants coming onto stage to the 'teller's chair' rather than speaking from the auditorium/audience. Four stories follow.

An Australian-born woman tells the first.

She recounts her childhood expedition to Oman where she lived for a year. She remembers feeling very white and conspicuous. Her telling ends with this juxtaposition: while at the airport she is admitted with minimal scrutiny, she observes the different treatment of a Pakistani man. He is searched mercilessly, his possessions spread all over the counter. Eventually, a well-bound package is ripped opened, scattering nuts all over the floor. She tells of her distress as she watches him on the floor recovering the nuts.

The next story is told by Misha, a girl of 11 years.

She shares her experience of leaving Iraq; her family is split up and she is separated from her father and brothers. Her mother, sister and she go on a journey through Pakistan, Indonesia and eventually to Christmas Island. She recalls an incident in which her mother almost fell into the water as she stepped from a pier onto a small boat. The absence of her father had been unbearable. The story ends with her memory of arriving, '[W]e are welcomed with open arms.'

This story has evoked the war in Iraq and the consequences of war in the world.[12] Audience members share a variety of responses that are enacted as dynamic sculptures. One says she feels ashamed of being Australian. Another is angry; she shouts across the action, '[T]hese are not stories these are people's lives.' Another shares her feelings about missing her own father. I return my gaze to the girl sitting with her family in the audience and hold her father's gaze. I nod. His voice is a whisper as he says, 'We suffered. We still suffer.'

The transition after this is slow and deliberate; I feel that we are on uncertain ground. As conductor, I invite a story from an Ethiopian man. He is seated in the front row; his face is alert with emotion; he is in a wheelchair. He declines. Another man strides quickly from the back of the room.

An experienced worker in the field, he settles into the teller's chair and expresses how he feels about missing Hong Kong. His Australian-born teenage son is not treating him the way sons treat their fathers in Hong Kong. He feels a loss of connection to his son and grief about not being in Hong Kong at this time.

After this the Ethiopian man whom I had invited earlier signals that he will now speak. I am aware of an increase in tension in the room. He expresses his deep sadness and hopelessness as he recounts his experiences at the hands of Australian officials. Due to his disability, he has not been able to qualify for entry; he is not considered a worthwhile resident. This has resulted in his being in pain for long periods because he cannot access services and appropriate treatment for his back. His pleas for a fair hearing have been futile. His story is so very different from that of the little girl earlier, he feels abjectly unwelcome.

There are many moments within this performance that deserve analysis in relation to inclusive democracy.[13] For the purposes of this chapter I will limit the discussion to those areas that have been raised by audience members during and after the event. These include the moment some time into the performance where I stated the intention to hear from a diverse range of storytellers/voices, the spontaneous shout by an audience member and my action to invite a specific teller.

Telling stories: A currency for inclusion

In playback theatre there are certain conditions that guide the telling of the personal story,[14] e.g., the audience participant who elects to tell a story tells it from their own point of view and their story features themselves. In Frank's (1995) terms, this positions the playback theatre teller as ethical. Drawing on the work of Kierkegaard, Frank states: '[T]o tell one's life is to assume responsibility for that life' (1995: xii). He also draws on the rights discourse to argue that everyone has the right to speak in his or her own words. When applied to the refugee context, the assumptions implicit in these simplistic conceptions of the storytelling act demand scrutiny. Ariel's[15] commentary in response to my direct invitation to Marcus, the man from Ethiopia leads this scrutiny. She said:

> Asylum seekers are so vulnerable. [This man] is disabled, a refugee and African. He is very vulnerable. He doesn't know the audience; he doesn't have any feeling of trust in his life yet, doesn't know how he can entrust his story. I am his caseworker and it still takes time. There are the language problems, and his anxiety. Refugees all have disempowered status whether they have a visa, or are temporary protection visa holders, they are under consideration, and everything you say in public could go back in weird and wonderful ways to the powers-that-be. They don't even know what to say, or when to keep quiet […] They have no voice, or they are not heard – the government doesn't listen, the community doesn't hear, the media misinterpret, and misunderstand. You are familiar with expressing yourself. You've gone through the rigours of how to speak out or how to be heard. From where asylum seekers come, they were punished for using their voice, by the government, the media, their neighbours …

Central to Ariel's comment is the idea that the refugee story is a complex resource and that the storytelling act reaches well beyond this performance. The experience refugees have of repeatedly telling their story, where they come to understand this act as a kind of currency, where each telling promises a move along the continuum from refugee to resident, means that there is an ambiguity in the value invested in the 'telling of a story' during the performance.

Playback theatre is contingent on people telling their stories as if this is a good thing. In his assessment of the use of personal narratives as resources, Rappaport (1995) claims we should be able to see who is controlling the stories and who gives them social value otherwise there is a risk of social control, oppression and disenfranchisement. As Ariel emphasizes, the refugee context is structured around the repeated requirement to tell within a culture of institutional disbelief; a story is presented as currency to earn the next stage of entry. She announces the various vulnerabilities of Marcus through a series of labels – disabled, refugee, African – yet her principle concern is not about who the man is in this context, rather she is concerned about who the listeners/witnesses to his story are and how an unplanned telling may jeopardize his status. She appears worried that the playback performance could perpetrate the same issues of social control that the organizers are claiming to remedy in this performance.

Haedicke and Nellhaus (2001) are very clear about the responsibility of the community-based artist/practitioner in this situation. They say everyone – 'actors and spectators, facilitators and participants – are involved in shifting social relations' and conclude:

> Inherent in the interaction between these groups is a dynamic of authority based on knowledge and/or expertise [… which demands] that the stance, assumptions, motivations of those involved, the discourse surrounding the event, and the relationships between groups and between language and issues of knowledge and power must be constantly interrogated (Haedicke and Nellhaus 2001: 15).

One way in which playback theatre might trouble these structures of power and control is through the actions of a conductor. In the opening sequence of the performance, I undertook a systematic inquiry that revealed who some of the listeners were. As the show progressed, this information guided my decision to state that it was necessary to include the diverse range of experiences from the audience in order to facilitate the participation by all (Young) and the engagement with difference (Phillips), characteristic of inclusive democracy. Yet my actions did not overcome the complex challenge within the refugee audience where inherent power structures were in play.

Context and the complexity of power

Numerous people in the audience at *Celebrating Colourful Communities* were in a client-professional relationship based on the one-way telling of stories. For many, the event created a tension between the socially formed value that demands they protect the client/refugee and the value implicit in community-based performance that advocates participation by refugees in the ritual space offered by the playback theatre performance; a tension that I drew on as conductor.[16]

Hoesch (1999) claims that playback offers a space where stories 'will not be judged or evaluated'; that each story, each storyteller 'carries equal weight'; and that 'everyone has the right to the teller's chair' (Hoesch 1999: 63). Overly simplistic claims about playback theatre that appear poignant in other contexts do not measure up in the refugee context. Broad claims about rights and equality are difficult to substantiate. The purpose of the performance was not to focus on refugee stories but to facilitate a dialogue across a range of voices within the community. However, after the performance, it was clear that the refugee-tellers and their stories were the focus for many professionals present. Indeed, throughout the performance, I, too, was constantly aware of whether a teller had had experience as a refugee.

Writing about people with severe learning disabilities, Clough (1996) cautions that the personal stories of vulnerable populations can be so compelling that we cannot leave them alone. He attributes this to our deep and abiding curiosity for that rare glimpse into the complex diversity and rich texture of the lives of others; a real possibility in this event staged for the purposes of mixing across difference. This raises the prospect of protective action. During the interviews conducted after the show, one informant suggested that professionals elected to tell stories during the performance to alleviate pressure on the refugee and asylum-seeker audience members. Alternatively, another admitted that she resisted volunteering because others needed to tell more than she did. Neither position was checked for validity. Both suggest a perception of the refugee participant as extremely fragile, serving to circumvent their agency in the performance zone. Like Ariel's, these critiques came from workers from within the sector whose perspectives were strongly influenced by their professional roles and experience in this context. Conducting such an audience is a political process. As conductor, my choices revealed the presence of various stakeholders, yet they have not revealed the way in which professional or client identities interacted to help or hinder participation.

Issues of power and control are also implicated in my role as conductor and in the actors' part as interpreters and animators. When, during the performance, I acknowledged the present or absent voices and when I made a specific invitation, did my contribution silence others or perhaps more significantly did my influence within the complex rules of engagement lead someone to feel pressured to tell? During the early stages of the performance as we were negotiating the rules of engagement, each teller and each enactment revealed the rhythm and repetition in the method. The repetitive pattern in the playback method induced a degree of familiarity that enabled the refugee participant to join in. Turner (1982) suggests that establishing a ritual frame in this way serves to announce that certain sets of rules are at play. As these rules are made visible they *release* participants to act beyond their habitual roles with each other. This can result in a disruption of everyday power structures that are governing the relationships among refugees and service providers. For example, the first four or five contributions came from people with migrant rather than refugee experience, some of whom also worked within the sector. When I acted on my artistic intuition, my values and my understanding of the method and announced this, professionals in the audience became anxious. This was not a neutral act, of course. In Victor Turner's terms I was directing the ritual momentum and asking the group to change their pattern of relating. As such, hierarchies and power positions were constantly being negotiated. Ariel elaborated these complexities in her comment above, suggesting that the public and creative dimensions of the event had introduced additional issues for refugees, stating that the refugee teller's story 'may not come out how they want' due to English being their second language as well as the pressures of performance. There was also the risk of the story being decontextualized if the teller found it too hard, complex or painful to elaborate, which might lead to something 'very integral' to be missing from the tale and increase the risk of the refugee-teller being misrepresented. Perhaps the key issue for Ariel was that there was no clear way to intervene from her position in the audience. Yet maybe there was.

An audience listens: Inclusive democracy, consuming difference

Seated towards the back, Leeann[17] had come to the performance as a gesture of support. Unfamiliar with the politics of the Brisbane refugee context and playback theatre, she found the performance disturbing. Unlike Ariel, who felt unable to act, Leeann was *released* to call out in the midst of the performance. My journal notes report it thus:

> People are angry and hostile [...] it's all come from workers in the sector [...] [and] none of who told a story. One woman [...] called out during the show, something about 'these are people's lives not stories.' She was angry.

Leeann's outburst coincided with what she considered to be an inaccurate enactment of Misha's story. Christmas Island was not a safe landing zone for a young girl; Australia was not welcoming; there were untold stories as we sat listening to and watching Misha's version. Perhaps Leeann's shout was also a public resistance to the demands placed on refugees and asylum seekers to tell stories. Her comment suggests that we were consuming the stories. Leeann's intervention demanded that the focus be returned to the person telling the story. After the performance a number of audience members commented on the inherent 'pressure' that the refugee audience member might feel, saying that it was not appropriate for me to invite anyone directly. Leeann did not wait till 'after' but spoke out at the moment she felt uncomfortable. As reported in the text of the performance above, the contravening forces at work at this moment in the show elicited various responses, including feelings of shame in relation to the action of the Australian Government and feelings of complicity as we sat watching and listening. Perhaps Leeann's shout coincided with a ritual disturbance among professionals who found themselves on unfamiliar terrain with regard to feelings and emotions. Another reading positions the outburst as an attempt to maintain professional control of the intimacy and sharing. Meanwhile the issues Ariel raised reveal the problematic nature of the event for refugee tellers and also the degree of intervention that the service worker might assume on behalf of the refugee participant. Aware of the fragility of truth in this context, and not wanting to see Marcus's 'boat' turned away, Ariel is cautious. Is this just an example of protective concern or is the community-based performance event exposing a culture of censorship in the refugee sector?

Offering a different take altogether, Mercy[18] did not construct the event as risky at all. She applauded the opportunity for the diverse stakeholders within the sector to listen to one another's stories and spoke of the way playback freed us collectively to experience what is hard to feel in day-to-day living.

> The beauty of playback theatre – or that which I saw – was that it focused on feelings. [People don't understand] the refugee life experiences, because the refugee experience is so different to many Australians' life experience. People remain detached and simply can't understand or see relevance in terms of their own lives. The great thing about your playback theatre was that it really focused on emotion – sitting in the audience it was impossible for me not to feel moved. Yes, my life journey and story is different – but I have experienced at one time or another all of the emotions that came out of people's stories – anxiety, fear, loneliness, disbelief, happiness, sense of security, political awakening – thus I felt really connected and better able to understand.

Mercy says that placing the emotional dimension at the forefront of the discussion has resulted in her feeling connected to others at the event. In contravention to Ariel's concern, she expresses appreciation on hearing about the refugee experience. Mercy is not preoccupied with protecting the refugee audience member. She did not see a stranger; she does not position the refugee as 'other'; rather she seems to have been able to encounter all of those present in the spirit of Phillips' radical democracy, 'as an exciting engagement with difference' (Phillips 1996: 144). Despite this positive spin, Mercy makes no reference to how the event might have been for the refugee audience member. In order to affect some redress, a final voice I wish to weave into this discussion is that of Marcus, the teller.

Marcus's reply – right, option or obligation

Marcus sat in the front row of the raked auditorium, probably not by choice as much as functionality linked to the limited access of the building and the needs of his wheelchair. Before he came forward to tell his story, he looked at me and expressed that he thought his story was 'too big.' He said, 'I don't know where to start.' While my approach to him during the show had been in response to what I had interpreted as keen eye contact and other non-verbal cues, I was well aware that my invitation to him made him visible and placed him in a position of having publicly to refuse. And he did refuse at first. While Marcus eventually told his story, my interaction with him made explicit the needs of the performance; a moment when the demands of the method and the agenda of the event converged to place the participant at risk of exploitation. My direct approach to Marcus was a breach of the social/professional boundaries of the group. His story presented a view of Australia that contested the idea of Australia as 'lucky' or welcoming, reinforcing the Australia of the 'children overboard' episode. Were his actions political in Cohen-Cruz's terms? Did he really speak, in Young's terms, 'for all those affected by problems and their proposed solutions' (Young 2002: 10)?

Writing Marcus into this paper has presented a similar kind of challenge to that of conducting him into the performance. I have the pen, the authorial control. I actively sought Marcus out in the foyer after the performance and he was nowhere to be found. I felt determined to 'check in' with him but was quickly reminded of my own visitor status in this (liminal) world of refugee and TPV holders when my request for an introduction to him was denied. I can proffer second-hand reports from the gatekeepers who were prepared to speak on his behalf. Are these valid inclusions in this discussion? Does using them reinforce the futility of refugee voice and agency? The following two excerpts are from Nina and Ariel, professionals in the refugee sector[19] who spoke to Marcus in the immediate post-performance period and on the next day. One reports:

> I spoke with him afterwards. Even though the past was incredibly painful he wants to look to the future. There was some pressure on him to tell because new refugees think they *have* to tell. I could feel his discomfort.

And another says:

> I saw him on the weekend and I asked what happened (to him after the show) and he said, 'I went out to have a drink.' We spoke about it, he said it's really important that stories have been told.

In the first excerpt the gatekeeper is focused on the structural power and appears to be acting on the assumption that the teller is at risk, whereas the second comment seems to capture Marcus's autonomy and agency. The structural safety net provided by Nina and Ariel has both protected and excluded Marcus again. Perhaps there has been value in telling his story. I cannot say. This exempts neither me as artist nor the playback theatre company as facilitators from the responsibility of unpacking the power dynamics, but it does raise questions about how the processes of negotiation embedded in community-based performance practice might be genuinely accessed by vulnerable populations.

Within this context, far from being empowering for the teller, the act of storytelling might become dangerous or arduous. I am conflicted as I recall Phillips' construction of democracy as 'an exciting engagement with difference: the challenge of "the other"; the disruption of certainties; the recognition of ambiguities within one's self as well as one's differences with others' (1996: 144), and question the value of these experiences. Is it merely that I have had an experience of democracy because of Marcus's presence and courage to tell part of his story? Such is the scope for inequity and the undermining of any democratic potential within the performance. Ariel suggests a possible way to mediate this risk. As part of her comments after the performance she points to the value of indirect representation of the refugee experience as one way to include their perspective without undue pressure being placed on them to narrate.

The [story about the] woman at the airport, that was powerful. We all knew. We all could see. It was just as powerful as having a Pakistani man tell the story but without risk of him being further humiliated.

It is not uncommon in playback theatre for a more vulnerable person to feature in a story someone else tells. The more vulnerable person can then be present in the enactment. The enactment provides a place for them to be seen, a place for their story to be shown, without any pressure being placed on them to recount. Could this translate into a different form of exclusion – how might these decisions be mediated? There is a naiveté, a child's perspective, in the story told by the young woman who lived in Oman. The teller remembers when she was a thirteen-year-old. In her memory she is living in Oman with her family and she is white and conspicuous, and has implicit power. Yet alongside this, in her memory, the Pakistani man is more conspicuous. She remembers him searched mercilessly, possessions spread all over the counter; eventually a precious, well-bound package filled with nuts is ripped open. The nuts scatter to every corner of the room, all over the floor. She remembers him on his knees retrieving the nuts. We now all imagine him on his knees retrieving the nuts. What would he have said? What might the government official tell if he were in the teller's chair? How would he describe Marcus? Could this adequately represent Marcus's experience?

I feel self-conscious and uncertain about the value of community-based performance in this context. Ahmed (2000) writes of uncertainty in her new vision for civil society. She advocates an engagement with the uncertainty and a commitment to struggle with feelings of estrangement and difference. She writes of estrangement as a kind of flux; or out of place-ness, and of how the 'not quite comfortable' feeling yields community through our 'reaching across different spaces, toward other bodies' (Ahmed 2000: 94). The purpose of the *Celebrating Colourful Communities* performance was in the spirit of this 'reaching across' difference and engagement with uncertainty. The playback theatre performance event was positioned as a bridge; a reaching beyond notions of similarity and unity so that a democratic model that fosters what Young (1990) calls a politics of difference might be nurtured. The key element to the bridging was the sharing of personal stories, not a fiction but a real, past experience; an exchange within the complexity of a context in which stories of the past represent a different currency – exchanged for entry to the new world; exchanged for access to a new future; exchanged for a chance to re-story a life that has been disassembled by war and terror; a context in which a story is evidence, is proof, is a justification that someone is worthy of refuge in (a safe) Australia.

The issues that have emerged from the *Celebrating Colourful Communities* performance are not unique. Facilitating a ritual rupture in the social hierarchy has represented a form of momentary democratic potential in the gathering. There is no evidence that the refugee audience members have benefited in a practical way towards identifying any solution to the problems of a hostile foreign policy in Australia. However, they have shared an experience with participants who are not marginalized by the political reality of being a refugee in Australia. Participants have witnessed each others' stories and some have told some of their own. A reflexive moment has occurred for some. Others have been trapped by their roles and power positions, by their care and concern, by their anger and confusion. Where does this leave the argument with regard to inclusive democracy within the community-based performance event if it is contingent on participation through personal story? I am left with a list of questions. Is the voluntary participatory tenet implicit in the playback method ever immune from the broader sociopolitical narrative? Can a teller be ethical in the way Frank describes? Can a teller have the rights that Hoesch writes about? How might my efforts to resist the traps of reinforcing the dominant voices and alienating minority voices make the minority voices vulnerable to exploitation?

There is still much to consider in the application of playback theatre within the refugee and asylum seeker context. Such audiences will always require sophisticated conducting based on inquiry and risk taking; the kind of deliberate and thoughtful practice that repeatedly makes explicit who is there, who is missing, who has told, what voices are absent, what stories are absent, what assumptions we are making and so enable moments of inclusive and radical democracy. But at what cost?

References

Ahmed, S., *Strange Encounters: Embodied Others in Post-coloniality*, London: Routledge, 2000.

Clough, P., 'Again fathers and sons: the mutual construction of self, story and special educational needs', *Disability & Society*, 11: 1 (1996), pp. 71–81.

Cohen-Cruz, J., *Local Acts: Community-based Performance in the United States*, New Brunswick, New Jersey and London: Rutgers University Press, 2005.

Dennis, R., 'Big clumsy feet: shame, caution and fear in performing for peace building', *Studies in Theatre and Performance* 29:1 (2008) pp. 53–66.

———, 'Crossing the threshold: tensions of participation in community-based playback theatre performance', *Journal of Interactive Drama*, 2:1 (2007), pp. 56–70.

Feldhendler, D., 'Augusto Boal and Jacob L. Moreno: theatre and therapy', in M. Schutzman and J. Cohen-Cruz (eds.), *Playing Boal: Theatre, Therapy & Activism*, London: Routledge, 1994, pp. 87–109.

Frank, A., *The Wounded Storyteller: Body, Illness and Ethics*, Chicago: University of Chicago Press, 1995.

Haedicke, S., 'The challenge of participation', in S. Kattwinkel (ed.), *Audience Participation: Essays on Inclusion in Performance*, London: Praeger, 2003, pp. 72–87.

Haedicke, S., and Nellhaus, T. (eds.), *Performing Democracy: International Perspectives on Urban Community Performance*, Ann Arbor: The University of Michigan Press, 2001.

Heddon, D., and Milling, J., *Devising Performance: A Critical History*, Hampshire: Palgrave Macmillan, 2006.

Hoesch, F., 'The red thread: storytelling as a healing process', in J. Fox and H. Dauber (eds.), *Gathering Voices: Essays on Playback Theatre*, New Platz, NY: Tusitala Publishing, 1999, pp. 46–66.

Marr, D., and Wilkinson, M., *Dark Victory*, Melbourne: Allen & Unwin, 2003.

O'Toole, J., *Negotiating Art and Meaning*, London: Routledge, 1992.

Phillips, A., 'Dealing with difference: a politics of ideas, or a politics of presence,' in S. Benhabib (ed.), *Democracy and Difference*, Princeton, NJ: Princeton Paperback, 1996, pp. 139–152.

Rappaport, J., 'Empowerment meets narrative: listening to stories and creating settings,' *American Journal of Community Psychology*, 23:5 (1995), pp. 795–808.

Salas, J., *Improvising Real Life*, New York: Tusitala Publishing, 1993.

Salverson, J., 'Change on whose terms?: Testimony and an erotics of inquiry,' *Theater* 31:3 (2001), pp. 119–125.

Sheer, E., 'Introduction: the end of ethics,' *Performance Paradigm* 3 (2007), http://www.performanceparadigm.net/journal/issue-3/articles/the-end-of-ethics/ (accessed 15 June 2007).

Turner, V., *From Ritual to Theatre: The Human Seriousness of Play*, New York: PAJ Publications, 1982.

Young, I. M., *Justice and the Politics of Difference*, Princeton, NJ: Princeton University Press, 1990.

———, *Inclusion and Democracy*, New York and Oxford: Oxford University Press, 2002.

Notes

1. Implicit in this chapter is the assumption that the readership will have some level of familiarity with the basic playback theatre method. For an elaboration of specific technical details about the form, see Salas (1993).

2. This chapter takes as its focus the place of personal story in the community-based event and the teller's relationship to others and to the context overall. Elsewhere I have examined the dramatization of the stories in this performance and analysed the position of the performer in relation to the teller and context. See Dennis (2006).

3. The place of personal stories has become progressively more prominent in rehabilitation and resettlement contexts. This is linked to the principles of inclusion and social justice like participation, individual agency, voice and identity, and sustainable empowerment that informs this work and where story-based processes are seen as a way to enact these principles.

4. 'Children overboard' is an infamous media headline from September 2001 that became the catch phrase used to refer to the approach of the Norwegian freighter, *Tampa*, into Australian waters. The captain of the *Tampa* had acted in accordance with the mariners' humanitarian code and rescued 433 refugees from a sinking fishing boat in Australian waters in August 2001. They were within 2 kilometres from the coast of Christmas Island (an Australian territory in the Indian Ocean) when Prime Minister John Howard refused them entry. Most of the refugees on board were redirected to the Pacific Island, Nauru, with others going to New Zealand. The *Tampa* crisis dominated local political debate and was prominent in the international arena until it was displaced by the shocking events of September 11. For a detailed analysis of the political manoeuvring underpinning the *Tampa* crisis, see Marr and Wilkinson (2003).

5   As in the United Kingdom, the formal stranger-danger campaigns in Australia include child safety campaigns that raise awareness of the danger of child sex offenders. However, as Ahmed states, there are multiple constructions of stranger embedded in the discourse, and in her deconstruction she claims that it has come to broadly refer to the stranger as invader and as a threat to the otherwise 'safe neighbourhood.'

6   *Celebrating Colourful Communities* was produced by the local non-government organization responsible for multicultural affairs with funding from the federal government's Department of Immigration and Multicultural Affairs (DIMA).

7   In the lead-up to the event, Rhada (name has been changed), an agent of the organizing body, spoke of her desire for the event to be seen as 'a good experience.'

8   That the playback theatre company has been invited is of particular importance here. If the work had been initiated by the playback company, this places them as host of the event. From its inception Fox has spoken about playback theatre in terms of 'service' publishing his own treatise *Acts of Service* in 1994. However, in being invited there is a chance that the company members are present as citizens/community members. As such, there is scope for the performer to be positioned as 'part of' rather than 'apart from' the community of participants.

9   The event was promoted through all agencies working with refugees, asylum seekers and newly arrived migrants, and the 'ethnic community' agencies.

10 There were 35 women, 22 men and 3 children.

11 This section is informed by my reflective notes and does not purport to be a comprehensive analysis of the stories told during this event. Rather it is an abbreviated description designed to situate the reader.

12 The opening tableau in the enactment invoked a representation of war, converging epic cinematic references with an aesthetic indicative of television news.

13 People were formally invited to supper as a way to wrap up the event. English was the second language for about half of the audience participants, which led to people gathering in language groups. More than half the audience completed a feedback form.

14 It is important to emphasize the non-fictional nature of story within the playback method; unlike drama, generally, and many applied and process theatre methodologies and other community-based performance practices, where there is a clear differentiation between the fiction and the real and a concerted effort to ensure fictionalized narratives feature as a way to ensure distancing for participants (see O'Toole 1992), in playback it is the personal story that is central.

15 Ariel is an advocate for refugee and asylum seekers who do not yet have status as a citizen of the state. Previously from Germany, she has been a resident of Australia for some years. The excerpts here are from an interview conducted with her after the performance.

16 Previously I have written about how the tension of participation in a playback theatre performance is derived from the ritual framing inherent in the community-based event that both drives and is driven by the audience-performer interaction. (See Dennis, 2007).

17 Leeann is a newcomer to the sector, recently appointed to facilitate a community art project with refugees and asylum seekers. It is her first commission. The excerpt here is informed by a telephone interview conducted with her after the performance.

18 Mercy is a worker within the resettlement agenda and works supporting people who have secured temporary protection visas. Having emigrated from Iran, she has been a resident in Australia for some time. The excerpt here is from an interview conducted with her a few days after the performance.

19 As explained earlier, Ariel is an advocate working with asylum seekers and the agency manager. As she states earlier, she is Marcus' caseworker. Nina is Ariel's colleague, working part-time in the same agency. She knows Marcus through this association. Nina was sitting alongside Marcus during the performance and her comment about him feeling pressured comes from her observations during the performance.

Chapter 17

Hospitable Stages and Civil Listening: Being an Audience for Participatory Refugee Theatre

Alison Jeffers

Introduction

The role of the audience has been under-explored in much writing about participatory refugee theatre that has emerged in recent years. An understandable emphasis on the participants, their experience as refugees, and on the ways in which being involved in participatory theatre projects has been considered beneficial, has meant that the act of being the audience for this work has not been considered in any detail. In the absence of any significant body of writing about the audience for refugee theatre, it has been presumed to fall into two broad camps: one, an audience that is ignorant about refugees and needs to be educated, and the other, an audience that is knowledgeable about 'refugee issues' and is therefore said to be 'converted.' Neither of these categories is accurate or helpful in developing participatory theatre with refugees and asylum seekers. This chapter suggests that there is a need to shift the focus from the participants onto the audience in order to challenge these assumptions, and it aims to do this by examining *the practice of being an audience* at a refugee theatre event. Using writing on theatre audiences helps to develop an understanding about the relationships between audience members and refugee performers to show how the act of *listening* at a refugee theatre event can be construed as a civil act that simultaneously challenges notions of togetherness and opens up tough questions about responsibility.

This exploration will be developed by thinking through the proxemics of the theatre event in a participatory refugee theatre project; that is considering bodies and space and the intersubjective relationships that develop through distance, proximity and the gaze in that space. This will involve not thinking about what an audience *is* so much as what an audience *does* and about the *process of being an audience*. Exploring this leads to an emphasis on the importance of the act of listening, of giving audience. Kershaw's notion of the radical potential of theatre is an important part of this argument, as examining how 'the audience gathers for a performance, and disperses when it is over, may be as important to its ideological reception of the show as, say, the performing style itself' (Kershaw 1992: 23). Within these activities of gathering, watching, listening and dispersing that are part of the process of being an audience, a picture emerges that leads to a reflection on the proxemics of the face-to-face relationship between performers and audience members and the notion of being shoulder-to-shoulder with other audience members. Combining these two proxemic positions shows how providing a hospitable stage for refugee stories and the act of *civil listening* at a refugee theatre event provides the grounds for an optimistic reading of the ethical potential of participatory refugee theatre.

Refugee arts and participatory theatre

Since the early 1990s there has been a significant growth in arts and cultural activities in Britain among community groups made up of refugees and asylum seekers (Barnes 2009; Blaker 2003; Harrow and Field 2001; Gould 2005; Kidd et al. 2008). In 2005 Creative Exchange[1] identified 76 refugee arts projects in Britain with a high concentration of projects in London (Gould 2005). By 2008 the authors of *Arts and Refugees in the UK: History, Impact and the Future* were able to report that over 200 arts projects existed in the UK, most in Britain's urban centres: London, Manchester, Birmingham and Glasgow (Kidd et al. 2008). Considerable amounts of public money have been made available to support a broad range of refugee projects generally. In London alone the Community Fund of the Big Lottery (the body that awards lottery cash to community groups) had awarded 138 grants totaling £15 million by 2000 (Harper 2001). In the arts, schemes like the Reaching Communities Fund and the Young People's Fund directly finance arts projects with refugees in the belief that arts activities have the potential to generate the power to improve access to training and education, promote active citizenship, improve the environment and create healthier individuals and communities.[2] In addition to this, a large amount of charitable money is available for refugee arts initiatives: the Paul Hamlyn Foundation and the Baring Foundation have given £3.5 million between them to such activities (Kidd et al. 2008). Similar to the Big Lottery Fund, the impact of these projects is said to be through participation, which builds social and community cohesion and capacity. Refugee arts projects are also thought to be a way of challenging negative representations of refugees and asylum seekers among non-refugee audiences.

An important feature of many refugee arts initiatives is participatory drama and theatre projects with refugee groups (Cohen-Cruz and Schutzman 2006; Kurahashi 2004; Salverson 1999 and 2006; Schinina 2002; Thompson et al. 2009; Wehle 2004). Within the academy these usually fall into the category of applied or social theatre although they would more commonly be called community or participatory theatre, which is the preferred term here. Typically projects involve a group of refugees, often with little or no experience of theatre or performing, working with artists to create and perform a piece based on their own ideas, stories and experiences. This is often staged for a small 'known' audience where the participants are somewhat protected, although the outcome of some participatory projects, including the one discussed here, can also be relatively high-profile public performances in theatres and other public buildings. Participatory theatre with refugee groups is thought to fulfill many similar functions to refugee arts more generally, and these include building participants' confidence and encouraging the development of social and language skills among individuals who get involved and challenging negative stereotypes of refugees and asylum seekers. In addition, participatory theatre projects are said to provide a safe space in which to explore and experiment with identity creation and a place in which participants can begin to understand and order their experiences.

Audiences for participatory theatre with refugees

The emphasis here does not lie exclusively with the participants of refugee theatre because I am concerned with exploring the experience of being an audience for this theatre form. Having suffered the frustrations of gathering information on audiences for two refugee theatre festivals in Manchester in 2006 and 2010, I am convinced that, while the quantitative and qualitative data gathered might be deemed necessary to illustrate some kind of efficacy to funding bodies, as a way to understand the complexities of the encounters at a refugee theatre event, it is a largely fruitless exercise.[3] There is a lack of clarity about who makes up the audience for refugee theatre (Gould 2005). This is compounded, rather than clarified, by the gathering of information about the audience at these events because questions are often predicated on unspoken assumptions about the audience from the outset. Many questions asked of audience members allude to possible changes in outlook towards refugees and asylum seekers, based on the idea that seeing the theatre piece will have produced a deeper understanding of refugees' experience and therefore a greater sense of empathy. The transactions at a refugee theatre event are much more complex than this and go to the heart of questions about responsibility and even citizenship.

In recent years there has developed a growing interest in theatre audiences and there has been some work that challenges assumptions about the monolithic nature of 'the audience', suggesting that 'there may be several distinct co-existing audiences to be found among the people gathered together to watch a show' (Freshwater 2009: 9). There is also a broad questioning about the assumptions of a link between seeing and understanding but this complexity seems to be largely ignored in participatory refugee theatre and audiences are broadly thought to occupy two possible positions.[4] In the first of these, the audience is in need of education – an uninformed body of people who must be told about the difficulties that refugees and asylum seekers face in the process of claiming asylum, in dealing with 'trauma' and in 'integrating' into the new lives and circumstances in which they find themselves. As I have already suggested, many rather vague claims are made about the potential of performance projects to help to combat negative stereotypes of refugees, often tackling them 'head on' with an emphasis on truth-telling and 'myth-busting' in the performances. The second audience position is the opposite, a more knowing audience who attend refugee theatre events in a spirit of solidarity, in sympathy with the 'plight' of refugees, the audience that is often accused of being 'converted' because they have knowledge of 'refugee issues' before attending the theatre.

Neither of these possible audience positions is adequate for exploring the very complex sets of negotiations, expectations and outcomes that are involved in a refugee theatre event, especially one in which the performers are themselves refugees. This question is more complex than simply deciding how best to address a 'non-refugee audience' and this chapter represents an attempt to find a way to conceptualize and discuss audiences for refugee theatre more clearly, precisely and usefully. Freshwater suggests that theatre scholars 'have yet to step up to the challenge of addressing the question of what we really know about what theatre does for those who witness, watch or participate' (Freshwater 2009: 74). Freshwater's emphasis here is on the visual, and she does not add listening to her list of activities, but

I will argue that paying attention to the under-explored action of *listening* in the context of participatory refugee might lead to a better understanding of the potential of the audience for this activity.

Hospitable stages

There are many examples of refugees being represented on stage by actors where the intention of that representation is to draw attention to human rights abuses or to negative perceptions of refugees and asylum seekers. *The Bogus Woman* by Kay Adshead might be one example among many where the actor Noma Dumezweni[5] played multiple characters in a story of seeking asylum in Britain as seen through the eyes of the Young Woman (Adshead 2001). *Asylum Monologues* by Ice and Fire uses actors to voice the edited verbatim stories of refugees and asylum seekers with minimal theatrical apparatus and no attempt to embody the speakers.[6] I would draw a comparison between performances like these and participatory theatre projects with refugees, not to diminish the potential impact of theatre created by non-refugee actors, nor to suggest that it is in any way unethical for actors to represent refugees on stage, but to pay attention to the possibilities inherent in seeing the face of a refugee in performance which is also a face that can be encountered *as a refugee* beyond the moment of performance. This clearly evokes Levinas's notions of the face-to-face encounter. Levinas fears that his 'place in the sun' is somehow granted at a cost to 'the other man' whom he has usurped, who becomes 'oppressed or starved, or driven out into a third world' (Levinas 1989: 82). This leads him to contemplate the face of the Other which 'summons me, calls for me, begs for me' and, in doing so, reminds him of his responsibility to that Other (Levinas 1989: 83). Levinas describes his responsibility for his neighbour, 'for the other man, for the stranger or soujourner' as an 'anarchic responsibility' (Levinas 1989: 84), evoking a sense of responsibility with no rules, with no limits, what he calls total responsibility. A theatrical face-to-face encounter is perhaps more literal and more embodied than Levinas was thinking but his ideas can be used to question the implications of the audience's responsibility for the Other in a theatrical encounter with refugees. How do we listen to refugee theatre and respond ethically as audiences to the idea that, to evoke Levinas's terms, 'our place in the sun' can only be made possible by the 'driving out' of refugees to the margins?

As already suggested above, assumptions about the monolithic nature of the audience are becoming increasingly unhelpful in understanding what is actually taking place in a theatrical exchange, and this complexity is further deepened if the relationship between the performers and the audience is as unstable as it is in this irregular theatre form. It is inadequate to configure the audience as a single mass or body, as an 'it,' because that suggests stability and turns a complex relationship into a simple one (Rayner 1993). As individual audience members, we hear 'with varying capacities, from varying positions, from different interests from one moment to the next' (Rayner 1993: 4) but we also hear with other people, as a 'we.' In pointing to the collective nature of being an audience in the theatre, we might be said to recognize that 'the joining together of multiple individuals [creates] another possible dimension for human action in which the group has more force than the individual' (Rayner 1993: 11). When we come together to listen to refugees in a theatre event, we are signalling a willingness to listen, but also the desire to listen *as a group*.

What happens then if we shift the focus to look at this body of people, at 'us', from the point of view of the performers? The 'we' of the audiences becomes a 'you' and when the audience is a 'you' the performers are also a 'you' which creates a 'simultaneous subjectivity in which each subject is also an other' (Rayner 1993: 13). This is the situation in which the face-to-face encounter between performer and audience member, or between refugee and non-refugee in the terms of this study, becomes possible. This simultaneous subjectivity creates the grounds for a dialogic relationship. In not being afraid to categorize refugee performers as 'you' in the sense of 'not us', the otherness of the Other becomes 'not a datum for knowledge but a condition of interest and dialogue' (Rayner 1993: 15). Maintaining the 'you-ness' of the refugee participants also excites questions about our apparent stability: in what ways and to what extent are 'we' a 'we'?; how do 'we' respond to questions about responsibility for the other that addresses us from the stage?

To examine these ideas in practice, it is helpful to look at the work of Afrocats, an African Caribbean dance group based in Manchester in the North West of England. Renowned for their lively and exuberant performances, which are mostly derived from traditional African forms and performed in 'authentic' costume, the Afrocats are a popular act at refugee music festivals in the city, where they have performed for enthusiastic crowds on a number of occasions. The membership of Afrocats is made up of young British women of colour and young women from Rwanda and Burundi who were classed as 'unaccompanied minors', young people under the age of eighteen who have arrived alone in Britain to claim asylum.

Figure 1: Scene from *Nyubani Wapi? Where is Home?* by Afrocats. Photograph reproduced with the permission of Community Arts North West.

Under British law the state is bound to look after these young refugees until their eighteenth birthdays when they officially move into adulthood and make the transition into the adult asylum system. If they do not have a convincing story of individual persecution by which they can gain refugee status, they face the threat of removal back to their country of origin.

In 2005 Afrocats created a theatre piece called *Nyubani Wapi? Where is Home?*[7] a play inspired by the personal situations of some of the young women who faced an uncertain future as they reached their eighteenth birthdays and the challenge of proving their refugee status. The impulse for the project lay in a certain frustration with what the Afrocats saw as the limitations of working solely in dance and the way in which, despite the immediacy of their performance style and their strong audience rapport, they could not achieve the level of sophistication in communication with their audience that they wanted. There was a strong feeling that the interaction between dance and drama was what gave *Nyubani Wapi? Where is Home?* its strength, as one of the directors commented:

[With] only a dance piece, we couldn't put that [complexity] on, show all of it, because we couldn't give the true portrayal [...] the stories were far too rich to put it on through dance, they were far too rich. [But] it didn't conflict, I think it added to it, and I couldn't [have done] the project through either/or, it wouldn't have been very fulfilling. There wasn't a clash, there was a combination that really worked.[8]

The directors and performers felt the need to develop a more narrative style of performance in which they could tell complex stories that could be *listened to* by an audience. *Nyubani Wapi? Where is Home?* was built on a mixture of the partial re-telling of some of the young women's personal stories, theatrical representations of asylum issues including the poor image of asylum seekers in the national press and a celebratory element of dance (Thompson et al. 2009: 99). It was staged in an episodic way to show scenes from life 'back home,' dealing with the challenges of entering the British education system and developing relationships with foster families. The play was punctuated by self-referential scenes called 'Afrocats Chit-Chat' in which the young women emulated their casual conversations that included gossip, reflections on what they wanted to do when they left school, and for the refugee actors, fear of what might happen if their claims to remain in Britain were unsuccessful. The play was performed a number of times in medium sized theatre venues in and around Manchester to a mixed audience made up of young people and adults from refugee and non-refugee backgrounds. This analysis is based on three viewings of the performance, interviews with the two directors and an evaluation with the participants after the project, part of which involved in-depth interviews with some of the young women involved.

It is useful to focus on the work of Afrocats because their experience of performing in festivals led them to theatre where they could place their dance skills into a narrative frame that they hoped would help them to communicate more clearly to a non-refugee audience. Neither the level of emotion captured in *Nyubani Wapi? Where is Home?* nor the political complexity of their situation could be evident in the Afrocats' performances at big refugee festivals like the Exodus Festival with their emphasis on visual spectacle and themes of celebration and togetherness (Jeffers 2011). The Afrocats were not content with being *seen*; they also wanted to be *heard* and it this aspect of speaking and listening in the context of thinking about audiences for refugee theatre that is important here. The experience of Afrocats provides the framework for a consideration of the experience of being an audience to refugee theatre, because developing a fuller understanding of audiences for refugee theatre demonstrates some of the ways in which we can look for, and understand, the potential that lies within these performances for an ethical encounter with refugees. This is important because an ethical encounter requires that we think about relationships and responsibilities.

Nyubani Wapi? Where is Home? opens with the scene called 'The Women Speak Out' which begins:

Cue music loud and clear. Simultaneously slow fade lights up full. Enter Afrocats one by one. All women start to murmur/whisper building their sound to a loud crescendo.
SABRA: Will someone listen to me?
They all abruptly stop. As does the music with a very quick fade. Music very slow fade back in to very low so actors are audible over music.
KIA: I am on your ground.
I am drinking your water.
I am an asylum seeker and I get benefits. And you call me illegal. Bogus. What's bogus? Boogey man.
Asylum seeker. Refugee. Immigrant. Illegal immigrant. Alien. Illegal alien. Ha! I do have a name and it's not Illegal.
My name is Kia … aha … yes. (*spells*) K-I-A
So you think coming to this country, living here, I chose to do?
I had nothing better to do – I want to come here and make a nuisance?
You think it is fun to hide in a lorry for 14 days? No air. Little water and food? You think it is fun to watch your family killed right in front of you?
I have the right to be here as much as you. The name is Kia.
Not illegal. Not liar. Not outsider. Not thief. Not terrorist.
Don't look at me like that. You know and you know and you know.[9]

As the actors move onto the stage one by one and stand downstage making eye contact with members of the audience, the first spoken line of the play, 'Will someone listen to me?' is a question, a challenge and a plea all at once. The direct audience address, looking into the faces of individuals in the audience, instead of staring into the darkness of the auditorium produced by traditional stage lighting, showed how these young refugee women faced the audience and, from the outset, demanded to be listened to even if what they had to say was challenging or uncomfortable. The urge to tell the audience about their experience is reflected in how the young women talked about the play. One young woman spoke about the challenge of 'giving a whole load of me out there' during the performance but was happy that the audience was 'going to get our message.' Another participant spoke of being happy to have the opportunity to 'put my view and opinions across' while another said she thought the play expressed 'talk about us, about who we are and that made me really strong.' One young woman summed up the opportunity of being involved in the project as a chance to have 'one big explain of what happened to people like me.'[10]

Civil listening

On first viewing the play, it seemed to me that the group and the artists with whom they worked had made an error of judgement with this opening; they were positioning the audience as ignorant of the prejudice towards refugees despite the fact that audience members were signalling their will to listen simply by their presence at the event. Yet, it is evident this was not a simple transaction. In challenging the decision to stage such a provocative opening, I had placed myself and my fellow audience members in the second audience position outlined above, of being a 'we' who were 'already aware' and in sympathy with the performers' stories of forced migration and prejudice. Feeling pushed into the alternative position of being 'unconverted,' I resented being positioned as ignorant or in need of education. But must audiences of refugee theatre always fall somewhere around these two polar positions or are there any other possibilities? As an audience member, I was looking for some way to indicate that these stories had been heard and understood, maybe a way to show some sense of solidarity and a desire to move forward together. However, it is vital to acknowledge something of the impossibility of that desire and to understand that that solidarity has the potential to be most effective if it remains in the auditorium, built up through the common act of listening to these stories and working out among 'us' the best way to respond.

This is because we cannot assume that simply by being there or by holding the gaze of the refugee actor it is possible to somehow bridge any gap that might exist between performer and audience, or between citizen and refugee, or to create any sense of togetherness. Separation between self and Other is essential for maintaining an ethical relationship and, according to Levinas, the collapsing of boundaries is inimical to developing an ethical relationship with the Other. He says 'one begins with the idea that duality must be transformed into unity and that social relations must culminate in communication,' adding that this notion is the 'last vestige of idealism' (Levinas 1989: 164). This presents a rather stern challenge for participatory refugee theatre. How can audiences ethically engage with the Other in a theatrical context, and how can we address otherness without resorting to bland discourses of togetherness or 'moral maxims or notions of community' (Wade 2009: 16)? Audiences sit or stand shoulder-to-shoulder in the face-to-face theatrical encounter.[11] One way to approach this is to think about the proxemic relationships *within* the auditorium as much as those between audience and stage. Thinking about the ways in which I sit shoulder-to-shoulder with my fellow audience members suggests Levinas's third party, the body which brings my face-to-face encounter with the refugee performer into the social and political arena. When the 'thou is posited in front of a we,' I discover the Other and a host of potential Others is revealed to me (Levinas 1969: 213). In watching theatre about refugees being performed by refugees themselves, I make that journey of discovery shoulder-to-shoulder with fellow audience members rather than with the refugee performers, because the 'host of potential Others' in this case is made up of other citizens. In gaining a better understanding of the ways in which refugees are treated in the name of protecting state borders, in the name of protecting us as citizens, we gain some understanding of our role in this and ways in which we can choose to be complicit or not: we stand shoulder-to-shoulder in the act of considering how to respond to the face-to-face interaction of the performance both in the moment and afterwards. The act of watching a piece of refugee theatre therefore challenges audience members to make a relationship with the others *in the audience* which leads to the suggestion that any potential actions that arise from this relationship should be focused on the activity of listening and couched in images of amplification, echoes and reverberations.

In offering a hospitable stage on which refugees can re-enact the stories that matter to them, we enter into a set of relationships that have been called 'a complicated ballet of proposals [and] expectations' (Rosello 2001: 127). Audience members cannot escape the fact that it is in their 'gift' to be able to offer theatre as a space for reflection and expression. At the same time, the offer of a 'hospitable stage' on which refugee stories can be re-enacted is just that, a stage, not substantial, not 'real.' Refugees who accept the offer understand to varying degrees that speaking their story in front of an audience will probably not materially affect their political standing in this place of refuge, but the act of standing shoulder-to-shoulder shows a willingness to listen on the part of the audience. The presence of the audience in the act of listening to refugee stories constitutes a form of commitment through an act of trust and generosity on its part as listeners. Of course, an even greater level of trust and generosity is needed on the part of those refugee speakers brave enough to share their thoughts, opinions and experiences with an audience: in the words of one of the Afrocats, 'giving a whole load of me out there.' In truth, we can offer very little *but* to listen and to amplify these stories by giving them a voice through theatre.

Thinking about the ways in which this amplification might work focuses ideas about listening and hearing in the participatory refugee theatre event in order to suggest that the offering of a hospitable stage from which to hear refugee voices constitutes an act of civility. The term 'civility' is used not in the contemporary sense to indicate polite indifference but in the archaic sense. The root of the word is the Latin *civilis* meaning 'of or belonging to the citizens' which, in seventeenth- and eighteenth-century English, developed into *civility* having the meaning of 'community.' Williams (1983: 58) points out the way in which the word developed into civilization, used increasingly to describe both a process and a state of being but it is the processual nature of the word that interests me most in relation to refugee theatre work. In the process of listening to refugee stories told through the medium of theatre, we are providing a civil audience for the tellers of these stories but we are also building a civility, going through a process of becoming civil. That process is not about creating exclusivities but about coming to an understanding of the ways in which these stories also become part of our civility. Civil listening allows us to distance ourselves from feelings of togetherness and false bonhomie while still demonstrating interest in refugee stories and commitment to dialogue.

Erikson (1999) suggests that one of the most important lessons for theatre that emerges from Levinas's ideas of face-to-face contact lies in the non-reciprocity of the relationship between performer and audience. Whether performers and audience are there for each other or not their relationship is not reciprocal, moment for moment, because of their inability speak up as an audience member in the moment of performance. We 'give audience' (Rayner 1993: 20) in the sense of our silence, a space in which refugee subjects can be heard but also one in which they are *seen to be speaking*. Giving audience is not a purely auditory experience but is also an activity, indicating presence in the act of listening. An audience at a refugee theatre event actively indicates their willingness and capacity to listen within an event that is framed as an act of listening. The desire not only to listen but to hear and create meaning, places the emphasis on attempt and effort, not on success or failure, because listening is not simply an auditory activity but a way to frame speech (Rayner 1993: 20). In the moment of listening, we constitute ourselves as an audience in the 'joint venture [of] opening towards meaning, not recovering it' (Rayner 1993: 21): put crudely, we have to shut up and listen. The ways in which the conventions and proxemics of theatre operate make this a very powerful activity.

Shifting the focus away from the participants and onto the audience means that we have to think about what that audience is actually doing at a refugee theatre event. The way in which the audience is compelled to 'give audience' shows how polarities of ignorance and knowledge have become redundant, inadequate for the relationships that are built up through a complex act of theatrical listening. If we are truly listening in the theatre event we are also listening ethically because the face-to-face encounter with refugees on stage makes audience members aware that they are sitting shoulder-to-shoulder with other audience members. It reminds us that we have a civil responsibility to provide an echo chamber for those refugee voices that reach us from the stage, to make them reverberate, and to amplify what we hear.

References

Adshead, K., *The Bogus Woman*, London: Oberon, 2001.
Barnes, S., *Drawing a Line. A Discussion of Ethics in Participatory Arts with Young Refugees*, London: Oval House, 2009.
Blaker, C., *Senses of the City. London's Support for Refugees, 1999–2002*, London: London Arts, 2003.

Cohen-Cruz, J., and Schutzman, M. (eds.), *A Boal Companion. Dialogues on Theatre and Cultural Politics*, London and New York: Routledge, 2006.

Erikson, J., 'The Face and the Possibility of an Ethics of Performance,' *Journal of Dramatic Theory and Criticism* (Spring 1999), pp. 5–21.

Freshwater, H., *Theatre and Audience*, Basingstoke: Palgrave Macmillan, 2009.

Gould, H., *A Sense of Belonging, Arts, Culture and the Integration of Refugees and Asylum Seekers*, London: Creative Exchange Network, 2005.

Harper, R., *Refugees and Asylum Seekers in London: The Impact of Community Fund Grants*, London: Community Fund Research, 2001.

Harrow, M., and Field, Y., *Routes Across Diversity. Developing the Arts of London's Refugee Communities*, London: London Arts, 2001.

Jeffers, A., *Refugees, Theatre and Crisis: Performing Global Identities*, Basingstoke: Palgrave Macmillan, 2011.

Kershaw, B., *The Politics of Performance: Radical Theatre as Cultural Intervention*, London: Routledge, 1992.

Kidd, B., Zahir, S., and Khan, S., *Arts and Refugees: History, Impact and Future*, London: Arts Council England, The Baring Foundation, The Paul Hamlyn Foundation, 2008.

Kurahashi, Y., 'Theatre as healing space. Ping Chong's *Children of War*,' *Studies in Theatre and Performance* 24:1 (2004), pp. 23–36.

Levinas, E., *Totality and Infinity*, Pittsburgh, PA: Duquesne University, 1969.

———, 'Ethics as First Philosophy,' in S. Hand (ed.), *The Levinas Reader*, Oxford: Blackwell, 1989a.

———, 'The other in Proust,' in S. Hand (ed.), *The Levinas Reader*, Oxford: Blackwell, 1989b.

Rayner, A., 'The audience: subjectivity, community and the ethics of listening,' *Journal of Dramatic Theory and Criticism* (Spring 1993), pp. 3–24.

Rosello, M., *Postcolonial Hospitality. The Immigrant as Guest*, Stanford: Stanford University Press, 2001.

Salverson, J., 'Transgressive storytelling or an aesthetics of injury: performance, pedagogy and ethics,' *Theatre Research in Canada* 20:1 (1999), pp. 35–51.

———, 'Witnessing subjects: a fool's help,' in J. Cohen-Cruz and M. Schutzman (eds), *A Boal Companion*, London and New York: Routledge, 2006.

Schinina, G., 'Cursed communities, rituals of separation and communication as vengeance,' in C. Bernardi, M. Dragone and G. Schinina (eds), *War Theatres and Actions for Peace. Community-based Dramaturgy and the Conflict Scene*, Milan: Euresis Edizioni, 2002.

Thompson, J., Hughes, J., and Balfour, M., *Performance in Place of War*, London, New York, Calcutta: Seagull Books, 2009.

Wade, L. A., 'Sublime trauma: the violence of the ethical encounter,' in P. Anderson and J. Menon (eds), *Violence Performed. Local Roots and Global Routes of Conflict*, Basingstoke: Palgrave Macmillan, 2009.

Wehle, P., 'Children of the World. Ping Chong's Travels,' *Performing Arts Journal* 76 (2004), pp. 22–32.

Williams, Raymond, *Keywords. A Vocabulary of Culture and Society*, London: Flamingo, 1983.

Notes

1 Creative Exchange is a charity which is concerned with creating networks and support projects in which arts and culture can influence social policy and practice. http://www.creativexchange.org/about (accessed 4 January 2008).

2 See http://www.biglotteryfund.org.uk/prog_reaching_communities for more information.

3 See Freshwater (2009: 29–30) for further information on the ways in which audience data is gathered and used for marketing purposes.

4 I am not exempting myself from this criticism and have indeed experienced this phenomenon myself from the point of view of a practitioner and theatre maker with refugee groups.

5 Dumezweni was born to South African parents in Swaziland and brought up and educated in Britain. http://www.thenewblackmagazine.com/view.aspx?index=158 (accessed 28 November 2011).

6 See http://iceandfire.co.uk/outreach/scripts/asylum-monologues (accessed 22 November 2011).

7 *Nyubani Wapi?* is the Swahili translation of the play's English title.

8 The project was initiated and the performance produced by Community Arts North West in Manchester. The interview with Magdalen Bartlett and Cilla Baynes, directors *of Nyubani Wapi?/Where is Home?* was carried out as part of the In Place of War project at the University of Manchester (2004–2008).

9 From the script of *Nyubani Wapi?/Where is Home?* (unpub.)

10 All these quotations are from the evaluation exercise which took place after the project.

11 I initially came to this idea through hearing about the Men's Shed movement in Australia where men have apparently found a sense of purpose and community in working practically shoulder-to-shoulder where the face-to-face encounter seen in various talking therapies has been rejected. See http://www.mensheds.com.au/ for more information.

Index